ESSAYS ON LITERATURE AND POLITICS 1932-1972

ESSAYS ON LITERATURE AND POLITICS 1932-1972

PHILIP RAHV

Edited by Arabel J. Porter
and Andrew J. Dvosin

With a Memoir by Mary McCarthy

HOUGHTON MIFFLIN COMPANY BOSTON 1978

Library of Congress Cataloging in Publication Data

Rahv, Philip, date.
   Essays on literature and politics, 1932–1972.
   Includes index.
     1. Literature, Modern — History and criticism — Ad-
dresses, essays, lectures.   2. Politics and literature —
Addresses, essays, lectures.   I. Porter, Arabel J.
II. Dvosin, Andrew J.   III. Title.
PN710.R327   1978   809   78–13373
ISBN 0–395–27270–X

Printed in the United States of America

s 10 9 8 7 6 5 4 3 2 1

Acknowledgments

Acknowledgment is made to the Louisiana State University Press for permission to reprint from *Southern Review* "Proletarian Literature: A Political Autopsy" (1939); to *The New Republic* for permission to reprint "The Education of Anton Chekhov" (July 18, 1955); to *The Brandeis Folio* for permission to reprint "On Pornography, Black Humor, Norman Mailer, Etc." (1966); to *Kenyon Review* for permission to reprint "Paleface and Redskin" (Summer 1939) and "Mrs. Woolf and Mrs. Brown" (Winter 1943); to *Commentary* for permission to reprint "Liberal Anticommunism Revisited" (1967) and "The Princess" (1970).

The following essays and reviews are reprinted by permission of *Partisan Review*: "Trials of the Mind" (April 1938); "Dostoevsky and Politics" (July 1938); "Twilight of the Thirties" (Summer 1939); "The Cult of Experience in American Writing" (November–December 1940); "The Dark Lady of Salem" (September–October 1941); "The Heiress of All the Ages" (May–June 1943); "Concerning Tolstoy" (September–October 1946); "Religion and the Intellectuals" (March 1950); "Our Country and Our Culture" (May–June 1952); "The Sense and Nonsense of Whittaker Chambers" (July–August 1952); "The Legend of the Grand Inquisitor" (1954); "Dostoevsky in *Crime and Punishment*" (Summer 1960).

The following essays and reviews are reprinted from *The New York Review of Books*: book review, Solzhenitsyn's *One Day in the Life of Ivan Denisovich* (August 29, 1963); "The Great Outcast" (January 23, 1964); "Crime Without Punishment" (March 25, 1965); "T. S. Eliot in His Posthumous Essays" (March 3, 1966); "On F.R. Leavis and D.H. Lawrence" (September 26, 1968); "Delmore Schwartz: The Paradox of Precocity" (May 20, 1971); "Henry James and His Cult" (February 10, 1972); "The Other Dostoevsky" (April 20, 1972); "In Dubious Battle" (October 5, 1972).

Excerpts from "The Literary Class War" are reprinted from *New Masses* (August 1932); "You Can't Duck Hurricane Under Beach Umbrella" is reprinted from *The Daily Worker* (May 5, 1934); "What and Where Is the New Left" and "Dostoevsky: Descent into the Underground" are reprinted from *Modern Occasions* 1971 (1972); the book review of Andrei Sinyavsky's *The Trial Begins* is reprinted from *Book Week* (May 1, 1966).

"Philip Rahv (1908–1973)" by Mary McCarthy is reprinted from *The New York Times Book Review* (February 17, 1974) by permission of the author and *The New York Times Book Review*.

Philip Rahv, 1908–1973*
by Mary McCarthy

So HE's GONE, that dear phenomenon. If no two people are alike, he was less like anybody else than anybody. A powerful intellect, a massive, overpowering personality and yet shy, curious, susceptible, confiding. All his life he was sternly faithful to Marxism, for him both a tool of analysis and a wondrous cosmogony; but he loved Henry James and every kind of rich, shimmery, soft texture in literature and in the stuff of experience. He was a resolute modernist, which made him in these recent days old-fashioned. It was as though he came into being with the steam engine: for him, literature began with Dostoevsky and stopped with Joyce, Proust, and Eliot; politics began with Marx and Engels and stopped with Lenin. He was not interested in Shakespeare, the classics, Greek city-states; and he despised most contemporary writing and contemporary political groups, being grumblingly out of sorts with fashion, except where he felt it belonged — on the backs of good-looking women and girls.

This did not overtake him with age or represent a hardening of his mental arteries. He was always that way. It helped him be a Trotsky-ite (he was a great admirer of the Old Man, though never an inscribed adherent) when Stalinism was chic. Whatever was "in" he threw out with a snort. Late in his life, serendipity introduced him to the word "swingers," which summed up everything he was against. With sardonic relish he adopted it as his personal shorthand. If he came down from Boston to New York and went to a literary party and you asked him, "Well, how was it?" he would answer, "Nothing but swingers!" and give his short soft bark of a laugh.

Yet he had a gift for discovering young writers. I think of Saul Bellow, Elizabeth Hardwick, Randall Jarrell, John Berryman, Bernard

* This memoir of Philip Rahv appeared on the front page of *The New York Times Book Review* on February 17, 1974, several months after his death.

Malamud. There were many others. He was quickly aware of Bob Silvers, editor of *The New York Review of Books,* and became his close friend — counselor, too, sometimes. To the end of his life, he remained a friend of young people. It was middle-aged and old swingers he held in aversion; young ones, on the whole, he did not mind.

He had a marvelous sensitivity to verbal phrasing and structure. What art dealers call "quality" in painting he would recognize instantly in literature, even of a kind that, in principle, ought to have been foreign to him. I remember when I first knew him, back in the mid-thirties, at a time when he was an intransigent (I thought), pontificating young Marxist, and I read a short review he had done of *Tender Is the Night* — the tenderness of the review, despite its critical stance, startled me. I would not have suspected in Rahv that power of sympathetic insight into a writer so glamorized by rich Americans on the Riviera. Fitzgerald, I must add, was "out" then and not only for the disagreeable crowd at the *New Masses.*

That review was delicately, almost poetically written, and this too was a surprise. I would have expected him to write as he talked, pungently, harshly, drivingly, in a heavy Russian accent. It was as though another person had written the review. But as those who knew him discovered, there were two persons in Rahv, but solidly married to each other in a long-standing union — no quarrels. It would be simplifying to say that one was political, masculine, and aggressive, one feminine, artistic, and dreamy, but those contrasts were part of it.

Perhaps there were more than two, the third being an unreconstructed child with a child's capacity for wonder and amazement. Philip marveled constantly at the strangeness of life and the world. Recounting some story, seizing on some item in a newspaper, he would be transported, positively enraptured, with glee and offended disbelief. His black eyes with their large almost bulging whites would roll, and he would shake his head over and over, have a short fit of chuckling, nudge you, if you were a man, squeeze your arm, if you were a woman — as though you and he, together, were watching a circus parade of monstrosities and curious animals (in the form of human behavior) pass through your village.

His own childhood in the Russian Ukraine had stayed fast in his mind. He used to tell me how his grandmother (his parents were Jewish shopkeepers living in the midst of a peasant population) ran into the shop one day saying, "The Czar has fallen," and to him it was as if she had said, "The sky has fallen"; he hid behind the counter. Then, when the civil war began, he remembered staying in the shop for weeks, it seemed, with the blinds pulled down, as Red and White troops took and retook the village.

His parents were early Zionists, and after the civil war they emigrated to Palestine, where in the little furniture factory his father opened he got to know those strange people — Arabs. In 1922 he went to America, alone, to live with his older brother. There, in Providence, Rhode Island, already quite a big boy, he went to grade school still dressed in the old-fashioned European schoolboy style, in long black trousers and black stockings, looking like a somber little man among the American kids. Starting to work early, as a junior advertising copywriter for a small firm out in Oregon, he had no time for college and got his education alone, in public libraries. In the Depression, he migrated to New York. Standing in breadlines and sleeping on park benches, he became a Marxist.

This education — Russia, the Revolution, Palestine, books read in libraries, hunger — shaped him. He read several languages: Russian, German (his family on its way to Palestine had spent a year or two in Austria), probably some Hebrew, and French, which he picked up by himself. He had a masterly sense of English and was a masterful copy editor — the best, I am told by friends, they ever knew. American literature became a specialty with him, and he came to it curious and exploratory, like a pioneer. Hawthorne, Melville, James, these were the main sources that fed his imagination. His insights, never random but tending to crystallize in theory, led him to make a series of highly original formulations, including the now famous distinction between redskins and palefaces among our literary men. He himself, being essentially a European, was neither.

Though he knew America intimately, he remained an outsider. He never assimilated, not to the downtown milieu of New York Jewish intellectuals he moved in during his early days, not to the university, although in time he occupied a professor's chair. When he lived in the country, which he did for long stretches, he was an obstinate city man and would hold forth darkly on the theme of "rural idiocy." He never learned to swim. This metaphorically summed up his situation: he would immerse his body in the alien element (I have nice pictures of him in bathing trunks by the waterside) but declined, or perhaps feared, to move with it. His resistance to swimming with the tide, his mistrust of currents, were his strength.

Remaining outside the American framework, his mind had a wider perspective, and at three critical junctures in our national intellectual life, its reflections were decisive. First, at the time of the Moscow trials, when he and William Phillips broke with the Communists and "stole" *Partisan Review,* which they had edited as an organ of the John Reed Club. Second, during the war, when he broke with his former collaborators Dwight Macdonald and Clement Greenberg on the issue of whether the war against Hitler should be supported by American radicals or not. We had all been affirming the negative, but Rahv in a long meditative article moved toward the opposite position: I remember the last sentence, with which I did not agree at the time but which struck on my mind nevertheless and reverberated: "And yet in a certain sense it is our war." Third, in the McCarthy time, when so many of his old friends in the anti-Stalinist left were either defending McCarthy or "postponing judgment," Rahv, alone in his immediate circle, came out in print with an unequivocal condemnation and contemptuous dismissal. On Vietnam, so far as I remember, he did not pronounce at any length; his characteristic voice is lost to my recollection, having mingled with so many others.

The words *radical* and *modern* had a wonderful charm for Philip; when he spoke them, his sometimes grating tone softened, became reverent, loving, as though touching prayer beads. He was also much attached to the word *ideas.* "He has no ideas," he would declare, dismissing some literary claimant; to be void of ideas was for him the worst disaster that could befall an intellectual. He found this deficiency frequent, almost endemic, among us. That may be why he did not wish to assimilate.

I said, just now, that he was unlike anybody, but now I remember that I have seen someone like him — on the screen. Like the younger Rahv anyway: Serge Bondarchuk, the director of *War and Peace,* playing the part of Pierre. An uncanny resemblance in every sense and unsettling to preconceived notions. I had always pictured Pierre as blond, pink, tall, and fat; nor could I picture Philip as harboring Pierre's ingenuous, embarrassed, puzzled, placid soul — they were almost opposites, I should have thought. And yet that swarthy Russian actor was showing us a different interior Philip and a different exterior Pierre. Saying good-bye to my old friend, I am moved by that and remember his tenderness for Tolstoy (see the very Rahvian and beautiful essay "The Green Twig and the Black Trunk") and Tolstoy's sense of Pierre as the onlooker, the eternal civilian, as out of place at the Battle of Borodino in his white hat and green swallowtail coat as the dark little man in his long, dark East European clothes eyeing the teacher from behind his grammar school desk in Providence.

Preface

ANY APPPRECIATION of Philip Rahv and his role in American letters must begin with his founding and for over thirty years editing the best and most influential literary magazine in America, *Partisan Review*. In his own right he was one of the finest literary critics of his generation. But it is of greater historical importance that he was a leader of that articulate band of left-wing intellectuals Norman Podhoretz called "the Family" — most of them Jews who began their careers as the Depression dawned, and whose style and commitments were shaped by its pressures and disputes — Lionel Trilling, Edmund Wilson, Sidney Hook, Meyer Shapiro, William Phillips, Harold Rosenberg, Lionel Abel . . .

Rahv was exceptional among them; he was the only one who for a long period had been a Communist. Later, he was somewhat circumspect about his faded party card but, during the thirties, he wrote essays and reviews (and even a few poems!) for the *New Masses* and the *Daily Worker,* and even for such fugitive publications as *Prolit* and the *Rebel Poet*. These writings were never reprinted in book form nor, Communist though their viewpoint is, were they reprinted in any of the retrospective left-wing anthologies that came out in later decades; by the Rahv, who had left the party, was a well-known apostate. An odd footnote in literary history! Odder still: for unexplained reasons, Rahv omitted from his three collections of criticism most of the subsequent essays which dealt directly with politics.

The inclusion of a sampling of these essays is one of the main reasons for bringing out an anthology of his writings now. They range from his first essays, full of strident revolutionary optimism, to attacks on Stalinism from the Left written in the late thirties and early forties, to articles written in the mid-fifties and early sixties to propound a doubt that mere *anti*communism formed an actual political doctrine, and finally to the essays of his last years, in which Rahv returned to many of his youthful Marxist-Leninist ideas. All of them have great political insight; together they constitute a remarkable document of this century's history. But it is not just the purely political essays which are unavailable: all three volumes of essays Rahv published in his lifetime are now out of print.

Included in this anthology of his best writing, then, are the essays which introduced Kafka to this country and Rahv's classic interpretations of the great Russian writers. Several of the articles on Dostoevsky appear in book form for the first time: Rahv, who was saving them for a long study of Dostoevsky, never lived to complete it. There is a generous sampling of his work on particular American authors, Hawthorne, Eliot, James, and others, and of the brilliant far-reaching essays like "Paleface and Redskin" and "The Cult of Experience," which more than any other work have won him a permanent place in American literary criticism.

These general essays form a prelude to Rahv's essays on American literature, since their themes are repeatedly sounded in his later articles on individual writers. They constitute the opening section devoted to "American Writers and Writing." We have grouped together all of Rahv's commentaries on Dostoevsky, a group that amounts to a book within a book. A scrutiny of his private papers shows that with only several more chapters Rahv would have considered his long-awaited book on Dostoevsky finished. After these two sections, the rest of the essays, under broad headings, are in chronological order.

Many people know Philip Rahv's writing; few of them knew Philip Rahv. In fact, one of his friends said that he was "so secretive as to be almost unknowable." But the Philip Rahv who struck Mary McCarthy as an "intransigent . . . pontificating young Marxist" may have struck his early readers as precisely that, too. With their lack of literary sophistication, his fervid declamations often sounded as if they came from inside a burning bush. In the *Daily Worker,* he praises proletarian literature (which later he anatomized so mercilessly) and hails its founder, Maxim Gorky, as a "great leader of the cultural revolution." In the *Rebel Poet* (subtitled "The Internationale of Song"), he declares that next to Gorky such bourgeois writers as Joyce and Lawrence appear "tangential to the concrete course of history." Eliot's devotional poetry in *Ash Wednesday* proves that "in the twentieth century it is" no more "possible to be a religious poet" than "to be a feudal knight." This anthology includes two examples of this militant period. There are excerpts from "The Literary Class War," in effect

Rahv's literary debut — an audacious attempt to superimpose Karl Marx on the Aristotelian theory of katharsis. From a 1934 issue of the *Daily Worker,* a review of F. Scott Fitzgerald's *Tender Is the Night.*

When Rahv and his friend William Phillips founded *Partisan Review* in 1934, the aims of the magazine announced in its opening editorial were to defend the Soviet Union, to combat fascism and war, and to promote a literature which would express the viewpoint of the working class. But in 1937, the aims of the magazine, which had folded once and now reappeared with a new editorial board, including Mary McCarthy, Dwight Macdonald, and F. W. Dupee, were to concern itself with the intellectuals, rather than with the proletarians.

Dismayed by the first of the Moscow trials, and by the Popular Front's policy of avoiding all revolutionary activity, Rahv had severed his ties with the Communist Party of the United States. The *New Masses,* in an attack on the new *Partisan Review,* informed its readers that "Mr. Rahv has been expelled from the Communist Party as a Trotskyite."

In the *Partisan Review,* proletarian literature was replaced by intellectual literature, Maxim Gorky and *The Rebel Poet* by Kafka, Dostoevsky, T. S. Eliot, and the works of Henry James. Political revolution was abandoned for literary revelation. The paradox that ran through Rahv's life in the 1940s and 1950s is that this conservative era, deeply antipathetic as it was to his central political instincts, was nevertheless by all external indications the most successful and satisfying period of his life. The forties in particular were Rahv's most productive time as a writer, and he was also at the height of his influence as an editor of *Partisan Review.* As his faith in radicalism eroded, he turned his energy to other efforts: in the early forties he wrote brilliant general essays on the classic writers of American literature; in the postwar period he virtually abandoned literature for the politics of anti-Stalinism; later in the fifties, he engaged in a struggle with the New Critics over how literature should be read and criticized; by the late fifties he almost suspended his critical labors. In all this time no controlling idea sustained him, no idea inspired him like the Marxism of his early years.

In the sixties, with the advent of the New Left, Rahv came alive again as a critic, although it was the New Left's advocacy of a political revolution rather than its concern with a revolution in consciousness which excited him, and although he often said that the New Left leaders were merely playing at revolution. However, when his connection with *Partisan Review* grew tenuous to the breaking point in

1970, he founded *Modern Occasions.* The last of the literary magazines founded on the radical ethos of the thirties, *Modern Occasions* came to a stop after six issues.

Philip Rahv did not outlive his magazine for many months. He had exercised a considerable influence upon American literary intellectuals as long as he could think and talk and write. For fifteen years the writer and critic had also been a professor at Brandeis, near Cambridge, Massachusetts. Much as he groused about his students from time to time, he was always interested in the most promising of these. They found in him the powerful intellect and the generosity of spirit that had characterized him and his work from the beginning.

Philip Rahv died suddenly in Boston on December 23, 1973. He had been born sixty-five years before with a different name — Ivan Greenberg. This name, with its marvelous blend indicative of his dual Russian-Jewish heritage, he had changed to Philip Rahv when he became a Communist in America. His grandmother had been devoutly religious in the fanatically orthodox style; in his mother this was transmuted and secularized into an ardent Zionism, and the name "Rahv" itself in Hebrew (רַב) means rabbi; it was a name quite different from the prototypically American names most American Jewish Communists chose for themselves in the thirties. In his will, Rahv left his money not to any person or cause, but to the state of Israel. It was a confounding gesture that went against the grain of much of his mature life, but in a sense it returned him to where he began.

ANDREW J. DVOSIN

Contents

III. POLITICS, RELIGION, AND CULTURE

I
AMERICAN WRITING AND WRITERS

Paleface and Redskin

Viewed historically, American writers appear to group themselves around two polar types. Paleface and redskin I should like to call the two, and despite occasional efforts at reconciliation no love is lost between them.

Consider the immense contrast between the drawing-room fictions of Henry James and the open-air poems of Walt Whitman. Compare Melville's decades of loneliness, his tragic failure, with Mark Twain's boisterous career and dubious success. At one pole there is the literature of the lowlife world of the frontier and of the big cities; at the other the thin, solemn, semiclerical culture of Boston and Concord. The fact is that the creative mind in America is fragmented and one-sided. For the process of polarization has produced a dichotomy between experience and consciousness — a dissociation between energy and sensibility, between conduct and theories of conduct, between life conceived as an opportunity and life conceived as a discipline.

The differences between the two types define themselves in every sphere. Thus while the redskin glories in his Americanism, to the paleface it is a source of endless ambiguities. Sociologically they can be distinguished as patrician versus plebeian, and in their aesthetic ideals one is drawn to allegory and the distillations of symbolism, whereas the other inclines to a gross, riotous naturalism. The paleface is a "highbrow," though his mentality — as in the case of Hawthorne and James — is often of the kind that excludes and repels general ideas; he is at the same time both something more and something less than an intellectual in the European sense. And the redskin deserves the epithet "lowbrow," not because he is badly educated — which he might or might not be — but because his reactions are primarily emotional, spontaneous, and lacking in personal culture. The paleface continually hankers after religious norms, tending toward a refined estrangement from reality. The redskin, on the other hand, accepts his environment, at times to the degree of fusion with it, even when rebelling against one or another of its manifestations. At his highest level the paleface moves in an exquisite moral atmosphere; at his lowest he is genteel, snobbish, and pedantic. In giving expression to the vitality and to the aspirations of the people, the redskin is at his best; but at his worst he is a vulgar anti-intellectual, combining aggression with conformity and reverting to the crudest forms of frontier psychology.

James and Whitman, who as contemporaries felt little more than contempt for each other, are the purest examples of this dissociation.* In reviewing *Drum Taps* in 1865 the young James told off the grand plebeian innovator, advising him to stop declaiming and go sit in the corner of a rhyme and meter school, while the innovator, snorting at the novelist of scruples and moral delicacy, said "Feathers!" Now this mutual repulsion between the two major figures in American literature would be less important if it were mainly personal or aesthetic in reference. But the point is that it has a profoundly national and social-historical character.

James and Whitman form a kind of fatal antipodes. To this, in part, can be traced the curious fact about them that, though each has become the object of a special cult, neither is quite secure in his reputation. For most of the critics and historians who make much of Whitman disparage James or ignore him altogether, and vice versa. Evidently the high valuation of the one is so incongruous with the high valuation of the other that criticism is chronically forced to choose between them — which makes for a breach in the literary tradition without parallel in any European country. The aristocrat Tolstoy and the tramp Gorky found that they held certain values and ideas in common, whereas James and Whitman, who between them dominate American writing of the nineteenth century, cannot abide with one another. And theirs is no unique or isolated instance.

The national literature suffers from the ills of a split personality. The typical American writer has so far shown himself incapable of escaping the blight of one-sidedness: of achieving that mature control which permits the balance of impulse with sensitiveness, of natural power with philosophical depth. For the dissociation of mind from experience has resulted in truncated works of art, works that tend to be either naive and ungraded, often flat reproductions of life, or else

---

* According to Edith Wharton, James changed his mind about Whitman late in life. But this can be regarded as a private fact of the Jamesian sensibility, for in public he said not a word in favor of Whitman.

products of cultivation that remain abstract because they fall short on evidence drawn from the sensuous and material world. Hence it is only through intensively exploiting their very limitations, through submitting themselves to a process of creative yet cruel self-exaggeration, that a few artists have succeeded in warding off the failure that threatened them. And the later novels of Henry James are a case in point.

The palefaces dominated literature throughout the nineteenth century, but in the twentieth they were overthrown by the redskins. Once the continent had been mastered, with the plebeian bourgeoisie coming into complete possession of the national wealth, and puritanism had worn itself out, degenerating into mere respectability, it became objectively possible and socially permissible to satisfy that desire for experience and personal emancipation which heretofore had been systematically frustrated. The era of economic accumulation had ended and the era of consummation had arrived. To enjoy life now became one of the functions of progress — a function for which the palefaces were temperamentally disqualified. This gave Mencken his opportunity to emerge as the ideologue of enjoyment. Novelists like Dreiser, Anderson, and Lewis — and, in fact, most of the writers of the period of "experiment and liberation" — rose against conventions that society itself was beginning to abandon. They helped to "liquidate" the lag between the enormous riches of the nation and its morality of abstention. The neohumanists were among the last of the breed of palefaces, and they perished in the quixotic attempt to re-establish the old values. Eliot forsook his native land, while the few palefaces who managed to survive at home took to the academic or else to the "higher" and relatively unpopular forms of writing. But the novelists, who control the main highway of literature, were, and still are, nearly all redskins to the wigwam born.

At present the redskins are in command of the situation, and the literary life in America has seldom been so deficient in intellectual power. The political interests introduced in the 1930s have not only strengthened their hold but have also brought out their worst tendencies; for the effect of the popular political creeds of our time has been to increase their habitual hostility to ideas, sanctioning the relaxation of standards and justifying the urge to come to terms with semiliterate audiences.

The redskin writer in America is a purely indigenous phenomenon, the true-blue offspring of the Western Hemisphere, the juvenile in principle and for the good of the soul. He is a self-made writer in the same way that Henry Ford was a self-made millionaire. On the one hand he is a crass materialist, a greedy consumer of experience, and on the other a sentimentalist, a half-baked mystic listening to inward voices and watching for signs and portents. Think of Dreiser, Lewis, Anderson, Wolfe, Sandburg, Caldwell, Steinbeck, Farrell, Saroyan: all writers of genuine and some even of admirable accomplishments, whose faults, however, are not so much literary as faults of raw life itself. Unable to relate himself in any significant manner to the cultural heritage, the redskin writer is always on his own; and since his personality resists growth and change, he must continually repeat himself. His work is ridden by compulsions that depress the literary tradition, because they are compulsions of a kind that put a strain on literature, that literature more often than not can neither assimilate nor sublimate. He is the passive instead of the active agent of the *Zeitgeist*, he lives off it rather than through it, so that when his particular gifts happen to coincide with the mood of the times he seems modern and contemporary, but once the mood has passed he is in danger of being quickly discarded. Lacking the qualities of surprise and renewal, already Dreiser and Anderson, for example, have a "period" air about them that makes a rereading of their work something of a critical chore; and one suspects that Hemingway, that perennial boy-man, is more accurately understood as a descendant of Natty Bumppo, the hero of Fenimore Cooper's *Leatherstocking Tales*, than as the portentously disillusioned character his legend makes him out to be.

As for the paleface, in compensation for backward cultural conditions and a lost religious ethic, he has developed a supreme talent for refinement, just as the Jew, in compensation for adverse social conditions and a lost national independence, has developed a supreme talent for cleverness. (In this connection it is pertinent to recall T. S. Eliot's remark about Boston society, which he described as "quite refined, but refined beyond the point of civilization.") Now this peculiar excess of refinement is to be deplored in an imaginative writer, for it weakens his capacity to cope with experience and induces in him a fetishistic attitude toward tradition; nor is this species of refinement to be equated with the refinement of artists like Proust or Mann, as in them it is not an element contradicting an open and bold confrontation of reality. Yet the paleface, being above all a conscious individual, was frequently able to transcend or to deviate sharply from the norms of his group, and he is to be credited with most of the rigors and charms of the classic American books. While it is true, as John Jay Chapman put it, that his culture is "secondary and tertiary" and that between him and the sky "float the Constitution of the United States and the traditions and forms of English literature" — nevertheless, there exists the poetry of Emily Dickinson, there is *The Scarlet Letter*, there is *Moby Dick*, and there are not a few incomparable narratives by Henry James.

At this point there is no necessity to enter into a discussion of the historical and social causes that account for the disunity of the American creative mind. In various contexts a number of critics have disclosed and evaluated the forces that have worked on this mind and shaped it to their uses. The sole question that seems relevant is whether history will make whole again what it has rent asunder. Will James and Whitman ever be reconciled, will they finally discover and act upon each other? Only history can give a definite reply to this question. In the meantime, however, there are available the resources of effort and understanding, resources which even those who believe in the strict determination of the cultural object need not spurn.

Kenyon Review, 1939

The Cult of Experience

in American Writing

Every ATTENTIVE READER of Henry James remembers that highly dramatic scene in *The Ambassadors* — a scene singled out by its author as giving away the "whole case" of his novel — in which Lambert Strether, the elderly New England gentleman who had come to Paris on a mission of business and duty, proclaims his conversion to the doctrine of experience. Caught in the spell of Paris, the discovery of whose grace and form is marked for him by a kind of meaning and intensity that can be likened only to the raptures of a mystic vision, Strether feels moved to renounce publicly the morality of abstention he had brought with him from Woollett, Massachusetts. And that mellow Sunday afternoon, as he mingles with the charming guests assembled in the garden of the sculptor Gloriani, the spell of the world capital of civilization is so strong upon the sensitive old man that he trembles with happiness and zeal. It is then that he communicates to little Bilham his newly acquired piety toward life and the fruits thereof. The worst mistake one can make, he admonishes his youthful interlocutor, is not to live all one can — "Do what you like so long as you don't make my mistake ... Live! ... It doesn't so much matter what you do in particular, so long as you have your life. If you haven't had that, what *have* you had? ... This place and these impressions ... have had their abundant message for me, I have just dropped *that* into my mind. I see it now ... and more than you'd believe or I can express ... The right time is now yours. The right time is any *time* that one is still so lucky as to have ... Live, Live!"

To an imaginative European, unfamiliar with the prohibitive American past and the long-standing national habit of playing hide-and-seek with experience, Strether's pronouncements in favor of sheer life may well seem so commonplace as scarcely to be worth the loving concentration of a major novelist. While the idea that one should "live" one's life came to James as a revelation, to the contemporary European writers this idea had long been a thoroughly assimilated and natural assumption. Experience served them as the concrete medium for the testing and creation of values, whereas in James's work it stands for something distilled or selected from the total process of living; it stands for romance, reality, civilization — a self-propelling, autonomous "presence" inexhaustibly alluring in its own right. That is the "presence" which in the imagination of Hyacinth Robinson, the hero of *The Princess Casamassima,* takes on a form at once "vast, vague, and dazzling — an irradiation of light from objects undefined, mixed with the atmosphere of Paris and Venice."

The significance of this positive approach to experience and identification of it with life's "treasures, felicities, splendors and successes" is that it represents a momentous break with the then dominant American morality of abstention. The roots of this morality are to be traced on the one hand to the religion of the Puritans and, on the other, to the inescapable need of a frontier society to master its world in sober practice before appropriating it as an object of enjoyment. Such is the historical content of that native "innocence" which in James's fiction is continually being ensnared in the web of European "experience." And James's tendency is to resolve this drama of entanglement by finally accepting what Europe offers on condition that it cleanse itself of its taint of evil through an alliance with New World virtue.

James's attitude toward experience is sometimes overlooked by readers excessively impressed (or depressed) by his oblique methods and effects of remoteness and ambiguity. Actually, from the standpoint of the history of the national letters, the lesson he taught in *The Ambassadors,* as in many of his other works, must be understood as no less than a revolutionary appeal. It is a veritable declaration of the rights of man — not, to be sure, of the rights of the public, of the social man, but of the rights of the private man, of the rights of personality, whose openness to experience provides the sole effective guaranty of its development. Already in one of his earliest stories we find the observation that "in this country the people have rights but the person has none." And insofar as any artist can be said to have had a mission, his manifestly was to brace the American individual in his moral struggle to gain for his personal and subjective life that measure of freedom which, as a citizen of a prosperous and democratic community, he had long been enjoying in the sphere of material and political relations.

Strether's appeal, in curiously elaborated, varied, as well as ambivalent forms, pervades all of James's work; and for purposes of critical symbolization it might well be regarded as the compositional key to the whole modern movement in American writing. No literature, it might be said, takes on the qualities of a truly national body of expression unless it is possessed by a basic theme and unifying principle of its own. Thus the German creative mind has in the main been actuated by philosophical interests, the French by the highest ambitions of the intelligence unrestrained by system or dogma, the Russian by the passionately candid questioning and shaping of values. And since Whitman and James the American creative mind, seizing at last upon what had long been denied to it, has found the terms and objects of its activity in the urge toward and immersion in experience. It is this search for experience, conducted on diverse and often conflicting levels of consciousness, which has been the dominant, quintessential theme of the characteristic American literary productions — from *Leaves of Grass* to *Winesburg, Ohio* and beyond; and the more typically American the writer — a figure like Thomas Wolfe is a patent example — the more deeply does it engulf him.

It is through this preoccupation, it seems to me, that one can account, perhaps more adequately than through any other factor, for some of the peculiarities of American writing since the close of its classic period. A basis is thus provided for explaining the unique indifference of this literature to certain cultural aims implicit in the aesthetic rendering of experience — to ideas generally, to theories of value, to the wit of the speculative and problematical, and to that new-fashioned sense of irony which at once expresses and modulates the conflicts in modern belief. In his own way even a writer as intensely aware as James shares this indifference. He is the analyst of fine consciences, and fine minds too, but scarcely of minds capable of grasping and acting upon those ineluctable problems that enter so prominently and with such significant results into the literary art developed in Europe during the past hundred years. And the question is not whether James belonged among the "great thinkers" — very few novelists do — but whether he is "obsessed" by those universal problems, whether, in other words, his work is vitally associated with that prolonged crisis of the human spirit to which the concept of modernity is ultimately reducible. What James asks for, primarily, is the expansion of life beyond its primitive needs and elementary standards of moral and material utility; and of culture he conceives as the reward of this expansion and as its unfailing means of discrimination. Hence he searches for the whereabouts of "Life" and for the exact conditions of its enrichment. This is what makes for a fundamental difference between the inner movement of the American and that of the European novel, the novel of Tolstoy and Dostoevsky, Flaubert and Proust, Joyce, Mann, Lawrence, and Kafka, whose problem is invariably posed in terms of life's intrinsic worth and destiny.

The intellectual is the only character missing in the American novel. He may appear in it in his professional capacity — as artist, teacher, or scientist — but very rarely as a person who thinks with his entire being, that is to say, as a person who transforms ideas into actual dramatic motives instead of merely using them as ideological conventions or as theories so externally applied that they can be dispensed with at will. Everything is contained in the American novel except ideas. But what are ideas? At best judgments of reality and at worst substitutes for it. The American novelist's conversion to reality, however, has been so belated that he cannot but be baffled by judgments and vexed by susbstitutes. Thus his work exhibits a singular pattern consisting, on the one hand, of a disinclination to thought and, on the other, of an intense predilection for the real: and the real appears in it as a vast phenomenology swept by waves of sensation and feeling. In this welter there is little room for the intellect, which in the unconscious belief of many imaginative Americans is naturally impervious, if not wholly inimical, to reality.

Consider the literary qualities of Ernest Hemingway, for example. There is nothing Hemingway dislikes more than experience of a make-believe, vague, or frigid nature, but in order to safeguard himself against the counterfeit he consistently avoids drawing upon the more abstract resources of the mind, he snubs the thinking man and mostly confines himself to the depiction of life on its physical levels. Of course, his rare mastery of the sensuous element largely compensates for whatever losses he may sustain in other spheres. Yet the fact remains that a good part of his writing leaves us with a sense of situations unresolved and with a picture of human beings tested by values much too simplified to do them justice. Cleanth Brooks and Robert Penn Warren have recently remarked on the interrelation between qualities of Hemingway's style and his bedazzlement by sheer experience. The following observation in particular tends to bear out the point of view expressed in this essay: "The short simple rhythms, the succession of coordinate clauses, the general lack of subordination — all suggest a dislocated and ununified world. The figures which live in this world live a sort of hand-to-mouth existence perceptually, and conceptually, they hardly live at all. Subordination implies some exercise of discrimination — the sifting of reality through the intellect. But Hemingway has a romantic anti-intellectualism which is to be associated with the premium which he places upon experience as such."*

But Hemingway is only a specific instance. Other writers, less gifted and not so self-sufficiently and incisively one-sided, have come to grief through this same creative psychology. Under its conditioning some of them have produced work so limited to the recording of the unmistakably and recurrently real that it can truly be said of them that their art ends exactly where it should properly begin.

"How can one make the best of one's life?" André Malraux asks in one of his novels. "By converting as wide a range of experience as possible into conscious thought." It is precisely this reply which is alien to the typical American artist, who all too often is so absorbed in experience that he is satisfied to let it "write its own ticket" — to carry him, that is, to its own chance or casual destination.

In the first part of *Faust* Goethe removes his hero, a Gothic dreamer, from the cell of scholastic devotion in order to embroil him in the passions and high-flavored joys of "real life." But in the second part of the play this hero attains a broader stage of consciousness, reconciling the perilous freedom of his newly released personality with the enduring interests of the race, with high art, politics, and the constructive labor of curbing the chaotic forces in man and nature alike. This progress of Faust is foreshadowed in an early scene, when Mephisto promises to reveal to him "the little and then the great world [*Wir sehen die kleine, dann die grosse Welt*]." The little world is the world of the individual bemused by his personal experience, and his sufferings, guilt feelings, and isolation are to be understood as the penalty he pays for throwing off the traditional bonds that once linked him to God and his fellowmen. Beyond the little world, however, lies the broader world of man the inhabitant of his own history, who in truth is always losing his soul in order to gain it. Now the American drama of experience constitutes a kind of half-*Faust*, a play with the first part intact and the second part missing. And the Mephisto of this shortened version is the familiar demon of the Puritan morality play, not at all the Goethian philosopher-sceptic driven by the nihilistic spirit of the modern epoch. Nor is the plot of this half-*Faust* consistent within itself. For its protagonist, playing Gretchen

* Cf. "The Killers," by Cleanth Brooks and Robert Penn Warren, in *American Prefaces*, spring 1942.

as often as he plays Faust, is evidently unclear in his own mind as to the role he is cast in — that of the seducer or the seduced?

It may be that this confusion of roles is the inner source of the famous Jamesian ambiguity and ever-recurring theme of betrayal. James's heroines — his Isabel Archers and Milly Theales and Maggie Ververs — are they not somehow always being victimized by the "great world" even as they succeed in mastering it? Gretchen-like in their innocence, they nonetheless enact the Faustian role in their un-interrupted pursuit of experience and in the use of the truly Mephis-tophelean gold of their millionaire-fathers to buy up the brains and beauty and nobility of the civilization that enchants them. And the later heroes of American fiction — Hemingway's young man, for in-stance, who invariably appears in each of his novels, a young man posing his virility against the background of continents and nations so old that, like Tiresias, they have seen all and suffered all — in his own way he, too, responds to experience in the schizoid fashion of the Gretchen-Faust character. For what is his virility if not at once the measure of his innocence and the measure of his aggression? And what shall we make of Steinbeck's fable of Lennie, that mindless giant who literally kills and gets killed from sheer desire for those soft and lovely things of which fate has singularly deprived him? He combines an unspeakable innocence with an unspeakable aggression. Perhaps it is not too farfetched to say that in this grotesque creature Steinbeck has unconsciously created a symbolic parody of a figure such as Thomas Wolfe, who likewise crushed in his huge caresses the deli-cate objects of the art of life.

The disunity of American literature, its polar division into above and below or paleface and redskin writing, I have noted elsewhere. Whit-man and James, who form a kind of fatal antipodes, have served as the standard examples of this dissociation. There is one sense, how-ever, in which the contrast between these two archetypal Americans may be said to have been overdrawn. There is, after all, a common ground on which they finally, though perhaps briefly, meet — an essential Americanism subsuming them both that is best defined by their mutual affirmation of experience. True, what one affirmed the other was apt to negate; still it is not in their attitudes toward expe-rience as such that the difference between them becomes crucial but rather in their contradictory conceptions of what constitutes experi-ence. One sought its ideal manifestations in America, the other in Europe. Whitman, plunging with characteristic impetuosity into the turbulent, formless life of the frontier and the big cities, accepted experience in its total ungraded state, whereas James, insisting on a precise scrutiny of its origins and conditions, was endlessly discriminatory, thus carrying forward his ascetic inheritance into the very act of reaching out for the charms and felicities of the great European world. But the important thing to keep in mind here is that this plebeian and patrician are historically associated, each in his own incomparable way, in the radical enterprise of subverting the puritan code of stark utility in the conduct of life and in releasing the long compressed springs of experience in the national letters. In this sense, Whitman and James are the true initiators of the American line of modernity.

If a positive approach to experience is the touchstone of the modern, a negative approach is the touchstone of the classic in American writing. The literature of early America is a sacred rather than a profane literature. Immaculately spiritual at the top and local and anecdotal at the bottom, it is essentially, as the genteel literary historian Barrett Wendell accurately noted, a "record of the national inexperience" marked by "instinctive disregard of actual fact." For this reason it largely left untouched the two chief experiential media — the novel and the drama. Brockden Brown, Cooper, Hawthorne, and Melville were "romancers" and poets rather than novelists. They were incapable of apprehending the vitally new principle of realism by virtue of which the art of fiction in Europe was in their time rapidly evolving toward a hitherto inconceivable condition of objectivity and familiarity with existence. Not until James did a fiction writer appear in America who was able to sympathize with and hence to take advantage of the methods of George Eliot, Balzac, and Turgenev. Since the principle of realism presupposes a thoroughly secularized relationship between the ego and experience, Hawthorne and Melville could not possibly have apprehended it. Though not religious men themselves, they were nevertheless held in bondage by ancestral conscience and dogma, they were still living in the afterglow of a religious faith that drove the ego, on its external side, to aggrandize itself by accumulating practical sanctions while scourging and inhibiting its intimate side. In Hawthorne the absent or suppressed experience reappears in the shape of spectral beings whose function is to warn, repel, and fascinate. And the unutterable confusion that reigns in some of Melville's narratives (*Pierre, Mardi*) is primarily due to his inability either to come to terms with experience or else wholly and finally to reject it.

Despite the featureless innocence and moral enthusiastic air of the old American books, there is in some of them a peculiar virulence, a feeling of discord that does not easily fit in with the general tone of the classic age. In such worthies as Irving, Cooper, Bryant, Longfellow, Whittier, and Lowell there is scarcely anything more than meets the eye, but in Poe, Hawthorne, and Melville there is an incandescent symbolism, a meaning within meaning, the vitality of which is perhaps only now rightly appreciated. D. H. Lawrence was close to the truth when he spoke of what serpents they were, of the "inner diabolism of their underconsciousness." Hawthorne, "that blue-eyed darling," as well as Poe and Melville, insisted on a subversive vision of human nature at the same time as cultivated Americans were everywhere relishing the orations of Emerson who, as James put it, was helping them "to take a picturesque view of one's internal possibilities and to find in the landscape of the soul all sorts of fine sunrise and moonlight effects." Each of these three creative men displays a healthy resistance to the sentimentality and vague idealism of his contemporaries; and along with this resistance they display morbid qualities that, aside from any specific biographical factors, might perhaps be accounted for by the contradiction between the poverty of the experience provided by the society they lived in and the high development of their moral, intellectual, and affective natures — though in Poe's case there is no need to put any stress on his moral character. And the curious thing is that whatever faults their work shows are reversed in later American literature, the weaknesses of which are not to be traced to poverty of experience but to an inability to encompass it on a significant level.

The dilemma that confronted these early writers chiefly manifests itself in their frequent failure to integrate the inner and outer elements of their world so that they might stand witness for each other by way of the organic linkage of object and symbol, act and meaning. For that is the linkage of art without which its structure cannot stand. Lawrence thought that *Moby Dick* is profound *beyond* human feeling — which in a sense says as much against the book as for it. Its further defects are dispersion, a divided mind: its real and transcendental elements do not fully interpenetrate, the creative tension between them is more fortuitous than organic. In *The Scarlet Letter* as in a few of his shorter fictions, and to a lesser degree in *The Blithedale Romance*, Hawthorne was able to achieve an imaginative order that otherwise eluded him. A good deal of his writing, despite his gift for precise observation, consists of fantasy unsupported by the conviction of reality.

Many changes had to take place in America before its spiritual and material levels could fuse in a work of art in a more or less satisfactory manner. Whitman was already in the position to vivify his democratic ethos by an appeal to the physical features of the country, such as the grandeur and variety of its geography, and to the infinite detail of common lives and occupations. And James too, though sometimes forced to resort to makeshift situations, was on the whole successful in setting up a lively and significant exchange between the moral and empiric elements of his subject matter. Though he was, in a sense, implicitly bound all his life by the morality of Hawthorne, James nonetheless perceived what the guilt-tossed psyche of the author of *The Marble Faun* prevented him from seeing — that it is not the man trusting himself to experience but the one fleeing from it who suffers the "beast in the jungle" to rend him.

The Transcendentalist movement is peculiar in that it expresses the native tradition of inexperience in its particulars and the revolutionary urge to experience in its generalities. (Perhaps that is what Van Wyck Brooks meant when, long before prostrating himself at his shrine, he wrote that Emerson was habitually abstract where he should be concrete, and vice versa.) On a purely theoretical plane, in ways curiously inverted and idealistic, the cult of experience is patently prefigured in Emerson's doctrine of the uniqueness and infinitude, as well as in Thoreau's equally steep estimate, of the private man. American culture was then unprepared for anything more drastic than an affirmation of experience in theory alone, and even the theory was modulated in a semiclerical fashion so as not to set it in too open an opposition to the dogmatic faith that, despite the decay of its theology, still prevailed in the ethical sphere. "The love which is preached nowadays," wrote Thoreau, "is an ocean of new milk for a man to swim in. I hear no surf nor surge, but the winds coo over it." No wonder, then, that Transcendentalism declared itself most clearly and dramatically in the form of the essay — a form in which one can preach without practicing.

Personal liberation from social taboos and conventions was the war cry of the group of writers that came to the fore in the second decade of the century. They employed a variety of means to formulate and press home this program. Dreiser's tough-minded though somewhat arid naturalism, Anderson's softer and spottier method articulating the protest of shut-in people, Lewis' satires of Main Street, Cabell's florid celebrations of pleasure, Edna Millay's emotional expansiveness, Mencken's worldly wisdom and assaults on the provincial pieties, the early Van Wyck Brooks's high-minded though bitter evocations of the inhibited past, his ideal of creative self-fulfillment — all these were weapons brought to bear by the party of rebellion in the struggle to gain free access to experience. And the secret of energy in that struggle seems to have been the longing for what was then called "sexual freedom"; for at the time Americans seeking emancipation were engaged in a truly elemental discovery of sex whose literary expression on some levels, as Randolph Bourne remarked, easily turned into "caricatures of desire." The novel, the poem, the play — all contributed to the development of a complete symptomatology of sexual frustration and release. In his *Memoirs,* written toward the end of his life, Sherwood Anderson recalled the writers of that period as "a little band of soldiers who were going to free life...from certain bonds." Not that they wanted to overplay sex, but they did want "to bring it back into real relation to the life we lived and saw others living. We wanted the flesh back in our literature, wanted directly in our literature the fact of men and women in bed together, babies being born. We wanted the terrible importance of the flesh in human relations also revealed again." In retrospect much of this writing seems but a naive inversion of the dear old American innocence, a turning inside out of inbred fear and reticence, but the qualities one likes in it are its positiveness of statement, its zeal and pathos of the limited view.

The concept of experience was then still an undifferentiated whole. But as the desire for personal liberation, even if only from the less compulsive social pressures, was partly gratified and the tone of the literary revival changed from eagerness to disdain, the sense of totality gradually wore itself out. Since the 1920s a process of atomization of experience has forced each of its spokesmen into a separate groove from which he can step out only at the risk of utterly disorienting himself. Thus, to cite some random examples, poetic technique became the special experience of Ezra Pound, language that of Gertrude Stein, the concrete object was appropriated by W. C. Williams, super-American phenomena by Sandburg and related nationalists, Kenneth Burke experienced ideas (which is by no means the same as thinking them), Archibald MacLeish experienced public attitudes, F. Scott Fitzgerald the glamor and sadness of the very rich, Hemingway death and virile sports, and so on and so forth. Finally Thomas Wolfe plunged into a chaotic recapitulation of the cult of experience as a whole, traversing it in all directions and ending nowhere.

Though the crisis of the 1930s arrested somewhat the progress of the experiential mode, it nevertheless managed to put its stamp on the entire social-revolutionary literature of the decade. A comparison of European and American left-wing writing of the same period will at once show that whereas Europeans like Malraux and Silone enter deeply into the meaning of political ideas and beliefs, Americans touch only superficially on such matters, as actually their interest is fixed almost exclusively on the class war as an experience which, to them at least, is new and exciting. They succeed in representing incidents of oppression and revolt, as well as sentimental conversions, but conversions of the heart and mind they merely sketch in on the surface or imply in a gratuitous fashion. (What does a radical novel like *The Grapes of Wrath* contain, from an ideological point of view, that agitational journalism cannot communicate with equal heat and facility? Surely its vogue cannot be explained by its radicalism. Its real attraction for the millions who read it lies elsewhere — perhaps in its vivid recreation of "a slice of life" so horridly unfamiliar that it can be made to yield an exotic interest.) The sympathy of these ostensibly political writers with the revolutionary cause is often genuine, yet their understanding of its inner movement, intricate problems, and doctrinal and strategic motives is so deficient as to call into question their competence to deal with political material. In the complete works of the so-called "proletarian school" you will not find a single viable portrait of a Marxist intellectual or of any character in the revolutionary drama who, conscious of his historical role, is not a mere automaton of spontaneous class force or impulse.

What really happened in the 1930s is that due to certain events the public aspects of experience appeared more meaningful than its private aspects, and literature responded accordingly. But the subject of political art is *history*, which stands in the same relation to experience as fiction to biography; and just as surely as failure to generalize the biographical element thwarts the aspirant to fiction, so the ambition of the literary Left to create a political art was thwarted by its failure to lift experience to the level of history. (For the benefit of those people who habitually pause to insist on what they call "strictly literary values," I might add that by "history" in this connection I do not mean "history books" or anything resembling what is known as the "historical novel" or drama. A political art would succeed in lifting experience to the level of history if its perception of life — any life — were organized around a perspective relating the artist's sense of the *society* of the dead to his sense of the *society* of the living and the as yet unborn.)

Experience, in the sense of "felt life" rather than as life's total practice, is the main but by no means the total substance of literature. The part experience plays in the aesthetic sphere might well be compared to the part that the materialist conception of history assigns to economy. Experience, in the sense of this analogy, is the substructure of literature above which there rises a superstructure of values, ideas, and judgments — in a word, of the multiple forms of consciousness. But this base and summit are not stationary: they continually act and react upon each other.

It is precisely this superstructural level which is seldom reached by the typical American writer of the modern era. Most of the well-known reputations will bear out my point. Whether you approach a poet like Ezra Pound or novelists like Steinbeck and Faulkner, what is at once noticeable is the uneven, and at times quite distorted, development of the various elements that constitute literary talent. What is so exasperating about Pound's poetry, for example, is its peculiar combination of a finished technique (his special share in the distribution of experience) with amateurish and irresponsible ideas. It could be maintained that for sheer creative power Faulkner is hardly excelled by any living novelist, yet the diversity and wonderful intensity of the experience represented in his narratives cannot entirely make up for their lack of order, of a self-illuminating structure, and obscurity of value and meaning. One might naturally counter this criticism by stating that though Faulkner rarely or never sets forth values directly, they nonetheless exist in his work by implication. Yes, but implications incoherently expressed are no better than mystifications, and nowadays it is values that we can least afford to take on faith. Moreover, in a more striking manner perhaps than any of his contemporaries, Faulkner illustrates the tendency of the experiential mode, if pursued to its utmost extreme, to turn into its opposite through unconscious self-parody. In Faulkner the excess, the systematic inflation of the horrible is such a parody of experience. In Thomas Wolfe the same effect is produced by his swollen rhetoric and compulsion to repeat himself — and repetition is an obvious form of parody. This repetition compulsion has plagued a good many American writers. Its first and most conspicuous victim, of course, was Whitman, who occasionally slipped into unintentional parodies of himself.

Yet there is a positive side to the primacy of experience in late American literature. For this primacy has conferred certain benefits upon it, of which none is more bracing than its relative immunity from abstraction and otherworldliness. The stream of life, unimpeded by the rocks and sands of ideology, flows through it freely. If inept in coping with the general, it particularizes not at all badly; and the assumptions of sanctity that so many European artists seem to require as a kind of guaranty of their professional standing are not readily conceded in the lighter and clearer American atmosphere. "Whatever may have been the case in years gone by," Whitman wrote in 1888, "the true use for the imaginative faculty of modern times is to give ultimate vivification to facts, to science, and to common lives, endowing them with glows and glories and final illustriousness which belong to every real thing, and to real things only." As this statement was intended as a prophecy, it is worth noting that while the radiant endowments that Whitman speaks of — the "glows and glories and final illustriousness" — have not been granted, the desired and predicted vivification of facts, science, and common lives has in a measure been realized, though in the process Whitman's democratic faith has as often been belied as confirmed.

It is not the mere recoil from the inhibitions of puritan and neo-puritan times that instigated the American search for experience. Behind it is the extreme individualism of a country without a long past to brood on, whose bourgeois spirit had not worn itself out and been debased in a severe struggle against an old culture so tenacious as to retain the power on occasion to fascinate and render impotent even its predestined enemies. Moreover, in contrast to the derangements that have continually shaken Europe, life in the United States has been relatively fortunate and prosperous. It is possible to speak of American history as "successful" history. Within the limits of the capitalist order — until the present period the objective basis for a different social order simply did not exist here — the American people have been able to find definitive solutions for the great historical problems that faced them. Thus both the Revolutionary and the Civil wars were complete actions that virtually abolished the antagonisms which had initially caused the breakdown of national equilibrium. In Europe similar actions have usually led to festering compromises that in the end reproduced the same conflicts in other forms.

It is plain that until very recently there has really been no urgent need in America for high intellectual productivity. Indeed, the American intelligentsia developed very slowly as a semi-independent grouping; and what is equally important, for more than a century now and especially since 1865, it has been kept at a distance from the machinery of social and political power. What this means is that insofar as it has been deprived of certain opportunities, it has also been sheltered and pampered. There was no occasion or necessity for the intervention of the intellectuals — it was not mentality that society needed most in order to keep its affairs in order. On the whole the intellectuals were left free to cultivate private interests, and, once the moral and aesthetic ban on certain types of exertion had been removed, uninterruptedly to solicit individual experience. It is this lack of a sense of extremity and many-sided involvement which explains the peculiar shallowness of a good deal of American literary expression. If some conditions of insecurity have been known to retard and disarm the mind, so have some conditions of security. The question is not whether Americans have suffered less than Europeans, but of the quality of whatever suffering and happiness have fallen to their lot.

The consequence of all this has been that American literature has tended to make too much of private life, to impose on it, to scour it for meanings that it cannot always legitimately yield. Henry James was the first to make a cause, if not a fetish, of personal relations; and the justice of his case, despite his vaunted divergence from the pioneer type, is that of a pioneer too, for while Americans generally were still engaged in "gathering in the preparations and necessities" he resolved to seek out "the amenities and consummations." Furthermore, by exploiting in a fashion altogether his own the contingencies of private life that fell within his scope, he was able to dramatize the relation of the new world to the old, thus driving the wedge of histori-cal consciousness into the very heart of the theme of experience. Later not a few attempts were made to combine experience with conscious-ness, to achieve the balance of thought and being characteristic of the great traditions of European art. But except for certain narratives of James and Melville, I know of very little American fiction which can unqualifiedly be said to have attained this end.

Since the decline of the regime of gentility many admirable works have been produced, but in the main it is the quantity of felt life com-prised in them that satisfies, not their quality of belief or interpretive range. In poetry there is evidence of more distinct gains, perhaps be-cause the medium has reached that late stage in its evolution when its chance of survival depends on its capacity to absorb ideas. The modern poetic styles — metaphysical and symbolist — depend on a conjunction of feeling and idea. But, generally speaking, bare expe-rience is still the *leitmotif* of the American writer, though the literary depression of recent years tends to show that this theme is virtually ex-hausted. At bottom it was the theme of the individual transplanted from an old culture taking inventory of himself and of his new sur-roundings. This inventory, this initial recognition and experiencing of oneself and one's surroundings, is all but complete now, and those who persist in going on with it are doing so out of mere routine and inertia.

The creative power of the cult of experience is almost spent, but what lies beyond it is still unclear. One thing, however, is certain: whereas in the past, throughout the nineteenth and well into the twentieth century, the nature of American literary life was largely determined by national forces, now it is international forces that have begun to exert a dominant influence. And in the long run it is in the terms of this historic change that the future course of American writing will define itself.

Partisan Review, 1940

F. Scott Fitzgerald on the Riviera

F. Scott Fitzgerald made a name for himself in the literature of the last decade as the voice and character of the jazz age. This,
in a sense, was his strength, as he showed himself capable of quickly
responding to features of American life that other writers assimilated
rather slowly, but also proved to be his greatest defect, since he failed
to place what he saw in its social setting. He himself was swept away
by the people he described and he bewitched himself with them.
Hence the critic who, at his appearance on the literary scene, saw in
him a major talent in postwar American literature, soon realized that
here was another creative promise petering out. The fever of the boom
days settled in his bones. In the end he surrendered to the standards
of the *Saturday Evening Post*.

In these days, however, even Fitzgerald cannot escape realizing how
near the collapse of his class really is. In his new work he no longer
writes of expensive blondes and yachting parties, lavish surroundings
and insane love affairs from the same angle of vision as in the past.
These things are still there but the author's enthusiasm has faded, giving way to the sweat of exhaustion. The rich expatriates who trail
their weary lives across the pages of the novel breathe the thin air of a
crazy last autumn. The author is still in love with his characters, but
he no longer entertains any illusions concerning their survival. Morally, spiritually, and even physically they are dying in hospitals for
the mentally diseased, in swanky Paris hotels, and on the Riviera
beaches. Yet, having immersed himself in the atmosphere of corruption, Fitzgerald's eye discerns a certain grace even in their last con-
tortions. The morbid romance of death sways his mind, and the signs
are not wanting that instead of severing the cords that bind them to
their degradation, he prefers to stick it out with them to the end. Even
while perceiving their doom he still continues to caress them with

soft words uttered in the voice of a family doctor pledged to keep the
fatal diagnosis from his patients.

A number of things happen in *Tender Is the Night*. First, let us introduce Mr. Warren, a Chicago millionaire who rapes his sixteen-year-
old daughter Nicole. This nonplebeian act drives the girl out of her
mind, and she is sent to a sanitarium in Switzerland, where she is
partially cured, and where she meets Dick Diver, a young American
psychologist who marries her. Nicole is extremely wealthy and the
Divers lead a model parasitic life, flitting from one European high
spot to another, accompanied by a varied assortment of neurotics and
alcoholics. Wherever they go they are intent on smashing things up.
Dick Diver's strength and charm fall apart in the insufferable atmosphere of sophisticated brutality. In the course of time he realized his
role as a live commodity bought by the Warren family to act as hus-
band-doctor to their crazy daughter. And Nicole, sensing Dick's growing despair, flies from him to the arms of Tommy Barban, the stylized
young barbarian who is potentially an ideal leader of a Nazi storm
troop.

When the plot is thus bluntly stated, stripped of its delicate, intro-
spective wording, of its tortuous style that varnishes rather than reveals
the essential facts, we can easily see that the book is a fearful indictment of the moneyed aristocracy. But Fitzgerald's form blunts this
essence, transforming it into a mere opportunity for endless psychologizing. And on account of it many a reader will let himself feast on the
novel's tender surface, without gauging the horror underneath.

The reviewer is inclined to think that in creating the figure of Dick
Diver, Fitzgerald has created — perhaps unconsciously — the image
of a life closely corresponding to his own. The truth is that Nicole
can be understood as a symbol of the entire social system to which
Fitzgerald has long been playing Dick Diver.

And lastly, a not too private postscript to the author. Dear Mr.
Fitzgerald, you can't hide from a hurricane under a beach umbrella.

Daily Worker, 1934

The Dark Lady of Salem

Because I seek an image not a book
W. B. YEATS

Hawthorne is generally spoken of as a novelist of sin, but the truth is that he is not a novelist, at least not in the sense in which the term is commonly used, nor is sin wholly and unequivocally his subject. What that subject is remains to be defined, though by way of introduction it might be said that it is less a subject than a predicament. Or, better still, the predicament is the subject.

What is the intention of the novel as we have come to know it? In the broadest sense, it is to portray life as it is actually lived. Free access to experience is the necessary condition of the novel's growth as well as the objective guaranty of its significance; experience is at once its myth and its reason; and he who shuns experience is no more capable of a convincing performance in its sphere than a man unnerved by the sight of blood is capable of heroic feats on the battlefield. Now Hawthorne lived in an age when it was precisely experience — or, at any rate, those of its elements most likely to engage the interests of an artist — that was least at the disposal of the imaginative American, whose psychic resistance to its appeal was everywhere reinforced by the newness and bareness of the national scene, by its much-lamented "paucity of ingredients." It is this privation that accounts for Hawthorne's chill ideality, for his tendency to cherish the fanciful at the expense of the substantial and to reduce the material world to the all-too-familiar abstractions of spiritual law and the moral conscience. Two strains mingle in his literary nature: the spectral strain of the Gothic tale and the pietistic strain of Christian allegory, and both contribute to his alienation from the real.*

---

* In his *American Prose Masters,* W. C. Brownell observes that Hawthorne's particular genius took him out of the novelist's field altogether. "His novels are not novels. They have not the reality of novels, and they elude it not only in their personages but in their picture of life in general." But the fact is that Hawthorne's

Yet there is in this writer a submerged intensity and passion — a tangled imagery of unrest and longing for experience and regret at its loss which is largely ignored by those of his critics who place him too securely within the family circle of the New England moralists. His vision of evil carries something more than a simple, one-way assertion of traditional principles; it carries negation as well. He was haunted not only by the guilt of his desires but also by the guilt of his denial of them. The puritan in him grappled with the man of the nineteenth century — historically a man of appetite and perspective; and the former did not so easily pacify and curb the latter as is generally assumed.

The whole tone and meaning of Hawthorne's work, it seems to me, turns on this conflict.

In his own estimate he was a "romancer," and his insistence on designating himself as such should not be overlooked. Time and again he admonished his readers not to expect from him that "fidelity, not merely to the possible, but to the probable and ordinary course of man's existence" which is the mark of the novelist. He took pains to distinguish between the romance and the novel in order to lay claim, though not without due apologies, to the latitude inherent in the earlier genre. Yet he was fully aware of its deficiencies, aware that the freedom it afforded was more apparent than real, committing him to all sorts of dodges and retreats to which his artist's conscience could not be reconciled. This explains his habit of referring to his own compositions in a disparaging manner as "fancy-pictures" that could not survive a close comparison with the actual events of real lives.

Even while writing *The Scarlet Letter*, the theme of which suited him perfectly, he publicly regretted the "folly" of flinging himself back into a distant age and attempting to create "a semblance of a world out of airy matter." He would have been far better served, he goes on to confess in that superb essay, *The Custom House*, had he sought his themes in the "warm materiality" of the daily scene. "The fault," he concludes, "was mine. The page of life that was spread out before me seemed dull and commonplace, only because I had not fathomed its deeper import. A better book than I shall ever write was there ... At some future day, it may be, I shall remember a few scattered fragments and broken paragraphs, and write them down, and find the

---

particular genius cannot be assessed apart from the forces that shaped its expression. If we accept Brownell's definition of the novel as the medium of the actual, it can be stated flatly that neither Hawthorne nor any of his contemporaries succeeded in mastering it.

letters turn to gold upon the page." But he was fated to be disappointed. The golden flow of reality never suffused his pages. Instead of entering the waking world of the novel, he remained to the last a "romancer" under the spell of that shadowy stuff which he at once loved and hated.

In the development of narrative prose his place is decidedly among the prenovelists — a position which he holds not alone but in the company of Poe and Melville and virtually the entire clan of classic American writers who, at one time or another, turned their hand to the making of fiction. The fact is that no novels, properly speaking, were produced in America until late in the nineteenth century, when the moralistic, semiclerical outlook which had so long dominated the native culture-heroes finally began to give way. The freedom promised by the Transcendentalist movement of the mid-century had not gone beyond a certain philosophical warmth and ardor of purpose. Though this movement expanded American thought, in itself this did not suffice to release the novelistic function. The release was effected only after the Civil War, when the many-sided expansion of American life created a new set of circumstances more favorable to artists whose business is with the concrete manifestations of the real and with its everyday textures. Then it was that James and Howells, susceptible, in different degrees, to the examples of European writing, came forward with new ideas, plans, and recipes.

Hawthorne's isolation from experience incapacitated him as a novelist. Yet he longed to break through this isolation, searching for the key that would let him out of the dungeon and enable him to "open intercourse with the world." "I have not lived," he cried, "but only dreamed of living ... I have seen so little of the world that I have nothing but thin air to concoct my stories of ..." Even the moderately candid biographies of him show that such protests were typical of his state of mind. And since these protests also inform his fiction, even if only in a tortuous and contradictory fashion, it can be said that his basic concern as a writer, though expressed in the traditional-moral terms of the problem of sin, was at bottom with the problem of experience — experience, however, not in the sense of its open representation in the manner of a novelist, but simply in the sense of debating its pros and cons, of examining good and evil, its promise and threat.

This preparatory scrutiny of experience constitutes his real subject, which is obscured by his creative means of allegoric construction and lavish employment of fantasy. His subject and the method he adopted to give it fictional form are incongruously related, but it was the only method available to him in his situation and, despite its faults, it permitted the growth of a novelistic embryo in each of his romances. That which is most actual in his work is comprised in these embryos; the rest — coming under the head of "romance" — is composed by his Gothic machinery and fed by the ceaseless pullulations of the sin-dogma. Knowingly or not, he indicated his own practice in remarking: "Realities keep in the rear, and put forward an advance-guard of show and humbug."

But the split in his emotional and intellectual nature prevented him from ever resolving the conflict of value and impulse implicit in his subject. All he could do was reproduce his predicament within his creations. On the one hand he thought it desirable "to live throughout the whole range of one's faculties and sensibilities" and, on the other, to play the part of a spiritualized Paul Pry "hovering invisible around men and women, witnessing their deeds, searching into their hearts, borrowing brightness from their felicity and shade from their sorrow, *and retaining no emotion peculiar to himself.*" In other words, he wanted the impossible — to enjoy the warmth and vitality of experience without exposing himself to its perils. His entire heritage predisposed him to regard a welcoming and self-offering attitude to experience as the equivalent of a state of sin; and though he was inclined to doubt the justice and validity of this cruelly schematic equation, its sway over him nevertheless told in the end. It barred him from any patent commitment to that program of personal liberation which his successors in the American creative line were later to adopt and elaborate into peculiarly indigenous forms of literary art. Is experience identical with sin? — and if so, is sin the doom of man or his salvation? To these queries he provided no clear rejoinder, but his bent was to say one thing on the surface of his work, on the level of its manifest content, while saying something else in its depths, in its latent meanings. He tried to serve at once the old and the new gods, and in the main it is within the active play of this ambivalence, of this sundered devotion, that he achieved his unique color and interest. His incubus he taught to poetize.

The constraint under which he labored had its source, of course, in the old Calvinist faith, but he was born too late to know it for what it once was. Of religion, indeed, he knew little beyond its fears. Originally a powerful vision of man's relation to God, the puritan orthodoxy was now reduced to a narrow moral scheme with clerical trappings. And Hawthorne's dilemma was that though the supernatural hardly existed for him in any realm save that of the fanciful, he was nonetheless unable to free himself from the perception of human destiny in terms of sin and redemption, sacrilege and consecration. The sacramental wine had turned to poison in his cup. His dreams abounded in images of his ancestors rising from their graves and of himself walking down Main Street in a shroud. No wonder, then, that he tended to conceive of the past as a menace to the living, as a force the ghastly fascination of which must be resisted.

The House of the Seven Gables is one long symbolization of this feeling. "In this age," preaches Holgrave, the young man who stands for the renovation of life, "the moss-grown and rotten Past is to be torn down, and lifeless institutions to be thrust out of the way, and their dead corpses buried, and everything to begin anew ... What slaves we are to bygone times — to Death ... We live in dead men's houses ... as in this of the Seven Gables ... The house ought to be purified with fire, — purified till only its ashes remain." Still, at the same time as Hawthorne abused the past and remonstrated against its morbid influences, he continued to indulge his taste for gloom and moldiness — for "old ideals and loitering paces and muffled tones." And as the years passed he yielded more and more to this tendency, with the result that in his last phase his mind faltered — it had lost, as he himself admitted, its fine edge and temper — and he could produce nothing but such fragmentary and essentially pointless allegories as *Septimius Felton* and *The Dolliver Romance*.

The conflict in him is clearly between a newborn secular imagination, as yet untried and therefore permeated with the feeling of shock and guilt, and the moribund religious tradition of old New England. It is a conflict which has seldom been detected by his critics, who have for the most part confounded his inner theme of experience with the all-too-apparent theme of sin. Yet the two themes, regardless of their mutual relation from a theological standpoint, are quite distinct as life-elements — though Hawthorne could not but confuse them. Perhaps it is this that was intuitively sensed by D. H. Lawrence, when he spoke of the duplicity of that "blue-eyed *Wunderkind* of a Nathaniel," thus construing as double-dealing a double-mindedness the roots of which lie deep in American history. But the melodramatic twist of Lawrence's insights is scarcely a valid reason for discounting them. He accurately noted the split in Hawthorne between his outward conformity and the "impeccable truth of his art-speech," between his repressed undermeanings and the moonshiny spirituality of his surface.

The evidence, of course, is in the tales and romances. There is one heroine they bring to life who is possibly the most resplendent and erotically forceful woman in American fiction. She dominates all the other characters because she alone personifies the contrary values that her author attached to experience. Drawn on a scale larger than reality, she is essentially a mythic being, the incarnation of hidden longings and desires, as beautiful, we are repeatedly told, as she is "inexpressibly terrible," a temptress offering the ascetic sons of the puritans the "treasure-trove of a great sin."

We come to know this dark lady under four different names — as Beatrice in the story *Rappaccini's Daughter,* Hester in *The Scarlet Letter,* Zenobia in *The Blithedale Romance,* and Miriam in *The Marble Faun.* Her unity as a character is established by the fact that in each of her four appearances she exhibits the same physical and mental qualities and plays substantially the same role. Hawthorne's description of her is wonderfully expressive in the fullness of its sensual imaginings. He is ingenious in devising occasions for celebrating her beauty, and conversely, for denigrating, albeit in equivocal language, her blonde rival — the dovelike, virginal, snow-white maiden of New England. But the two women stand to each other in the relation of the damned to the saved, so that inevitably the dark lady comes to a bad end while the blonde is awarded all the prizes — husband, love, and absolute exemption from moral guilt. There is obviously an obsessive interest here in the psychosexual polarity of dark and fair with its symbolism of good and evil — a polarity which in Fenimore Cooper's treatment (in *The Last of the Mohicans* and *The Deerslayer*) is little more than a romantic convention but which both in Hawthorne and in Melville (Hautia and Yillah in *Mardi* and Isabel and Lucy in *Pierre*) acquires a newly intensive meaning.

Beatrice, of *Rappaccini's Daughter,* is as luxuriant as any of the gemlike flowers in her father's garden of poisonous plants. She looks "redundant with life, health, and energy ... beautiful as the day, with a bloom so deep and vivid that one shade more would have been too much"; her voice, "rich as a tropical sunset," makes her lover Giovanni "think of deep hues of purple or crimson and of perfumes heavily delectable." Hester, of *The Scarlet Letter,* is "tall, with a figure of perfect elegance on a large scale. She had dark and abundant hair, so glossy that it threw off the sunshine with a gleam, and a face which besides being beautiful from regularity of feature and richness of complexion, had the impressiveness belonging to a marked brow ... She had in her nature a rich, voluptuous, Oriental characteristic." In the redundancy of her charms Zenobia, of *The Blithedale Romance,* is fully the equal of Hester Prynne. "Zenobia was an admirable ... a magnificent figure of a woman, just on the hither verge of her maturity ... her hand, though very soft, was larger than most women would like to have ... though not a whit too large in proportion with the spacious plan of her development ... the native glow of coloring in her cheeks, and even the flesh-warmth of her round arms, and what was visible of her full bust — in a word, her womanliness incarnate — compelled me sometimes to close my eyes ... One felt an influence breathing out of her such as we might suppose to come from Eve, when she was just made ... a certain warm and rich characteristic ... the whole woman was alive with a passionate intensity in which her beauty culminated. Any passion would have become her well; and passionate love, perhaps, best of all." And Miriam, of *The Marble Faun,* also had "a great deal of color in her nature ... a beautiful woman ... with dark eyes ... black, abundant hair ... a dark glory."

It is plain that the physical characteristics of these four heroines are interchangeable, and this cannot be due to poverty of invention on Hawthorne's part. What it suggests, rather, is a strong fixation on a certain type of woman, in every way the opposite of the sexually anesthetic females to whom he officially paid homage.* The dark lady is above all an ambivalent love-object;† but beyond that she makes visible that desire for an open-handed conduct of life and individual fulfillment which was in later years to become the major concern of American writing. Reduced to more realistic proportions but nonetheless still invested with mythic powers, she reappears, in such novels as Sherwood Anderson's *Dark Laughter* and *Many Marriages,* in the part of the ideal love partner for whom thwarted husbands desert their wives; and a character like Hemingway's Maria (*For Whom the Bell*

* In this connection a revealing passage from W. D. Howells' *Literary Friends and Acquaintance* is worth citing. Howells is telling of his first meeting with Hawthorne in 1860: "With the abrupt transition of his talk throughout, he [Hawthorne] began to speak of women, and said he had never seen a woman whom he thought quite beautiful. In the same way he spoke of the New England temperament, and suggested that the apparent coldness in it was also real, and that the suppression of emotion for generations would extinguish it at last." Psychologically speaking, the second remark might be taken as a sufficient explanation of the first. On the other hand, perhaps Hawthorne meant to say that no woman he had ever met in the flesh was quite as resplendent as his imagined dark lady.

† Her type is not unknown of course in Victorian fiction, from Trollope to Hardy. She also enters the folklore of the Anglo-Saxon countries as the villainous "dark vampire" of the early American films and popular romances. It is interesting to note that in the 1920s the glamorous (the "hot") blonde replaces the mysterious and voluptuous brunette as the carrier of the sexually potent and dangerous. In Anita Loos's *Gentlemen Prefer Blondes* the usurpation has already gone so far that it is taken for granted. This reversal of roles may well be due to the newly won sexual freedom of the postwar era, a freedom which brought the sexual element to the light of day and thus ended its hitherto exclusive identification with the secrets of the night.

Tolls) — likewise not a "real" person but a dream-image of sexual bliss — is clearly in her line of descent. In her latter-day mutations, however, the sinister side of this heroine has been obliterated. She is now wholly affirmed.

But insofar as they no longer threaten us, these idealized modern women have also ceased to be thoughtful. The Anderson and Hemingway girls leave us without any distinct impression of their minds, whereas the dark lady of Salem displays mental powers that are the counterpart of her physical vitality. Invariably she dominates, or seeks to dominate, the men she loves, and her intellectual range equals and at times even exceeds theirs. She not only acts but thinks passionately, solving the problem of the relation between the sexes in a radical fashion and subverting established values and standards. After being cast out by the community, Hester, we are told, "assumed a freedom of speculation . . . which our forefathers, had they known it, would have held to be a deadlier crime than that stigmatized by the scarlet letter"; Zenobia, who is something of a littérateur and a crusader for women's rights,* has an aptitude for extreme ideas that fill her interlocutors with dismay; and Miriam evolves a conception of sin which amounts to a justification, for she takes the view that sin is a means of educating and improving the personality.

The dark lady is a rebel and an emancipator; but precisely for this reason Hawthorne feels the compulsion to destroy her. *He thus converts the principle of life, of experience, into a principle of death.* Incessantly haunted by the wrongs of the past, by the memory of such brutal deeds directly implicating the founders of his family as the witchcraft trials and the oppression of the Quakers, this repentant puritan is nevertheless impelled by an irresistible inner need to reproduce the very same ancestral pattern in his work. Roused by long-forgotten fears and superstitions, he again traces the footprints of the devil and hears demonic laughter in the woods as darkness falls. His story of the dark lady renews, in all essentials, the persecution of the Salem witches. Beatrice is "as lovely as the dawn and gorgeous as the sunset," yet the "rich perfume of her breath blasts the very air" and to embrace her is to die. Passionate love becomes Zenobia best, yet through insinuating symbols she is pictured as a sorceress. She wears an exotic flower in her hair, and perhaps if this talismanic flower were snatched away she would "vanish or be transformed into something

---

* This is the basis of the widespread impression that she is modeled after Margaret Fuller. Henry James thought there was no truth in the legend. Hawthorne's references to the Boston sibyl in his notebooks are uniformly unkind; he describes her as devoid of the "charm of womanhood" and as a "great humbug" to boot.

else." Miriam, too, has the "faculty of bewitching people." When her nerves give way and she fancies herself unseen, she seeks relief in "fits of madness horrible to behold." Such is the twice-told tale of the dark lady. The victim, in her earlier incarnations, of grim black-browed puritan magistrates, she is now searched out by a secluded New England author who condemns her because she coerces his imagination.

Her figure is first evoked by Hawthorne in *Rappaccini's Daughter* (1844), an entirely fantastic tale generally ranked among the most brilliantly effective of his earlier writings. Beatrice is the daughter of a malignant old professor, who, in his search of fearsome secrets, is experimenting with the medicinal properties of poisonous plants. On coming to Padua, the student Giovanni rents a room the window of which overlooks Rappaccini's garden. Though unaware of the real nature of the flowers in this garden, he is at once troubled by their strange and rampant bloom — "The aspect of one and all of them dissatisfied him; their gorgeousness seemed fierce, passionate, and even unnatural. There was hardly an individual shrub which a wanderer, straying by himself through a forest, would not have been startled to find growing wild, as if an unearthly face had glared at him out of the thicket." His initial impression of Beatrice is that she is but another flower — "the human sister of these vegetable ones, as beautiful as they, more beautiful than the richest of them, but still to be touched only with a glove, nor to be approached without a mask"; and when night closes in, he dreams of a rich flower and a lovely girl. "Flower and maiden were different and yet the same, and fraught with some peculiar peril in either shape." In time, as Giovanni ventures into the garden, he learns that the flowers are deadly. But he is now in love with Beatrice and tormented by the suspicion that she possesses the same fatal attributes. Can such dreadful peculiarities in her physical nature exist, he asks himself, without some corresponding "monstrosity of soul"? The day comes when after many tests he is at last sure that not only is she poisonous but that she had begun to instill her poison into his system. He procures an antidote which he forces her to drink. But it is too late to save her, for "so radically had her earthly part been wrought upon by Rappaccini's skill, that as poison had been her life, so the powerful antidote was death; and thus the poor victim of man's ingenuity and of thwarted nature ... perished there, at the feet of her father and Giovanni."

No summary can give an adequate sense of the exotic light in which this story is drenched, nor of the extravagantly erotic associations of its imagery. It opens with the "peephole" motif, so typical of Hawthorne. ("Sometimes through a peephole I have caught a glimpse of the real world . . ." he wrote to Longfellow.) At first it is only from the outside — through a window — that Giovanni dares to peer into this "Eden of poisonous flowers," which Freudians would have no trouble at all translating into a garden of genitalia. But whether interpreted in a Freudian manner or not, its mystery is easily unraveled. What is this Eden if not the garden of experience, of the knowledge of good and evil. Giovanni is tempted to enter it, only to discover that its gorgeous flowers are emblems of sin and that the gorgeous Beatrice embodies all that is forbidden. She has succeeded in enticing him into a "region of unspeakable horror," but it is she who is doomed, while he, being innocent, escapes. The wages of sin is death.

To be sure, there are other readings of this story. The traditional one simply takes at face value Hawthorne's stated intention, his "message" warning against such unscrupulous love of power and knowledge as is manifested in Rappaccini. The old professor, who is a shadow character, is thus put in the foreground, while Beatrice, who is the real protagonist, is reduced to the role of a mere passive victim of her father's monomaniacal ambition. Needless to say, this approach ignores the story's specific content for the sake of its abstract and, it should be remarked, utterly commonplace moral. It fails to account for the mystic sensuality, the hallucinated atmosphere, and the intertwining symbolism of flower and maiden. No, this business of the wizard Rappaccini and his poisons is just so much flummery and Gothic sleight-of-hand. Its use is that of an "alibi" for the author, who transforms Beatrice into a monster in order to punish her for tempting Giovanni. Actually it is her beauty that Hawthorne cannot forgive her.

The flower-symbolism of this tale is repeated in the later romances of the dark lady. So resplendent is the scarlet token of shame worn by Hester Prynne that it might well be a flower in Rappaccini's garden formed to spell the letter A. ("On the breast of her gown, in fine red cloth, surrounded with an elaborate embroidery and fantastic flourishes of gold thread, there appeared the letter A. It was so artistically done, and with so much fertility and gorgeous luxuriance of fancy . . .") And, again, much is made in *The Blithedale Romance* of the single flower that adorns Zenobia's hair — "It was a hothouse flower, an outlandish flower, a flower of the tropics, such as appeared to have sprung passionately from a soil the very weeds of which would be fervid and spicy . . . so brilliant, so rare, so costly . . ." It is manifestly a flower of a preternatural order, a kind of *mana*-object, an instrument of magic and witches' work.

As compared to the subsequent full-length versions of the same theme, the story of Beatrice is but a primitive fantasy. There is a gap between *Rappaccini's Daughter* and *The Scarlet Letter*, which was written six years later and which is the most truly novelistic of Hawthorne's romances. Its concrete historical setting gives it greater density of material and sharpness of outline; and largely because of this gain in reality, Hester Prynne is the least symbolically overladen and distorted of the four heroines who share in the character of the dark lady. There is nothing satanic about her motives and she is the only one who, far from being ultimately spurned, is justified instead.

There are ambiguities in *The Scarlet Letter,* as in all of Hawthorne, yet it is possible to say that it represents his furthest advance in affirming the rights of the individual. Known as a story of the expiation of a sin, it is quite as much an analysis of this sin as a "kind of typical illusion." It is the Reverend Mr. Dimmesdale, his brain reeling from ghostly visions, who in his repentance plies a bloody scourge on his own shoulders; Hester, on the other hand, is ready to reject the puritan morality altogether, to make a clean sweep of the past and to escape from the settlement in order to fulfill her love without shame or fear. Her pariah status in the community is not productive of remorse and humility. On the contrary, we are told that "standing alone in the world . . . the world's law was no law for her mind . . . In her lonesome cottage, by the seashore, thoughts visited her, such as dared enter no other dwelling in New England."

This is best shown in Chapters 17 and 18 of the novel when Hester finally persuades the minister that the only way he could rid himself of Chillingsworth's persecution is to desert his congregation and return to England. At first he thinks that she bids him go alone, whereupon he protests that he has not the strength or courage to embark on such a venture. At this point she reveals her plan, proving that she does not recognize her guilt, that for her nothing has changed, that in fact "the whole seven years of outlawry and ignominy had been little other than a preparation for this very hour." But some of the passages that follow are worth quoting at length.

> He repeated the word.
> "Alone, Hester!"
> "Thou shalt not go alone!" answered she, in a deep whisper.
> Then all was spoken!
> Arthur Dimmesdale gazed into Hester's face with a look in which hope and joy shone out, indeed, but with fear between them, and a kind of horror at her boldness, who had spoken what he vaguely hinted at but dared not speak.
> But Hester Prynne, with a mind of native courage and activity, and for

so long a period not merely estranged, but outlawed from society, had habituated herself to such latitude of speculation as was altogether foreign to the clergyman ... For years past she had looked from this estranged point of view at human institutions, and whatever priests or legislators had established ... The tendency of her fate has been to set her free.

"Thou wilt go," said Hester calmly, as he met her glance.

The decision once made, a glow of strange enjoyment threw its flickering brightness over the trouble of his breast. It was the exhilarating effect — upon a prisoner just escaped from the dungeon of his own heart — of breathing the wild, free atmosphere of an unredeemed, unchristianized, lawless region ...

"Do I feel joy again?" cried he, wondering at himself. "Methinks the germ of it was dead in me! O, Hester, thou art my better angel! I seem to have flung myself — sick, sin-stained, and sorrow-blackened — down upon these forest-leaves, and to have risen up all made anew, and with new powers to glorify Him that hath been merciful! This is already the better life. Why did we not find it sooner?"

"Let us not look back," answered Hester Prynne. "The past is gone! ... See! With this symbol I undo it all, and make it as it had never been!"

So speaking, she undid the clasp that fastened the scarlet letter, and taking it from her bosom, threw it to a distance among the withered leaves ... The stigma gone, Hester heaved a deep, long sigh, in which the burden of shame and anguish departed from her spirit. O exquisite relief! ... By another impulse she took off the formal cap that confined her hair; and down it fell upon her shoulders, dark and rich ... There played around her mouth and beamed out of her eyes, a radiant and tender smile, that seemed gushing from the very heart of womanhood. A crimson flush was glowing on her cheeks, that had been long so pale. Her sex, her youth, and the whole richness of her beauty, came back from what men call the irrevocable past, and clustered themselves, with her maiden hope and a happiness before unknown, within the magic circle of this hour.

This unregenerate temptress knows her power, but in the end Dimmesdale cheats her of her triumph by publicly confessing his sin on the scaffold; and that, of course, is *his* triumph. This thin-skinned clergyman is the ancestor of all those characters in Henry James who invent excruciatingly subtle reasons for renouncing their heart's desire once they are on the verge of attaining it. But in James there are also other characters who, while preserving Dimmesdale's complex qualities of conscience and sensibility, finally do succeed in overcoming this tendency to renunciation. Lambert Strether of *The Ambassadors* and Milly Theale of *The Wings of the Dove*, whose ideal aim is "to achieve a sense of having lived," are plainly cases of reaction against Hawthorne's plaint: "I have not lived but only dreamed of living!"

This link with James is further evidence that, though in no position to show his hand and not even fully conscious of what was at stake, Hawthorne dealt with the problem of sin mainly insofar as it served him as a mold for the problem of experience. It is difficult to believe in the sins committed by his characters for the simple reason that he hardly believes in them himself. Consider how he stacks the cards, how he continually brings up extenuating circumstances and even lapses into telltale defensive statements, so that before long we cannot but lose the conviction of evil and corruption. Who, actually, are his sinners? The minor figures cannot, of course, be taken into account in this respect, for, like Chillingsworth, Westervelt, Miriam's model, and even Judge Pyncheon, they are nothing more than conventional villains, and at that most of them are so unreal that their conduct is of little consequence. It is only the protagonists, then, who count. But of these, with the exception of Dimmesdale, there is scarcely one who can be objectively regarded as a wrongdoer. Among the women only Hester's guilt is definitely established, yet even she is shown to have so many rights on her side that it is impossible to see in her anything more portentous than a violator of the communal *mores*. It is not, however, by their flouting of the communal *mores* that we judge the great transgressors pictured in literature. These big biters into the apple inevitably sin against the Holy Ghost.

Zenobia and Miriam wholly exemplify Hawthorne's bias against the dark lady, a bias which, instead of being supported and objectified by a credible presentation of her misdeeds, is limited in its expression to atmospheric effects, insinuations, and rumors. He wants to destroy the dark lady at the same time that he wants to glorify her; hence his indictment of her is never really driven home. This divided intention cannot but impair the dramatic structures of *The Blithedale Romance* and *The Marble Faun*, and these two narratives are in fact much inferior to *The Scarlet Letter*.

But the *Romance*, with its marvelous sense of place and weather and with its contrasted tableaux of town and country, has a unique appeal of its own. Both James and Lawrence have testified to its attraction. The former speaks of it as "leaving in the memory an impression analogous to that of an April day — an alternation of brightness and shadow, of broken sun-patches and sprinkling clouds." James also thought that in Zenobia Hawthorne made his nearest approach to the complete creation of a character. But this vivid brunette is treated with much less sympathy than Hester — and perhaps the reason is that since she exerts greater sexual power she must needs be subjected to firmer measures of control. At any rate, his attitude toward her is markedly more subjective, and this note of subjectivity is one of the charms of the *Romance,* the unfailing charm of the confessional tone and of the personal modulation. The story is told through a narrator by the name of Miles Coverdale, a minor Boston poet in whom one easily discerns many features of the author.

No sooner does Coverdale come upon Zenobia in Blithedale — a utopian colony inhabited by a "little army of saints and martyrs" — than her beauty moves him to rhapsodic appreciation; he is in a fever of susceptibility, and the very next day a fit of sickness lays him low. His illness and exhaustion render him even more sensitive — morbidly so — to what he calls "Zenobia's sphere." (What a master stroke, this episode of Coverdale's illness, with its suggestions of a rite of passage from one mode of life to another!) Obviously infatuated with her, he is not the man to submit to such a feeling. By what is plainly a psychological detour — analysts would see in it an example of protective displacement — he persuades himself that his real attachment is to Zenobia's half-sister, the mediumistic, shadowy snow-maiden who is the Prissy of the tale. This convenient self-deception permits him to covet Zenobia and to pry into her affairs without in any way committing himself to her — for how could he, a paleface poet with overcharged scruples, make up to a woman who is "passionate, luxurious, lacking simplicity, not deeply refined, incapable of pure and perfect taste"? Moreover, as if to spare him further trouble, both females fall in love not with him but with the fanatical reformer Hollingsworth, who is a mere stick of a character, a travesty as a reformer and even worse travesty as a lover. The emotional economy of this story is throughout one of displacement. It is evident on every page that the only genuine relationship is that of Coverdale to Zenobia; the rest is mystification. But the whole point of Coverdale's behavior is to avoid involvement. As Zenobia tells him in one of the final bang-up scenes, his real game is "to grope for human emotions in the dark corners of the heart" — strictly in the hearts of other people, to be sure. He plays perfectly the role of the ideal Paul Pry that Hawthorne envisaged for himself in the earlier passages of his journals.

Though vowing that he adores the ethereal Priscilla, Coverdale is nevertheless quite adept at belittling her by means of invidious comparisons that strike home despite their seemingly general reference. Some finicky people, he reflects after his first encounter with Zenobia, might consider her wanting in softness and delicacy, but the truth is that "we find enough of these attributes everywhere; preferable . . . was Zenobia's bloom, health, and vigor, which she possessed in such overflow that a man might well have fallen in love with her for their sake only." And again: "We seldom meet with women nowadays, and in this country, who impress us as being women at all; — their sex fades away and goes for nothing . . . a certain warm and rich characteristic seems to have been refined away out of the feminine system." Finally, in view of these frequent digs at Prissy, there can be no doubt that Westervelt, the villain of the piece, is really speaking for Coverdale when he describes her as "one of those delicate, young creatures, not uncommon in New England, and whom I suppose to have become what we find them by the gradual refining away of the physical system among young women. Some philosophers chose to glorify this habit of body by terming it spiritual; but in my opinion, it is rather the effect of unwholesome food, bad air, lack of outdoor exercise, and neglect of bathing, on the part of these damsels and their female progenitors, all resulting in a kind of hereditary dyspepsia. Zenobia, with her uncomfortable surplus of vitality, is far the better model of womanhood."

But this "better model of womanhood" commits suicide for want of love, while the obstreperous Hollingsworth is collared by Prissy and dragged to the altar. The puritan morality of predestination takes its toll as the story closes. Humanity is divided into the damned and the saved, irretrievably so, and never the twain shall meet. Yet the *Romance*, despite its mechanically enforced moral lessons, stands out among Hawthorne's works for its outspokenness and for its bold and free characterization of Coverdale and Zenobia. In its painful doubleness, in its feeling of combined attraction and repulsion, the relationship between these two characters is one of the most meaningful and seminal in American literature. It is intrinsically the relationship between New England and the world, and again the connection with James comes to mind. Zenobia can be understood as an earlier and cruder version of Madame de Vionnet (of *The Ambassadors*), whose worldly motives and passionate nature Lambert Strether finally comes to understand and to accept; and Coverdale, too, is reproduced in James, and not in one type alone. One recognizes his kinship with Strether, who has overcome the obsession with sin and is priming himself to enter forbidden territory, no less than with such a curious figure as the spying, eavesdropping protagonist of *The Sacred Fount*, whose neurotic fear and envy of life find an outlet in a mania of snooping and prying into the lives of his neighbors. In this nameless Jamesian snooper the "peephole" motif reaches its culmination: it has become his medium of existence and his intellectual rationale besides.

In *The Marble Faun* Hawthorne resumes his story of the dark lady, and his attitude to her is now formulated in more logical terms. The conception of sin as an "instrument most effective in the education of intellect and soul" is openly expounded and affirmed by Miriam, whereas the snow-maiden Hilda, who is a purist and perfectionist, defends to the last the old puritan ethic. What Miriam advocates is the right of the personality to that self-knowledge and self-development which only the process of experience can provide. But she too, like Hester, is in the end sentenced by the author to life-long suffering and expiation of her sin. Unlike Hester's sin, however, Miriam's is utterly chimerical, fabricated out of whole cloth by the Gothic machinery of horror; what alone is real is her defiance of the ancestral taboos.

The part of the male evildoer in *The Marble Faun* is taken by Donatello, the innocent, faunlike, quasi-mythical Italian who is drawn by Miriam to commit a crime and is thus brought within the confines of "sinful, sorrowful mentality." It is the story, of course, of the fall of man, with the dark lady cast in the dual role of Eve and the serpent. Hilda and the sculptor Kenyon are the onlookers and commentators on the action. Presented as models of virtue, they are actually an insufferable pair of prigs, especially Hilda, who is in fact one of the grimmest figures in Hawthorne, despite all the proper talk about her dovelike nature. Symbolically enough, this militant virgin dwells in a tower which is continually referred to as the "young girl's eyrie," and from this high vantage point she surveys the conduct of mankind with the self-assurance of a moral millionaire. The sculptor, to be sure, tends to sympathize with Miriam, but Hilda never fails to pull him up short. The whole issue is summed up perfectly in the following dialogue between them:

> "Ah, Hilda," said Kenyon, "you do not know, for you could never learn it from your own heart, which is all purity and rectitude, what a mixture of good and evil there may be in things evil; and how the greatest criminal, if you look at his conduct from his own point of view, or from any side-point, may seem not so unquestionably guilty, after all. So with Miriam, so with Donatello. They are, perhaps, partners in what we must call awful guilt; and yet, I will own to you, — when I think of the original cause, the motives, the feelings, the sudden concurrence of circumstances thrusting them onward, the urgency of the moment, and the sublime unselfishness on either part, — I know not well how to distinguish it from much that the world calls heroism. Might we not render some such verdict as this? — 'Worthy of Death, but not unworthy of Love!' "
>
> "Never!" answered Hilda, looking at the matter through the clear crystal medium of her own integrity. "This thing, as regards its causes, is all a

mystery to me, and must remain so. But there is, I believe, only one right and only one wrong; and I do not understand, and may God keep me from understanding, how two things so totally unlike can be mistaken for one another; nor how two mortal foes, such as Right and Wrong surely are, can work together in the same deed . . ."

"Alas for human nature, then!" said Kenyon, sadly . . . "I have always felt you, my dear friend, a terribly severe judge, and have been perplexed to conceive how such tender sympathy could coexist with the remorselessness of a steel blade. You need no mercy, and therefore know not how to show any."

"That sounds like a bitter gibe," said Hilda, with the tears springing to her eyes. "But I cannot help it. It does not alter my perception of the truth. If there be any such dreadful mixture as you affirm — and which appears to me almost more shocking than pure evil, — then the good is turned to poison, not the evil to wholesomeness."

It is against such pharisaical moralism as Hilda displays that Hawthorne reacted in creating the figure of the dark lady, yet he could never muster the resolution to repudiate Hilda openly. Hence the dark lady, too, is inevitably stricken down by the same minatory code. Miriam pleads that the crime joining her to Donatello was "a blessing in disguise" in that it brought "a simple and imperfect nature to a point of feeling and intelligence which it could have reached under no other discipline." But her pleas are of no avail — in the end she is destroyed. And how illusory is the crime of which she is accused, with its horror-romanticism of the murder of a timeless wizard who has in some inexplicable way gained an ascendancy over her. And this in what is presumably a serious novel of crime and punishment! One might claim, of course, that the failure of actuality at this crucial turn of the plot is nothing more than a defect in the storyteller's art, a carryover from the obsolescent Gothic technique. But it is precisely Hawthorne's persistent reliance on this technique which is so revealing of his real situation. It seems to me that he is unable to authenticate Miriam's guilt for the quite obvious reason that her beauty and love of life already sufficiently condemn her in his eyes. In other words, it is not her deeds but her very existence which is the supreme provocation and the supreme crime.

The critics of the school of "original sin" have for some years now tried to present Hawthorne as a kind of puritan Dostoevsky. But this comparison will not stand the test of analysis. In their eagerness to make ideological capital out of Hawthorne's "traditionalism," these critics overlook one vital distinction: whereas in Dostoevsky's case the awareness of sin flows from a mighty effort to regain a metaphysical and religious consciousness, in Hawthorne this awareness is at the point of dissolution. What is behind it is no genuine moral passion nor a revival of dogma but a fear of life induced by narrow circumstances and morbid memories of the past. The faith of his forefathers had lost its rational appeal, yet psychologically it still ruled and confined him. Hence the inherited beliefs appear in his work as specters rather than as convictions.

A literature of sin is more naturally developed in a society suffering from a surfeit of experience — an excess which it cannot control because of a derangement of values. This was the condition of Russian society in Dostoevsky's time; and it is this unlimited availability of experience, amounting almost to anarchy, which enabled the Russian novelist to materialize his themes of sin and evil. We believe in the sins of Stavrogin, Raskolnikov, and the Karamazovs because they are actualized within the experiential realm, the only realm in which significant actions can be truly confirmed. Now if regarded from this point of view, the American romancer must be placed at the opposite pole from the Russian novelist. The society to which he belonged suffered not from a surfeit but from poverty of experience; and, far from being too fluid, its values were altogether too rigid. His problem was simpler than Dostoevsky's as well as radically different in nature. It was not an exceptional but necessarily a typical problem — typical, despite all variations, of America's creative writers in the nineteenth century and in the early decades of the twentieth. It can be defined as the problem of the reconquest, of the reacquisition of experience in its cultural, aesthetic, and, above all, subjective aspects. For this is the species of experience which had gradually been lost to the migrant European man in the process of subjugating and settling the new world.

Van Wyck Brooks has described Hawthorne as the "most deeply planted of American writers." But this is true only in the sense that he is the most deeply and vividly local. He rifled the hive of New England honey, but he was quite indifferent to the wider ranges of the national scene. His is the "sweet flavor," to use one of his own similes, of "a frost-bitten apple, such as one picks up under the tree in December." It is the chill yet mellow flavor of the Salem centuries. On this side of him he indeed sums up and closes the puritan cycle; but from another angle of vision he can be seen to be precursive of the later and more positive interests of American letters. Times past are mirrored in the dark lady's harsh fate, yet in her mystic sensuality she speaks of things to come.

Partisan Review, 1941

The Heiress of All the Ages

H<small>ENRY</small> J<small>AMES</small> is not fully represented in his novels by any one single character, but of his principal heroine it can be said that she makes the most of his vision and dominates his drama of transatlantic relations. This young woman is his favorite American type, appearing in his work time and again under various names and in various situations that can be taken as so many stages in her career. Hence it is in the line of her development that we must study her. Her case involves a principle of growth which is not to be completely grasped until she has assumed her final shape.

This heroine, too, is cast in the role, so generic to James, of the "passionate pilgrim," whose ordinary features are those of the "good American bewildered in the presence of the European order." But bewilderment is not a lasting motive in this heroine's conduct; unlike most of her fellow pilgrims in James's novels, she soon learns how to adjust European attitudes to the needs of her personality. Where she excels is in her capacity to plunge into experience without paying the usual Jamesian penalty for such daring — the penalty being either the loss of one's moral balance or the recoil into a state of aggrieved innocence. She responds "magnificently" to the beauty of the Old World scene even while keeping a tight hold on her native virtue: the ethical stamina, goodwill, and inwardness of her own provincial background. And thus living up to her author's idea both of Europe and America, she is able to mediate, if not wholly to resolve, the conflict between the two cultures, between innocence and experience, between the sectarian code of the fathers and the more "civilized" though also more devious and dangerous code of the lovers. No wonder James commends her in terms that fairly bristle with heroic intentions and that in the preface to *The Wings of the Dove* he goes so far as to credit her with the great historic boon of being "that certain sort of young American," exceptionally endowed with "liberty of action, of choice, of appreciation, of contact . . . who is more the 'heir of all the ages' than any other young person whatsoever."

If James's relation to his native land is in question, then more is to be learned from this young woman's career than from any number of discursive statements quoted from his letters, essays, and autobiographies. "It's a complete fate being an American," he wrote. Yes, but what does this fate actually come to in his work? The answer, it seems to me, is mostly given in his serial narrative of the heiress of all the ages.

The initial assignment of this heroine is to reconnoiter the scene rather than take possession of it. As yet she is not recognized as the legitimate heiress but merely as a candidate for the inheritance. Such is the part played by Mary Garland, for instance, a small-town girl from New England who herself feels the pull of the "great world" even as she tries to save her errant lover from its perils (*Roderick Hudson*, 1875). Daisy Miller, a young lady whose friends are distressed by the odd mixture of spontaneous grace, audacity, and puerility in her deportment, is also cast in this role, though with somewhat special and limited intentions. Bessie Alden (*An International Episode*, 1878), a more cultivated and socially entrenched figure than the famous Daisy, voyages to England — inevitably so — for the sake of enjoying its picturesque associations; and she is noteworthy as the first of the James girls to reap the triumph of turning down the proposal of an Old World aristocrat. But it is in Isabel Archer (*The Portrait of a Lady*) that we first encounter this heroine in a truly pivotal position, comprising the dramatic consequences of a conflict not merely of manners but of morals as well. In Isabel her heretofore scattered traits are unified and corrected in the light of James's growing recognition of the importance of her claims. Two decades later, at the time when his writing had settled into the so portentously complex style of his ultimate period, she reappears as the masterful though stricken Milly Theale of *The Wings of the Dove* and as the impeccable Maggie Verver of *The Golden Bowl*, to whom all shall be given. These last displays of her age are by far the most accomplished, for in them her function as "princess" and "heiress" is fully defined and affirmed.

The evolution of our heroine thus gives us the measure of James's progressively rising estimate of that American fate to the account of which he devoted the greater part of his work. The account opens with the simple, almost humble, instances of Mary Garland and Daisy Miller, who are baffled and shamed by Europe, and closes with the "prodigious" success of Maggie Verver, to whom Europe offers itself as a dazzling and inexhaustible opportunity. What is the heiress, then, if not a character-image of aggrandizement on every level of meaning and existence? She is that in her own right, as the representative American mounting "Europe's lighted and decorated stage"; but she also serves James as the objective equivalent of his own increase and expansion as man and artist. This is all the more striking when we consider that both author and heroine entered upon their careers under seemingly inauspicious circumstances. At the start they are beset by the traditional scruples of their race, by fits of enervation and recurrent feelings of inferiority; yet as both mature he achieves a creative dignity and consciousness of well-nigh lordly dimensions, while she comes to value herself and to be valued by the world at large as the personage appointed by history to inherit the bounty of the ages. Francis Fergusson has aptly summed up this entire process of growth in remarking that James "developed a society manner into a grand manner much as he developed a rich American girl into a large, sober, Bérénice-like stage queen."

Such exceptional prosperity is hardly to be explained in terms of individual aptitude alone. Certain large conditions make it possible, such as America's precipitant rise as a national power in the late nineteenth century; its enhanced self-knowledge and self-confidence; and, more particularly, the avid desire of its upper classes to obtain forthwith the rewards and prerogatives of high civilization. The truth is that for qualities of a surpassingly bourgeois and imperial order James's heiress is without parallel in American fiction. Note that this millionaire's daughter is an heiress in moral principle no less than in material fact, and that James, possessed of a firmer faith in the then existing structure of society than most novelists and wholly sincere in his newly gained worldliness, tends to identify her moral with her material superiority.* Yet in the long run she cannot escape the

---

* Some critics writing about James in the early 1930s sought to put him in line with the leftist trend of the times. This sort of intention is evident in Robert Cantwell's several essays of that period and to a lesser extent in Stephen Spender's study, *The Destructive Element.* These critics overlook, it seems to me, a depth of the conservative idea in James, and that is why they are forced to exaggerate the meaning of novels like *The Ivory Tower* and *The Princess Casamassima.* Even though in the latter the atmosphere of class conflict is genuine enough, its revolutionary theme cannot be taken at face value. For imbedded in this novel is the more familiar theme of the passionate pilgrim — the pilgrim being the hero, Hyacinth Robinson, who sees the "immeasurable misery of the people" but who also sees, even more clearly and passionately, "all that has been, as it were, rescued and redeemed from it: the treasures, the felicities, the splendors, the successes of the world"; and in the end, when the final choice is put to him, he takes his stand not with the people but with the "world" resting upon their misery. Thus Robinson is enticed by the same image that draws the Jamesian Americans to Europe.

irony — the inner ambiguity — of her status. For her wealth is at once the primary source of her so lavishly pictured "greatness" and "liberty" and the source of the evil she evokes in others. There is no ignoring the consideration, however, that in the case of the heiress, as in the case of most of James's rich Americans, money is in a sense but the prerequisite of moral delicacy. What with her "higher interests" and pieties, the rigor of her conscience and the nicety of her illusions, what is she really if not a graduate of the school of Boston Transcendentalism? Her author's imagination operated according to the law of the conversion of the lower into the higher, and by means of this ideal logic his heroine's debut in the "social successful worldly world" is transformed into a kind of spiritual romance. What James knew best of all is, of course, how to take things immensely for granted; and not to appreciate the wonder of his beguilement is to miss the poetry, the story, the very life of his fictions.

To grasp the national-cultural values implicit in the progress of his heroine is to be done once and for all with the widely held assumption that to James the country of his birth always signified failure and sterility. Edmund Wilson is surely right in contending that it is America which really "gets the better of it in Henry James." Such an interpretation is consistent with his return to the theme of the heiress at the turn of the century, with his honorific treatment of her, his enamored tone and laudatory report of her aims and prospects — her aims and prospects being not merely those of a typical Jamesian aspirant but of an American emissary endowed with a character "intrinsically and actively ample . . . reaching southward, westward, anywhere, everywhere." As the years passed James's awareness of the American stake in the maintenance of civilization grew increasingly positive and imposing. In his later writings old Europe serves once more as the background for young America, and his restored interest in the nuclear fable of the passionate pilgrim is now worked out on a more ambitious scale and with more intricate artistic intentions. His last great novels are remarkable, too, for the resurgence in them of

---

The one variation is that he constructs this image out of class rather than national or, so to speak, hemispheric differences.

So far as the political estimate of James is concerned, one cannot but agree with Joseph Warren Beach that he is basically a "gentleman of cultivated and conservative, not to say, reactionary instinct, who will generally be found to favor the same line of conduct as that favored by the ecclesiastical and civil law, as far as the law goes" (*The Method of Henry James*). So blunt a characterization is likely to offend the James cultists, but I think it can stand so long as we take it in a strictly political sense, not as a judgment of his moral realism. On that score Spender is closer to the truth in observing that James "saw through the life of his age" but that he "cherished the privilege that enabled him to see through it."

that native idealism — that "extraordinary good faith" — the effect of which in his early fiction was to link him with the classic masters of American literature. In *The Wings of the Dove, The Ambassadors,* and *The Golden Bowl* the motives and standards of this idealism are applied to the mixed disorder and splendor of the "great world," now no longer simply admired from afar but seen from within.

But the question whether the ultimate loyalty of James is claimed by Europe or America is hardly as meaningful as it has appeared to some of his interpreters. For actually his valuations of Europe and America are not the polar opposites but the two commanding centers of his work — the contending sides whose relation is adjusted so as to make mutual assimilation feasible. It is the only means by which the Jamesian idea of heritage can be brought to fruition. What his detractors can never forgive him, however, is his bursting the bounds of that autarchic Americanism of which Whitman is the chief exponent. Never having fallen into the habit of "glowing belligerently with one's country," he is able to invest his characters with a historic mission and propel them into spheres of experience as yet closed to them at home. They are the people named as the Ambassadors — and the nationalist critics who make so much of his expatriation should be reminded that there is a world of difference between the status of an ambassador and the status of a fugitive.

James's all-inclusive choice is dramatized in his recurrent story of the marriage of an eminent New World bride to an equally eminent Old World groom. The marriage is symbolic of the reconciliation of their competing cultures; and if it sometimes turns out badly, as in *The Portrait of a Lady,* or if it fails to come off altogether, as in *The Wings of the Dove,* James still holds fast to his scheme, continuing his experiments in matchmaking till finally, in *The Golden Bowl,* all the parts fall into their proper place, the marriage is consummated and bears luxurious fruit. Observe, though, that this happy ending is postponed again and again until the American wife, in the person of Maggie Verver, has established herself as the ruling member of the alliance.

The advancement of this heroine takes on historical form against the period background of the American female's rise to a position of cultural prestige and authority. She it was who first reached out for the "consummations and amenities" of life while her male relatives were still earnestly engaged in procuring its "necessities and preparations." No wonder W. D. Howells declared that "the prosperity of our fiction resides in the finer female sense." Now James's so-called feminine orientation is to be explained partly by this social fact and

partly by his instinct, the most exquisite possible, for private relations
and for their latent refinement of fact and taste. So estranged was he
from typical masculine interests that he could not but fall back more
and more on the subject of marriage, a subject dominated, in his
treatment of it, by the "social" note and meeting the "finer female
sense" on its own preferred ground.* Moreover, he could have found
no better framework of realistic detail for his picture of "young
American innocence transplanted to European air." And if his stories
of marriage are mostly stories, as he himself once put it, about "very
young women, who, affected with a certain high lucidity, thereby
become characters," it is because all the conditions of his art made for
such a choice.

His male figures are, generally speaking, to be identified with his
less masterful side, with the negative component of his sense of experience and the masochistic tendency to refuse the natural gifts of
life. It is in deviating from this code of refusal that Roderick Hudson goes to pieces. In *The Ambassadors* Lambert Strether learns the
lesson of *not* refusing, but his adventure in Paris gains its point from
the sheer process of his learning that lesson rather than from his
application of it. Nor can one overlook the repeated appearance in
James of certain sad and uncertain young men who vie with each
other in devising painfully subtle motives for renouncing their heart's
desire once it is within their grasp. One such specimen is the young
man (Bernard Longmore in *Madame de Mauves*) who is revolted
by the idea of making love to the woman whose happiness he tries
to save. Another is the incredibly appealing though emotionally dense
Mr. Wendover, who has "no more physical personality than a con-
sulted thermometer" and who, courting the girl he loves with more
propriety than imagination, fails her when she needs him most (*A
London Life*). In point of fact, the heiress is the one native Jamesian
who knows exactly what she wants. She, too, is confronted, to be
sure, with "beautiful difficulties," but they are never of the kind that
spring from some crucial frustration or of the kind that can be translated into some moral issue, which is then to be carefully isolated
and solved in a chessboard fashion. In her case the "beautiful diffi-

---

* In *The Point of View*, a story published in the early eighties, James inserts the
following ironic reference to himself into the Paris-bound letter of a French visitor
to New York: "They have a novelist here with pretensions to literature, who writes
about the chase for the husband and the adventures of the rich Americans in our
corrupt old Europe, where their primeval candor puts the Europeans to shame.
C'est proprement écrit; but it's terribly pale." In later years he would hardly have
enjoyed any such ironic play at his own expense, for with age self-depreciation
gave way to portentousness in his estimate of himself.

culties" spring out of her very search for self-fulfillment and impetuosity in "taking full in the face the whole assault of life."

It is with a bright and sudden flutter of self-awareness that Mary Garland reveals, in a brief passage of dialogue, the state of mind of the heiress as she sets out to meet her fate. The occasion for it is a night scene in *Roderick Hudson,* when Mary confesses to Rowland Mallet that her stay in Italy has induced a change in her conception of life:

> Mary: "At home ... things don't speak to us of enjoyment as they do here. Here it's such a mixture; one doesn't know what to believe. Beauty stands here — beauty such as this night and this place and all this sad strange summer have been so full of — and it penetrates one's soul and lodges there and keeps saying that man wasn't made, as we think at home, to struggle so much and to miss so much, but to ask of life as a matter of course some beauty and some charm. This place has destroyed any scrap of consistency that I ever possessed, but even if I must say something sinful I love it!"

> Rowland: "If it's sinful I absolve you — insofar as I have power. We should not be able to enjoy, I suppose, unless we could suffer, and in anything that's worthy of the name of experience — that experience which is the real *taste* of life, isn't it? — the mixture is of the finest and subtlest."

The pathos of this dialogue is the pathos of all the buried things in the American past it recalls us to. It recalls us, moreover, to one of the most telling and precise relations in our literature, that of the early James to Hawthorne.* Consider how this relation is at once contained and developed in Mary's vision of what life holds for those bold enough to ask for it as a matter of course "some beauty and some charm." For Mary is essentially a figure from a novel such as *The Blithedale Romance* or *The Marble Faun* brought forward into a later age; and because of the shift of values that has occurred in the meantime, she is able to express in a mundane fashion those feelings and sentiments that in Hawthorne are still somewhat hidden and only spoken of with a semiclerical quaver, as if from under a veil. In Mary's confession the spectral consciousness of the perils of beauty, of the evil it hides, is at long last being exorcised, the mind

---

* Among the first to notice the connection was William James. In 1870 he wrote to his brother: "It tickled my national feeling not a little to note the resemblance of Hawthorne's style to yours and Howells's.... That you and Howells, with all the models in English literature to follow, should involuntarily have imitated (as it were) this American, seems to point to the existence of some real mental American quality."

is being cleared of its homegrown fears and mystifications. The reality of experience can no longer be resisted: "Even if I say something sinful I love it!" And having said it, she is absolved of her "sin" by Rowland, who in this scene is manifestly acting for the author. It is Rowland, too, who describes experience as the "real *taste* of life," thus disclosing its innermost Jamesian sense. For in this sense of it the idea of experience is emptied of its more ordinary meanings, of empirical reference, and made to correspond to pure consummation, to that "felt felicity" so often invoked by James, to something lovingly selected or distilled from life — all of which is perfectly in line with the indicated function of the heiress as the prime consumer of the resources, material and spiritual, of both the Old and the New World. And though it is not within the power of even this superior brand of experience to exempt one from suffering, still the risk is well worth taking so long as "the mixture is of the finest and subtlest."

But in Mary the ferment of experience is as yet more potential than actual. At this stage James is already sure of his heroine's integrity and liveliness of imagination, knowing that in this fine flower of a provincial culture he had gotten hold of a historical prodigy admirably suited to his purpose as a novelist. He is still doubtful, however, of her future, uncertain as to the exact conditions of her entry into the "great world" and of the mutual effect thus created. Daisy Miller and Bessie Alden represent his further experiments with her character. Daisy's social adventures make for a superb re-creation of manners and tones and contrasts and similitudes. Spontaneity is her principal quality — a quality retained by the heiress through all her mutations and invariably rendered as beautifully illustrative of the vigor and innocence of the national spirit. But Daisy is altogether the small-town, the average American girl; and by virtue of this fact she lays bare the lowly origin of the heiress in the undifferentiated mass of the New World democracy. Winterbourne, Daisy's admirer and critic, observes that "she and her mamma have not yet risen to the stage — what shall I call it? — of culture, at which the idea of catching a count or a *marchese* begins."

Bessie, on the other hand, seizes upon this conception only to rise above it. This "Bostonian nymph who rejects an English duke" combines the primal sincerity of her forebears with a Jamesian sensitivity to the "momentos and reverberations of greatness" in the life of ancient aristocracies — and this amalgam of values proves to be beyond the comprehension of Lord Lambeth's simple matter-of-fact mind. Bessie's behavior was resented, of course, by English readers, just as Daisy's was resented by American readers. But the so-challenged author, far from being flustered by the protests that reached him, took it all in with gloating satisfaction, delighted by the contrast, with its "dramas upon dramas...and innumerable points of view," thus brought to light. He felt that the emotion of the public vindicated his faith in the theme of the "international situation."

As the 1870s come to a close, James is done with the preliminary studies of his heroine. Now he undertakes to place her in a longer narrative — *The Portrait of a Lady* — the setting and action of which are at last commensurate with the "mysterious purposes" and "vast designs" of her character. In the preface to the New York edition (written nearly a quarter of a century later) he recalls that the conception of a "certain young woman affronting her destiny had begun with being all my outfit for the large building of the novel"; and he reports that in its composition he was faced with only one leading question: "What will she 'do'?" But this is mainly a rhetorical question, for naturally "the first thing she'll do will be to come to Europe — which in fact will form, and all inevitably, no small part of her principal adventure." *The Portrait* is by far the best novel of James's early prime, bringing to an end his literary apprenticeship and establishing the norms of his world. Its author has not yet entirely divorced himself from Victorian models in point of structure, and as a stylist he is still mindful of the reader's more obvious pleasure, managing his prose with an eye to outward as well as inward effects. It is a lucid prose, conventional yet free, marked by aphoristic turns of phrase and by a kind of intellectual gaiety in the formulation of ideas. There are few signs as yet of that well-nigh metaphysical elaboration of the sensibility by which he is to become known as one of the foremost innovators in American writing.

Isabel Archer is a young lady of an Emersonian cast of mind, but her affinity as a fictional character is rather with those heroines of Turgenev in whose nature an extreme tenderness is conjoined with unusual strength of purpose.* No sooner does Isabel arrive at the country house of her uncle Mr. Touchett, an American banker residing in England, then everyone recognizes her for what she is — "a delicate piece of human machinery." Her cousin Ralph questions his mother: "Who is this rare creature, and what is she? Where did you find her?" "I found her," she replies, "in an old house at Albany,

---

* The influence may well be conscious in this case, though in the preface to the novel James admits to being influenced by the Russian novelist only on the technical plane, with respect to the manner of placing characters in fiction. James's critical essays abound with favorable references to Turgenev, whose friendship he cultivated in Paris and of whom he invariably spoke with enthusiasm.

sitting in a dreary room on a rainy day ... She didn't know she was bored but when I told her she seemed grateful for the hint ... I thought she was meant for something better. It occurred to me it would be a kindness to take her about and introduce her to the world." The American Cinderella thus precipitated from the town of Albany into the "great world" knows exactly what she must look forward to. "To be as happy as possible," she confides in Ralph, "that's what I came to Europe for." It is by no means a simple answer. On a later and more splendid occasion it is to be repeated by Maggie Verver, who proclaims her faith, even as the golden bowl crashes to the ground, in a "happiness without a hole in it ... the golden bowl as it *was* to have been ... the bowl with all our happiness in it, the bowl without a crack in it." This is the crowning illusion and pathos, too, of the heiress, that she believes such happiness to be attainable, that money can buy it and her mere good faith can sustain it. And even when eventually her European entanglements open her eyes to the fact that virtue and experience are not so charmingly compatible after all, that the Old World has a fierce energy of its own and that its "tone of time" is often pitched in a sinister key, she still persists in her belief that this same world will yield her a richly personal happiness, proof against the evil spawned by others less fortunate than herself; and this belief is all the more expressive because it is wholly of a piece with the psychology of the heiress as a national type. The ardor of Americans in pursuing happiness as a personal goal is equaled by no other people, and when it eludes them none are so hurt, none so shamed. Happiness, one might say, is really their private equivalent of such ideals as progress and universal justice. They take for granted, with a faith at once deeply innocent and deeply presumptuous, that they deserve nothing less and that to miss it is to miss life itself.

The heiress is not to be humbled by the tests to which life in Europe exposes her. The severer the test the more intense the glow of her spirit. Is she not the child, as Isabel proudly declares, of that "great country which stretches beyond the rivers and across the prairies, blooming and smiling and spreading, till it stops at the blue Pacific! A strong, sweet, fresh odour seems to rise from it ..." The Emersonian note is sounded again and again by Isabel. She is truly the Young American so grandly pictured by the Concord idealist in his essay of that title, the Young American bred in a land "offering opportunity to the human mind not known in any other region" and hence possessed of an "organic simplicity and liberty, which, when it loses its balance, redresses itself presently ..." Witness the following passage of character analysis, with its revelation of Isabel's shining beneficent Emersonianism:

> Every now and then Isabel found out she was wrong, and then she treated herself to a week of passionate humility. After that she held her head higher than ever; for it was of no use, she had an unquenchable desire to think well of herself. She had a theory that it was only on this condition that life was worth living: that one should be the best, should be conscious of a fine organization . . . *should move in a realm of light, of natural wisdom, of happy impulse, of inspiration fully chronic. It was almost as unnecessary to cultivate doubt of oneself as to cultivate doubt of one's best friend.* . . . The girl had a certain nobleness of imagination which rendered her a good many services and played her a good many tricks. She spent half her time in thinking of beauty, and bravery, and magnanimity; *she had a fixed determination to regard the world as a place of brightness, of free expansion, of irresistible action; she thought it would be detestable to be afraid or ashamed.* [Italics not in the original.]

Still more revealing is the exchange between Isabel and the thoroughly Europeanized Madame Merle on the subject of the individual's capacity for self-assertion in the face of outward circumstances:

> Madame Merle: "When you have lived as long as I, you will see that every human being has his shell, that you must take the shell into account. By the shell I mean the whole envelope of circumstances. There is no such thing as an isolated man or woman; we're each of us made up of a cluster of circumstances. What do you call one's self? Where does it begin? Where does it end? It overflows into everything that belongs to me — and then it flows back again. I know that a large part of myself is in the dresses I choose to wear. I have a great respect for *things!*"

> Isabel: "I don't agree with you . . . I think just the other way. I don't know whether I succeed in expressing myself, but I know that nothing else expresses me. Nothing that belongs to me is a measure of me; on the contrary, it's a limit, a barrier, and a perfectly arbitrary one."*

In *The Portrait* James is still hesitating between the attitude of Madame Merle and that of Isabel, and his irony is provoked by the excessive claims advanced by both sides. But in years to come he is to be drawn more and more to the "European" idea of the human self, his finer discriminations being increasingly engaged by the "envelope of circumstances" in which it is contained.

---

* Note the close parallel between Isabel's reply to Madame Merle and the Emersonian text. "You think me the child of my circumstances: I make my circumstances. Let any thought or motive of mine be different from what they are, the difference will transform my condition and economy . . . You call it the power of circumstance, but it is the power of me." (*The Transcendentalist*)

Isabel is above all a young lady of principles, and her most intimate decisions are ruled by them. In refusing the proposal of the grandiose Lord Warburton, she wonders what ideal aspiration or design upon fate or conception of happiness prompts her to renounce such a chance for glamor and worldly satisfaction. Never had she seen a "personage" before, as there were none in her native land; of marriage she had been accustomed to think solely in terms of character — "of what one likes in a gentleman's mind and in his talk ... hitherto her visions of a completed life had concerned themselves largely with moral images — things as to which the question would be whether they pleased her soul." But if an aristocratic marriage is not to Isabel's liking, neither is the strictly hometown alternative of marrying a businessman. The exemplary Gaspar Goodwood, who owns a cottonmill and is the embodiment of patriotic virtue, likewise fails to win her consent — "His jaw was too square and grim, and his figure too straight and stiff; these things suggested a want of easy adaptability to some of the occasions of life."

Isabel having so far lacked the requisite fortune to back up her assumption of the role of the heiress, her cousin Ralph provides what is wanting by persuading his dying father to leave her a large sum of money. "I should like to make her rich," Ralph declares. "What do you mean by rich?" "I call people rich when they are able to gratify their imagination." Thus Isabel enters the uppermost circle of her author's hierarchy, the circle of those favored few who, unhampered by any material coercion, are at once free to make what they can of themselves and to accept the fullest moral responsibility for what happens to them in consequence. Now the stage is set for the essential Jamesian drama of free choice. In this novel, however, the transcendent worth of such freedom is not yet taken for granted as it is in *The Wings of the Dove* and *The Golden Bowl*. There is the intervention, for instance, of the lady correspondent Henrietta Stackpole, who is no passionate pilgrim but the mouthpiece, rather, of popular Americanism. It is she who questions Isabel's future on the ground that her money will work against her by bolstering her romantic inclinations. Henrietta is little more than a fictional convenience used to furnish the story with comic relief; but at this juncture of the plot she becomes the agent of a profound criticism aimed, in the last analysis, at James himself, at his own tendency to romanticize the values to which privilege lays claim. And what Henrietta has to say is scarcely in keeping with her habitual manner of the prancing female journalist. Characteristically enough, she begins by remarking that she has no fear of Isabel turning into a sensual woman; the peril she fears is of a different nature:

> "The peril for you is that you live too much in the world of your own dreams — you are not enough in contact with reality — with the toiling, striving, suffering, I may even say, sinning world that surrounds you. You are too fastidious, you have too many graceful illusions. Your newly-acquired thousands will shut you up more and more in the society of selfish and heartless people, who will be interested in keeping up those illusions . . . You think, furthermore, that you can lead a romantic life, that you can live by pleasing others and pleasing yourself. You will find you are mistaken. Whatever life you lead, you must put your soul into it — to make any sort of success of it; and from the moment you do that it ceases to be romance, I assure you; it becomes reality! . . . you think we can escape disagreeable duties by taking romantic views — that is your great illusion, my dear."

The case against the snobbish disposition of the Jamesian culture seekers and their overestimation of the worldly motive has seldom been so shrewdly and clearly stated. But Isabel is not especially vulnerable to criticism of this sort. It is only in her later incarnations that the heiress succumbs more and more to precisely the illusions of which Henrietta gives warning — so much so that in the end, when Maggie Verver appears on the scene, the life she leads may be designated, from the standpoint of the purely social analyst, as a romance of bourgeois materialism, the American romance of newly got wealth divesting itself of its plebeian origins in an ecstasy of refinement!

Henrietta's words, moreover, are meant to prefigure the tragedy of Isabel's marriage to Gilbert Osmond, an Italianate American, virtually a European, whom she takes to be what he is not — a decent compromise between the moral notions of her American background and the glamor of the European foreground. Osmond, whose special line is a dread of vulgarity, employs a kind of sincere cunning in presenting himself to Isabel as the most fastidious gentleman living, concerned above all with making his life a work of art and resolved, since he could never hope to attain the status he actually deserved, "not to go in for honors." The courtship takes place in Rome and in Florence, where Isabel is swayed by her impression of Osmond as a "quiet, clever, distinguished man, strolling on a moss-grown terrace above the sweet Val d'Arno . . . the picture was not brilliant, but she liked its lowness of tone, and the atmosphere of summer twilight that pervaded it . . . It seemed to speak of a serious choice, a choice between things of a shallow and things of a deep interest; of a lonely, studious life in a lovely land." But the impression is false. Only when it is too late does she learn that he had married her for her money with the connivance of Madame Merle, his former mistress, who had undertaken to influence her in his behalf. This entrapment of Isabel illustrates a recurrent formula of James's fiction. The person springing the trap is almost invariably driven by mercenary motives, and, like Osmond, is capable of accomplishing his aim by simulating a sympathy and understanding that fascinate the victim and render her (or him) powerless.* Osmond still retains some features of the old-fashioned villain, but his successors are gradually freed from the encumbrances of melodrama. Merton Densher (*The Wings of the Dove*) and Prince Amerigo (*The Golden Bowl*) are men of grace and intelligence, whose wicked behavior is primarily determined by the situation in which they find themselves.

Osmond reacts to the Emersonian strain in Isabel as to a personal offense. He accuses her of willfully rejecting traditional values and of harboring sentiments "worthy of a radical newspaper or a Unitarian preacher." And she, on her part, discovers that his fastidiousness reduced itself to a "sovereign contempt for every one but some two or three or four exalted people whom he envied, and for everything but half-a-dozen ideas of his own . . . he pointed out to her so much of the baseness and shabbiness of life . . . but this base, ignoble world, it appeared, was after all what one was to live for; one was to keep it forever in one's eye, in order, not to enlighten, or convert, or redeem, but to extract from it some recognition of one's superiority." Isabel's notion of the aristocratic life is "simply the unison of great knowledge with great liberty," whereas for Osmond it is altogether a "thing of forms," an attitude of conscious calculation. His esteem for tradition is boundless; if one was so unfortunate as not to be born to an illustrious tradition, then "one must immediately proceed to make it."† A sense of darkness and suffocation takes hold of Isabel as her husband's rigid

---

* It seems to me that this brand of evil has much in common with the "unpardonable sin" by which Hawthorne was haunted — the sin of *using* other people, of "violating the sanctity of a human heart." Chillingsworth in *The Scarlet Letter* is essentially this type of sinner, and so is Miriam's model in *The Marble Faun*. In James, however, the evil characters have none of the Gothic *mystique* which is to be found in Hawthorne. Their motives are transparent.

† The significance of Osmond's character has generally been underrated by the critics of James. For quite apart from his more personal traits (such as his depravity, which is a purely novelistic element), he is important as a cultural type in whom the logic of "traditionalism" is developed to its furthest limits. As a national group the American intellectuals suffer from a sense of inferiority toward the past, and this residue of "colonial" feeling is also to be detected in those among them who raise the banner of tradition. It is shown in their one-sided conformity

system closes in on her. She believes that there can be no release from the bondage into which she had fallen and that only through heroic suffering is its evil to be redeemed. On this tragic note the story ends.

Yet the heiress is not to be turned aside from her quest by such inevitable encounters with the old evils of history. On the lighted stage the bridegroom still awaits his New World bride.

In few of his full-length novels is James so consummately in control of his method of composition as in *The Wings of the Dove* and *The Golden Bowl*. It is a method all scenic and dramatic, of an "exquisite economy" in the architectonic placing of incidents, which eliminates any "going behind or telling about the figures" save as they themselves accomplish it. Indulgence in mere statement is banned; the motto is: *represent, convert, dramatize.* By means of this compositional economy the story is so organized that it seems to tell itself, excluding all material not directly bearing on the theme. This despite the "complication of innuendo and associative reference," as William James called it, by which the author communicates the vital information needed to understand the action. Complications of this sort so confuse some readers that they see nothing but surplus matter and digression where, in fact, everything is arranged in the most compact order. Nor is the occasional wordiness and vagueness of James's prose germane to our judgment of his novelistic structure. Even the thoughts of his characters are reproduced along exclusive rather than inclusive lines, as in *The Golden Bowl,* where the interior monologues of Maggie and the Prince are in reality a kind of speech which no one happens to overhear, showing none of the rich incoherence, haphazardness, and latitude of Joyce's rendering of the private mind, for example.

The principle of free association is incompatible with the Jamesian technique, which is above all a technique of exclusion. One can best describe it, it seems to me, as the fictional equivalent of the poetic modes evolved by modern poets seeking to produce a "pure poetry." In this sense the later James has more in common with a poet like Mallarmé than with novelists like Joyce and Proust, whose tendency

---

to the idea of tradition, in their readiness to inflate the meanings that may be derived from it. Their tendency is to take literally what their European counterparts are likely to take metaphorically and imaginatively. My idea is that James tried to overcome this bias which he suspected in himself by objectifying it in the portrait of Osmond. To this day, however, the shadow of Gilbert Osmond falls on many a page of American writing whose author — whether critic, learned poet, or academic "humanist" — presents himself, with all the exaggerated zeal and solemnity of a belated convert, as a spokesman of tradition.

is to appropriate more and more material and to assimilate to their medium even such nonfictional forms as the poem and the essay. In Proust the specific experience is made use of to launch all sorts of generalizations, to support, that is, his innumerable analyses — by turn poetic and essayistic — of memory, love, jealousy, the nature of art, etc. In Joyce this impulse to generalization finds other outlets, such as the investing of the specific experience with mythic associations that help us to place it within the pattern of human recurrence and typicality. James tightens where Joyce and Proust loosen the structure of the novel. In their hands the novel takes on encyclopedic dimensions, surrendering its norms and imperialistically extending itself, so to speak, to absorb all literary genres. It might be claimed, in fact, that *the novel as they write it ceases to be itself, having been transformed into a comprehensive work from which none of the resources of literature are excluded.* Not that they abandon the principle of selection; the point is rather that they select material to suit their desire for an unrestricted expansion of the medium, whereas James selects with a view to delimiting the medium and defining its proper course. He confirms, as very few novelists do, Goethe's observation that the artistic effect requires a closed space. It is true that at bottom it is culture and the history of culture, which constitute the inner theme of all three writers, but while Joyce and Proust express it by continually revealing its universality, James expresses it by limiting himself, through an extraordinary effort of aesthetic calculation, to its particularity.

One need not go so far as to say that the formal character of the Jamesian novel is determined by its social character in order to emphasize the close relation between the two. Both manifest the same qualities of particularity and exclusiveness. But why, it might be asked, is Proust's work so different in form, given the fact that he, too, is drawn by the resplendent image of the "great world" and, presumably, is quite as responsive to some of the values attributed to James? The answer would be that even on this ground the American and the French novelist are more at variance than would seem at first glance.

Proust's picture of society contains elements of lyricism as well as elements of objective analysis. He is a more realistic painter of social manners than James, perhaps for the reason that he permits no ethical issues to intervene between him and the subject, approaching the world *ab initio* with the tacit assumption that ethics are irrelevant to its functions. By comparison James is a traditional moralist whose insight into experience turns on his judgment of conduct. If sometimes, as in *The Golden Bowl,* we are made to feel that he is withholding judgment or judging wrongly, that may be because he is either conforming, or appears to conform, to certain moral conventions of the world's making by which it manages to flatter itself. In Proust such conventions are brought out into the open, but not for purposes of moral judgment. The sole morality of which the protagonist of his novel is conscious grows out of the choice he faces between two contrary ideals. He must decide whether to pursue the art of life or the life of art, and the novel can be said to be an epical autobiography of his effort to come to a decision. But it is not until the end-volume that the world is finally renounced; and through a kind of optical illusion induced by the novel's astonishing unfoldment, we seem to participate in this renunciation of the world at the precise moment when its alternative — i.e., the work of art — actually comes into being, or, more accurately, is at last fully realized. Since in this work the world is overcome only after it has been possessed, the unity of life and art is affirmed in it despite the author's attempt to divorce them by closing with a purely subjective account of the artistic process. No matter what Proust intended this account to mean, taken in its context it affects us as an ironic expression of the artist's triumph over his material, a mocking valediction addressed to that recalcitrant angel — the objective spirit of reality — with whom the artist grappled through the long night of creation and, having gotten the better of him, can now treat with disdain.

But if in Proust art and life are unified by the contradiction between them, in James they are initially combined in his root-idea of experience. His passionate pilgrims, such as the heiress, are driven, despite all vacillations and retractions, by their need to master the world (which is identified with experience and the "real *taste* of life"), and in art they recognize the means by which the world becomes most richly aware of itself. As Americans they have come to it so belatedly that they can ill afford either the spiritual luxury or spiritual desperation of looking beyond it. This is the reason, I think, that except for the early example of *Roderick Hudson* and later of *The Tragic Muse,* the theme of art and artists enters significantly and independently only into some of James's short stories, in which he deals not with his representative figures but with his own case as a professional writer somewhat estranged from society by his devotion to his craft. Though these stories testify to the artistic idealism of their author, they can scarcely be taken as a serious challenge to the authority of the world.

Now at this point it should be evident that James's inability to overcome the world, in the sense that most European writers of like caliber overcome it, is due not to his being too much of it, but, paradoxically enough, to his being too little of it. And for that the explanation must be sought in his origins. For he approaches the world with certain presumptions of piety that clearly derive from the semireligious idealism of his family background and, more generally, from the early traditions and faith of the American community. But in James this idealism and faith undergo a radical change, in that they are converted to secular ends. Thus one might venture the speculation that his worldly-aesthetic idea of an elite is in some way associated, however remotely and unconsciously, with the ancestral-puritan idea of the elect; hence the ceremoniousness and suggestions of ritual in the social display of a novel like *The Golden Bowl*. So with the ancestral ideas of sin and grace. Is it not possible to claim that the famous Jamesian refinement is a trait in which the vision of an ideal state is preserved — the state of grace to be achieved here and now through mundane and aesthetic means? It is the vision by which Milly Theale is transported as she rests in her Venetian garden — the vision of "never going down, of remaining aloft in the divine dustless air, where she could but hear the plash of water against the stone." And through the same process, as I have already had occasion to remark, the fear of sin is translated in James into a revulsion, an exasperated feeling, almost morbid in its sensitiveness, against any conceivable crudity of scene or crudity of conduct.

Yet whatever the sources and implications of the social legend in James, I have no doubt that it enabled him as nothing else could to formulate his creative method and to remain true, even on his lower levels, to the essential mood and sympathy of his genius. There is an essay on Proust by Paul Valéry in which he speaks of the French novelist's capacity "to adapt the potentialities of his inner life" to the aim of expressing "one group of people . . . which calls itself Society," thus converting the picture of an avowedly superficial existence into a profound work. But I have always felt that what Valéry is saying in this essay could more appropriately be said about the later James than about Proust:

> The group which calls itself Society is composed of symbolic figures. Each of its members represents some abstraction. It is necessary that all the powers of this world should somewhere meet together; that *money* should converse with *beauty*, and *politics* become familiar with *elegance;* that *letters* and *birth* grow friendly and serve each other tea . . . Just as a banknote is only a slip of paper, so the member of society is a sort of fiduciary money made of living flesh. This combination is extremely favorable to the designs of a subtle novelist.

... very great art, which is the art of simplified figures and the most pure types; in other words, of essences which permit the symmetrical and almost musical development of the consequences arising from a carefully isolated situation — such art involves the existence of a conventional milieu, where the language is adorned with veils and provided with limits, where *seeming* commands *being* and where *being* is held in a noble restraint which changes all of life into an opportunity to exercise presence of mind. (*A Tribute*)

This is, however, a peculiarly one-sided view of the Proustian scene, as Valéry allows himself to be carried away by the comparison between the old French literature of the court and *À la recherche du temps perdu*. Proust balances his poetic appreciation of the Guermantes way with a more than sufficient realism in portraying the rages of Charlus, the passions of Saint-Loup, the schemes of Mme. Verdurin, Bloch, Morel, Jupien, etc.; nor is he averse to showing the pathological condition of that "group which calls itself Society"; he, too, is infected, after all, with the modern taste for excess, for speaking out with inordinate candor. The truth is that it is in James, rather than in Proust, that we often find it difficult to make certain of the real contours of *being* behind the smooth mask of *seeming*. It is *his* language which is "adorned with veils and provided with limits," and it is the conversation of *his* characters which is so allusive that it seems more to spare than to release the sense.

And Valéry continues: "After a new power has gained recognition, no great time passes before its representatives appear at the gatherings of society; and the movement of history is pretty well summarized by the successive admissions of different social types to the salons, hunts, marriages, and funerals of the supreme tribe of a nation." What an apt description of the rise of the heiress — of, say, Milly Theale entering a London drawing room and being greeted by Lord Mark as the first woman of her time, or of Maggie Verver gravely telling the prince to whom she has just become engaged that he is an object of beauty, a *morceau du musée*, though of course she hasn't the least idea of what it would cost her father to acquire him, and that together they shall possess the "world, the beautiful world!"

Partisan Review, 1943

Saul Bellow's Progress

With this new work, *Herzog*, his sixth novel, Saul Bellow emerges not only as the most intelligent novelist of his generation but also as the most consistently interesting in point of growth and development. To my mind, too, he is the finest stylist at present writing fiction in America.

For some time now the critical consensus has been, expressed not so much formally in writing as in the talk of literary circles, that *Seize the Day*, published some nine years ago, was his best single performance. However, I think *Herzog* is superior to it, even if not so tightly organized and in fact a bit loose on the structural side. For one thing, it is a much longer and fuller narrative than *Seize the Day*, which is hardly more than a novella. For another, it is richer in content, in the effective disposition of tone and language, as well as in intellectual resonance and insight of a high order in the makeup of modern life — insight into what is really new and perhaps all too hazardous about its strange, almost inconceivable mixture of greater freedom and maddening constriction.

Above all, this novel positively radiates intelligence — not mere brightness or shrewdness or that kind of sensitiveness which all too often passes for mind among us. This intelligence is a real endowment, coherent, securely founded, and of a genuine intellectual quality which, marvelously escaping the perils of abstractions, is neither recondite nor esoteric. It is directed toward imaginative ends by virtue of a true and sharp sense of the pain that rends the human world, of its ills both curable and incurable, and equally by a bracing, unfailing sense of humor and irony serving to counteract such chronic vulnerabilities of intelligence as oversolemnity of mind on the one hand and perversity of sensibility on the other.

It is important to stress this element of intellectual mastery in Bellow, for in the milieu of our creative writers intellect has by no means played a conspicuous part. Hence the immaturity of even the best, like Hemingway for instance, and the aborted careers of not a few other gifted writers, aborted among other things by the repetition compulsion that results not so much from neurotic disturbance, though that may be present too, as from thematic poverty and narrowness of the mental horizon. To be sure, intellect is not art; in some ways it might even be said to be corrosive in its effect on artistic production. But without intellect it becomes impossible for the artist, the verbal artist particularly, to transform into consciousness what is offered by experience and the manifold and at times infinitely varied and subtle emotions it gives rise to. After all, thinking too is an experience. Without thought the writer may be able to relate the particulars of experience well enough, though usually at inordinate length, but he is at a loss when it comes to extracting values from experience that will make it meaningful to the reader (and perhaps to himself also).

Herzog is far and away the most personal novel Bellow has written, and the most immediate in self-reference. But the personal element in this case in no way strikes us as an intrusion, as it makes for a clear gain in impact and reality-mindedness. By comparison, *The Adventures of Augie March* seems like a wonderfully inventive exercise in mere narrative fantastication, projecting an affirmative message that falls short of conviction. *Herzog,* moreover, despite its deeply personal provenance, betrays none of that orgastic self-glorification that you may find in our hipster writers who make do with the self (the ravenous, raging self of erotic fantasy and adolescent daydreams of power) when talent and moral intelligence fail them. As a maker of prose fiction, Bellow is far too scrupulous and his personality too complicated to engage in such capers. He has put a great deal of himself into his protagonist Herzog, but always with a twist of irony and a minimum of self-display.

Herzog is a Chicago professor, author of a work entitled *Romanticism and Christianity* (a good stroke, that, for the novel is in its own way a kind of exploration of latter-day versions of romanticism), who is suffering a near breakdown when his second wife, Mady, leaves him. She appropriates house and child to take up with his best friend, Gersbach, a purveyor of the latest cultural goodies, like Buber's "I and Thou" relationship, the more portentous varieties of existentialism, and Yiddishisms of phrase and stance. At the very start of the story we are told that some people thought Herzog was cracked, and he himself is uncertain whether this is so. The truth is, however, that he "had fallen under a spell and was writing letters to everyone under the sun," feeling an irresistible need "to explain, to have it out, to justify, to put in perspective, to clarify, to make amends." The letters teem with ideas, thus converting Herzog's personal crisis into the more impersonal crisis of modern thinking. Herzog moves from place to place carrying a valise full of papers, which he takes with him from New York to Martha's Vineyard and back again almost at once. Two days later he flies to Chicago, keyed up to the highest pitch, to have it out with his wife and her lover (at this stage the latent violence almost erupts), and then back again to a village in western Massachusetts where, hidden in the country, he again "writes endlessly, fantastically, to the newspapers, to people in public life, to friends and relatives, and at last to the dead, his own obscure dead and finally the famous dead." The story ends in this village, where Herzog evades his brother's efforts to get him to a psychiatrist even as he makes ready for a visit from his New York mistress, a superbly rendered figure of "sex and swagger."

There is nothing in any novel I have read quite like these letters Herzog writes. In no sense formal in tone, they represent at once a fictional device and a prodigiously productive aggression of the mind. The writer is richly ironic, at his own expense too, and intolerant of the typical platitudes of modern thought, letting go in a strange intermixture of "clairvoyance and spleen, *esprit de l'escalier,* noble inspiration, poetry and nonsense, ideas, hyperaesthesia ..." To the philosopher Heidegger he addresses himself, "I should like to know what you mean by the expression, 'The Fall into the Quotidian.' When did this fall occur? Where were we standing when it happened?" Another letter, to Nietzsche, opens with the sentence, "Dear Herr Nietzsche — my dear sir, may I ask a question from the floor?," followed by an outburst against the German thinker's celebration of the Dionysian spirit's pride in allowing itself the luxury of pain and evil. In still another letter, to a fellow scholar named Shapiro, he writes that "we must not forget how quickly the visions of genius become the canned goods of the intellectuals. The canned sauerkraut of Spengler's Prussian socialism, the commonplaces of the Wasteland outlook, the cheap mental stimulants of Alienation, the cant and rant of the pipsqueaks about Inauthenticity and Forlornness. I can't accept this foolish dreariness. We are talking about the whole life of mankind. The subject is too great, too deep, for such weakness, cowardice.... A merely aesthetic critique of modern history! After the wars and mass killings! You are too intelligent for this. You inherited rich blood. Your father peddled apples."

Herzog, with his talent for polemics, bears down with particular force on those German existentialists who tell you that guilt and dread are good for you; their story is that "God is no more but Death is." Human life, writes Herzog, "is far subtler than any of its models. Do we need *theories* of pain and anguish?" Now such ideas will scarcely please our academic popularizers of existentialism who imagine that with delusions of concreteness borrowed from Germany and France, they are actually escaping the basic and very comfortable abstraction of their professorial stance. Herzog protests vehemently against the seeming profundities of the modern cult of pain and suffering. Himself in a state of extreme anguish, he needs no theories to rub it in.

Among the characters of the novel other than Herzog (of whom there is a richly varied cast, some beautifully drawn), Ramona, his mistress, is an outstanding creation. Mady, the treacherous wife, does not really come through except as an object of hostility, though a weirdly interesting one, whereas Ramona is the best portrait I have encountered in contemporary fiction of the modern woman *par excellence* who has made good on the sexual revolution. That kind of woman is the chief beneficiary of the revolution, made mostly by men. How is it possible, muses Herzog, to run out "on fragrant, sexual, high-minded Ramona? Never in a million years. She has passed through the hell of profligacy and attained the seriousness of pleasure." She believes in no sin but "the sin against the body, for her the true and only temple of the spirit." If you are under stress and Ramona likes you, then the only thing to do, the perfect restorative indeed, is to fly to her at once; she will "feed you, give you wine, remove your shoes, flatter you, put down your hackles, pinch your lips with her teeth. Then uncover the bed, turn down the lights, disclose the essentials."

In his state of feeling betrayed, Herzog voices a certain animus against women, and this animus is not without heuristic value. He notes: "Will I never understand what women want? What do they want? They eat green salad and drink human blood." This short last sentence, with its startling juxtaposition of the tame and the fierce, is good vivid writing and by no means purely rhetorical. For nowadays women do expect all the privileges of the sex-inhibited past plus all the freedoms of the swinging present. In other words, the modern female is hugely avid and expects nearly everything, and from her husband most of all. She expects him to provide nightly erotic "gratification, safety, money, furs, jewelry, cleaning women, drapes, dresses, hats, night clubs, automobiles, theater!"

As the story progresses it becomes clear that poor Ramona will receive none of those valuable things from Herzog, who is much too ironically observant of her modern ways to fall in love with her, even though, far from young, she is touching enough as a woman who more than once has taken matters into her own hands. It is scarcely easy to live on an ideological diet of permanent sex, and Ramona is "fairly fanatical about that." On the theme of the erotic, Herzog has his mordant say: "The erotic must be admitted to its rightful place, at last, in an emancipated society," but why put such a great value on the sexual act as "actually socially constructive and useful, an act of citizenship" no less? Salvation through sex is among the more fatuous illusions of our age. In this novel there are sexual scenes galore, but none of them clinical, none of them fired with the vulgar *ne plus ultra* fervor of our contemporary sexologists in fiction.

Bellow's style in this narrative, as in most of his fiction, provides a very meaningful pleasure in its masterful combination of the demotic and literary languages. At once astringent and poetic, it neither muffles nor distends his themes. Among the elements back of it is, no doubt, a deep sense of humor derived from his Jewish background and thoroughly assimilated to his sensibility. This style is sensibility in action.

From *The Myth and the Powerhouse,* 1964

Crime without Punishment

An *American Dream* is, to my mind, the most eccentric of the four novels Norman Mailer has written. It is far more eccentric, I think, than *Barbary Shore* — his second novel and a better one than literary opinion has generally taken it to be — which alienated readers not so much by personal singularity as by the extreme sectarianism of its political theme. In the case of that work it might well be said that the reader, wholly unprepared for that kind of statement, was in a certain sense quite as much at fault for its failure as the author. This latest book, however, has very few if any of the qualities that redeemed *Barbary Shore* as well as Mailer's other fiction.

There is nothing here like the brilliantly observed comic episodes in *The Deer Park* (involving the Hollywood producers Teppis and Munshin), or the powerfully sustained narrative sequence comprising the second part of *The Naked and the Dead* (the Sergeant Croft section). And the title, *An American Dream,* strikes me as a misnomer. It implies a generalization about the national life palpably unsupported either by the weird and sometimes ludicrous details of the story or by the low-level private mysticism informing its imaginative scheme. That mysticism is more or less pseudonymously presented in Mailer's articles under the flashy and ostensibly impersonal heading of Hip. Now whatever the origin of the term in the underworld of jazz and narcotics, the explication of it that he has been engaged in for some years is at bottom scarcely a report on something that exists outside himself but in basically a programmatic statement of his own desires, power drives, and daydreams. It amounts to a kind of personal mythology projected unto something he chooses to call Hip. I venture to say that real-life hipsters, not romantic youths reading Mailer with relish, would hardly recognize themselves in his free-wheeling description of their motivation and behavior.

The time span of this new novel is thirty-two hours, and its frantic action consists of a great deal of sexual exertion and is centered on a murder — the protagonist's killing of his wife, a bitchy wealthy heiress, during a violent tussle in which hard words and harder blows are exchanged. It is true enough that the murder is unpremeditated, but neither can it be said that this act of ultimate violence committed by Stephen Rojack, the protagonist, is merely an accident; and he commits it with enormous exhilaration. Already on page 8, before the episode of the killing is introduced, Rojack acknowledges that he had long known there was murder within him, and he speculates that the exhilaration accompanying it must come "from possessing such strength." "Besides," he adds, "murder offers the promise of vast relief. It is never unsexual." (How would he know that, since these thoughts occur to him prior to the experience itself?) Moreover, the long paragraph describing Rojack's choking of Deborah to death is full of positive imagery, and it closes with the following sentences: "I was weary with a most honorable fatigue, and my flesh seemed new. I had not felt so nice since I was twelve. It seemed inconceivable at this instant that anything in life could fail to please. But there was Deborah dead beside me . . ." And immediately after absorbing this to him so ecstatic experience, a true renewal, Rojack rushes to the maid's room to engage her in sex acts both plain and fancy. It is not that he had been having an affair with her; killing excites him sexually. Then he returns to the scene of the killing and dumps the corpse out of the tenth-floor window to the East River Drive. So much for hipster heroics!

The curious thing about it is not only that this murder goes unpunished (Crime without Punishment) but that it is also without any kind of consequence, either public or private. Clearly the plot is all too intentionally manipulated by the author so as to free Rojack from paying any sort of price, even if only psychologically, for what he had done. At the last moment and even as the detectives are closing in on him, they are held back by a call from Washington. We are astonished to learn — just as the husband is — that Deborah had all along been engaged in "amateur espionage." As the maid, Ruta, explains to him: "Last night they must have had electricity burning in government offices all over the world . . . Yes, they had to let you go . . . Since nobody can know if you know a little or a lot, a real investigation would be ending *der Teufel* knows where." But this novel is not designed as a spy-thriller nor as a wacky tale the absurd happenings of which are not meant to produce consequences; it is written in the realistic convention and without a trace of irony. The business about espionage, arbitrarily introduced at the last moment, is simply the author's *deus ex machina* — a device confirming Rojack in his lordly "existentialist" freedom at the same time as it confirms him in his ecstasy of violence. Only in a hipster's fantasy is society so easily cheated of its prey and only in his fantasy can the self become so absolutized, so unchecked by reality, as to convert itself with impunity into the sole arbiter of good and evil.

It is evident that Mailer has repressed in this novel his common sense as well as the moral side of his nature. He has of late been arguing in his neoprimitivistic fashion, that civilization threatens to "extinguish the animal in us." This yea-saying to instinct is a common error of neoprimitivism. It is well known that patterns of instinct are rigid and conservative; the original and spontaneous are virtually a monopoly of human consciousness. Moreover, neoprimitivists seem unaware that not only "the animal in us" but also our Superego, as Freud and other analysts have repeatedly shown, is subject to repression. If Freud's motto was: "Where the Id once was there shall Ego be," Mailer's should read: "Where the Ego once was there shall Id be." Nor is the objection to the imaginative scheme of this novel a matter of morality pure and simple. It is also a matter of the novelist's primary responsibility to his craft. A writer like Mailer, who aspires to be something more than an intellectual version of Mickey Spillane, who takes himself seriously and in turn expects us to take him seriously, cannot without self-stultification center a story on so portentous a theme as murder (think of what novelists like Dostoevsky and Stendhal and Faulkner, among others equally pre-eminent, have made of this theme!) and then proceed to evade its multiple consequences in the dimensions of character and fate by means of sheer plot manipulation. But I suppose this kind of thing was more or less in the cards ever since a number of our literary people have gone in in a big way for what is known as swinging. The swingers want to make the scene, to be "in," to be "with it." Their great pretension is that they are protesting against a genteel, conventional, and conformist society, but the fact is that they are not truly protestants or rebels at all. What they are doing is expressing the fickle moods of a certain sector of American society, by no means the least affluent, which in every sphere but the political has collapsed into total permissiveness. There is money in it and fun too, though in the long run the fun runs out as the law of diminishing returns takes over. And as the shock of riotous explicitness in the handling of sexual subject matter by writers wears off, murder and other forms of brutal sadism beckon from the wings. Engaged in raising the ante all the time, the swingers must come to that.

Who is this protagonist of Mailer's? He is not at all the anti-hero of modern fiction but one of the most lamentably old-fashioned heroes, in the dictionary meaning of a man of distinguished valor and performance, I have come across in years. Hence as a novelistic character he never quite comes to life: he remains a vacuity. He is "the one intellectual in America with a Distinguished Service Cross," an ex-Congressman, a television celebrity, a professor of "existentialist psychology with the not inconsiderable thesis that magic, dread and the perception of death were the roots of motivation," author of a work entitled *The Psychology of the Hangman,* and, needless to say, a prepotent lover and expert in fisticuffs. Though as conformist as anyone else in his bedazzlement by power and success ("there's nothing but magic at the top"), he is so full, however, of obsessions almost clinical in nature, and outright superstitions to boot, that the last thing one can say about him is that he stands generically for Americans at large. On all levels but that of literal biography he is a facsimile of the author, down to the most absurd details of his personal mythology; and some of the secondary characters, like his girl friend Cherry and his millionaire wheeler-dealer father-in-law, are also mere mouthpieces on occasion. The national experience, whether conceived in the broadly typical manner of Dreiser and Dos Passos or in a latent imaginative form, is not to be found in this novel. Its true *raison d'être* is a dream of romantic omnipotence, in which what is projected is a mana-figure, a being of occult and enchanting powers. Mailer is testing here (or acting out, to be more precise) a whole cluster of notions to which he has committed himself. But unfortunately for him the fictional medium is far more exacting in its demands than the discursive form of the article, in which charm and personal vehemence take you a long way.

To make sense of *An American Dream* one must use as a gloss the articles he has collected in *Advertisements for Myself* and *The Presidential Papers.* There he declares that "the existentialist moment, by demanding the most extreme response in the protagonist, tends to destroy psychotic autonomies . . . and then one is returned to the realities of one's personal strength or weakness." Also, "whether the life is criminal or not, the decision is to encourage the psychopath in oneself." Also: "Postulate a modern soul marooned in constipation, emptiness, boredom and a flat, dull terror of death. It is a deadened existence, afraid precisely of violence, cannibalism, loneliness, insanity, libidinousness, perversion and mess, because these are states which in some way must be passed through, digested, transcended, if one is to make one's way back to life." The language here is a bit circumlocutory, a bit on the "tactical" side, but its meaning is clear enough. It appears that the way to "transcend" violence is to commit it, the way to overcome perversion is to indulge in it: get it out of your system once and for all. The "extreme response" (presumably not excluding murder) is regarded as therapeutic and heuristic. The psychopath in oneself is to be encouraged, and if that is indeed Mailer's program he has certainly succeeded only too well so far as this latest novel at least is concerned. And the most curious thing about it all is the way in which all his invocations of violence he nearly always identifies with its perpetrators, almost never with its victims. And violence, however extreme, is plainly for him a testing ground of courage which he is inclined to understand, with excessive reiteration and emphasis, in a strictly physical sense. Yet because of such ideas Mailer has been saluted by some people as a "moralist" no less, an expositor of sacred mysteries, a religious type in fact.

The one religious notion of the novel is expressed by the girl friend Cherry in this wise: "There is no decent explanation for evil. I believe God is just doing His best to learn from what happens to us. Sometimes I think He knows less than the Devil because we're not good enough to teach him. So the Devil gets most of the best messages we think we are sending up." This same belief is elaborated by Rojack's father-in-law, who holds that God is engaged in a war with the Devil and God may lose — "God might be having a very bad war, with troops defecting everywhere." Thus when the God-Devil relationship is not conceived of as a kind of celestial prize fight it is conceived of as a scene from a war novel. This echo of an old Christian heresy, a sort of flattened out Manichaeism, is solemnly offered as a contribution to theology. It also seems to contain a vague, distorted, late American military-style reminiscence of *Paradise Lost*. More than ever, then, we should now cry out with Wordsworth: "Milton! thou shouldst be living at this hour . . ."

Then there is Mailer's obsession with explaining cancer in his own inimitable manner, here repeated by Rojack: "In some madness must come with breath . . . In some it goes up to the mind. Some take the madness and stop it with discipline. Madness is locked beneath. It goes into the tissues, is swallowed by the cells. The cells go mad. Cancer is their flag." With what ease Mailer thus outmaneuvers the biochemists! And there are other far less "original" beliefs of a magical nature in the book, such as Rojack's compulsive involvement with "the phases of the moon," which now and then invites him to commit suicide; but these thoughts of suicide, induced by the guileful moon, appear to have nothing to do with guilt-feelings or remorse; in fact they occur to him before the murder. Rojack also hears voices and messages from some unspecified beyond, which at one point order him to walk three times around a parapet twelve inches wide at the Waldorf Towers thirty stories above the street, and this feat he virtually manages to accomplish too. Then there is a whole series of extravaganzas of the olfactory sense, a kind of olfactory mysticism, permitting Rojack to smell what are really states of mind rather than states of the body.

On the technical side what the novel obviously lacks is verisimilitude, even in the most literal sense. In his thirty-two hours in New York, Rojack, a man no longer young, engages in feats of strength — consuming vast quantities of alcohol, fighting, making strenuous love to two different girls, not to mention murder — that would lay low not one but several younger men. The characters don't emerge into reality, especially Rojack and his girl Cherry; Deborah is drawn rather better than the rest. In Chapter 7 the Negro singer Shago Martin engages in a near-monologue of hipster talk which is worldly-wise, heady, and strangely effective. It is a pity that he does not stay around long enough, for he is soon beaten up by Rojack and thrown downstairs. Eventually, in the very last paragraph, the words "I was something like sane again" occur, but here Rojack is referring not to the main action in New York but to his last and least credible experience in Las Vegas, where the story ends. It is important to stress that Rojack is not considered by his author to be insane — inspired, if you please, but not mad.

But Mailer is no ordinary swinger. For one thing, he cannot be accused of pornographic intent, as the sex-writing in his more recent work, however rank and dense, is so mixed up with concepts of the self's salvation that it cannot be mistaken for exploitative commercialized sexology. For another, he is a prose writer of considerable gifts; and this novel is likewise written with a certain sharpness, though to my taste there are too many purple passages in it. The trouble with Mailer, to my mind, is that he has let himself become a victim of ideas productive of "false consciousness"; and these ideas are willful, recklessly simple, and too histrionic. He has too many ambition-fed notions and he does not sufficiently value the artistic function. His habitual stance of toughness and the "advertisements" of his own special brand of excruciated sexology have not been helpful in resolving the discords of his creative personality. Salvation is not to be seized by force of heroics or diabolics. Life's cruel and inexorable processes can be arrested neither by the brain nor by the phallus, least of all by the phallus. But if Mailer ever extricates himself from his entanglement with the hocus-pocus of power and the glamor-dream of the romantic domination, physical and psychic, of existence, he might yet emerge as one of our greater talents.

New York Review of Books, 1965

Postscript 1969 — There is surely something to be said about Mailer's development since the publication of *An American Dream.* His next novel, *Why Are We in Vietnam?,* struck me as an even worse performance. The author's frenetic language, the failure to discover in the youthful hero-narrator anything but one more souped-up version of himself and, above all, the extravagant and (to my mind) wholly unfounded claim of having gained deep insights into the American psyche — what does all that come to but more play-acting, more gimmickry? The fact is that though Mailer is overly fascinated by the actuality of America, he has no real ideas about it. All you find in him on this subject are outlandish notions, mostly psychosexual projections of his own confused inner life; nor has the personality cult which the media have by now secured for him proven to be anything but damaging to that inner life. And in the literary world he has become the hero of a claque whose outrageous puffery cannot but abort his creative career in the long run. If he takes it seriously, that is. And I am afraid he does. He is not very discerning in distinguishing his talent for self-promotion from his genuine talents as an imaginative writer.

However, Mailer appears to have recovered somewhat his élan in his more recent journalistic works, *Armies of the Night* and *Miami and the Siege of Chicago.* For Mailer is really far more effective as an observer and reporter of immediate situations than as an ideologue. In the latter role he seldom conveys an impression of authenticity; what you mostly get is mere idea mongering in a dashing manner. In this respect he reminds me of what T. S. Eliot once said about Chesterton: that his "brain swarms with ideas; I see no evidence that it thinks." At bottom Mailer is a man of divided consciousness, ambivalent in the extreme. Instinctively an extremist of the Left, if not a complete anarchist, he nevertheless prefers to speak of himself as a "Left conservative," whatever that may mean. So he strives with might and main to seem more "original" in his political and intellectual attitudes than it is within his power to be. Even in *Armies of the Night* he by no means overcomes his besetting vice of playing ego games and flaunting his personality. Yet the famous Mailer personality is not actually very interesting. It affects animal vitality and pride of life, but what comes through mainly, apart from all-too-obvious charm, is unbounded egocentrism and flamboyance of phrase and posture. It is only in *Miami and the Siege of Chicago* that he manages to stick to the job at hand and thus succeeds in checking his bent for self-exploitation. For this reason I think it is a far better book than *Armies of the Night*.

From *Literature and the Sixth Sense,* 1969

On Pornography, Black Humor,
Norman Mailer, Etc.*

Interviewer: Is there any particular way in which contemporary literature can be characterized?

Rahv: The present situation in American literature is one of perplexity and confusion, of marking time, actually, while most of the attention goes to the hipsters, militant homosexuals, and pornographers, who claim the title of avant-garde even while trying to "make it" in a big way in the worldly world. They are tremendqusly concerned with publicity and success at the same time as they come on as moral and literary rebels. But what exactly would you like to talk about?

Interviewer: How about the pornographers?

Rahv: The pornography written today, as well as the old pornography, like *Fanny Hill,* reissued in new editions and widely distributed, is being played up as a form of literature, but it still remains pornography no matter what the label.

Terry Southern's book, *Candy,* consists of a series of dirty jokes. It uses one of the standard gimmicks of pornography. The main character is not in any sense a person. She is supposed to be a liberal type, all too open to experience, anxious to help the deprived, and the novel is ostensibly a satire on liberal credulity. This is simply a gimmick making it easy for Southern to take her through a whole series of scabrous incidents. None of the other people in the book are real characters either. The humor of the story, real enough on a low

* This interview appeared in the undergraduate Brandeis literary magazine, *Folio.*

level, has nothing to do with literature. Yet *Candy* was built up by the reviewers as a spoof on pornography, some kind of sophisticated product no less. In my judgment its impulse is basically commercial, and we know, in fact, that it was originally written for a few hundred dollars to feed the Olympia Press in Paris.

Actually, it is not possible for pornography to be a literary form because its aim is too "practical," so to speak. Its aim is to appeal to prurient interests and to satisfy the public's inexhaustible interest in sexual details; nor does the public care whether the information given is in any sense accurate or not. Now literature can never have such a limited and "practical" goal.

Interviewer: Do you think that pornography is bad on moral grounds?

Rahv: As a critic, I am not concerned with the question whether pornography is good or bad for young people, or old people for that matter. This is something for the courts or other governmental bodies to worry about. Nor am I a sociologist. I have opinions on the subject but they are no better qualified than yours. As a literary critic I am qualified — or at least I think I am — to judge whether it is a form of literature, as it now claims to be, or not.

The publishers have succeeded in putting something over on reviewers and critics who are confused by the cultural atmosphere of the 1960s and who live in mortal fear of being called squares or philistines. Now the reviewers have nothing to gain when a pornographic work becomes a best seller. The publishers, however, stand to make a lot of money; yet reviewers, and even some academic types, have apparently chosen to play their game.

There is a large distinction to be made between a novel like *Candy* and one like *Lolita*. The latter work has a literary framework within which the sexual events take place. The characters are interesting and credible, the author's sensibility is superb, and the erotic scenes are validated by the context. But *Candy* is a novel with sex but no people, no psychology; it is mere organ-grinding in words, as pornography inevitably tends to be; even the book's sexology is not real, because you can't have sexuality without relationships, without people. You can't create a character by limiting yourself to purely physical sexual acts. People are not reducible to their private parts.

It is in the nature of novelists — American novelists especially — to be very competitive with one another. And now that the clinical sex scene has virtually become obligatory, most novelists feel that they must bring this scene into their work, whether it belongs there or not, or risk losing out in the competitive game. I think this situation is causing a good deal of damage to the literary effort, for what you have here in consequence is a new and terribly tyrannical literary convention imposed by commercial considerations.

Pure physical sensation is very difficult to render in literature anyhow. The sensation tends to be pretty much the same no matter who is involved, and this leads to monotony or else to totally irrelevant rhapsody. On the other hand, desire and erotic states in general can be rendered with far more interest and variety, as for instance in *Madame Bovary*, where actual intercourse is not described though an air of sensuality pervades the novel.

Pornography is essentially a subliterary form. All it has in common with literature is the written word.

Interviewer: What about the black humorists?

Rahv: Black humor seems to me — as a phrase — to have become a mere fashionable label for elevating all kinds of shoddy work to artistic status. The best piece of black humor in American literature that I know of is *Miss Lonelyhearts* — a very good book published in the early 1930s. But why use the expression anyway? Most of the writers called black humorists today are mere buffoons of one sort or another. To call them black humorists is to flatter them. The expression suggests a desperate state of negation, but our writers are far too wordly-wise and ambitious for that sort of thing. They are still immersed in the cult of experience.

Interviewer: Do you have any thoughts as to why Mailer's novel, *An American Dream*, did not become a best seller?

Rahv: Not because it was too shocking but rather because it was so childish. There is a small literary clique which is furious because it did not make the best-seller list, and the members of that clique, mostly hangers-on of Mailer, are very angry at Bellow for the success of his novel, *Herzog*.

In his novel Mailer is out to show that he can outsex all the sexologists. But the sex scenes are not sexy; they are mostly repulsive. But that is not important as such. Rojack (the novel's hero who is so closely identified with his author in his ideas and general demeanor) appears to consider bed an arena in which to show off his prowess as a male. What he is after is domination, not pleasure; he wants to subdue women, to bring them to subjection by exercising some kind of magic. The feeling of competition with other men is very prominent throughout the work, and one of the women tells Rojack that he is a sexual genius.

On the question of murder, the main event of the book, Mailer indulges himself in pure uninhibited fantasy. He pretends that the act of murder has no moral relevance. But whatever may be true of life, where people both literally and figuratively sometimes "get away with murder," this cannot be true of the novel, a literary form that cannot ignore moral experience. This is not just moralizing. The prohibition of murder is not a mere convention of society, a pious prejudice or some kind of bourgeois leftover: it has existed in every society, however primitive. The serious novelist must see it as a significant act with consequences. Now Mailer does not attempt to re-evaluate murder morally. He presents it as self-justified. Why does his hero kill his wife? Because she makes some sarcastic remarks about his virility. No wonder Professor Coser has called the novel "an apologia for murder." Actually, Rojack is the comic-strip fantasy of an adolescent. The neoprimitivism, which has played a considerable role in modern literature, is reduced in this work to mere gratuitous violence and sexual braggadocio.

1966

T. S. Eliot in His

Posthumous Essays

THERE IS MUCH to interest and even fascinate students of T. S. Eliot in his posthumously published collection, *To Criticize the Critic and Other Writings,* consisting for the most part of public lectures and addresses delivered between 1942 and 1961. Of the earlier articles not heretofore reprinted only two, both dating back to 1917 — one on *vers libre* and the other on the metrics of Ezra Pound — are included in this volume. The analysis of *vers libre* is as lively as it is discriminating, keyed to the highest pitch of poetic intelligence; but the essay on Pound's metrics is less satisfactory. It is full of technical argumentation that somehow steers clear of any truly evaluative judgment. It has generally been my impression that, in his various statements on Pound, Eliot seems to be laboring under an intolerable burden of personal indebtedness that inhibits candor. As a result, what we get is a kind of embarrassed formalism that makes more for the appearance than the substance of criticism. He is always ready to praise Pound; yet the grounds of his praise, apart from the purely technical points involved, remain obscure.

The title essay of the volume is indispensable for the understanding of Eliot's development. He reviews in it the entire corpus of his critical writing with great tact and a good deal of humor. The self-deprecatory manner characteristic of his later years is also much in evidence in his remarks on errors of judgment and errors of tone: "the occasional note of arrogance, of cocksureness and rudeness, the braggadocio of the mild-mannered man safely entrenched behind his typewriter." As he grew older Eliot was never fanatical about his literary ideas and opinions, and he mixed grace with courage in retracting quite a few of them, as on the subject of Milton, for instance;

nor did he ever lose sight of the literary object in expounding his religious convictions. The one interlude of fanaticism in his career that I recall occurred in the early 1930s, and its upshot was *After Strange Gods*. This book, harsh and even supercilious in tone, has not been reprinted for a long time, probably because its author regretted its publication in the first place. The fanaticism has been voiced mainly by his disciples, who did their master little good by converting his insights, perhaps inseparable from their specific contexts, into dogmas; and Eliot does in fact express here his irritation at having his words, uttered decades ago, quoted as if he had written them yesterday. Even the famous statement (in the preface to *For Lancelot Andrewes*) that proclaimed him to be "a classicist in literature, a royalist in politics, and an Anglo-Catholic in religion," is considerably hedged in 1961 — the Anglo-Catholicism is still firmly retained, while the royalism is reduced to an empty gesture, and the classicism is brushed aside altogether. It is clear that Eliot is no system builder, has no great flair for logical consistency, and is scarcely if ever concerned with the more abstract concepts of aesthetic theorizing. If a number of influential commentators have insisted on deriving a system from his work, it is largely due, it seems to me, to their willfully confusing his religious ideas, which belong to an entirely different order of discourse and are even at best quite unoriginal, with his literary and critical ones. There is no real interdependence, either logical or substantive, between the two orders of ideas. For it can be shown, I think, that his more valuable literary ideas are mostly empirical in nature and can easily be disengaged from his religious commitments. That this disengagement is stubbornly resisted by some people points to the vested interest in Eliot that the religious ideologists have acquired. The religious experience that he records in his poetry is validated by the poetry, not the other way around; the ideology, insofar as it enters his criticism, is something else again, and should be separated out if we are to make the best use of it. Deliberately or not, it is exactly in this fashion that we proceed with Dr. Johnson, with Coleridge, and with Arnold. Why not with Eliot, who, to my mind, is as good a critic as any of them?

Eliot distinguishes three periods in his criticism, and attributes the "enduring popularity" of his earlier essays, in which, as he says, he was implicitly defending the sort of poetry he was then writing, to a kind of "urgency, the warmth of appeal of the advocate," which his later, "more detached and judicious essays cannot claim." (Of course, there is more to it than that: The authority and enormous influence of that earlier criticism, though it must always be considered in close relation to the poetry, are by no means fully accounted for by his successful poetic practice.) In the first period the influences he was chiefly aware of were those of Irving Babbitt and Ezra Pound, "with a later infusion of T. E. Hulme and of the more literary essays of Charles Maurras" — influences apparent in the recurrent theme of classicism versus Romanticism, an opposition he later abandoned when he realized that its literary implications were meager indeed, and that its origins lay mainly in political conservatism. As for the emphasis on "tradition" — transmogrified by the disciples, of whom there were far too many until very recently, into a reactionary status symbol — it came about, he states, as a result of his reaction against the poetry, in English, of the nineteenth and early twentieth centuries, and his "passion" for the poetry, both dramatic and lyric, of the late sixteenth and early seventeenth centuries. But this much we have known for a long time. He is "certain of one thing," however: that he wrote best about the poets who influenced his own poetry.

The essay "To Criticize the Critic" is full of very informative asides and excellent formulations. Thus he comments on his varying attitudes toward D. H. Lawrence through the years, confessing that, in spite of Mr. Leavis' repeated animadversions, his antipathy to Lawrence remains, "on the grounds of what seems to be egotism, a strain of cruelty, and a failing in common with that of Thomas Hardy — the lack of a sense of humor." This may not be the last word on Lawrence, but it surely adumbrates a more realistic approach, and a more sensible one, than can be inferred from the overwrought opinions of Dr. Leavis, whose addiction to a limited, social-moralistic, edifying interpretation of Lawrence has now for the most part prevailed in academic circles. Eliot persists in his view that it is impossible "to fence off literary criticism from criticism on other grounds," that standards other than those of "literary merit" cannot be excluded in the long run. I think that he made this point with greater precision in an earlier essay, "Religion and Literature": "The greatness of literature cannot be determined solely on literary grounds; though we must remember that whether it is literature or not can be determined only by literary standards." Certainly the practice of most literary critics, past and present, bears out this simple but very important truth.

It is disturbing to observe that this simple truth, substantiated by the whole history of literature, is hardly understood any longer by our younger, articulate critics of art and letters, whose twaddle about something they call "aesthetic bliss," setting immediate sensation above thought and feeling, has lately acquired a fashionable ring. What this represents, finally, is a falling back to *fin-de-siècle* aestheticism, only in a souped-up, modish version. Now in the van of fashion — and fashion invariably goes in for change for its own sake and novelty at all costs — these people are not critics at all but the tastemakers of the newly affluent whose vulgar yearning it is to consume culture, as it consumes any product that makes for "excitement." Since these tastemakers have learned that "culture" goes down all the more easily if diluted with *kitsch*, they exhibit no reluctance whatever to issuing certificates of aesthetic chastity to *kitsch* of all sorts. The true function of criticism, however, is more frequently to resist the *Zeitgeist* rather than acquiesce in its now rampant aberrations. As Eliot notes in his book, criticism at its best acts "as a kind of cog regulating the change of literary taste," since it is well aware of "the antiquarianism of the old and the eccentricity and even charlatanism of the new . . ."

It is necessary to add that the parts of this volume dealing with nonliterary subjects are not very impressive, reminding us, unhappily, of such laborious compositions as *Notes towards the Definition of Culture* and *The Idea of a Christian Society*. In such works the author's superior intelligence and ironic bent recede before his sense of duty as a responsible Anglican churchman. An example is the long piece, "The Aims of Education," which, though bristling with carefully staged definitions, does not really get us very far beyond Arnold's "the best that has been said and thought in the world." But the literary essays are as superb as ever. Even if more "detached and judicial" than Eliot's earlier work, certainly they display no falling off in the assured grasp of issues relevant to a literary discussion, no loss of vigor in the tactful but firm avoidance of concerns that are basically academic. For instance, in the short essay on "American Literature and Language," he dissects a number of questions which most of our critics are not properly equipped even to identify. Thus Eliot persuades us once again that he is the finest literary critic of this century in the English language. His only possible rival is Edmund Wilson. But the comparison is not quite to the point, because Wilson's merits and demerits are of a different order. In the future the comparison will no doubt be made often enough, but only after essential distinctions between *kinds* of criticism have been drawn.

To my mind the most admirable piece of criticism in the book is the essay "From Poe to Valéry" — a marvel of precision and insight. Eliot begins by giving us his impression of Poe's status among English and American readers and critics, an impression accurate enough, and then proceeds to develop his own estimate of him. I take it to be the definitive estimate; I certainly find it far more convincing than either the wholly negative, virtually demolishing, view that Yvor Winters adopted in *Maule's Curse,* or the somewhat implausibly positive opinion of Poe to which Wilson has committed himself. In some of Poe's poems Eliot detects "an irresponsibility towards the meaning of words," and he has no trouble refuting in detail the theory of the impossibility of writing a long poem. According to Eliot, that Poe had a powerful intellect is undeniable, but it was also a fatally immature intellect. Though the variety and ardor of his curiosity delight and dazzle, yet in the end the eccentricity and lack of coherence of his interests tire. There is just that lacking which gives dignity to the mature man: a consistent point of view. An attitude can be mature and consistent, and yet be highly skeptical: but Poe was no skeptic. He appears to yield himself to the idea of the moment: the effect is, that all his ideas seem to be *entertained* rather than believed.

But the heart of the essay is in Eliot's consideration of the manner in which three French poets, Baudelaire, Mallarmé, and Valéry, representing three different generations, responded in different ways to Poe. Their response is, of course, the truly significant factor in his reputation. As Eliot sees it, Baudelaire primarily appreciated Poe as a prototype of *le poète maudit,* and in this sense he was first of all interested in Poe the man. With Mallarmé the interest shifts to Poe the poetic technician, while with Valéry "it is neither the man nor the poetry but the theory which engages the attention." Thus Eliot arrives at the strategic point where he can undertake a thorough analysis of *la poésie pure* and all the possible relations between subject matter and poetic language grown increasingly self-conscious. Eliot does not come down on the side of purity. On the contrary, he thinks that "poetry is only poetry so long as it preserves some 'impurity' in this sense: that is to say, so long as the subject matter is valued for its own sake." Valéry represents above all a change of attitude toward the subject matter. It is not so much that it has become less important but rather that its importance is that of a means only — the end is the poem. Furthermore, in Valéry, the interest in the compositional process, and in observing himself in the act of composition, finally displaces even the belief in ends. This represents the culmination of ideas that can be traced back to Poe. And what about the future? Eliot holds it as "a tenable hypothesis that this advance of self-consciousness, the extreme awareness of and concern for language which we can find in Valéry, is something which must ultimately break down, owing to an increasing strain against which the human

mind and nerves will rebel . . ." That in this respect Eliot is essentially
right is shown by the work of the latest generation of poets, post-
Eliot and post-Auden, who are in full retreat from the more complicated verbal and structural modes of the recent past.

Eliot is dead, and we will not soon see his like again. He was one
of the principal educators of the imaginative life of his age, a uniquely
great shaping influence both as poet and critic. In the latter capacity
he was never deceived by the stratagems and artifices of "methodology," and taught us to understand that the only method is to be
very, very intelligent, that, in the words of Henry James, "the deepest
quality of a work of art will always be the quality of the mind of
the producer." His commitment to orthodox beliefs must have answered an irresistible inner demand of his nature for a discipline to
shore him up against chaos, against his fears of "shape without form,
shade without color/ Paralysed force, gesture without motion." In this
sense it was no more than an anodyne, yet we who have not suffered
his pains are seldom in a position to reproach him. No, it was not in the
titanic ambition to steal fire from heaven that he sought his inspiration
but rather in a kind of patience of suffering and wonderment of scruples
forbidding him ever to try purloining the things that rightly belong to
the gods.

New York Review of Books, 1966

Delmore Schwartz:

The Paradox of Precocity

THIS BOOK, a selection of the late Delmore Schwartz's essays and reviews, has been much too long in the making. Its author, who died of a heart attack in 1966 at the age of fifty-three, was an exceptionally able literary critic. Far too sophisticated intellectually and too much at home with conceptual matters to turn himself into an exponent of any given exclusive method, he also understood the pitfalls to which critical discourse is exposed when it oversteps its limits to indulge in philosophical or sociological divagations. Sound in his literary judgments, he wrote without pretension or solemnity and without ever divesting himself of his fine and highly original sense of humor.

But it is precisely as a critic that he was grievously underrated, and for reasons not too difficult to identify. In the first place, readers were mainly aware of him as a poet and short-story writer, and only marginally as a critic; and, secondly, he himself put no particular emphasis on his critical work, conceiving of himself as primarily a creative writer. Yet in no sense can he be considered an amateur in criticism; he wrote a great deal of it, quite as much as he wrote fiction. However, we now learn from the editors of this volume that in his later and terribly lonely years he was rather anxious to see his better essays reprinted, while at the same time he was continually inventing new grounds for delay, withholding himself from the task of selection and arrangement until "the plan for publication had regretfully to be suspended."

To some extent these circumstances (in which the pathogenic element is scarcely to be missed by anyone who knew him well) account for the fact that even his most noteworthy essays are hardly ever to be found in any of the all too numerous anthologies of criticism that have appeared in the past two decades. Hence it is only now that his critical aptitudes and inclinations can be properly appreciated.

I first met Schwartz in 1938, when he was only twenty-four years old, and I was at once struck by his extreme precocity. It was his most conspicuous trait. There can be no disagreement with the opinion of the editors of the *Selected Essays* that Schwartz had "an extraordinary intelligent and sensitive mind, nutured on Joyce, Yeats, Rilke, Eliot, the heroes of modernism, but alert to change in the tradition before and after World War II. . . ." They wholly miss, however, his precocity, which does not even enter their discussion. Yet it might be claimed that it is this very precocity which lifted him to such high ground when he was relatively very young and which began to fail him rather rapidly precisely when others reach their creative maturity.

It is not my intention here to generalize either about the causes or consequences of precocity: I am merely noting an outstandingly paradoxical case of it. Whether Schwartz's early literary triumph and later decline stand in any significant relation to his deepening neurosis and final collapse into paranoia I have no means of knowing. My concern is primarily with his career as a writer who made a brilliant debut in several literary genres and with the singular circumstances surrounding the debacle that ensued.

Let us take a closer look at that career. At the age of twenty-four he had already written some of his finest poems as well as "In Dreams Begin Responsibilities," the most captivating and, in the judgment of most people who know his work well, the best short story he was ever to compose. What is even more surprising is that in that very year he also published what, in my view, are three superb critical pieces: "The Critical Method of R. P. Blackmur" is a definitive essay; another is the long and thoroughly cogent analysis of Yvor Winters' *Primitivism and Decadence*; and still another, entitled "John Dos Passos and the Whole Truth," is as fair in its argument as it is perceptive of that novelist's strengths and weaknesses — perhaps the most plausible single evaluation of Dos Passos as yet available to us.

Now while it is well-known that many poets have produced their best work in their early twenties, it is only very rarely that a critic has contributed anything memorable at that age. Usually it is not until their early thirties that critics are able to write anything really substantial exhibiting a mature cast of mind. And this is exactly where the paradox of Schwartz's precocity calls attention to itself in a striking way. The criticism he wrote even as late as 1953 (such as "The Duchess' Red Shoes," for instance, an essay on Lionel Trilling as notable for its humor as for its insight into that critic's social bias) has enduring value, while the poetry he published in his thirties and forties is clearly inferior to his earlier work in that medium. Thus the thematic richness as well as the diction, versification, and rhythmic range of the verse contained in *Vaudeville for a Princess* (1950) is almost embarrassingly feeble in comparison with such earlier poems in his first collection as "The Heavy Bear That Goes with Me," "In the Naked Bed, in Plato's Cave," or "Tired and Unhappy, You Think of Houses."

The same goes for his later fiction. In my reading of it only four of his stories are truly superior: "In Dreams Begin Responsibilities," "America! America!," "The Statues," and "A Bitter Farce," all written, I believe, before the age of thirty. Moreover, in the later stories, such as "The Child Is the Meaning of This Life" and those collected in his last volume *Successful Love,* the prose becomes flatter and flatter, the narrative movement slows down, dramatic impact is lost in tiresome repetitiousness; and in the novella *The World Is a Wedding* some of the characters are barely distinguishable from one another as they carry on a prolonged dialogue that is excessively, even compulsively, "literary" in the pejorative sense of that term.

No, it cannot be said of Schwartz that he was a born writer of fiction. He was not endowed with the capacity to create a solid fictional world seemingly self-governing in structure and possessed of an energy supple enough to establish a necessary congruity between interior and external event and circumstance. In Schwartz's narratives the best writing (and effects) is mostly achieved in lyrical moments and in passages embodying the emotional and intellectual pathos of self-recognition or self-identification.

This is of particular pertinence to the volume under review, which opens with Dwight Macdonald's essay in appreciation, comprising a personal impression of its subject rather than a literary or critical portrait. Macdonald's appreciation is generous and just on the whole, but in some ways it strikes me as wide of the mark and deficient in the comprehension of his friend's difficult and extremely problematical character. Above all, Macdonald appears to be quite unaware of Schwartz's intricate inner life, which might be described as a kind of unremitting self-reflexive internal labor and to which, I believe, both the origin and the imaginative source of his most expressive stories can be traced.

Consider the climactic scene in "In Dreams Begin Responsibilities," where the protagonist, easily identifiable with the author himself, watching on the movie screen a series of incidents in the courtship of his future parents, stands up in the theater, much to the discomfiture of his neighbors in the audience, and loudly cries: "Don't do it. It's not too late to change your minds, both of you. Nothing will come of it, only remorse, hatred, scandal and two children whose characters are monstrous." This startling intervention by the dreaming protagonist is by no means to be taken as a literary flourish, a finely devised ending, or some kind of symbolic statement concerning the human condition. It is the writer's adverse yet most intimate confession, the one psychodynamic form open to him for attaining transcendence.

Schwartz, with whom I was associated for more than ten years in the editorial enterprise of *Partisan Review,* was an off-and-on friend of mine. His rambling talk during the long walks we took from the office of the magazine on West 47th Street to the Village, where we both lived, is still vivid in my mind, and everything he told me about his parents, his brother, and his early experiences tended to reinforce the impression of him I had on first reading his story. Saturnine by temperament, he took an exceedingly comfortless view of the conduct of human beings, of whose motives he was chronically distrustful; and his habit was to denounce endlessly what he saw as their moral lapses even while taking care to exculpate himself.

It is only within his creative work that the vein of self-accusation is to be discovered. At times it comes through even in his poetry, as the following lines, for example, that appear in *Genesis*:

> ... I could endure
> My dark body's awkward brutality,
> I could endure my soul's black
>   guilt which hoped
> The world would end, and all things,
>   screaming, die
> Because I was in my ambition stopped
> The while my brother, friend, and
>   enemy
> Succeeds with seeming spontaneity,
> And wins the girl, acclaim, the
>   world's applause!

Oddly enough these deep suspicions of himself never entered his conversation, in which he invariably presented himself as a person perpetually harassed but exempt of all blame.*

* If Macdonald's impression of him differs so drastically from mine, it may well be because Schwartz cultivated two quite distinct modes of behavior in his relationship with people. When the relationship was in the main social, as I think it was with Macdonald, his manner was chiefly adapted to attract and entertain, as by piling one funny story upon another in a deadpan fashion, with his talk im-

Schwartz, in his more abstract musings, dreamed of a different kind of life, a life in which "the idea of love" held sway, but at the same time he was persuaded that "the ideas of success and failure are the two most important things in America." This distressing state of affairs, in which the real so crudely mocks the ideal, is among the more haunting themes of his creative work. In his stories it is often wistfully alluded to and is directly, though briefly, spoken of in *The World Is a Wedding*. Two characters, Jacob and Edmund, participate in the following dialogue:

> "Nevertheless the fact remains that practically everyone is unhappy. Now if the idea of love supplanted the ideas of success and failure, how joyous everyone might be! and how different the quality of life!"
>
> "You're just dreaming out loud," said Edmund to Jacob, thinking again how he had failed once more to be appointed a teacher.

Thus ideal hopes are sardonically dismissed by the real, which the author resists so little as to implicate even small children in his disconsolate submission to the pessimism it evokes in him. For instance, in "The Statues" the protagonist Faber Gottschalk, an unsuccessful dentist of thirty who is clearly another persona of the writer, speaks to a crowd assembled on a street corner:

> So I say to you . . . those who have been in favor of getting rid of this statue, which they avow to be obscene, tell us that the children will be corrupted by it. I will not say in reply that we cannot permit our lives to be determined by what the children will or will not see. Such an argument would be easy, although true enough. I will not advance the argument that those of us who really know children and have lived with them know very well that it is the children, not the adults, nor the statues, who are corrupt, whence it is that our adult lives are a long suffering and chiefly unsuccessful attempt to free ourselves from the utter corruption

---

parting a sense of rueful detachment. No wonder Macdonald can write: "There was a genial shimmer in Delmore's talk . . . generous, easy and, no matter how outrageously exaggerated, never envious or malicious; like Jove's laughter. He was egotistic without vanity. . . ." This benign impression is not at all artificial, but in being entirely synthetic it excludes any attempt at analysis.

Schwartz's bearing was quite different in truly intimate relations, as for example with the women he lived with and the male friends he knew since boyhood, or with someone like myself, with whom he was involved in a practical enterprise in which role playing could scarcely be maintained for very long. I am inclined to believe that this second Delmore was the more genuine one, for in these more familiar circumstances his genial tone and effort to amuse receded as his dark and somber moods and entanglement in various and sometimes fantastic intrigues connected with both his literary and academic life came frequently to the fore. The editors of the *Selected Essays* come close to the truth in stating that though "a passionate believer in the supreme importance . . . of love, Delmore proved himself incapable of permanent relationships."

of childhood, infancy, and the egotism contracted in the womb. I myself remember very well, how at the age of eight, on a visit at my aunt's, my two female cousins, twins, took me into the closet and taught me certain things of which I must already have been somewhat aware, because I was scarcely surprised by what they did to me.

In writing this speech Schwartz, an assiduous reader of Freud, was probably inspired by his theory of "infantile sexuality," but if so he had gone considerably beyond it, showing that he had got more out of that theory than Freud had put into it. Actually, there is nothing in Freud's theory that allows one to draw a moral condemnation of childhood as utterly corrupt, for in Freud's view "infantile sexuality" belongs to the natural order of things. I think that it was really not sexuality that Schwartz had in mind in the above passage. It seems to me that here he was indirectly affirming his conviction that the delinquency, as he saw it, of his character — the egotism and bound-less ambition as well as the guilt — had been entirely determined by his earliest experience. The "family romance," which he never ceased lamenting, extended beyond the limited Freudian conception of it.

Manifestly, in his mind's long reflection on itself, a true *inspectio mentis,* he could conceive of the idea of freedom, especially liberation from an apparently coercive past, the fatality of his childhood, only as a nebulous hope, the inconceivable dream of redemption of a fore-doomed life. Yet at the same time he was disposed to consider his precocity as an endowment conferred upon him once and for all, in compensation perhaps for the delinquencies he detected in himself. Even in this regard he was fated to be disappointed, for he never anticipated the decline of that precocity and to acknowledge it was beyond his powers.

But the boundless ambition that was part of the precocity never left him. He wanted to be a great poet and because of this aspiration he was fascinated above all by T. S. Eliot's career — the paradigmatic instance of the success he craved. That he greatly admired Eliot's poetry goes without saying, but what struck me in his truly obsessive talk about Eliot was the note of suspicion it sounded, the elusive hints of literary politics and the gossipy stories that plainly had no founda-tion in fact about the man behind the career, a man, by the way, he had never known. There was something in these palpably absurd stories, abounding with "delusions of reference," to use a Freudian phrase, that contained in embryo the paranoia that later overwhelmed him.

Even his singular personal charm, and the slight stutter that served only to draw attention to his frequently extravagant speech, whose undercurrent of humor accentuated all the more his exigent sense of being-in-the-world, could seldom obliterate the worried self-concern that possessed him. And as he grew older his self-concern mounted, so much so that the tendency to ritualize, if I may put it that way, his own unhappiness became more and more marked in the later poetry and fiction. This may help to explain the evident flatness of style and debility of emotional force.

However, he did not falter to the same degree in his criticism. After all, the critical medium permits only a minimum of subjectivity. Moreover, in any case, regarding himself as a creative writer above all and therefore attaching no ultimate importance to articles and reviews, he was able to approach the writing of them with greater relaxation and, curiously enough, in a more disciplined spirit. On the surface his essays are marked by a kind of deceptive simplicity, yet an attentive reading cannot but verify their rare precision of statement and shrewdness of insight.

I have already noted the excellence of his earliest essays, those dealing with Blackmur, Winters, and Dos Passos, and it is necessary to add that later on he wrote extremely well on Eliot's poetry and literary ideas, on Yeats, and on prose writers like Faulkner and Ring Lardner; and he was among the first to lay bare the class bias or impulse informing Trilling's account of the novel, that is, of the social ethos implicit in the genre.

Notable also is his essay on Edmund Wilson, which to my mind is the one truly exhaustive and percipient appraisal of that author's work in its totality that we have. Toward the end of the piece, after distinguishing clearly between different types of literary criticism and disclosing occasional failures of taste and sensibility in Wilson, Schwartz finally sees him as being something more and something less than a literary critic in the accepted sense of the term. His conclusion is worth quoting, at least in part:

> But it does not matter, because the whole of Wilson's work actually represents something else and just as important as literary history and literary criticism. Once we have seen both history and criticism as a device or pretext or convenient form, we can see how Wilson has provided a history of the American of "fundamental decency," who has come from "the old American life" and has borne this feeling about Life throughout the America of his time, Princeton, the first World War, the Greenwich Village and the New York of the Twenties, the social ferment and the moral disillusion of the Thirties. The actuality of this experience is to be found nowhere else in the writing of our time.
>
> It is as if we were provided . . . with the history of one of the sons of

a hero of Henry James; but this character has not only gone to Europe to bring back the art treasures of the Old World in *Axel's Castle* — he has had his moral experience in the Soviet Union, rather than in the Italy of Milly Theale, or the France of Lambert Strether. . . . Another comparison worth taking with the utmost literalness is to *The Education of Henry Adams,* for in Wilson we have another and later and more difficult education under circumstances which Adams foresaw but did not live to experience. It is an education without conclusion, but fruitful and illuminating in the concreteness of its experience: the Soviet Union, for example, as something lived through by one kind of American.

In his function as a critic Schwartz was far more disinterested than most of his contemporaries. Indifferent to "grand theory" and fashions in "methodology," he was singularly free of ideological prejudice. Also, he was sufficiently well-educated in philosophy to spot with ease the metaphysical presuppositions that some critics unknowingly let slip into their work, perhaps because of a simple misunderstanding of philosophical terms or sheer ignorance of the rules of the game. Thus he was able to reproach both Blackmur and Winters for indulging in "philosophy-mongering," that is for habitually referring to philosophical ideas and definitions in a manner "unfailingly inexact." Though highly sensitive to fallacies of discourse, he was never an unkind critic of the sort who is ever on the lookout for faults by way of displaying his superiority. Despite a certain moral insecurity that sometimes retarded his creative efforts, he not only understood literature thoroughly but also loved it passionately.

So Delmore, whom I remember as being more depressed by life than fearful of death, is no longer with us. His fate calls to mind certain lines of a sixteenth-century French poet, author of *Les Tragiques*:

> Avorté avant les jours,
> D'une âme pleine d'angoisse.

New York Review of Books, 1971

Henry James and His Cult

With this fifth volume, perhaps somewhat too brashly and summarily entitled *The Master,* Leon Edel at long last brings to a close his biography of James which has been appearing serially since 1953. In its way it is a phenomenal production, if only because of the truly exhaustive research that has gone into it and because it is probably the longest biography in English, and for all I know in any other language, of any single writer — of a writer, moreover, of whom it cannot be said that he really "lived," as even Edel himself admits albeit reluctantly and apologetically.

With so exiguous a life, what James mostly did was to spend his time alone in a room writing, subsisting on impressions and perceptions, which he insisted, with a fervor all too plainly defensive, on equating with what most of us mean by "experience." That Edel makes too much of James, that he overestimates his importance in the most extravagant manner possible, that he is much too expansive, even rapturous, about him, has been evident all along.

The excessive length of this biography is explained by its ·glut of detail, of which much is only of minor interest. No wonder that the effect of far too many of its pages is that of supersaturation. James was a prolific correspondent, and was it really necessary for Edel to present us with a surfeit of information about every one of his correspondents, friends, and acquaintances? After all, we are interested not in every casual person who came his way, but only in his principal literary and social relationships. Moreover, the few happenings that might be regarded as "events" in James's life are treated at inordinate length. Thus in his penultimate volume, *The Treacherous Years,* Edel describes the failure of the play *Guy Domville,* James's only strenuous theatrical venture, at such length and in such detail as to make one think that he is recounting an event comparable, say, to Napoleon's retreat from Moscow.

The same can be said of his voluminous account of James's move from his London flat to Lamb House at Rye. Why treat this as if it had world-shaking implications? Nor does Edel persuade me when he goes so far as to read into the anxieties occasioned by this move the psychic motivation that impelled James to write *The Turn of the Screw*.

In general Edel's numerous excursions into the psychoanalytic investigation of James both as author and as personality strike me as neither very apt nor convincing. The metaphorical couch on which he all too readily lays James out yields surprisingly meager results. In James's case there is simply too little attestable clinical material (on this score he was remarkably reticent in his autobiographical writings) to permit us to arrive at conclusions that are not vague or amateurish.

The biography also contains its full quota of literary criticism of James's work — and here too Edel cannot rest 'without bringing in every item of his writings, even the most obviously contrived and lacking in perceptible value. Moreover, the critical effort is all too often directed to tracing or detecting the personal sources of James's works rather than to the precise evaluation of their merits and demerits. It goes without saying that when the demerits do come up for discussion they are for the most part given short shrift.

For instance, William James showed no small measure of critical acumen in his negative reaction to his brother's later manner, as did a good many other resistive respondents, including Edith Wharton who, for all her admiration of James, did confront him with a leading question concerning *The Golden Bowl*: "What was your idea in suspending the four principal characters in a void? What sort of life did they lead when they were not watching each other and fencing with each other? Why have you stripped them of all the human fringes we necessarily trail after us through life?" James answered in a disturbed voice: "My dear — I didn't know I had. . . ."

Surely this lame reply tells us much about the peculiar assumptions underlying James's creative consciousness. It may well be that he had so stringently refined his singularities as to cease understanding susceptibilities of a more normal order. Yet Edel treats virtually all such remonstrances in cavalier fashion, as if they were irrelevant or else actuated by motives unduly personal. He does not even extend them the courtesy of a closely reasoned rejoinder — a rejoinder which, in my view, is not even very difficult to draw up. Disregarding Edith

Wharton's pointed query, he persists in characterizing *The Golden Bowl* as "the richest" of all of James's novels. But, after all, Edith Wharton was not alone in questioning the art of that novel. More than a few critics of stature have been taken aback by it. Still, Edel ignores them all.

However, there are certain revelations in the last volumes of this biography that are of immense biographical importance. I am referring, especially, to the story of Miss Constance Fenimore Woolson, who was in love with James and committed suicide in Venice because of his failure to respond to her. (The reverberations of this event in the story "The Beast in the Jungle" are apparent though the roles of male and female are changed.)

Then there is the tantalizing question of James's homo-erotic tendencies that surfaced only very late in his life. It is to Edel's credit that he treats these belated "romances" with candor, uncommon tact, and good judgment. There can be no doubt any longer that James was in love (or thought he was) with two exceedingly handsome young men: the sculptor Hendrik Andersen and the socialite Jocelyn Persse. Account must also be taken of his very ambiguous relationship with the young writer Hugh Walpole. Edel quotes extensively from the passionate letters James wrote to all three, but unfortunately their replies are mostly lost. Thus to the question of what was the exact nature of these "affairs" — "just romantic or also physical?" — Edel can only answer that at this late date it is impossible to establish the facts on any kind of firm basis.

On his part he is inclined to see in these attachments "the love of an aging man for his lost youth and evocation of it in figures of masculine beauty" that were, however, lacking in intellectual endowments. (At least two of them were.) Perhaps this very lack might serve as a key to the real nature of these attachments, but this is no more than nebulous speculation. On the whole Edel seems to have given us a fairly plausible account of these episodes, to which very little can be added unless further documentation becomes available.

Hugh Walpole, who certainly knew James as well as anyone else did, said more than once that his life was chiefly dominated by his "inevitable loneliness" and the persistent conflict in him between his "intellectual curiosity" and his inbred "reticent puritanism." And in my reading of his life and career it is his loneliness that comes through as the most ascertainable reality, even though Edel tries very hard to mitigate this impression. Still, I don't see how one can fail to recognize the psychogenic significance and therefore give due emphasis to the following remarks in James's letter to his Parisian friend Morton Fullerton, who asked him point blank to tell him his idea of the actual *point de départ* of his life. James felt that he could only "in a manner" reply to that:

> The port from which I set out was, I think, that of the *essential loneliness of my life* — and it seems to me the port also, in sooth, to which my course again finally directs itself! This loneliness was — what is it still but the deepest thing about one? Deeper, about me, at any rate, than anything else; deeper than my "genius," deeper than my "discipline," deeper than my pride, deeper, above all, than the deep counterminings of art. *

One can only regard this singular avowal — perhaps confession is the more proper term — as decisive for our understanding of James, certainly far more so than his belated "romances," conducted mostly in epistolatory form, which, in my effort at comprehension, appear to be no more than rather pathetic symptoms of senile sexuality, that is to say, of a sexuality so long and tenaciously suppressed that it could find an outlet only in the blessed safety of old age, when James could assure himself in good conscience that implementation was no longer a practical possibility.

Edel ends his biography with such an excessive tribute to the Jamesian *oeuvre* as to disclose, to me at least, his grave disabilities as a critic of the very subject to which he has devoted so many long years. For one thing, he is far too staunch an adherent of the James cult, which he assumes is destined to last forever. Thus he expresses no doubt whatever of James's "enduring fame." It seems to me, however, that the history of James's reputation fails to bear Edel out. It is a reputation that has waxed and waned, and precisely now it has already begun to wane. Though the taste of the young scarcely serves as a touchstone for me, I think it is none the less worth considering their taste in this period. It is clear to anyone in contact with young people that what they want from literature is mainly immediacy, spontaneity, and sensuality — the very qualities in which James is patently deficient. Hence the cult, which attained its peak in the forties and fifties, is already losing force and is rapidly drawing to a close. But of course Edel's involvement with James has been so close and prolonged that one cannot really expect him to perceive the strained nature of the cult of which he is now the leading hierophant.

---

* Italics in the original. The letter is quoted in part on page 350 of *The Treacherous Years.*

I myself was at one time engaged to some extent in helping to restore James's reputation after its long decline. But then the academy, with its characteristic lack of discrimination, took him over, displacing certain critics who entirely on their own, in the twenties and thirties, continued to insist on his importance. When it became apparent that the James boom was in full swing, I wrote in the foreword to my book *Image and Idea* (1948) that "the apotheosis of James is not quite what is wanted. For it appears that the long-standing prejudice against him is by now giving way to an uncritical adulation equally retarding to a sound appraisal of his achievement." Edmund Wilson, too, in the same year, spoke up quite sardonically about the cult in his appendix to his famous essay "The Ambiguity of Henry James," even while reaffirming his belief that we do well to be proud of him.

If I now enter a demurrer to Edel's approach it is because that approach consists almost wholly of uncritical adulation, approximately of the sort at present prevailing among the professors, who, let it be recalled, were strikingly inattentive to James when *The Little Review* devoted an issue to him in 1918 (with Eliot and Pound among the contributors) and, later, when in 1934 *The Hound and Horn* made a brave effort to revive the interest in James by presenting a collection of brilliant critical articles in an issue entirely given over to him. As usual the critics won out in the long run, but it was not until the early forties that the academics began suspecting that James was definitely "in." Since then they have been producing endless dissertations about him that are mostly wearisomely pedantic and that tend to take for granted exactly what requires the most rigorous proof.

If James is a great writer — and I believe he is one — it is strictly on a national scale that he can be most highly appreciated. In the literature of the world he is not a figure of the first order. European readers, lacking a deep background in American or at least Anglo-Saxon culture of the Victorian age, make very little of him. He is one of those writers, like the Russian novelist and storyteller Nikolai Leskov, the Austrian novelist Adalbert Stifter, and the Swiss Gottfried Keller, who have proven themselves incapable of readily crossing their own language frontiers. Indeed, nearly every literature counts among its luminaries writers of this special type. Though some of the works of Leskov, Keller, and Stifter are available in English, the response has been inconsiderable. The same can be said of the attempted translations of James, who is indissolubly at one not only with his language but with the determinate circumstances of his culture and background.

In German, for example, you find any number of elaborate scholarly and critical studies of Keller and Stifter (the latter was a favorite of Nietzsche). Yet without a broad knowledge of the cultural, social, and historical assumptions governing their mode of expression there is no way of comprehending their significance to German readers. Like James, and unlike such writers of fiction as Balzac, Stendhal, Flaubert, Proust, Mann, Joyce, Dostoevsky, Tolstoy, and Chekhov, Keller and Stifter have not become an intimate possession of the West.

Whereas American writers like Melville, Whitman, Poe, Faulkner, and Hemingway have attained international renown, James remains only a "name" even to the more cultivated Europeans, in spite of the best efforts of many foreign specialists in American letters. One can hardly conceive of Albert Camus, for instance, writing a highly laudatory essay about him, as he did about Melville in 1952, after reading him in a French translation. Camus put great stress on the following sentence in Melville: "To perpetuate one's name, one must carve it on a heavy stone and sink it to the bottom of the sea; depths last longer than heights."

Now though James sometimes liked to refer to the "abysses" of the artist's mind, it was mostly the heights, and those of a very selected kind, that struck him with wonder and excited his admiration. The depths only benumbed him. His work, for all its high refinement and felicity of style, is far too idiosyncratic to elicit universal assent; and the very special temperamental quirks and oddities of James the man sometimes spilled over into the products of his imagination, depriving them of the necessary "aesthetic distance" and the crowning effect of "objective" inevitability.

Moreover, for all his fond talk of "exquisite economy" in composition, in his later phase particularly his prose is frequently wrenched out of focus by undue loquacity in some places and undue reserve and restraint in others. As Yvor Winters once observed, at times James attempts to make "the sheer *tone* of speech and behavior carry vastly more significance than is proper to it," with the result that in novels like *The Awkward Age, The Sacred Fount,* and *The Sense of the Past* he pushes his feeling for nuances and discriminations to an unworkable extreme. James cannot be considered to have created a *novum organum* for encountering the richness, the depth, and the ultimately terrifying gratuity of man's being-in-the-world.

What is at times disturbing about him is his disposition to equate sheer naiveté or crudity of manners with innocence, which is a quality of a different sort altogether. We believe in Prince Myshkin's innocence, but can we really say without serious reservations that the

Ververs, with their bought-and-paid-for prince, a costly *morceau du musée,* are truly innocent? Their wealth, so concretely and almost piously dwelt upon, cannot as easily be conjoined with innocence as James assumes.

James took the social order of his time too much for granted, a position that is wholly contrary to the spirit of modern literature. This literature is inherently so radically suspicious of man as to make little of innocence, least of all the innocence of the rich and proud, American or not. Moreover, this literature is mainly concerned with ideas relating to the crisis of values by which the modern world is afflicted, while in James you find almost no awareness of this theme. His sense of history is static. One might sum up the peculiarities of his consciousness by saying that it is both intellectual and simultaneously indifferent to general ideas, and systematically unattached to any open philosophical theme. James made a metaphysic of private relations, giving the impression that they are immune to the pressures of the public and historical world.

The Americanness of his rich innocents and "passionate pilgrims" is by no means so decisive a factor in their characters as he is inclined to believe. Europe is to him romance, reality, and civilization, yet he cannot finally abandon his conviction that the spirit resides in America. Hence his notion of Old World corruption, which, as he sees it, can only be cured of its "taint of evil" if penetrated and cleansed by the New World conscience, inwardness, and, yes, innocence. This idea strikes us today as preposterous — a transient historical fantasy generated by an exaggerated sense of national security and a buoyant self-interpretative grandiosity from which at this late date one recoils with bewilderment.

In my view, James tended to confuse the genuine inwardness and good faith of his immediate family with the American character in general. As he himself pointed out, "downtown" was always strange territory to him; he only felt at home "uptown," where ladies of leisure sometimes read what he wrote. The consequence is a certain fond abstraction in his conception of the national character; and this unrealistic postulation led him to read too much meaning into his theme of "transatlantic relations" and to a variety of artificial complications in the plotting of his novels and stories.

The truth is that James differs so drastically in his creative contradictions from other great writers that numerous readers, not merely Europeans, are baffled by him. His attitude to experience especially mystifies them. They are put off by the tension in him between the impulse to consent to experience and the impulse to withdraw from it, by his dread of approaching it in its natural state, particularly love and marriage, where his "confounded renunciations" seem to them cerebrally calculated and too contrived to carry conviction. It is a sphere in which his scrupulosities, whatever their cultural, social, or psychic origin, are far too readily pressed into service.*

It might be said of James that though he protested more than once against the Genteel Tradition of the age he lived in, in the matter of sexual relations he coped with it all too successfully. My feeling is that he was deeply and irretrievably offended by the grossness of the flesh, and that in his novels he resorted to exploiting this very limitation, thus submitting himself to egregious self-exaggeration, the principal manifestation of which is his obsessive refinement, a veritable delirium of refinement. This may well be among the considerations that prompted his brother William to write about him to his wife Alice:

> Harry is a queer boy, so good and so limited, as if he had taken an oath not to let himself out to more than half his humanhood in order to keep the other half from suffering, and has capped it with a determination not to give anyone else credit for the half he had resolved not to use himself. Really it is not an oath or a resolve but helplessness.

Admittedly Henry always remained "powerless Harry" to William, who had no eye for his brother's masterful side, which was noted by many of his friends. Still, his observation is too perspicacious to be dismissed. The "poor sensitive gentleman" who appears again and again in Henry's fiction is not a mere narrative device. He is that too, but he is also a projection of his author's innermost sense of helplessness which he tried to conceal from himself.

Among the bad habits contracted by the James cultists is that of reading the famous prefaces he wrote for the New York edition entirely too literally, that is, without a trace of skepticism, as if their highly suggestive and illuminating ideas of dramatic method, structure, design, point of view, scene, and picture were in actual practice fully substantiated in his fictional texts. But that is by no means the case. While dismissing the work of the great Russians as "large, loose baggy monsters" (which they certainly are not), he fails to notice that at least some of his high-falutin' talk about the art of the novel is little more

---

* According to Edel, in his last years Henry started to refer to carnal love as "the great relation" — a euphemism typically Jamesian. Is the adjective "great" really appropriate? It is a fundamental relation, inescapable for most people, as tender and demonstrative as it is torturous and recurrently brutal.

than a defensive maneuver on his part — largely unconscious no doubt — a maneuver designed so firmly to fix our attention on the architectonics of the novel that we are apt to lose sight of the requirements of the hard stuff of experience it contains. How does he manage to accomplish that feat? By submitting his favorite theme, "the sacred mystery of structure," to an intensive process of idealization and sublimation. Yet we, as critical readers, are under no compulsion to play his game.

One question we ask, which James seldom pauses to ask himself, is whether the plotting of his last three "great" novels does actually come off so far as his choice of character, scene, and action is concerned. In my view each of his novels has its fascination, but that does not mean that they are without grave faults. In fact, in all three novels the author asks of us a "suspension of disbelief" that is so broad and inclusive, and so violates our sense of reality, that in the end we are forced to accept their basic situations as mere *données* — and that procedure, in view of the claims made for these works, is simply not good enough. After all, these works were written in the realistic convention, not as romances or fantasies.

The objections I have in mind are fairly specific. For instance, is it really likely that a woman as delightfully attractive, sophisticated, and aristocratic as Mme. de Vionnet of *The Ambassadors* would fall seriously in love with a young man as callow as Chad Newsome from Woollett, Massachusetts? In a perfunctory way James does try to persuade us, to be sure, that Chad has changed, that he is no longer the boy the "ambassador" Lambert Strether knew back home. The change, however, lacks the specifications that would be really convincing, and the effort on the author's part soon turns into sheer legerdemain when Chad, opting for the advertising "game" in America, prepares to desert his love while she puts a good face on it in her last interviews with Strether. Clearly, James has lost his touch here, proceeding in an arbitrary and manipulative fashion.

The same arbitrary manipulation is to be found in *The Wings of the Dove*. It is improbable that the handsome, hard, worldly, and ambitious Kate Croy — one of the very few women in James who strikes us as a truly sexual being — would love the "longish, fairish, leanish" journalist Merton Densher, of whom even Edel says, "For all his disguises as an active and even coercive lover, Merton Densher is in reality the classically passive, renunciatory Jamesian hero." One might accept Milly Theale's love of Densher, because her wealth gives her the inner security to permit any choice in love. But why should Kate

Croy, lacking that security and intent on making her way in the world, accept the vague and passive Densher? And when Ford Madox Hueffer asked James why he left out the last scene of Milly's confrontation with Densher, his reply was that he was afraid the novel might turn into a sentimental romance — surely an evasive reply in which there is more sophistry than truth.

The case seems to be, rather, that as James grew older his approach to the making of novels grew more and more artificial and self-willed, for he had lost his earlier intuitive feelings for the human combinations possible in fiction. As T. S. Eliot once put it: novelists need not necessarily understand people better than most of us, but what they must be is exceptionally aware of them. It is precisely this exceptional awareness that is missing in *The Golden Bowl*, especially in its last "Book" where rich little Maggie Verver gets the upper hand, emerging as the real master of Prince Amerigo, her husband. Here James appears to be unaware that the prince, an idle aristocrat (all ornamental being with no chance of becoming, that is, of growth and transformation) who married Maggie for her money and has little to do except play billiards at his club, is highly unlikely to remain faithful to his American wife, who in any case conveys the unmistakable impression of inveterate frigidity.

Even if we grant that Maggie has succeeded in shipping off Charlotte, her stepmother and her husband's mistress, to the Siberia which the latter takes America to be, James fails to consider that there are other Charlottes, any number of them, awaiting the prince's pleasure, and that therefore Maggie's triumph, so gloatingly rendered, is only temporary. For, lacking anything else to engage his full attention, adultery is the prince's real métier. After all, it is an occupation of sorts. That James fails to take this glaring fact into account is a consequence of his illusion of "the world, the beautiful world!"

Another bad habit of the James cultists is to overlook his snobbery; perhaps some of them have been so affected by it as to have wholly absorbed it. But of course snobbery, if accompanied by superior imaginative powers, is not necessarily as odious a trait as it is usually made out to be. It is a kind of idealism *manqué*. To use a Jamesian analogy, it might be likened to zero in a number: its significance depends on the figure preceding it. If we compare James's snobbery to Proust's, we can see how little it helps him. Proust started with the ambition to penetrate the highest social circles; aristocratic names enchanted him; yet he ended by turning his fiction into an exposure of the "worldly world" and the renunciation of it in favor of the artistic vocation.

What is really at stake here is the question of innocence. Proust was *never* innocent, while in some important ways James remained innocent to the very end. He was inclined to equate the sensibility of culture with aristocracy, yet unlike Proust he could never make himself understand that the aristocrat is a type in whom subtle manners and beautiful displays of consideration can easily go hand in hand with the crudest moral practices and presumptions. Hence we cannot imagine James writing the episode of "the red slippers" in which the Duc and Duchesse de Guermantes are shown up by Proust for what they really are. Like his heroine Bessie Alden in his early *nouvelle, An International Episode,* James himself was oversensitive to "the mementoes and reverberations of greatness in the life of noble families of ancient lineage."

The values of aristocracy bulked so large in his mind that he hated to be told that he belonged to the middle class, being the grandson of an impoverished Irish immigrant who succeeded in making a small fortune in Albany, New York. E. S. Nadal, a secretary at the American Embassy in London in the 1870s, relates in his memoirs that James often spoke to him "of the rudeness encountered from the London social leaders," and one time he told him that some lady of the English middle class had said to him: "That is true of the aristocracy, but in one's own class it is different," meaning, said James, "her class and mine." Rather than endure such insults, James declared, he preferred to be regarded as a foreigner. This incident is very expressive of James's social insecurity and snobbish preoccupations. He did, after all, belong to the middle class and his indignant reaction to the English lady is fully indicative of his staggering pretensions.

In spite of the innovations in the art of the novel that James can undoubtedly be credited with and a certain kind of psychological lyricism of a very high order, it is still true that he cannot be regarded as a truly modern writer. The Victorian strain was too strong in him. Fundamentally he belongs to the American nineteenth century, and hence he, too, is a queer duck, essentially an outsider, like all the important American creative writers of that era. Aside from freewheeling quasi-philosophical preachers like Emerson, there are actually very few of them — Hawthorne, Melville, Whitman, Poe, and James (Mark Twain and Emily Dickinson are borderline cases). All five are outside the mainstream of the society of their time, which was so singlemindedly devoted to the practical tasks of completing the conquest of the continent and industrializing its economy that it left virtually no room for the disinterested pursuits of the imaginative faculty and its seemingly irrelevant, if not downright dangerous, exuberances and dejections.

America was as yet in no position to sustain their gifts, and in their isolation each one of them either tried to overreach or suppress himself, thus developing certain *outré* tendencies. Hawthorne was at one and the same time fearfully inhibited and ridden by sex fantasies; the latent homosexuality of Whitman and Melville was a constriction of a singularly insidious sort in their milieu; Poe was sexually impotent and a dipsomaniac; and James found a way out by expatriating himself. His genius could not have come to fruition in his native land. He did succeed in saving himself, but at no small price.

New York Review of Books, 1972

II
RUSSIAN
AND EUROPEAN
LITERATURE

Dostoevsky in *The Possessed*

THE TENDENCY of every age is to bury as many classics as it revives. If unable to discover our own urgent meanings in a creation of the past, we hope to find ample redress in its competitive neighbors. A masterpiece cannot be produced once and for all; it must be constantly reproduced. Its first author is a man. Its later ones — time, social time, history.

To be means to recur. In the struggle for survival among works of art those prove themselves the fittest that recur most often. In order to impress itself on our imagination, a work of art must be capable of bending its wondrous, its immortal head to the yoke of the mortal and finite — that is, the contemporary, which is never more than an emphasis, a one-sided projection of the real. The past retains its vitality in so far as it impersonates the present, either in its aversions or ideals; in the same way a classic work renews itself by impersonating a modern one.

If of all the novels of Dostoevsky it is *The Possessed* which now seems closest to us, arousing a curiosity and expectation that belong peculiarly to the age we live in, it is because it deals with problems of radical ideology and behavior that have become familiar to us through our own experience. It is a work at once unique and typically Dostoevskyean. Shaken by the Karamazov fury and full of Dostoevsky's moral and religious obsessions, it is at the same time the one novel in which he explicitly concerned himself with political ideas and with the revolutionary movement.

The fact is that it really contains two novels. It was begun as an openly "tendentious" study of the evolution of ideas from fathers to sons, of the development of the liberal idealism of the thirties and forties of the past century into the nihilism and socialism of the sixties and seventies; but Dostoevsky encountered such difficulties in its writing that he finally incorporated into it many conceptions from *The Life of a Great Sinner,* a projected novel in several volumes which was to be his major effort on the subject of atheism. For that reason *The Possessed* might be said to have two sets of characters, one sacred and one profane, one metaphysical and one empirical — the group around Stavrogin, the great sinner, and the group around the Verhovenskys, father and son, who are defined socially and politically. While one set commits sins, the other commits crimes. Externally, in his melodramatic, sinister attractiveness and in the Byronic stress given to his personal relations, Stavrogin derives from early European Romanticism, but in his moral sensuality, in his craving for remorse and martyrdom, he is an authentic member of the Karamazov family. He is doubled within himself as well as through Shatov and Kirillov, his satellites in the story. Shatov represents his Russian, national-messianic side, and Kirillov his "religious atheism" — his experiments with God and eventual destruction of Him to make room for the man-god who kills himself to assert his divinity and prove it.

There can be no doubt that the introduction of Stavrogin into *The Possessed,* which in its first draft relied exclusively on the Verhovenskys for its interest, gives the novel a psychological depth and moral propulsion that brings it up to the level of Dostoevsky's best work in his later period, the period that opens with the appearance of *Notes from Underground* in 1864. For with the introduction of Stavrogin, Dostoevsky was able to double the theme of his novel, thus allowing sin and crime, religion and politics, to engage in a mutual criticism of each other. It should be added, however, that the two themes are not fused with entire success. Stavrogin is at times somewhat gratuitously implicated in the younger Verhovensky's political maneuvers; the link between them is often artificial, giving rise to superfluous intricacies of structure and episode. The plot, in part improvised, is insufficiently unified. But this defect is more than made up for — and precisely from the standpoint of plot, always so crucially important in Dostoevsky's creative scheme — by the opportunity provided in Stavrogin's accession to the role of principal hero for the employment of that technique of mystification and suspense, of narrative progression by means of a series of tumultuous scenes and revelations of an agonizing nature, on which the Dostoevskyean novel depends for its essential effects, its atmosphere of scandal and monstrous rumor, its tensions of thought no less than of act and circumstance resolved only when the ultimate catastrophe overwhelms the characters and rolls up the plot. Now Stavrogin, whose character is an enigma toward the solution of which everything in the novel converges, is the kind of central figure perfectly suited to this imaginative scheme.

If in the past social critics dismissed *The Possessed* as a vicious caricature of the socialist movement, today the emergence of Stalinism compels a revision of that judgment. Its peculiar "timeliness" flows from the fact that the motives, actions, and ideas of the revolutionaries in it are so ambiguous, so imbedded in equivocation, as to suggest those astonishing negations of the socialist ideal which have come into existence in Soviet Russia. Emptied of principle, the Communist movement of our time has converted politics into an art of illusion. Stalin's "socialism" is devoid of all norms; never acting in its own name, it can permit itself every crime and every duplicity. Its first rule is to deny its own identity and to keep itself solvent by drawing on the ideological credit of those revolutionary traditions and heroic struggles for freedom which its brutal totalitarianism repudiates in their very essence. In public the rapacious bureaucrat appears masked as the spokesman of the oppressed and exploited. Marxism, and not the savage doctrine of preserving and extending at all costs the power of the usurpers, is his official philosophy. It is a similar element of counterfeit, of a vertiginous interplay of reality and appearance, which makes Dostoevsky's story so prophetic in the light of what we know of the fate of the Russian Revolution.

Thus in its Verhovensky parts the novel reminds us of the most recent political phenomena; and it is not by chance that on the occasion of the Moscow trials the world press unanimously recalled to its readers the name of Dostoevsky, the great nay-sayer to the Revolution. This occurred twenty years after Dostoevsky's Russia — that realm of wood and dark furious souls — had been ostensibly demolished and a new harmonious society erected on its ruins. The principles of science and reason had triumphed, we were told. But now the creations of a novelist who considered these same principles to be the spawn of Satan were invoked to explain events which science and reason had apparently found inexplicable. It is not worthwhile, however, to examine *The Possessed* in order to appeal to the "Slav soul" for the divulgence of racial or national secrets. The "Slav soul" never explained anything. That swollen concept is the product of the historical romanticism of the Slavophil movement, which substituted brooding about history for making it. Dostoevsky, too, "brooded" in the Slavophil fashion, but that by no means exhausts his contribution to letters. As a suprahistorical essence the "Slav soul" is impartial in its testimony, drawing no distinctions between accusers and accused, or between oppressors and oppressed. If you make the unfathomable perversity of the Slav nature your premise, then logically your conclusion cannot exclude any explanation, no matter how wild and incredible. Hence it is futile to look to the author of *The Possessed* for revelations about specific historical events, such as the Moscow trials; but much can be learned from a study of the interrelationships between his work and the contending forces that he combined into such extraordinary patterns. Although this analyst of contradictions, who was ever vibrating between faith and heresy, made the revolutionary the object of his venom, there is a real affinity between them.

"In everything and everywhere," he wrote to his friend Maykov in 1867, "I go to the very last limit; all my life long I have gone beyond the limit." Whatever his conscious convictions about orthodoxy, monarchy, and the Russian folk, his temperament and the profoundly dissident if not daemonic force of his imaginative dialectic transformed him into a revolutionary influence in Russian life and culture. And it is precisely this "going beyond the limit" that explains why in spite of himself he became, in his very resistance to the Revolution, its herald and prophet. Into his Christianity, too, he injected, as Lunacharsky noted, "the maximum of his revolutionism." Thus Russian orthodoxy found in him a dangerous advocate and protector, for his championship of it took the form of ideas so apocalyptic as to disintegrate its traditional and institutional sanctions. There is no stasis in Dostoevsky's religiosity but rather a dynamism destructive of dogma and seeking fulfilment in the triumph of Christian love and truth in the human world. To be sure, this did not escape the notice of the more subtle partisans of orthodoxy, such as Konstantin Leontiev, an original thinker and religious philosopher who valued in religion its dogma more than its ethics. Leontiev accused Dostoevsky of deviating from Christianity in the spirit of Western humanism and of promoting an "earthly eudaemonism with Christian nuances." He wrote that "in the eyes of a Christian these hopes (of brotherhood and love) contradict the direct and very clear prophecy of the Gospels concerning the worsening of human relations right to the very end of the world. Brotherhood and humanitarianism are of course recommended by the New Testament for the saving of the individual soul; but in the New Testament it nowhere says that through these humanitarian efforts man will ultimately come to peace and love — *Christ did not promise us that ... that is not true! ...* Christ told or advised us to love our neighbor *in the name of God;* but on the other hand he prophesied that many will not obey Him. It is in this sense exactly that the new European humanism and the humanism of Christianity are clearly antithetical, and very difficult to reconcile." From the standpoint of orthodoxy Leontiev was doubtless right in his strictures. The truth is that Dostoevsky, despite the commitment of his will to reactionary principles, was at bottom so deeply involved in the spiritual and social radicalism of the Russian intelligentsia that he could not help attempting to break through the inner rigidity of the orthodox tradition toward a dynamic idea of salvation; and in a certain sense what this idea came to is little more than an anarcho-Christian version of that "religion of humanity" which continued to inspire the intelligentsia throughout the nineteenth century and by which Dostoevsky himself was inspired in his youth, when together with Belinsky, Petrashevsky, and other social enthusiasts of the 1840s, he took for his guides and mentors such heretical lovers of mankind as Rousseau, Fourier, Saint-Simon, and George Sand.

For if analysed in terms of his social milieu and affiliations, it becomes clear at once that Dostoevsky was the spokesman not of the *narod* — that is the mass of the Russian people, the peasantry — with which he fancied himself to stand in a relation of congenial intimacy, largely of his own imagining, but of the intelligentsia, a class so precariously situated in Russian society, so tightly squeezed between the feudal-aristocratic power above it and the elemental power of the peasant multitude below it, that it had virtually no social space in which to move and grow. It is this stiflingly narrow basis of the Russian intelligentsia which in some ways accounts for its extremes of thought and behavior — the deadly seriousness of its approach to theoretical and ideological issues, its moods of slackness, dreaminess, and passivity alternating with moods of political intransigence and boundless enthusiasm, its fanaticism and tendencies to schism and heresy-hunting combined with tendencies to self-depreciation and self-hatred. In Dostoevsky these characteristics of the Russian intellectuals are summed up to perfection, and that despite his continual quarrels with them, his nagging criticism of them for their alleged estrangement from the people. By his nagging criticism and contempt, which is really self-contempt, he is all the more identified as one of them. In common with many Russian intellectuals he regarded the mysterious power of the *narod* with a fascination that is precisely the negative of their self-contempt and awareness of their own helplessness. Dostoevsky, by idealizing submission, suffering, and the necessity of bowing down before the people, turned this very negativity inside out, endeavoring to convert it into a positive value. But his ambivalent nature did not permit his losing himself in the contemplation of this false though gratifying luster of the positive.

The fact is that it is not in the construction of harmonies but in the uncovering of antinomies that his genius found its deeper expression.

His children of light, like Sonia Marmeladov, Myshkin, Alyosha, and Zossima, are passionally and intellectually inferior to his children of darkness, such as Svidrigailov, Raskolnikov, Stavrogin, Kirillov, and Ivan Karamazov. (Myshkin, in whom his author aspired to create the image of a "positively good man," is no doubt the most alive of the children of light, though in saying this one must consider the telling fact that it is primarily from his malaise rather than from his goodness that he gains his vitality as a character.) Ivan Karamazov, transcending his novelistic framework, is a world-historical creation that overshadows all the saints and pseudo-saints in the Dostoevskyean canon; and one cannot but agree with D. Mirsky, who, in discriminating between the lesser and the greater Dostoevsky, notes that his tragedies are "irreducible tragedies that cannot be solved or pacified.... His harmonies and solutions are on a shallower level than his conflicts and tragedies.... His Christianity ... did not reach the ultimate depths of his soul." The distinction drawn by Mirsky, and indirectly supported from a theological standpoint by Leontiev, is essential to an accurate understanding of Dostoevsky's relationship to historical Christianity, though nowadays, of course, critics friendly to the new religiosity and aware of the uses to which the example of Dostoevsky may be put in the struggle against secular ideas, tend to ignore an insight so damaging to the cause of tradition and dogma.

Excluded from the sphere of practical life and confronted by the need of thinking their way out from the historical impasse into which backward and calamitous conditions had driven their nation, the Russian intellectuals lived in and through ideas. This almost predacious feeling for ideas and relatedness to them is actualized in Dostoevsky as in no other Russian novelist. To his characters ideas are a source of suffering. Such people are unknown in countries like America, where social tension is at a relatively low point and where, in consequence, the idea counts for very little and is usually dismissed as "theory." Only in a society whose contradictions are unbridled in temper do ideas become a matter of life and death. Such is the historical secret of that Russian intensity which Western critics find so admirable. Alyosha Karamazov, for example, was convinced "as soon as he reflected seriously, of the existence of God and immortality, and at once he said to himself: 'I want to exist for God, and I will accept no compromise.'" In the same way, adds Dostoevsky, "if he had decided that God and immortality did not exist he would at once have become an atheist and a socialist." As simply as that. And in *The Possessed*, Kirillov decides that God "is necessary and must exist," but at the same time he knows that "He doesn't and He can't." "Surely," he says, "you must understand that a man with two such ideas can't go on living." Kirillov shoots himself.

In *The Possessed* it is necessary above all to distinguish between its manifest and latent meaning. A counterrevolutionary novel in its manifest intention and content, what it actually depicts in terms of felt experience is the total disintegration of the traditional order and the inevitability of its downfall. The disintegration is of the soul no less than of the social order; and if Stavrogin, with his stupefaction of ennui and loss of the sense of good and evil, represents the decomposed soul, the decomposed society is represented mainly in Verhovensky together with his followers and easy victims. Disintegration is the real theme of the novel, as it is the real theme of *A Raw Youth, The Brothers Karamazov,* and other major works of Dostoevsky's later period. Thus in *The Possessed,* while setting out to report on the moral depravity of the Revolution, Dostoevsky was nevetherless objective enough to demonstrate that Russia could not escape it. The hidden ideologue of radicalism and social prophet in him would not be submerged. If it is true, as it has been repeatedly charged, that there was a good slice of the flunkey in his personal psychology, then he was the kind of flunkey, or rather superflunkey, who even while bowing and scraping says the most outrageous things to your face. This novel, which so delighted the autocratic regime, in reality generalized its breakdown in the political sphere as well as in the sphere of values and moral experience.

In reading this novel one is never quite certain that Pyotr Verhovensky, its chief revolutionary character, is not an agent of the Czar's secret police. Even as he is engaged in preparing an insurrection, this "authorized representative" of an invisible Central Committee, which is located somewhere abroad and turns out to be a myth, describes himself as "a scoundrel of course and not a socialist." He methodically uses blackmail, slander, drunkenness, and spying to achieve his ends. But what in reality are his ends? Give him state power and you get the kind of social type who makes his way to the top in the Soviet secret police. Verhovensky's plan is to organize a network of human knots whose task is to proselytize and ramify endlessly, and "by systematic denunciation to injure the prestige of local authority, to reduce villages to confusion, to spread cynicism and scandals, together with complete disbelief in everything and an eagerness for something better, and finally, by means of fire, a pre-eminently national method, to reduce the country at a given moment, if need be, to desperation." Verhovensky actually carries out this ingenious plan in the town where the scene of the novel is laid — an unnamed town which stands for the whole of Russia. His associate Shigalov — a character who fits Lenin's definition of the petty bourgeois "gone mad" but who at the same time, in view of the monstrous consistency of his revolutionary-utopian logic, reminds us if not of Lenin personally then surely of Leninism as an historical phenomenon — busies himself with constructing, on paper, a new form of social organization to guarantee complete equality. Starting with the idea of attaining "unlimited freedom" in his Utopia, he soon arrives at the conclusion that what it will actually produce is "unlimited despotism." This throws him into despair, yet he insists that there can be no other solution to the problems of society. Yulia Mihailovna, a well-born and well-to-do lady, wife of the governor of the province, dreams of reconciling the irreconcilable in her own person, of uniting in the adoration of herself "the correct tone of the aristocratic salons and the free-and-easy, almost pothouse manners" of the youthful nihilists, the system of big landed property with free-thinking socialist notions. (In the unsurpassable portrait of this vain woman Dostoevsky created the model of what has since evolved into a ubiquitous social type — the wealthy and thoroughly bourgeois "friend" or "sympathizer" of the Russian Revolution who in his befuddlement tries to reconcile his existing status in society with the self-conceit of playing a progressive role and being "in" on the secrets of history.) And what shall one say of Yulia Mihailovna's husband, the governor, who in his snobbish desire to associate himself with the cause of progress, can think of no other objection to the manifestoes urging the people to rebellion except that the ideas expressed in them are "premature." Verhovensky quickly and cruelly turns this objection aside by saying to him: "And how can you be an official of the government after that, when you agree to demolishing churches, and marching on Petersburg with staves, making it all simply a question of date?" Such people are the natural prey of a character like Liputin, an unwashed intriguer, at once a despot and a dreamer, who propounds the theory that there are people on whom clean linen is unseemly. Practicing petty usury, he at the same time holds forth in the language of "the universal republic and harmony of mankind." But the odd thing about him is that he is sincere.

It is exactly through such complex and conflicting motivation that the inevitability of the social breakdown is impressed on the reader's mind. Here the impulse to be rid of a rotting order and to break loose has reached such intensity that it has become objective; penetrating into the innermost, the most differentiated cells of human psychology, it has ceased to be incompatible with degenerate habits and desires. In one scene the writer Karmazinov, a figure through whom the author mercilessly derided Turgenev, describes Russia in terms that approximate the Marxist formula of a revolutionary situation. One must bear in mind that since the intent of the novel is counterrevolutionary, the perception that "Russia as she is has no future" and that "everything here is doomed and awaiting its end" is necessarily put into the mouth of a character, presented as a pompous and conceited coward, at whom we are supposed to laugh. Yet the author makes it plain, even if through indirect means, that Karmazinov is a man of acute intelligence. And Karmazinov so truly predicts what has since come to pass that he is well worth quoting at some length in order to demonstrate how powerfully his author's observation of Russian society was engaged with reality at the very time when he was ostensibly defending this society by writing a novel exposing and satirizing its liberal and socialist enemies. Karmazinov is addressing himself to Verhovensky:

"If the Babylon there (meaning Europe) really does fall, and great will be the fall thereof . . . there's nothing to fall here in Russia, comparatively speaking. There won't be stones to fall, everything will crumble into dirt. Holy Russia has less power of resistance than anything in the world. The Russian peasantry is still held together somehow by the Russian God; but according to the latest accounts the Russian God is not to be relied upon . . . And now, what with railways, what with you . . . I've no faith in the Russian God."

"And how about the European one?"

"I don't believe in any. . . . I was shown the manifestoes here. Every one looks at them with perplexity because they are frightened at the way things are put in them, but every one is convinced of their power even if they don't admit it to themselves. Everything has been rolling downhill, and every one has known for ages that they have nothing to clutch at. I am persuaded of the success of this mysterious propaganda, if only because Russia is now pre-eminently the place in the world where anything you like may happen without any opposition. . . . Holy Russia is a country of wood, of poverty . . . and of danger, the country of ambitious beggars in the upper classes, while the immense majority live in poky little huts. She will be glad of any way to escape; you have only to present it to her. It's only the government that still means to resist, but it brandishes its cudgel in the dark and hits its own men. Everything here is doomed and awaiting the end. Russia as she is has no future. I have become a German and am proud of it."

"But you began about the manifestoes. Tell me everything. How do you look at them?"

"Every one is afraid of them, so they must be influential. They openly unmask what is false and prove that there is nothing to lay hold of among us, and nothing to lean upon. They speak aloud while all is silent. What is most effective about them ... is the incredible boldness with which they look the truth straight in the face. To look facts straight in the face is only possible to Russians of this generation. No, in Europe they are not yet so bold; it is a realm of stone, there there is still something to lean upon. So far as I see and am able to judge, the whole essence of the Russian revolutionary idea lies in the negation of honor. I like its being so boldly and fearlessly expressed. No, in Europe they wouldn't understand it yet, but that's just what we shall clutch at. For a Russian a sense of honor is only a superfluous burden, and it always has been a burden through all his history. The open 'right to dishonor' will attract him more than anything. . . ."

If any character in *The Possessed* personifies the negation of honor, it is of course Pyotr Verhovensky. But can it be said that he is truly representative of the Russian revolutionary movement? Has it not been pointed out time and again that he is a monster and not a radical? Anyone who has studied Russian history cannot fail to agree that in presenting Verhovensky as typical of radicalism Dostoevsky was oblivious to the innumerable examples of idealistic self-sacrifice which the class struggle in Russia had to show. There can be no doubt of Dostoevsky's spiteful tendentiousness in this respect. Professor Ernest J. Simmons is entirely in the right when he observes, in his book on Dostoevsky, that Verhovensky is no socialist because his ideology is "the criminal creed of the absolutely self-willed man." But where Professor Simmons is wrong, to my mind, is in contenting himself with this observation, as if that disposed of the matter once and for all.

For if it is true that in a factual sense Verhovensky is altogether untypical of the revolutionary movement of Dostoevsky's time, is it not also true, on the other hand, that this same Verhovensky has since become all too typical — typical, that is, of the men whom the Bolshevik revolution has raised to power and established as Russia's ruling elite? There is an uncanny likeness, after all, between "the criminal creed of the absolutely self-willed man" and the creed, prevailing in practice though for obvious reasons unacknowledged in theory, which is the real motive force of Russia's self-styled socialist masters. And because this likeness has become an historical fact it is no longer possible to dismiss Verhovensky as a monster and not a radical, as Professor Simmons dismisses him in his book. The revolutionary process as it has taken shape in the new order of Stalinism has indisputably confirmed Dostoevsky's insight that the monstrous in human nature is no more incommensurable with the social revolution than it is incommensurable with institutional Christianity. In point of fact, the totalitarian potential of both is incorporated in the principal symbol of the legend of the

Grand Inquisitor — the symbol of the Tower of Babel that replaces the temple of Christ.

Thus it can now be seen that as a character-image Verhovensky is symbolically representative of the Revolution in its results, if not in its original motives. Of course, Dostoevsky was entirely tendentious when he ignored, in *The Possessed*, the role played in the socialist movement by such humanistic and libertarian personalities as Herzen, Chernichevsky, and Mikhailovsky; but here again, unfortunately, his bias is vindicated when it is brought home to us that the Revolution, not as it is presented in the Marxist textbooks but as it actually developed, followed the path not of the socialist humanists but of socialist Machiavellians like Tkachev and Nechayev. To be sure, if examined in the light of the struggle for freedom in czarist Russia, the "right to dishonor" of which Karmazinov speaks (and you may be sure that in this instance he speaks for his author) seems like a vile imputation. Yet the fact is that it is this right, in essence, that the triumphant revolutionaries arrogated to themselves — and precisely in the fashion of the Dostoevskyean man-gods — when they proclaimed moral standards to be a bourgeois prejudice, proceeding on the assumption that to them all is permitted. It is the tragedy of the Russian people that history has proven Dostoevsky to be a truer prophet than Lenin. Only in speaking out of the depths of negation, however, was Dostoevsky a true prophet. Of his positive prophecies none have been fulfilled. The national-Christian ideology of which Shatov is the mouthpiece in *The Possessed* has turned out to be no more than wishful thinking. In the novel Verhovensky murders Shatov, and in real life this crime, endlessly multiplied, has become the foundation of the new Russian state. In this sense Leontiev was again shown to be right against Dostoevsky when he declared that "Russia has only one religious mission, and that is to give birth to anti-Christ." Actually, the anguish of disintegration in Dostoevsky is the creative counterpart of this very idea, an idea strenuously denied in the consolatory and visionary parts of his writings.

But let us look further into Verhovensky's origins in the Russian revolutionary movement of the past century. The biographers of Dostoevsky tell us that the activity of Verhovensky's circle in the novel is an imaginative rendering of the Nechayev episode in the history of Russian radicalism. Now in Nechayevism the Revolution suffered its first formidable inroads of Machiavellian deception and double-dealing. Nechayev invented the slogan: "Everything for the revolution — the end justifies the means." He systematically cultivated criminal methods (which are in no way identical with the methods of underground struggle) in the pursuit of his radical ends. Verhovensky's murder of Shatov is patterned on Nechayev's murder of the student Ivanov; and if we know that one section of the *Catechism of a Revolutionary*, composed by Bakunin and Nechayev, calls for "acquaintance with city gossips, prostitutes, and other private sources" for gathering and disseminating information and false rumors, we realize to what an extent, even to the repetition of comic details, the archetype of Nechayev is reproduced in the portrait of Verhovensky.* The *Catechism*, moreover, contains something more than formulas of conspiracy and provocation. In that document it is written that "everything which promotes the success of the revolution is moral, everything which hinders it is immoral" — a dictum, at once savage and naive, that Lenin took over in toto, applying it with all the rigor of his political nature and never ceasing to defend it as the only possible ethic consistent with Marxist aims. Lenin's self-will was so inordinate that he always assumed perfect knowledge on his part as to what made for the ultimate success or failure of the Revolution. Thus what appeared to him like an objective test of morality rested on nothing whatever except his subjective assumption of perfect knowledge, judgment, and disinterestedness. We can grant him the disinterestedness, but not the knowledge or the judgment. Because of the absolutism of his revolutionary character he failed to look beyond the abstractions of historical materialism to the real interests that lurk behind the ideologies of individuals as well as social groups. He overlooked the inescapable fact that behind every doctrine or program, including his own, there are living men, with immediate and concrete desires, needs, and ambitions, and that this could only mean that Nechayev's dictum would eventually be altered to read that everything is moral which promotes the success, not of the Revolution, but of the men who choose to speak in its name, and that everything which hinders them is immoral. Lenin's disregard of the ethics of humanism was implicit in his self-will. The enormity

---

* In his political traits, that is. As a psychological type Verhovensky has Nechayev's ruthlessness and immoralism but none of his revolutionary asceticism. As a matter of fact, in his psychological aspects Verhovensky reminds us more of such famous *agents provocateurs* as Azev and Malinovsky, both of whom, long after Dostoevsky's time, rose to high positions in the revolutionary movement while in the pay of the *Okhrana,* the Czar's secret police. Azev became head of the powerful terrorist section of the Social Revolutionary Party; Malinovsky, who had Lenin's confidence, became the chief spokesman of the Bolsheviks in the Duma. Of both Azev and Malinovsky it may be said that they were truly Dostoevskyean in their doubleness of character, for they were not police spies pure and simple but men of ambiguous motivation and dual loyalties who did not know from one day to the other what they really believed in or whether their principal allegiance was to the Revolution or to their czarist paymasters.

and arrogance of that will is the peculiar sin of Bolshevism, the *hubris* for which Lenin has been paid out by the utter ruin of his revolutionary achievements.

The connection between Nechayevism and the Revolution is close indeed. When Bakunin finally repudiated his fanatical disciple he exposed him as one who believed that "in order to create a workable and strong organization one must use as a basis the philosophy of Machiavelli and adopt the motto of the Jesuits: 'Violence for the body; lies for the soul.'" It was not until the Grand Inquisitor himself, the dictator Stalin, gained supreme power that Nechayev's central thought was translated into the terms of real life. Still, the totalitarian virus is no doubt present in Lenin's moral opportunism, an opportunism exalted into a principle of socialist organization and propaganda and thus far more pernicious in its consequences than the casual, unthinking pragmatism and the recourse to expediency that as a rule prevail in political affairs. The Revolution is a means and not an end; and the outcome of Lenin's absolutizing of the Revolution was that the means so completely usurped the end that it was soon transformed into its exact opposite — into a system reminiscent of Shigalov's thesis rather than of the forecasts of Marx and Engels. What is Shigalov's thesis? That the only way to secure unlimited freedom is through unlimited despotism, or rather that the two concepts are ultimately identical. Therefore he proposes that nine-tenths of mankind be deprived of all freedom and individuality while one-tenth enjoys the unbounded power required for the compulsory organization of happiness. Shigalov's "earthly paradise" is nothing if not a remarkable prevision of Stalin's "workers' paradise." And when one comes to appreciate the fact that Dostoevsky's prognosis of the course of the Revolution, however crude in detail, is essentially correct in its main outlines, one cannot but admire his astonishing clairvoyance; and that despite his malicious tendentiousness, which we can now put in the proper perspective without in any way justifying it.

This malice, inherent in Dostoevsky's character, was strengthened by his polemical exertions as a writer. Still, there is no denying that he decided against socialism on a principled metaphysical basis. His antipathy to it had nothing in common with the habitual objections of conservative property holders, office holders, and ideologues. He understood that "socialism is founded on the principles of science and reason . . . that it is not merely the labor question, it is before all else the atheistic question, the question of the form taken by atheism today"; and in a variant passage of *The Possessed* we find the statement, attributed to Liputin, that "socialism is a substitute for Christianity, it is a new Christianity, which wants to renew the whole world. It is positively the same as Christianity, but without God." Nevertheless he was drawn to it, for he was as much fascinated as repelled by the demonstrations of reason. Like Stavrogin, he never really attained the peace of religious faith, and when he believed he could not actually believe that he believed. He hated socialism because it objectified his lack of belief and both his fear and heretical love of the boundless expansion and change of which the human mind is capable. In his compulsion to test theory by practice he came close to the methods of extreme rationality; and when he subjected Christianity to this rigorous test he found that only a special kind of "idiot" and genius of neuroticism could possibly undertake to lead a Christian life.

His plebeianism was another element that tended to subvert his support of the autocracy and the church. On his subjective-psychological side he remained a democrat, regardless of the shifts that took place in his political convictions; and for this reason he could not restrain himself from berating the older generation of Slavophils for their "aristocratic satiety." Like the critic Belinsky and the poet Nekrasov he belonged to the school of commoners, whose inner affinity was with the psychic distortions and the moral agitation and resentment of Gogol rather than with the objective art of Pushkin. In Dostoevsky's work we do not experience that sense of social hierarchies which affects us so strongly in the novels that Tolstoy wrote before his conversion. In modern times the plebeian world-feeling is one of the intrinsic conditions of heresy, and the spiritual equality which reigns in Dostoevsky's world seems like a kind of inverted socialism, a commune of the spirit.

In *The Possessed* liberal idealism receives the broadest and most perspicacious criticism in the history of political fiction. The comic strokes with which the portrait of the intellectual Stepan Trofimovitch, the elder Verhovensky, is executed, in no way diverts us from its enduring reality and social truth. This characterization has enormous contemporary meanings. It is only now, after fascism and communism have severely penalized Western culture for subjecting itself to the timorous and accommodating counsels of the liberals, that we can fully appreciate Stepan Trofimovitch.

A gentleman scholar and aesthete, he simultaneously abuses and adores the Revolution. His standing protest he makes by lying down; he is subtle in his feelings, a self-indulgent humanitarian and a parasite. He is superior to Thomas Mann's Settembrini, whose distant relative he is, for he is understood not argumentatively but through a tangible social milieu. And what a hazardous yet just simplification it was to place him in the position of being the charge of a rich and aristocratic lady, of making an assertive dramatic image out of Varvara Petrovna's support of him. This exchange of cash and culture, however, is not conceived as a simple transaction; on the contrary, it entails mutual distrust, bitterness, and emotional tempests — at one and at the same time it involves very real sentiments, even love, and "a mutual exchange of sloppiness."

Stepan Trofimovitch is a typical modern figure, the liberal intellectual with a tender social conscience and a taste for fine feelings and ideas, who, while pluming himself on his advanced position as a champion of the oppressed, is at once thrown into a state of collapse when forced to face the consequences of his own commitments and the cruel exigencies of the historical process. This dilettante of revolution is bound to end up among its first victims. He is unable to cope with his revolutionary son, Pyotr, nor with the nihilists whom the latter trains in his base methods. In *Fathers and Sons,* Turgenev's Bazarov, the prototype of the nihilists in the Russian novel, holds the view that a good chemist is worth twenty poets. But Bazarov's nihilism is only a form of moral empiricism; he is an individualist as yet unaware of the potency of political action. A few decades later, in the 1870s, the nihilistic adversaries of Stepan Trofimovitch had already translated Bazarov's moral empiricism into the formulas of political terror and demagoguery. During the fête — the description of which includes some of the novel's superb scenes — Stepan Trofimovitch defies the political mob by shouting at them: "What is more beautiful, Shakespeare or boots, Raphael or petroleum?" "*Agent provocateur!*" they growl in reply. It is a crushing reply and one that is all too indicative of the manner in which the revolutionaries in power will eventually dispose of the tender-minded intelligentsia. If in his generalizations Dostoevsky recognizes no difference between liberals, nihilists, and socialists, within the living organism of the novel he takes care to distinguish clearly between the elder and younger Verhovensky; paternity in this case is symbolic of a relation of ideas at once positive and negative. The revolutionary doctrine negates liberalism even as it grows out of it. In the historical sense what Pyotr represents is his father's ideas thought out to an outrageously logical conclusion, and for that very reason he becomes his father's worst enemy.

But the vitality of Stepan Trofimovitch's character is by no means confined to the political dimension. He is also a splendidly comical

creation, richly illustrating Dostoevsky's gifts as a humorous writer
that have been obscured by his accomplishments as psychologist and
dialectician. In Stepan Trofimovitch, this "most innocent of fifty-year-
old infants" who is capable of the most surprising and subtle insights,
Dostoevsky reached the apogee of his comic art — an art that produced
such figures as Foma Fomitch of *The Friend of the Family* and that
entire incredible collection of buffoons, like Lebedev of *The Idiot* and
Captain Lebyadkin of *The Possessed,* of whom at least one specimen
is invariably to be found in any Dostoevskyean cast of characters.
Stepan Trofimovitch does not belong to this species. For all his pol-
troonery, tormenting vanity, nervous outbreaks, and fondness for
French phrases, he is yet invested with a redeeming generosity and
openness of feeling that converts him into a figure of heroico-comical
proportions. We believe in him as we can never believe in his son
Pyotr, in whom there is something cold and amorphous, and whom we
can imagine only as a kind of abstract demon all the more terrible in
his fury for being doomed to beat his wings in a void. He has no
ability to transcend his situation, while his father has this ability above
all; and that so endears him to us that in our sympathy we are persuaded that even if he is a bundle of human failings in him the human
image is still the goad of love.

There are few scenes in Dostoevsky as marvelous as the scenes of
Stepan Trofimovitch's stormy interviews with his capricious patroness,
or of his appearance and declamations at the fête, or of his engagement
to Darya Shatova, and, in particular, of his flight and wanderings in
the countryside, where he meets the Bible-selling woman, wooing her
in his delirium and panic — the flight that ends with his breakdown
and the self-confrontation of those last great reconciling speeches in
which, as if summing up the rhetoric of a lifetime, he salutes "the
Eternal and Infinite Idea" at the same time that he confesses to the
lies he has told through all the years, summoning all to forgiveness,
for all are guilty, all have wronged one another, in the hope that he
too will be forgiven. In those last tremendous pages of the novel we
are made to feel as though Stepan Trofimovitch, lying on his deathbed,
has departed from his character in order to voice, in unison with his
author, a great cry of grief for Holy Russia, a prayer that her sick
men be freed of the demons that possess them so that, whole again and
much afraid, they may come and sit at the feet of Jesus.

It is significant that the passage from the Gospels, which forms the
epigraph to the novel, telling about the sick man cured of his devils
and sitting at the feet of Jesus, is made to resound through Stepan

Trofimovitch's last speeches, as if to indicate that the author, despite the vindictive spirit of his initial approach to him, is so taken with his creature that he cannot help lending him a modicum of his own faith and outlook. It is a case of sympathy between the creative artist and the created being, in the sense of Keats' notion of "the poetical Character," which forfeits its own identity in taking unto itself the identities formed by the imagination. ("What shocks the virtuous philosopher delights the chameleon poet," said Keats.) Now in Stepan Trofimovitch, modelled on a handsome Moscow professor by the name of Granovsky, a friend of Herzen and Belinsky, the "virtuous philosopher" in Dostoevsky wanted to score off the generation of the 1840s, whose rational humanism he regarded as a source of infection; but Stepan Trofimovitch turned out differently than is anticipated in the original design. Though his function in the novel is to stand as a reproach to the Westernizing intellectuals, he is creatively assimilated to such a degree that in surpassing himself he assumes other roles, not the least of which is to act as a foil to Dostoevsky in his farewell to the Schilleresque period of his own youth, the period of *Schwärmerei* and idealistic grandiloquence, when at one with his contemporaries he shared the exalted feelings inspired by the rational religion of humanity.

In Stavrogin and his alter egos, Kirillov and Shatov, Dostoevsky was reproducing the obsessions of his ultimate phase. As against radicals like Verhovensky and Karmazinov, they personify the "pure" Russians. Shatov, for instance, becomes the spokesman of the national destiny. What are the Russians like and what is their mission? — that is the problem tormenting him.

Three times, in *Fathers and Sons,* Turgenev essayed to define the "typical Russian," and each time he betrayed his sense of inferiority to the West and the complacent, moderate cast of his sensibility. (The three definitions occur in subordinate verbal constructions: *a.* ". . . a coarse, half-educated, but not ill-natured man, a typical Russian"; *b.* "the only good point in a Russian is his having the lowest possible opinion of himself"; *c.* ". . . a young man at once progressive and a despot, as often happens with Russians.") Dostoevsky was outraged by Turgenev's common sense and persistent depreciation of Russia. Into his own conception of Russia and Russians he injected his characteristic emotion of extremity. The Russians are to him a kingdom of priests and a chosen people; even God is appropriated to its uses. In Shatov's scheme of things God is merely "the synthetic personality of the whole people, taken from its beginning to its end." These national visions anticipate much that Europe was to experience later; and the same holds true of Stavrogin's "life, so to speak, of mockery," of his psychic conundrums that are precursive of many tendencies in twentieth-century European literature.

It is significant that Shatov, who patently speaks for the author in his affirmation of the Russians as a god-bearing people destined to regenerate the world, is unable to attain in his faith the completeness that Kirillov attains in his atheism. For Shatov, though believing in Russian Orthodoxy, in the body of Christ, and in the new advent that will take place in Russia, is nevertheless thrown for a loss when asked pointblank whether he actually believes in God. All he can say in reply is "I . . . I will believe in God." Thus he lays himself open to Stavrogin's gibe that he is preparing to cook an uncaught hare — "to cook your hare you must first catch it, to believe in God you must first have a god." Kirillov, on the other hand, is completely certain of his idea that God is dead, and in his obsession with this idea he challenges the universe, setting himself up as its master in the place of God.

Kirillov's atheism is of a desperate intensity without parallel in world literature. It is the atheism of a man so profoundly religious that once he is convinced of the impossibility of God's existence he must refuse at all costs to go on inventing Him; His absence is so agonizing a negation of meaning that he cannot help reacting to it by attempting to blow up the world, and since the world is not his to destroy he can only destroy himself. That seems to me to be the real motive of his suicide. To be sure, the commentators on Dostoevsky have mostly explained it as the consequence of Kirillov's logic of self-will, and it is indeed true that he makes of his suicide the climactic act of his self-willed accession to the role of the man-god. One must distinguish, however, between the logical and existential aspects of this act. Logically it is an assertion of the absolute freedom of his self-will; existentially it expresses the passionate indignation of his atheism, an atheism whose inescapable logic is beyond his endurance. His suicide is thus to be conceived as an explosion of subjectivity protesting the objective godlessness of the world. *Allein zu sein und ohne Götter, das ist er, ist der Tod,* said Hölderlin. To be alone and without gods — that is death; and it is this thought, literally, that compels Kirillov to kill himself. In reading the overpowering description of his suicide and the dialogue that precedes it one becomes aware that here Dostoevsky is picturing nothing less than the self-crucifixion of an atheistic Christ. Consider that shortly before firing his shot Kirillov recalls the crucifixion of old in words of ecstatic pain:

"Listen to a great idea: there was a day on earth, and in the midst of the earth there stood three crosses. One on the Cross had such faith that he said to another, 'Today thou shalt be with me in Paradise.' The day ended; both died and passed away and found neither Paradise nor resurrection. His words did not come true. Listen: that man was the loftiest of all on earth. He was that which gave meaning to life. . . . For that is the miracle, that there never was and never will be another like Him. And if that is so, if the laws of nature did not spare even Him, have not spared even their miracle and made even Him live in a lie and die for a lie, then all the planet is a lie and rests on a lie and on mockery. So then, the very laws of the planet are a lie and the vaudeville of devils. What is there to live for? Answer, if you are a man."

Kirillov's suicide is a parody of the crucifixion of Christ — a parody because in a universe whose laws are "a lie and the vaudeville of devils" there can be no meaningful acts, only parodies.

The atheism of Kirillov is not to be equated with that of some of the modern existentialists. Sartre, for example, defines existentialism as "nothing less than an attempt to draw all the consequences of a coherent atheistic position"; and the chief consequence of the atheistic position is that it forces man to confront his freedom in a world emptied of all values and commands not derived from himself. This idea of man alone in his freedom is of course not alien to Kirillov, but in his dialectic it is so hugely exaggerated that it is transformed into a notion of human omnipotence and made into the basis of the man-god's mad rationale. On this side of it his atheism is a sick phantasy of his soul suffering the ordeal of God's absence. At bottom, however, his atheism is really a form of negative religiosity. It is real nevertheless, and in considering its implications there is no way of absolving the author of complicity in it. If Shatov speaks for him, so does Kirillov; and if the latter manifests more spiritual vitality than the former it is no doubt because Dostoevsky imbued him with a deeper and more personal significance. V. V. Rozanov, a writer who brought exceptional gifts to the interpretation of Dostoevsky, was moved to say, in citing the passage from *The Possessed* quoted above, that "when Dostoevsky wrote those words you feel that through his soul, a single human soul, there passed such a terrifying atheism as has never been experienced before, or, if experienced, has not yet been uttered in words."

The curious thing about the ideas both of Shatov and Kirillov is that they are represented in the novel as emanations of Stavrogin's irony. To them his ideas have become altogether real, whereas he has forgotten them. Stavrogin experiments with life, only incidentally with ideas, and every experiment strengthens the demon of irony that possesses him. There are elements of Christian feeling in him, but only in the sense that at times he is inclined to believe in the devil, never in God. Everyone expects of him something unheard-of, something not expected from other people, for in truth he is a hero of charismatic authority, a leader-type who is bored, however, by his own charisma. That is what is really "new" in the character of Stavrogin, this refusal to make use of his own powers — a refusal caused by the recoil of his consciousness upon itself in the dreadful apprehension of its own limitless freedom. He is free of the sense of good and evil, being convinced that "good and evil do not exist . . . and are but a prejudice." Yet he knows that it is precisely in the attainment of this freedom that he will perish. He says of himself that he ought to commit suicide; but at the same time he rejects suicide for fear of showing greatness of soul, for such greatness could hardly be anything more than "another sham, the last deception in an endless series of deceptions." Dostoevsky, in creating the character-image of Stavrogin, reached the last frontier of the modern imagination, and it is perhaps for this reason, since life did not as yet contain him, that he could not make him "true to life" but was forced to rely almost entirely on his mastery of the devices of melodrama and mystification.

Nearly all the female characters in the novel are in love with Stavrogin, a love which he is incapable of reciprocating. Hence his desires are nothing less than crimes — the crime of murder above all. Thus it is through their love of him that both the imperious Liza and the crippled, half-witted Marya are done in; and Matryosha, the little girl whom he has violated, kills herself. Stavrogin, like Svidrigailov in *Crime and Punishment,* is a sexual marauder, but in his case too it is the *idea* of sex rather than the reality of it that absorbs the imagination. This Dostoevskyean idea of sex is not an abstraction; on the contrary, it is enormously creative in that it at once suggests and exceeds the reality behind it. But it is typical of Dostoevsky that he should have let nothing escape his ideological net, not even the cravings of the flesh and the aberrations of desire.

Of course, Dostoevsky paid for his ideological power by strictly limiting his incursions into the sensuous-material world. He gives us sensations of time, and only seldom of space. He has a prodigious appetite for people, but he is insensitive to textures and objects; his characters act sexually only when aroused by their own moral and spiritual sensuality. This overproduction of the spiritual makes for a constant inner crisis, for an analyzing attitude which shuts him off from nature. It is this quality which permits his narratives their breakneck pace — there is no need to stop when there is nothing to look at. The excessive sociability of his people has the same source. It has often been observed how perpetually dependent they are on externalization through talk and debate. Even in committing suicide they are not alone, and a love scene seldom takes place without the presence of a third person. Dostoevsky stages his climaxes only after he has assembled as many of his characters as possible into one room; and the action, in which the philosophical dialogue is inextricably involved with a story of mystery and crime, moves in a whirlwind manner toward a *dénouement* that consumes heroes and victims alike in a conflagration of hatred, pity, resentment, remorse, and love.

If the religious-minded critics of Dostoevsky have emphasized almost exclusively the Christian element in his work, the Marxist critics have permitted political considerations to influence them in disparaging and ignoring his achievements. Gorky spoke of Dostoevsky as "our evil genius," strictly limiting himself to his negative features. Even D. Mirsky, who before going over to a Marxist position wrote with fine insight and precision about Dostoevsky, later committed himself to views contradicting his previous evaluations. Thus, in his preface to Edward Hallett Carr's biography of Dostoevsky, he expresses his gratification with Carr for showing up, as it were, his subject. Carr had laid great stress on the literary and Romantic antecedents of Dostoevsky, and Mirsky concludes that he is "modern only in so far as the term modern can be extended to Rousseau, Byron, and Benjamin Constant." He was produced by Russia precisely because she was backward and because "he was a belated parallel in his country to what the Romantics had been in the West." To Mirsky it seems that by labeling Dostoevsky the belated Romantic of a backward country he has effectively removed him from the terrain of the modern; what he has further in mind, of course, is to connect him with the reactionary tendencies of the Romantic movement in Germany and to a lesser extent in France.

In relating Dostoevsky to Romanticism in the way he does, Mirsky suggests the use of the Marxist "law of combined development." But to invoke this law is to disprove Mirsky's approach. The "law of combined development" explains why a bourgeois revolution, when it occurs in a backward country, tends to go beyond itself and to be transformed into a socialist one. A backward country is thus enabled to make up for lost time and outstrip its advanced neighbors, at least politically. There is no reason, however, to confine this phenomenon of accelerated mutation to politics. It also operates on the spiritual plane. To say, then, in this sense, that Dostoevsky was a belated

Romantic does not at all mean that the Romantic world was his world or that he restored the Romantic state of mind.

Why is the Russian novel of the nineteenth century so great in its achievements? If the "law of combined development" has any application here, it would point to the need of the Russian novelist to break out ideologically and imaginatively from the blind alley in which his country found itself. This same need impelled him to augment his equipment by taking over as rapidly as he could whatever acquisitions of Western culture were open to him. Even when he rejected this culture, as Dostoevsky did, he was strongly affected by it. Before condemning it he still had to acquire some essential part of it.

To recognize the achievement of the Russian novel of the nineteenth century is to recognize Dostoevsky's supremacy as a modern writer. His one rival is Tolstoy. Only dogmatists of progress, who conceive of it as an even and harmonious development, could presume to commit Dostoevsky to a museum of Romantic antiquities. It is true that he labored to give his genius a religious sanctification, but it must be kept in mind that in the sphere of imaginative creation progress does not simply consist of knowing what is true and what is false from the standpoint of progressive or scientific thought. Dostoevsky not only renovated the traditional properties of Romanticism, but also discovered inversions and dissociations in human feeling and consciousness which literature has to this day only imperfectly assimilated. Reactionary in its abstract content, in its aspect as a system of ideas, his art is radical in sensibility and subversive in performance.

Moreover, Romanticism is far from being as dreadful as Mirsky makes out. Its impulse is partly reactionary, of course, but in approaching the old values through the self-consciousness of the new epoch, it responded to new emotions and invented new themes. There are numberless examples of this dual function of Romanticism. Chateaubriand, for instance, was faithful to throne and altar; he set out to defend tradition and belabor Rousseau. "I am not like Rousseau," he wrote in the introduction to *Atala*, "an enthusiast over savages. . . . I do not think that pure nature is . . . beautiful. . . . I have always found it ugly. Let us paint nature, but selected nature (*la belle nature*). Art should not concern itself with the imitation of monsters." This declaration, however, as Sainte-Beuve noted, was belied by the actual content of *Atala*, in which one encounters a crocodile on nearly every page.

Dostoevsky's "crocodiles" are thinking men.

Partisan Review, 1938

The Legend of
the Grand Inquisitor

UNTIL RECENTLY Dostoevsky's Western interpreters were open to the reproach of making far too little of his Legend of the Grand Inquisitor. The same, however, can hardly be said of his Russian critics, who repeatedly stressed its significance long before the onset of totalitarianism in our time brought on the widespread recognition, if not of the Legend's actual content and meaning, then surely of its close relevance to modern historical experience.

The late Nicolas Berdyaev, writing from a philosophical standpoint, maintained that in the Legend Dostoevsky reached the summit of his creation; and some five decades ago V. V. Rozanov, whose insight into Dostoevsky is unsurpassed among Russian commentators, declared it to be of exceptional profundity as a revelation of the structure of human destiny — "terrifying unbelief and the deepest and most ecstatic faith are inconceivably mingled in it." There is some evidence, too, that its author himself thought of it in such terms. In 1902 one witness (V. F. Putzikovitch) published an account of a conversation he had had with the novelist in the summer of 1879, while *The Brothers Karamazov* was still running serially in the *Russky Vestnik*, in which he speaks of the chapter on the Grand Inquisitor as the "culminating point" of his creative career; and when questioned as to his reasons for interpolating a devised legend of sixteenth-century Spain into a narrative of contemporary Russia, his reply was that its theme had haunted him since early youth and for fear that he might not live to complete another major work he had resolved to try his hand at it without delay and incorporate it in the novel he was then engaged in writing.

One need not agree with Berdyaev that the Legend of the Grand

Inquisitor represents the summit of Dostoevsky's creation in order to make out that as an excursus on the theme of man's historical fate, its terror, despair, and absurdity, it is nearly without equal in world literature. It enriches the ideological content of the novel in which it is embedded, enabling us to understand more fully the far-ranging implications of Ivan Karamazov's "rebellion," but it is even more meaningful in terms of Dostoevsky's development as a whole; and the figure of the Grand Inquisitor is dramatically compelling enough to stay permanently in our minds as a symbolic character-image of the dialectic of power. Moreover, the Legend lends itself to analysis, quite apart from its local narrative setting, as a unique essay in the philosophy of history. Deceptively easy on the surface, it is at bottom one of the most difficult texts in the Dostoevskyean canon. By the same token, however, it is also one of the most rewarding. And the difficulty is not in its dramatic form but in the complexity of the ideas, their immense suggestiveness and scope, and the dissonances of belief and emotional discords that sound in them.

But the dramatic form is indispensable to Dostoevsky. That he would have been capable of making substantially the same statement without recourse to the dramatized consciousness of a fictional character is extremely doubtful. For the truth is that this most daring of novelists is apt to decline abruptly to lower levels of performance whenever he puts himself in the position of addressing the reader directly — a stance that rarely suits him, as is shown by the inferior quality of most of the articles included in his *Diary of a Writer*. Now a disjunction of this sort would scarcely surprise us in a novelist deficient in intellectual force and stamina. In Dostoevsky's case, however, the felt disjunction between the qualities of his direct discourse and those emerging through the sustained imaginative projection of his fiction is due, I think, to the fact that when writing in the first person — out in the open so to speak — he at once loses the advantages of complicity. For it is complicity above all which is the secret of his creative triumph over the propagandist in himself. It arises in the process of his identification as novelist with his characters, but it is necessary to distinguish between its genesis and the larger uses to which he puts it. It saves him from the one-sidedness, the fanaticism of commitment, and the casuistry to which as an embattled reactionary ideologue he was all too prone. There is an ambiguity of feeling and attitude in him, a tension between sympathies and antipathies, finding its release in this complicity. He fully depends on it in the creation of his characters; and the few from whom he withholds it are reduced to stereotypes, as, for example, Grushenka's Polish suitor and the student-radical Rakitin in *The Brothers Karamazov*. Creatures of their author's political malice, they fall below the level of the world into which he injects them.

Ivan, on the other hand, it has frequently been observed, is the figure in the novel to whom as author he most readily gives himself in the process of identification.* This must be taken into account in examining the Legend recounted by Ivan to his brother Alyosha in the course of that prolonged dialogue which is perhaps the most audacious and masterful in the whole of Dostoevsky. Ivan calls the Legend "a poem in prose" that he had not written down but simply made up, as he says, and he tells it to Alyosha in order to support, in a manner at once dramatic and metaphysically provocative, his denial not so much of God as of His creation. The denial consists of a relentless scrutiny of man in general, and particularly Christian man, in the light of what he has made of history and history has made of him.

In his assault on God and the traditional faith Ivan proceeds in a way that transcends the rationalistic argumentation of the old-time atheists. For him it can no longer be a question of attempting to disprove God's existence logically. Ivan is not one to permit his intellectual faculties to linger in the modes of the past. He has made the essentially modern leap from the static framework of analytic thinking to thinking in terms of the historical process. But his leap is made in the typical Russian fashion of that epoch. That is to say, it lands him not in the somewhat placid "historicism" then prevailing in the consciousness of the West but in the eschatological frame of mind common to the Russian intelligentsia of the latter part of the past century. For whatever their outlook, whether revolutionary or not, inclined to nihilism or given to apocalyptic visions, in the main those people tended to see history as verging toward the ultimate and bringing forth a final solution compounded either of pure good or pure evil. "The orientation toward the end," as Berdyaev calls it, mastered the most sensitive spirits among them, some predicting the approach of anti-Christ and others fervently awaiting the imminent erection of the City of Man; and in the intensity of their longing for an incontrovertible decision they transform the historical realm into the realm of prophecy and revelation. This is the mood that Ivan's "rebellion" exemplifies to perfection.

---

* My impression is that the identification is more on the intellectual plane than on that of intimate subjectivity. But of course in Dostoevsky ideas are never divorced from feeling; in his critical statements he was wont to link them by inventing such new-fangled terms as "idea-forces" and "idea-feelings." In her memoirs Aimée Dostoevsky recalls the family tradition that her father, in looking back to his youth, "portrayed himself in the person of Ivan."

His version of atheism is all the more forceful in that it allows for God's existence, if need be, but not for the justifications of His world as revealed progressively *in* and *through* history. Ivan proclaims that no restitution is possible: that the ultimate harmony or reconciliation in the fullness of time could never expiate the suffering of even a single innocent child, let alone efface the innumerable horrors of injustice which humanity has endured through the ages. Hence he refuses God's creation ("returns his entrance ticket") thus proclaiming the right of indifference to the issue of His existence.

Nor does Ivan dispute the ideality and supreme goodness of Christian teaching. On the contrary, it is this very ideality and goodness that he turns into the motive of his dissent from it when he depicts the Grand Inquisitor upbraiding Christ for thinking much too highly of man in endeavoring to augment his freedom of choice between good and evil instead of heeding the counsel of the wise and dread spirit of the wilderness to strip man of his freedom so that he might at long last live in peace and brutish happiness. God, confronted by the radical proofs of the meanness of His world, the senseless suffering prevailing in it and man's congenital inability to enter the promised spiritual kingdom, is disposed of through His works.*

But if Ivan does not believe in God, neither does he believe in man. It is true that he loves man — there is no one else left to love and perhaps there has never actually been anyone else. Yet how can he believe in man's freedom in the face of the appalling testimony of history proving his incapacity to achieve it? And in what way does Ivan envisage the future? If we take the Grand Inquisitor as his *persona*, then he thinks that just as historical Christianity has failed man, so socialism — the Tower of Babel of the coming centuries — will fail him and afterwards the authoritarian theocrats will resume command. And the fault, from first to last, is in man himself because he is an "impotent rebel," a slave even if rebellious by nature. Implicit here is the idea of freedom as the consummation of rebellion and of happiness as the total renunciation of it. The choice is between freedom and happiness. But so long as man is unable to carry his rebellion through to the end,

---

* Dostoevsky appears to have been inordinately proud of Ivan's subversive intelligence. "Ivan is deep," he wrote in his private notebook; "he is not one of your present-day atheists whose unbelief demonstrates no more than the narrowness of their point of view and the obtuseness of their small minds." And again: "Those thickheads never dreamt of so powerful a negation of God as that embodied in the Inquisitor and in the preceding chapter, to which the entire novel serves as an answer. . . . Even in Europe there have never been atheistical expressions of such power."

or alternatively, renounce it once and for all, he will attain neither goal. Ivan torments himself with the question of what is to be done with man if you at once love and despise him. The ideology of the Grand Inquisitor, which repudiates freedom for the sake of happiness, is the means he devises for forcing a solution. Yet it also is a means of exposing it. The very manner in which Ivan develops this ideology expresses his loathing of it even as he despairingly accepts it.

This is but another way of saying that in the last analysis he is not really possessed by it, that his mind moves freely in and out of it. The Legend as a whole, in its interplay of drama and ideology, is to be taken, I think, as an experiment, one of those experiments in frightfulness with which modern literature has the deepest affinity. Dostoevsky stands at two removes from the Inquisitor, and Ivan at one remove; and this placing, or aesthetic "distancing," reflects precisely the degree of commitment we are entitled to assume. Therefore to identify Ivan wholly with the Inquisitor, as so many commentators have done, is an error, though a lesser one than that of wholly identifying Dostoevsky with him. The fact is that the Legend has not one but two protagonists, Jesus and the Inquisitor, and that Ivan makes no real choice between them. Jesus is freedom and transcendent truth, whereas the Inquisitor typifies the implacable logic of historical reality; but so stark a confrontation in itself demonstrates that Ivan's dilemma is absolute. After all, he has no God to whom he can appeal for a guaranty of his choice; Jesus is his hero but not his God. Ivan, like his creator, is split through and through, torn between love and contempt, pride and submission, reason and faith, teleology and the extremest pessimism. Inherently a stranger in the world of action, he is capable, however, of apprehending his thought with such urgency and fearlessness that it comes almost to resemble an action. And in his rage of love he invokes with prophetic violence a totalitarian elite whose rule is justified by humanity's refusal of Christ's tragic gift of freedom.

The scene of Ivan's "poem in prose" is Seville at the time of the Inquisition. On a day when nearly a hundred heretics had been burnt *ad majorem Dei gloriam* by the cardinal, the Grand Inquisitor, in a splendid *auto-da-fé*, Christ reappears in His human shape, as He appeared fifteen centuries earlier. The people, recognizing their Savior, welcome Him with cries of love and faith, but at that moment the cardinal — "an old man, almost ninety, tall and erect, with a withered face and sunken eyes, in which there is still a gleam of light" — orders the guards to seize and lead Him away to the dungeon of the Holy Inquisition. At night the door of the cell is suddenly opened and the aged cardinal comes in alone to confront his prisoner. On the morrow, he announces, he will condemn and burn Him at the stake as the worst of heretics: "And the very people who have today kissed Thy feet, tomorrow at the faintest sign from me will rush to heap up the embers of Thy fire." Throughout the long scene that follows Christ is speechless. Only the Inquisitor speaks, and his speech is an astonishingly coherent and complete apology for the total power of man over man. It has grandeur, penetration, and enormous audacity — thus would the Inquisitor's counterparts in real life speak if they had candor and were capable of making independent forays into the philosophy of history. The phenomenon of power has always been surrounded by taboos. Power is in some sense the deepest of mysteries, hence taboo, for whatever is behind it is at once holy and unclean. But the Inquisitor breaks all taboos. It was the recommendation of Edmund Burke, that enemy of extremism and of theory, that a "sacred veil" should ever be drawn "over the beginnings of all governments." Now if by "beginnings" we understand the motive force or inner principle of government, then the Inquisitor is bent on rending asunder the veil that shrouds it and letting us in on its secret. Not that he is not himself a firm believer in the beneficent uses of Burke's "politic, wellwrought veil." He is that above all, but in the séance with his speechless prisoner he is for once intent on putting all things plainly.

What he puts most plainly to his prisoner is the enormity of the error of rejecting coercion and domination for the sake of man's free love. The three powers with which Satan had tempted Him in the wilderness are miracle, mystery, and authority, the sole means of vanquishing the conscience of men forever and holding it captive for their own good. The churchly hierarchy has found it necessary to correct that error and to found its work on those powers. Never has anything truer been said than what was revealed by the wise and dread spirit of the wilderness in the three questions later recorded in the Gospels as "the temptation." For in those questions "the whole subsequent history of mankind is, as it were, brought together into one whole and foretold, and in them are united all the unsolved historical contradictions of human nature. . . ."

Man, hungering both for "earthly bread" and "common worship," and on no account wanting the one without the other, will gladly exchange his freedom for the promise that his double hunger will be appeased. He longs "to find someone quickly to whom he can hand over the gift of freedom with which the ill-fated creature was born"; and he prefers to worship the one who feeds him, the one performing the miracle rejected by Jesus, the miracle of turning stones into bread.

Yet man is so constituted that he seeks to worship only that which he believes to be established beyond dispute:

> For those pitiful creatures are concerned not only to find what one or the other can worship, but to find something that all would believe in and worship; what is essential is that all may be *together* in it. This craving for *community* of worship is the chief misery of every man individually and of all humanity from the beginning of time. For the sake of common worship they have slain each other with the sword. They have set up gods and challenged one another, "Put away your gods and come and worship ours, or we will kill you and your gods!" And so it will be to the end of the world, even when gods disappear from the earth; they will fall down before idols just the same.

Jesus' hope that man would cling to God and not crave miracles is futile. Man seeks not so much God as the miraculous, and when deprived of it he creates "new miracles of his own for himself, and will worship deeds of sorcery and witchcraft, though he might be a hundred times over a rebel, heretic and infidel." The Inquisitor foretells that the downfall of the church will come about exactly through such a deed of sorcery and witchcraft when men, declaring that there is no crime and no sin but only hunger, will erect the terrible Tower of Babel. But after a thousand years of suffering, of the confusion of free thought and of science ending in "cannibalism," the people will seek out the priestly elite hidden in their catacombs: "They will find us and cry to us, 'Feed us, for those who have promised the fire from heaven haven't given it!' And then we shall finish building their tower. . . . And we alone shall feed them in Thy name, declaring falsely that it is in Thy name. . . . And we shall sit upon the beast and raise the cup, and on it will be written, 'Mystery.'"

The Inquisitor sneers at the nihilists and socialists even while appropriating what he conceives to be their principal idea: materialism and technics, the miracle of turning stones into bread. In other words, ecclesiastical totalitarianism comes to terms with the socialist cause by absorbing it. Only then begins the reign of the universal state — "an harmonious antheap" — assuring peace for all. Its principle of organization is power. Jesus repudiated power, but not the theocrats of Rome, who have taken up the sword of Caesar, proclaiming themselves the lords of the earth. "We shall triumph and we shall be Caesars," the Inquisitor cries, "and then we shall plan the universal happiness of mankind." All will be happy except the members of the ruling caste, since it is they alone who are not absolved from the knowledge of good and evil. They keep that knowledge strictly to themselves, just as they keep the secret of their atheism. The millions whom they rule submit meekly to their commands and die peacefully believing in the rewards of heaven and eternity, as they have been told to believe, though of course beyond the grave nothing whatever awaits them.

The only answer the Inquisitor receives from his prisoner is a kiss on his withered lips. The old man shudders and, opening the door of the cell, exclaims: "Go, and come no more . . . come not at all, never, never!"

The Legend of the Grand Inquisitor did not of a sudden spring full-grown from Dostoevsky's imagination. For its sources, and that peculiar combination in it of elements seldom found in close association, we must look to his intellectual development and political and literary biography.

What is first to be accounted for is the strange amalgam of socialism and Catholicism. The critique of socialism is no more than insinuated in the Legend. Its specifications of time and place are such that socialism can come into it only through oblique references and allusions of an allegoric nature. Thus in the Inquisitor's gloss on the Gospel story of "the temptation" the motif of "stones turned into bread" is brought in again and again so as to convert it into the formula for socialism. The linkage of socialism with the Roman Church, though it may strike Western readers as fantastic, is integral to Dostoevsky's thought.

The connection he saw between these two apparently hostile forces actually dates back to the period of the 1840s, when in his youth he belonged to the Petrashevsky circle of intellectual conspirators. Even then, while reading such ideologues as Fourier, Saint-Simon, Proudhon, and Pierre Lerroux, he was still holding fast to the image of Christ and searching for a way of reconciling it with the socialist creed;* and he was doubtless influenced by the example of Lamennais, the Catholic priest and social philosopher, the apostle to the poor as he was called, who stood for a kind of theocratic democracy and preached the ideals of the French Revolution. His writings were well known to the members of the Petrashevsky circle, and so were such works as V. Menier's *Jésus Christ devant les conseils de guerre* and Cabet's *Le vrai christianisme suivant Jésus Christ.* Now after Dostoevsky's return from penal servitude in Siberia, as he gradually shed his radical views, he began interpreting the connection he had once seen between the Catholic Church and the socialist movement in a different sense, positing the authoritarian principle as the root idea of both. To

---

* In this he differed markedly from his fellow conspirators. Petrashevsky, for instance, once referred to Christ in a private letter as "that notorious demagogue who ended his career somewhat unfortunately."

be sure, the animus against Rome is partly explained by the anti-Western turn of his thought and his growing inclination to identify Christianity exclusively with the Russian people and their national Church. In the main, however, it was the authoritarian idea of the "compulsory organization of human happiness" that was the essential link in his conception of socialism and Catholicism as two aspects of the same heretical self-will driving toward the obliteration of human dignity and freedom of conscience. In *The Diary of a Writer* as in his private notebooks he predicted time and again that the Catholics, deserting the "earthly potentates" with whom they had been allied in the past, would inevitably join forces with the socialists. At other times he varied the prediction (and this is the variant given in the Legend) by saying that socialism would fail and that thereafter the Catholic hierarchy would adopt the socialist dogma of "earthly bread" and by uniting it with its own dogma of "common worship" forge an ideological instrument for the conquest of the universal power it had always striven for. And if we go further back into Dostoevsky's fiction we learn that in *The Idiot* (1868) he was already experimenting with the notions that more than ten years later found their definitive form in the Legend. Thus Myshkin, in a ranting monologue, denounces Catholicism as an unchristian religion that, preaching a "distorted Christ," is "even worse than atheism itself." "The Pope," he cries, "seized the earth ... and grasped the sword. ... How could atheism fail to come from them?" And socialism also comes "from despair in opposition to Catholicism on the moral side, to replace the lost moral power of religion ... and to save humanity not by Christ but by violence. ..."

The critique of socialism in the Legend has its source, too, in a crucial experience of Dostoevsky's youth. This was his relationship with Belinsky, the great radical critic and one of the most dominant and fascinating figures in Russian cultural history, who intervened decisively in Dostoevsky's early career by his laudatory appraisal of his first novel, *Poor Folk*. It can be shown that a key passage in the Inquisitor's speech is a direct transposition of arguments to which Belinsky had recourse in the passionate debates of that early period. Many years later, in a reminiscence entitled "Old People" (*The Diary of a Writer, 1873*), the intrinsic significance of which exceeds any interest we may have in it from the standpoint of provenience in the narrow sense, Dostoevsky summed up what was at stake for him in those debates by recollecting certain scenes involving Belinsky that had long haunted his mind; and the piece as a whole, with its marvelously vivid portrait of the radical critic, suggests, as no purely conceptual formulation could ever do, the agitation of soul and the importunity and immediacy with which those people grasped ideas, striving with might and main not so much to master them for their own sake as to extract from them at all costs a meaning or a truth that would dispel the darkness in which men live and redeem their suffering. "Old People" is in fact a little masterpiece that, in its recovery of the past, recalls us to the very origins of Dostoevsky's complex of ideas. It discloses, if not the personal, then at least the intellectual conditions under which he formed some of his powerful obsessions, as, for instance, the obsession with the personality of Christ to which he at all times yielded even at the expense of Christianity itself.

"Dost Thou know that ages will pass, and humanity will proclaim by the lips of their sages that there is no crime, and therefore no sin; there is only hunger. 'Feed men, and then ask of them virtue!' that's what they'll write on their banner, which they will raise against Thee." Thus begins the passage in the Legend directly echoing Belinsky's thought. It is by no means the only passage of its kind, as the account given in "Old People" sufficiently makes clear.*

> Belinsky was not primarily a reflective person. He was above all an enthusiast, always and throughout his life. My first novel, *Poor Folk,* delighted him ... but then, from the first days of our acquaintance, he threw himself with the most simple-hearted haste into the task of converting me to his creed. . . . I found him to be a passionate socialist, but it was his atheism rather that he at once began urging upon me. There is much that is noteworthy in that, for it reveals his astonishing intuition and extraordinary ability to sound an idea to its very depth. Some two years ago the International began one of its manifestoes with the significant declaration: "We are first of all a society of atheists," that is to say, it began with the essence of the matter. Likewise Belinsky. Valuing above all reason, science, and realism, he nevertheless understood better than anyone else that by themselves reason, science, and realism could produce an antheap but not the social "harmony" in which a human being would be able to dispose of his life properly. He knew that the moral principle is at the root of everything. As for the new moral principle of socialism . . . he believed in it fervently and without reflection; in this respect there was nothing but enthusiasm in his approach. But as a socialist, knowing as he did that the revolution must positively begin with atheism, it was his duty first of all to depose Christianity—the religion from which emerged the moral principles of the society he negated. And

---

* The translation is by the present writer. I have found the English version of *The Diary of a Writer,* brought out in this country in 1949, to be virtually unusable, inept in point of style and frequently far from accurate in rendering the plain meaning of the text.

he radically negated the family, property, the moral responsibility of the individual. (I might add that, like Herzen, he was himself a good husband and a good father.) No doubt he understood that in denying the moral responsibility of man he was depriving him of his freedom; yet at the same time he believed with his whole being that socialism not only does not wipe out the freedom of the individual but, on the contrary, that it actually raises it to unheard-of grandeur, establishing it on adamantine foundations.

All that remained then, was the glowing personality of Christ, with which it was most difficult to cope. As a socialist Belinsky was in duty bound to subvert the teaching of Christ, terming it a mendacious and ignorant idolatry of man, condemned by contemporary science and the principles of political economy. However, there still remained the luminous image of the Son of God, His ethical inaccessibility, His wondrous and miraculous beauty. Belinsky, in his constant, unquenchable enthusiasm, would not be stopped even by this insuperable barrier, as Renan was stopped, who, in his book *Vie de Jésus,* full of unbelief, none the less declared that Christ is the ideal of human beauty, an inaccessible type which humanity can never be expected to bring forth again.

"Do you know?" Belinsky screamed at me one evening (he was always screaming as he got excited). "Do you know that it is not ethical to heap sins upon man and to put him under all sorts of obligations, when society is so badly organized that man cannot help doing evil, since he is economically led to wickedness [*ekonomichesky priveden k zlodeistvu*]. It is inept and cruel to demand of man that which he cannot fulfill according to the laws of his nature, even if he wished to do so."

That evening we were not alone. A friend of Belinsky's was present, a person whom he greatly esteemed and listened to with attention.

"It hurts me to look at him," Belinsky suddenly interrupted his vehement discourse, pointing toward me. "Every time I mention Christ his face changes so, falling to pieces as if he were about to cry. Yes, believe me, simple-hearted man that you are," and here again he threw himself at me, "believe me that that Christ of yours, had he been born in our time, would be the most ordinary, inconsequential person; he would have to efface himself in the presence of contemporary science and leaders of humanity."

"Well, not quite," Belinsky's friend intervened. (I remember that we were sitting down while Belinsky was racing up and down the room.) "Well, no. If Christ were to appear now he would surely join the movement and become its head. . . ."

"Yes, that's it," Belinsky agreed with surprising alacrity. "He would follow the socialists and certainly join them."

"Feed men, and then ask of them virtue!" is the Inquisitor's blunt way of stating Belinsky's protest against the demands made on abused and hungry men in the name of the Christian ethic.* Dostoevsky, ignoring with typical guile the concrete political meaning of this protest, which lay in the struggle against arbitrary power and oppressive institutions, transposed the issue to the philosophical plane and applied himself to disclosing the implications of unfreedom and refusal of moral responsibility in his antagonist's position. He continued his quarrel with Belinsky through the years; but the particular formulation of "stones turned into bread" he first hit upon in the May 1876 issue of *The Diary of a Writer*, where he analyzed the case of a young girl by the name of Pisareva who had committed suicide and whose letter taking leave of her friends had been printed in the newspapers. Pisareva, the daughter of formerly well-to-do landowners, came to Petersburg, as Dostoevsky put it in his article, "to pay her respects to progress and become a midwife . . . but not finding enough significance in earthly medicine and undergoing moral fatigue took her life." He seized upon a part of her letter containing very precise instructions as to the disposal of her petty savings to preach a sermon on the materialistic leanings of the younger generation. "The importance attached to money is perhaps the last echo of the chief prejudice of her life, that of 'stones turned into bread.' In short, here we come upon the leading conviction that if all were economically secure all would be happy and if there were no poor people there would be no crime. There is no such thing as crime. It is a morbid state, induced by poverty and unfortunate circumstances, etc., etc. This comprises the small, conventional, terribly characteristic and ultimate catechism with which they enter life . . . a catechism which they substitute for the living life, for bonds with the soil, faith in the truth, everything, everything." Thereupon the musician V. V. Alexyev wrote to Dostoevsky to inquire about his quotation from the Gospels, the phrase "stones turned into bread." To this query from a reader he replied at length, explaining the import of "bread and stones" in terms of the social pathos of the age and outlining in some detail the main ideological theme of the Legend, which he did not actually write till three years later, in 1879.

The letter to Alexyev contains the ideas of the Legend but no hint of its plot. And of this plot of Christ's return to earth and His encounter with the Inquisitor it should be said that it is not quite so original as it appears at first sight, far less so in fact than the ideological content of the Legend. The return of Christ is a theme touched upon in one way or another by not a few writers whose work Dostoev-

---

* This is of course a recurrent theme of all radical literature, e.g., Bertolt Brecht's famous line in the *Dreigroschen Oper: Erst kommt das Fressen, dann kommt die Moral.*

sky knew well, among them Voltaire, Goethe, Schiller, Jean-Paul Richter, Balzac, Hugo, and Vigny. Here we can only indicate two possible sources that are of particular interest and that Russian scholars have remarked upon. The first is Jean-Paul's fantastic story, "A Dream," in which an atheist gives an account of finding himself in a cemetery at midnight and overhearing a colloquy between Jesus and the dead. The dead ask Him whether God exists and He replies that He had sought God in vain and that everywhere He had come upon nothing but emptiness. Then children rise from their graves and ask: "Jesus, are we really without a father?" "Yes," is the answer, "we are all orphans." The second source is Victor Hugo's poem *Le Christ au Vatican,* an anticlerical pamphlet published in Geneva in 1864. (Dostoevsky, an assiduous reader of Hugo, wrote a preface to the Russian translation of *Notre Dame de Paris.*) In this poem Christ, fearing that men had forgotten His message, resloves to return to earth in His human shape. (*Dépouillons, il le faut, ma divine nature/ Prenons l'habit modeste et l'humaine figure/ Que j'avais en Judée....*) He appears in Rome but is denied access to the Pope. In a conversation with some officials of the Vatican, among them a cardinal, he learns that the popes have long ago assumed the role of Caesar and that *La sainteté a d'autres choses à faire/ Que de penser au Christ, au ciel, au bréviaire.* Christ's retort to this startling news is rendered in the last stanza of the poem:

> Le cardinal parlait encore
> Que Jésus Christ comme sur le Thabor
> S'etait transfiguré. Dans son regard austère
> S'allumaient les éclairs de la sainte colère
> Qui l'anima lorsque jadis
> Il chassa les vendeurs loin du sacré parvis.

Hugo's Christ responds angrily to the cardinal's tale of betrayal, and this must have struck Dostoevsky as an egregious error on the part of the French poet, a symptom no doubt of the pride and self-will ruling the West. In his own version Christ kisses the cardinal and departs quietly — a meek exit entirely in keeping with Dostoevsky's conception of Russian Christianity.

But if Dostoevsky's Christ is so very Russian in his meekness, his Inquisitor is no less Russian in his cruelty. Though appearing in the role of a Catholic hierarch, he is in fact quite as Byzantine as he is Roman, if not more so. However considerable the part he has played in the history of the West, in Russian history he gained even greater ascendancy. From Ivan the Terrible to Stalin he has always known how to apply cruelty, violence, and deception, as well as how to make use of doctrine and dogma, in order to subjugate the people, depriving them of all rights but one — the right to practice the Christian virtue of meekness; and to this day that virtue is still widely practiced in Russia, though to call it a Christian virtue has now been forbidden. Why call it meekness when there are other words for it, such as obedience and discipline?

The historian Kliuchevsky once summed up Russian history in a single sentence: "The state thrives while the people grow sickly." It is this brutalizing national experience which makes for the compelling force of the Legend and is by far the deeper explanation of it. Whatever Dostoevsky's manifest intention, actually it is one of the most revolutionary and devastating critiques of power and authority ever produced. What it comes to in the end is a total rejection of Caesar's realm, a rejection of power in all its forms, in its actuality as in its rationalizations; and it exposes above all the fatal effect of power on such ideals and aspirations of humanity as are embodied in the original Christian teaching. Clearly, then, the Legend cuts under Dostoevsky's persistent efforts to present Eastern Orthodoxy as a viable alternative to the Orthodoxy of the West; the czars, autocrats of church and state alike, were after all quite as grand as any Roman pontiff in their inquisitorial absolutism. Hence it can be said, on this ground and other grounds too, that the implications of the Legend belie the "official" national-religious thesis of the novel as a whole.

For implicit in the Legend is another thesis altogether, that of Russian Christian anarchism. And apart from the Legend there are many intimations of this latent thesis in the novel. It almost emerges to the surface in Chapter 5 of Book II, where Ivan, beginning with an exposition of the ideas in his article on the ecclesiastical courts, ends up by advocating the dissolution of all "earthly states" and their absorption into a church that has in truth abjured "every purpose incongruous with its aims as a Church." To this sketch of a religious Utopia Father Zossima assents, if anything going even further than Ivan, while Father Paissy cries: "So be it, so be it!" One must know how to read the Aesopian language of this singular dialogue, with its undertones, political hints, and ideological anecdotes cunningly introduced at strategic moments and then deliberately cut short before their full intent is disclosed. One such anecdote, for example, is related by the liberal Miüsov whose very liberalism serves here as a screen behind which the author can have his say without too obviously compromising himself. Miüsov tells of meeting a Frenchman in Paris, an influential personage in the government, who confides in him that "we are not particularly afraid of all those socialists, anarchists, infidels and revolutionists. . . . But there are a few peculiar men among them who believe in God and are Christians, but at the same time are socialists. These are the people we are most afraid of. . . . The socialist who is a Christian is more to be dreaded than a socialist who is an atheist." In the given context this comes through as virtually a confession on Dostoevsky's part. The crypto-anarchist or socialist element in the novel was not noticed, to be sure, by Dostoevsky's reactionary mentors, such as Pobedonostsev for instance,* who lauded him for showing up the disrupters of the imperial authority without suspecting that he himself — or was it his double? — was inextricably involved with them. Merezhkovsky was essentially right, I think, in the claim he once made that the author of *The Brothers Karamazov,* though fearful of speaking out, was at bottom a religious revolutionist.

The Russian intelligentsia of the nineteenth century was deeply antagonistic to state and empire. It produced all sorts of libertarian ideas, secular and religious, which, while related to Western influences, at the same time reflect the elemental hatred of authority prevailing among the peasant masses, a hatred sometimes taking the form of blind anarchic revolt but more often that of meek submission; yet the submission has something about it so flagrant, a perfection of abjectness as it were, which is in itself a kind of challenge and provocation. It goes without saying that Dostoevsky was thoroughly infected with such feelings, and that their ambivalence suited his psychological make-up. And, in speaking of this anarchism, what is meant by it is nothing like a theoretically worked-out doctrine, as that of Bakunin or Kropotkin; he was hardly able to distinguish between anarchism and socialism. The one emphatic distinction he did make was between believing and unbelieving rebels; and if he was an opponent of the socialists it was, on the conscious level at any rate, because of their atheism, which he struggled to suppress in himself, and the totalitarian potential he discerned in their designs. Inevitably his religious anarchism brings to mind the anarchism of Tolstoy, and in this respect it is instructive to compare the two novelists. Dostoevsky's anarchism is fully as utopian as that of Tolstoy but with these important differences: it is latent rather than manifest in his work and it is mystical rather

* Pobedonostsev, at that time procurator of the Holy Synod and tutor of the crown prince, was an out-and-out reactionary authoritarian bearing in his role and personality a rather strong family-likeness to the Grand Inquisitor: so much so in fact that some Russian critics (e.g., Georgi Chulkov in *Kak rabotal Dostoevski*) have speculated on the possibility of Dostoevsky actually having had him in mind as a model even while enjoying his patronage and writing him letters of fulsome flattery.

than rational in conception; its political aims are ill-defined and ambiguous; intrinsically it is more the expression of an apocalyptic mood than of a radical will to revolution as a practical enterprise. The notion of a "free theocracy" expounded by Ivan is a contradiction in terms — a system of government by priests is scarcely the medium in which freedom might be expected to flourish. But if it is a contradiction, it is exactly of the type, holding in balance his conflicting impulses toward rebellion and submission, to which Dostoevsky was always irresistibly drawn.

In the late 1870s, the period of the composition of *The Brothers Karamazov,* his exasperation grew as he watched the continuing attraction of Russian youth to subversive doctrines. He felt the need to provide some kind of alternative to those godless doctrines, and one surmises that that was the motive for his advancing, even if tentatively, the idea of the regeneration of society through the rise of a "free theocracy." This idea, however, is so vaguely related to the real forces at work in Russian society, so utopian in essence, as to suggest its makeshift character as a hastily mounted countermove, from the position of religious radicalism, to the atheistical radicalism of his opponents among the intellectuals. On a deeper level, and without abandoning in any way his faith in the Russian Christ, he yet reacted to the signs of disintegration all around him by becoming more and more skeptical of man's capacity for salvation and the meaningfulness of his history. Thus he came to fear that the weakness of men would eventually bring on a successful attempt to organize their happiness by compulsion. This theme was not new to him. He had dealt with it before, in *Notes from Underground* and in *The Possessed.*

It is interesting to compare his earlier and later handling of this theme of "the compulsory organization of human happiness." Let us begin, then, by putting the Grand Inquisitor into relation with another and quite as famous protagonist of Dostoevsky's, the hero-narrator of *Notes from Underground.* It is for the content of their thought that they are worth comparing, and not primarily as novelistic creations. The aged cardinal of Seville, lacking the dimension of subjectivity so conspicuous in the underground man, is not a character in the proper sense of the term but simply the personification of a *Weltanschauung* — that of Ivan Karamazov in its most heretical and negative aspects. The undergroundling, on the other hand, is very far from being merely the embodiment of an idea. Still, in linking him with the Inquisitor, our concern is not with the undergroundling's prostrate personality, with his nausea of consciousness and enjoyment of his own degradation, but rather with the theory of human nature he propounds, a theory in which the bold affirmation of freedom is combined with the equally bold negation of "reason, progress and enlightenment."

What this theory has in common with that of the Inquisitor is that both are centered on the question of freedom. Where they differ is in their answers to this question, the undergroundling's answer being as positive as the Inquisitor's is negative. Hence the contrast between the two theories gives us the measure of the growth and change of Dostoevsky's thought between the early 1860s, when he wrote *Notes from Underground,* and the period of his last and greatest novel. The earlier work is written from the perspective of the isolated and perversely recalcitrant individual, who, in his "moral obliquity," will never consent to join the "universal and happy antheap" projected by the ideologues of rational self-interest and progress toward an harmonious society. Through the figure of this unconsoled and unconsolable individual Dostoevsky pointed to the chaos and irrationality of human nature, thus mocking the utilitarian formulas of the radicals and liberals. "Man everywhere and at all times . . . has preferred to act as he chose and not in the least as his reason and advantage dictated. . . . One's own unfettered choice, one's own caprice . . . is that very 'most advantageous advantage' . . . against which all systems and theories are shattered to atoms. . . . What man wants is simply *independent* choice, whatever that independence may cost and wherever it may lead." He readily admits that man "likes to make roads and to create," but this admission goes with the emphatic reminder that man also loves chaos and destruction. He is therefore convinced that the organization of a rational society — which, in his view, cannot but turn out to be a human antheap — will prove forever impossible.

Now this is a vision entirely at variance with that of the Inquisitor, whose idea it is that "independent choice" is exactly what men fear most; that is the source both of his contempt for them and his paradoxical determination to strip them of the useless gift of free choice so as to convert them into the childishly happy and ignorant members of a totalitarian collective. He proclaims the failure of historical Christianity to illuminate and sanctify human existence, but this failure he imputes not to the church but to the falsity of Christ's message in the light of the proven inadequacy of human nature. Consequently the church can have no function but that of an instrument of power in the hands of an elite that has taken up the sword of Caesar. Since man is feebler and baser than Christ believed him to be, it was senseless to bring him the gift of freedom. The weak soul is unable to benefit from such heady gifts. The Inquisitor is not a psychologist pure and simple, like the undergroundling. In his thought psychological insights are supported by historical facts. Another difference is that the primary object of his polemic is what he takes to be the illusion of human freedom, whereas the undergroundling makes reason the target of his devaluating analysis.

When it came to writing *The Brothers Karamazov* Dostoevsky had wholly surmounted the standpoint of defiant and obdurate individualism exhibited in *Notes from Underground*. He then thought that the Palace of Crystal (at that time his prime symbol of socialism, superseded later by the Tower of Babel, a more cheerless symbol) would never be built because men were too independent to permit its construction. This type of individualism, however, with its stress on the unfettered human will and the inexhaustible intransigence of self-pride, is not really consonant with the religious valuation of life. It is, in fact, a secular type of individualism which can be turned quite as effectively against Christian philosophies as against the philosophy of social progress; the recalcitrant individual may after all refuse to choose Christ in the same "irrational" way as he refuses to submit to the dictates of reason and self-interest. "Moral obliquity" provides as insecure a foundation for the Kingdom of God as for the Kingdom of Man. It is only in later years, as his religious consciousness became fully engaged in his creative effort, that Dostoevsky developed a new idea of freedom, based not on "moral obliquity" but on Christian love and the unviolated conscience.

Also, it is important to note that so far as socialism is concerned it is mainly the conception of it dramatized in *The Possessed* which is epitomized in the Legend, and that, in a sense, the figure of the Inquisitor also derives from that novel, being an elaborated and historically enriched variant of the sketchy figure of Shigalov. It will be remembered that Shigalov, an eccentric ideologue, comes to the conclusion that unlimited freedom can be attained only through unlimited despotism, or, rather, that the extremes of freedom and despotism are in reality identical. Accordingly he proposes, as no less than "a final solution of the social question," that mankind be divided into two unequal parts, one-tenth enjoying "absolute liberty and unbounded power over the other nine-tenths. The others have given up all individuality and become, so to speak, a herd, and, through boundless submission, will by a series of regenerations achieve primeval innocence, something like the Garden of Eden. They'll have to work, however." The society envisaged by the Inquisitor is plainly a later edition of Shigalov's herd, and the latter's elite is even further reduced in numbers by the Inquisitor: "There will be thousands of millions of happy babes, and a hundred thousand sufferers who have taken upon themselves the curse of the knowledge of good and evil." The reign of the "sufferers" will be cruel, of course, for they believe that their cruelty will guarantee the happiness of the rest of mankind. Moreover, as Albert Camus has remarked, they excuse their cruelty by claiming, like the Satan of the Romantics, that it will be hard for them to bear.

Yet there is no denying that even this mordant reading of the historical past and future did not deter Dostoevsky from asserting his belief that freedom of choice in the knowledge of good and evil is the essence of man's humanity and the essence of Christ's teaching. The kind of faith or obedience that is bought with bread is evil, and so is any constraint on man's conscience, in whatever form, even if the constraint is exercised for ostensibly good ends. Freedom is not to be confounded with goodness or happiness. Goodness festers if bred by constraint, and happiness turns into brutish contentment. Only when freely chosen do they acquire a human content. This is precisely what makes Dostoevsky a novelist of tragic freedom, his perception that genuine freedom, being open to the choice between good and evil, is unthinkable without suffering. That is the price of freedom, and he who refuses to pay it can only dream of freedom without experiencing it, without substantiating it within the actual process of living. It is a conception which on one side of it is close to existentialist thought. For Dostoevsky, as for the existentialists, it is above all through the experience of choice and decision, resolutely entered upon, that the individual comes to self-realization. But this grasp and possession of one's own being, which is the human creature's truest rapture, is at the same time inescapably associated with anxiety and suffering, and for this reason men are continually driven to shirk meaningful choices. However, the difference between some of the latter-day existentialists and Dostoevsky is that for him the act of choosing is wholly a moral if not always a religious act while for them it is an act unconditionally open to existence in all its sheerness and totality, not limited to any single sphere, ethical or otherwise.

Now in the Legend Dostoevsky so represents the truth of history — that is, the truth not of what ought to be but of what is and has been — that we see it as patently belonging to the Inquisitor, not to Christ. Dostoevsky nonetheless takes his stand with Christ. This should not surprise us; if we consider his biography in its temporal depth, so to speak, we find that he committed himself very early to this clinging to Christ in the face of all the malignant realities of history and man's nature. More than twenty-five years before composing the Legend he wrote in a letter from his place of exile in Siberia that if it were proven to him that Christ is "outside the truth, and if the truth really did exclude Christ, I should prefer to stay with Christ and not with the truth."

This paradoxical attitude is not to be taken as mere sentiment. It has its consequences. In the context of the Legend it means that if Dostoevsky rejects the wisdom of the Inquisitor, it is solely in the terms of the desperate paradox of his faith in Christ. Otherwise he apparently neither doubts nor denies that malign wisdom. What is to be observed, too, is that he thus indirectly fulfills his ideological aim of excluding any middle ground between Christ and the Grand Inquisitor. And the starkness and ultimatism of the choice he offers, which has the effect of shrinking our sense of historical possibilities and reducing our resourcefulness in the face of extremes, reminds us of other great thinkers of the nineteenth century, like Kierkegaard and Marx, who likewise made war, though from other standpoints, on that century's liberal humanism — Kierkegaard with his either-or formula that is spiritually quite as terroristic as that of the Russian novelist, and Marx with his inexorable idea that if humanity fails to choose socialism it will inevitably fall back into barbarism.

Partisan Review, 1954

Dostoevsky in
Crime and Punishment

When thought is closed in caves
The love shall show its roots in deepest hell.
WILLIAM BLAKE

Is THIS THE TYPE of narrative nowadays called a psycho-thriller? Yes, in a sense it is, being above all, in its author's own words, the psychological account of a crime. The crime is murder. But in itself this is in no way exceptional, for the very same crime occurs in nearly all of Dostoevsky's novels. Proust once suggested grouping them together under a single comprehensive title: The Story of a Crime.

Where this novel differs, however, from the works following it is in the totality of its concentration on that obsessive theme. Virtually everything in the story turns on Raskolnikov's murder of the old pawn-broker and her sister Lizaveta, and it is this concentration which makes the novel so fine an example of artistic economy and structural cohesion. Free of distractions of theme and idea, and with no confusing excess or overingenuity in the manipulation of the plot, such as vitiates the design of *A Raw Youth* and reduces the impact of *The Idiot, Crime and Punishment* is the one novel of Dostoevsky's in which his powerful appeal to our intellectual interests is most directly and naturally linked to the action.

The superiority of this work in point of structure has been repeatedly remarked upon, but what has not been sufficiently noted is its extraordinary narrative pace. Consider the movement of Part I, for instance. In this comparatively short section (coming to eighty-four pages in Constance Garnett's translation), we get to know the protagonist fairly well, to know the conditions of crushing poverty and isolation under which he lives and the complex origins of his "loathsome scheme"; we see him going through a rehearsal-visit to the victim's flat; we listen to Marmeladov's sermon in the pothouse, to the recital of his domestic woes, including the circumstances that forced his daughter Sonia to become a prostitute; we witness the drunken old man's homecoming and the hysterical violence with which he is received by his wife; then we read with Raskolnikov the long letter from his mother, learning a good deal about his family situation; we dream with him the frightful dream, looking at once to the past and to the future, of the beating to death of the little mare; finally, after several more scenes of the strictest dramatic relevance, we are brought to a close-up of the double murder, probably the most astonishing description of its kind in fiction, and watch the murderer returning to his lodgings where, after putting back the ax under the porter's bench, he climbs the stairs to sink on his bed in blank forgetfulness.

Thus in this first section of seven chapters a huge quantity of experience is qualitatively organized, with the requisite information concerning the hero's background driven into place through a consummate use of the novelistic device of foreshortening, and with the swift narrative tempo serving precisely as the prime means of controlling and rendering credible the wild queerness of what has been recounted. For this wild queerness cannot be made to yield to explanation or extrinsic analysis. To gain our consent — to enlist, that is, our poetic faith — the author must either dramatize or perish, and for full success he must proceed with the dramatic representation at a pace producing an effect of virtual instantaneousness. To have secured this effect is a triumph of Dostoevsky's creative method — a triumph because the instantaneous is a quality of Being rather than of mind and not open to question. As the vain efforts of so many philosophers have demonstrated, Being is irreducible to the categories of explanation or interpretation.

The artistic economy, force, and tempo of Part I is sustained throughout the novel. (The epilogue, in which hope and belief play havoc with the imaginative logic of the work, is something else again.) There is no wasted detail in it, none that can be shown to be functionally inoperative in advancing the action and our insight into its human agents. And it is important to observe that the attaining of this fullness and intensity of representation is conditional upon Dostoevsky's capacity to subdue the time element of the story to his creative purpose. Readers not deliberately attentive to the time lapse of the action are surprised to learn that its entire span is only two weeks and that of Part I only three days. Actually, there is no real lapse of time in the story because we are virtually unaware of it apart from the tension of the rendered experience. Instead of time lapsing there is the concrete flow of duration contracting and expanding with the rhythm of the dramatic movement.

Least of all is it a chronological frame that time provides in this novel. As the Russian critic K. Mochulsky has so aptly remarked, its time is purely psychological, a function of human consciousness, in other words the very incarnation of Bergson's *durée réele.** And it is only in Bergsonian terms that one can do it justice. Truly, Dostoevsky succeeds here in converting time into a kind of progress of Raskolnikov's mental state, which is not actually a state but a process of incessant change eating into the future and expanding with the duration it accumulates, like a snowball growing larger as it rolls upon itself, to use Bergson's original image.

This effect is partly accomplished by the exclusion from Raskolnikov's consciousness of everything not directly pertaining to his immediate situation. From beginning to end he is in a state of crisis from which there is no diversion or escape either in memory or fantasy. The import of what he thinks, feels, and remembers is strictly functional to the present. Thus he thinks of his mother, who is involved in the action, with distinct alternations of feelings, while his dead father hardly exists for him. He belongs to the past, and so far as Raskolnikov is concerned the past is empty of affect. The one time he evokes his father's figure is in the anguished dream of the beating to death of the little mare, and his appearance in that dream is singularly passive, manifestly carrying with it no charge of emotion. This dream, enacting a tragic catharsis, is introduced with calculated ambiguity. Is the dreamer actually remembering an episode of his childhood or is he imagining the memory? In any case, though the dream is of the past its meaning is all in the present. The pitiful little mare, whipped across the eyes and butchered by Mikolka and a crowd of rowdy peasants, stands for all such victims of life's insensate cruelty, in particular such victims as Sonia and Lizaveta whose appeal to Raskolnikov is that of "poor gentle things . . . whose eyes are soft and gentle." Also, the mare stands above all for Raskolnikov himself, and in embracing her bleeding head in a frenzy of compassion it is himself he is embracing, bewailing, consoling. He is present in the dream not only as the little boy witnessing an act of intolerable brutality but as at once its perpetrator and victim too. The dream's imagery is entirely prospective in that it points ahead, anticipating the murder Raskolnikov is plotting even while exposing it as an act of self-murder. Its

---

* K. Mochulsky, *Dostoevskii: zhizn i tvorchestvo* (Paris, 1947), p. 243 ff.

latent thought-content is a warning that in killing the pawnbroker he would be killing himself too, and it is indeed in this light that he understands his deed afterwards when, in confessing to Sonia, he cries out: "Did I murder the old woman? I murdered myself, not her! I crushed myself once and for all, forever." The cathartic effect of the dream is such that upon awakening he recovers the sense of his human reality, feeling "as though an abscess that had been forming in his heart had suddenly broken . . . he was free from that spell, that sorcery, that obsession." But the catharsis is momentary, and he no sooner hears that the pawnbroker will be alone in her flat the next evening than he is again gripped by his obsession.

Another instance of the functional character of Raskolnikov's memory is the way he recalls the invalid girl to whom he had once been engaged. "I really don't know," he says, "what drew me to her then . . . she was always ill. If she had been lame or hunchback, I believe I would have liked her even better." This is a meaningful admission, and it is curious that the numerous commentators on the novel should have unanimously ignored it. It is as if they all wanted to spare Sonia. For what prompts this memory if not his involvement with Sonia, who is in her own way ill too? In the eyes of the world and likewise of Raskolnikov in some of his moods she is a morally deformed creature, an outcast, and "a religious maniac" to boot. Physically, too, the description of the invalid girl has much in common with that of Sonia.

Yet, for all his living in the present, Raskolnikov wills and acts with his whole past back of him; and it is for a very good reason that we are not permitted to gain a privileged understanding of his past in the sense of entering a series of his mental states anterior to the action. By denying us such intimacy the author effectively prevents us from rationalizing the mystery of the crime and its motive — the mystery which is never really solved but toward the solution of which everything in the novel converges. Now the study of Dostoevsky's manuscripts has shown that he was himself disturbed no end by the indefiniteness and uncertainty of Raskolnikov's motive, and he wrote a note reminding himself that he must once and for all clear up the uncertainty and isolate the "real" motive in order "to destroy," as he put it, "the indefiniteness and explain the murder this way or that way [*tak ili etak*]." Fortunately he was able to forget this injunction as the novel progressed. For his basic idea of his hero's motivation is such as to identify it with the totality of his consciousness, and to have changed that conception to a more conventional one would have led to the withering of that fine insight; and what that insight comes to, in the last analysis, is that human consciousness is inexhaustible and incalculable. It cannot be condensed into something so limited and specific as a motive. The consciousness is ever obliging in generating a sufficiency of reasons, but it is necessary to distinguish between reasons and motives. Not that motives have no existence; they exist, to be sure, but only on the empirical plane, materializing in the actual practice of living, primarily in the commitment of action. Existentially speaking, the acting man can be efficient and self-assured only in so far as his consciousness is nonreflective. Raskolnikov, however, is above all a man of reflection, and his crime is frequently described in the book as a "theoretical" one, "theoretical" not only in the sense of its being inspired by a theory but also in the sense that theory, that is to say abstraction, is of its very essence: no wonder he carries out the murder in the manner of a sleepwalker or of a man falling down a precipice. The textual evidence shows that what his crime mainly lacks is empirical content, and that is what some critics had in mind, I think, in defining it as a pure experiment in self-cognition. Thus it can be said of this murderer that he produces a corpse but no real motive. His consciousness, time and again recoiling upon itself in a sickening manner, consumes motives as fast as it produces them.

Crime and Punishment may be characterized as a psycho-thriller with prodigious complications. It is misleading, however, to speak of it as a detective story, as is so often done. It is nothing of the sort, since from the outset we know not only the murderer's identity but are also made to enter into some of his innermost secrets. True, the story is almost entirely given over to detection — not of the criminal, though, but of his motive. Inevitably it turns out that there is not one but a whole cluster of motives, a veritable *embarras de richesses,* and if the criminal himself is in his own fashion constrained to take part in the work of detection it is because he is soon lost in the maze of his own motivation. Never quite certain as to what it was exactly that induced him to commit murder, he must continually spy on himself in a desperate effort to penetrate his own psychology and attain the self-knowledge he needs if he is to assume responsibility for his absurd and hideous act. And this idea of him as the criminal in search of his own motive is precisely what is so new and original in the figure of Raskolnikov.

His knowing and not knowing is in a sense the worst of his ordeal. He is aware of several motives that keep eluding him as his thought shifts among them, and there are times when they all seem equally unreal to him. To sustain himself in the terrible isolation of his guilt he must be in complete possession of a single incontrovertible motive representing his deepest self, his own rock-bottom truth. But he no sooner lays hold of this truth than he catches himself in a state of mind that belies it, as, for example, in the scene when right after burying the loot — a purse and some trinkets of jewelry — he suddenly stops in the street to confound himself with a simple and terrifying question:

> If it had all really been done deliberately and not idiotically, if I really had a certain and definite object, how is it that I did not even glance into the purse and didn't know what I had there. Then why have I undergone these agonies and have deliberately undertaken this base, dirty and degrading business?

This is but one of several passages in which the abstraction, so to speak, of the crime, its lack of empirical substance, is brought home to us. There is an intrinsic incongruity between this criminal and his crime which is exhibited by the author with masterful indirection, and nowhere to better effect than when Raskolnikov makes his confession to Sonia. In the course of it, though straining as hard as he can to discover and at long last seize the motive that impelled him, he still cannot stop wavering and giving various and contradictory explanations of his act. He begins by stating that he murdered "for plunder," but when Sonia cries: "You were hungry! It was to help your mother? Yes?" he at once retracts that explanation, muttering: "No, Sonia, no.... I was not so hungry.... I certainly did want to help my mother, but that's not the real thing either...." A little later he adds that if he had simply killed the old pawnbroker because of hunger he would be *happy* now, exclaiming that he really wanted to become a Napoleon and that is why he killed her. Yet still later we hear him say that the argument from Napoleon is "all nonsense" as he reverts to the explanation from poverty and simple need. Soon enough, however, he strikes again the Napoleonic note, accounting for the murder now as a matter of wanting to have the daring: "I only wanted to have the daring ... that was the whole cause of it"; he claims that he killed "not to gain wealth and power" but for himself alone so as to find out quickly whether "he was a louse like everybody else or a man," whether he was a "trembling creature" or one who has "the right" to step over barriers. Still another cause, more immediately psychological in bearing, is introduced when he speaks of his airless cupboard of a room, that room where he turned sulky and sat "like a spider," where he would not work but simply lay for hours thinking. It is chiefly this perpetual thinking, this desperate resort to sheer reflection, which is the source of the mystifications that torment him. Though it is his consciousness which did him in, it is to his empirical self that he absurdly looks for the justification it cannot supply; so that in the end, for all the keenness with which he explicates his act to Sonia, we are still left with a crime of indeterminate origin and meaning.

The indeterminacy is the point. Dostoevsky is the first novelist to have fully accepted and dramatized the principle of uncertainty or indeterminacy in the presentation of character. In terms of novelistic technique this principle manifests itself as a kind of hyperbolic suspense — suspense no longer generated merely by the traditional means and devices of fiction, though these are skillfully brought into play, but as it were by the very structure of human reality. To take this hyperbolic suspense as a literary invention pure and simple is to fail in comprehending it; it originates rather in Dostoevsky's acute awareness (self-awareness at bottom) of the problematical nature of the modern personality and of its tortuous efforts to stem the disintegration threatening it. Thus Raskolnikov, like Stavrogin and other protagonists of Dostoevsky's, is represented throughout under the aspect of modernity (the examining magistrate Porfiry Petrovitch sees him very specifically as "a modern case"), understood as spiritual and mental self-division and self-contradiction. It is in this light that the search for the true cause of the crime becomes ultimately intelligible, the search that gives the novel at once its form and meaning, taking us where no psycho-thriller before or after *Crime and Punishment* has ever taken us, into a realm where only the sharpest psychological perception will see us through and into another realm still where our response to ideas is impetuously solicited: ideas bearing on crime and its relation to psychic illness on the one hand and to power and genius on the other; ideas about two kinds of human beings, ordinary and extraordinary, with the former serving as mere material for the latter, who arrogate to themselves the right "to overstep the line" and remove moral obstacles at will; ideas concerning the supernal value of suffering and the promise of deliverance in Christ.

The principal characters (Raskolnikov, Svidrigailov, and others) are the carriers of these ideas, and if we are not to sever the unity of thought and action, theory and practice, prevailing in the Dostoevskyean world, it is necessary to take their ideas for what they are, without reducing them, with the purely psychological critics, to a species of "interesting" rationalizations, or, with the formalistic critics, to mere "fictive matter" drawn fortuitously from the intellectual sphere. That we must first of all regard the ideas as dramatic motivation goes without saying; but that should not deter us from also accepting them as given on the level of thought. "I killed not an old woman but a

principle," declares Raskolnikov. What is that principle and why does
he want to kill it? The answer to such questions has been much
simplified or, worse still, credulously taken for granted.

From the Christian standpoint Raskolnikov is easily enough perceived to be a kind of Lazarus whom Sonia strives to raise from the
dead. Yet if he comes forth from the tomb it is only after experiencing
the ecstasy and terror of having touched for one moment the secret
springs of freedom and power. "What, then, is to be done?" asks
Sonia. This is indeed the fateful question which reverberates throughout the whole of Russian literature and to which all the leaders of
Russian thought, from Chaadayev to Lenin, sought to provide an
answer. Raskolnikov, too, accepts the challenge. "Break what must
be broken," he replies, "once and for all, and take the suffering on
oneself.... Freedom and power! Over all trembling creation and all
the antheap!... That is the goal, remember that!" No wonder that
though apparently renouncing that goal in yielding to Sonia's entreat-
ies that he save himself through penance and submission, he nevertheless remains essentially unrepentant to the end. At the very least
it can be said that he remains so deeply divided in his mind as to
give himself up more because of confusion and despair than because
of any real change of heart. About his regeneration we are told only
in the epilogue, when at long last the pale sickly faces of the murderer
and the saintly prostitute become "bright with the dawn of a new
future." But this happy Siberian aftermath is the beginning of something altogether new and different. As the author observes in the last
paragraph of the text, it "might be the subject of a new story but our

---

* It might indeed have been the subject of a new story. However, Dostoevsky,
as a number of critics have noted, appears to have been incapable of carrying out
his declared intention to depict the renewal of life on Christian foundations. On
this score the late Leo Shestov made one of the most sardonic notations: "*Crime
and Punishment* ends with the promise to picture the Christian rebirth of the
hero. His words sound as if he were binding himself with a sacred vow. And,
in point of fact, as a professed teacher of humanity, was not Dostoevsky in duty
bound to let us in on the secret of the new reality and fresh possibilities that
opened up to Raskolnikov? Yet our preceptor never managed to fulfill that sacred
vow. The same promise is encountered again in his foreword to *The Brothers
Karamazov*, where we are told that in order to portray his real hero, Alyosha, he
would need to write still another volume, as if the existing book with its thousand
pages lacked sufficient space to accommodate the 'new life.' In the three novels
he produced after *Crime and Punishment* there is no mention of the sacred vow.
Prince Myshkin cannot be taken into account here. If he is the one representing
the 'renewal' awaiting mankind ... then there is no point whatever in looking
toward the future.... No, compared to Dostoevsky's other heroes Prince Myshkin is a misfit. This novelist understood only restless, fractious, stuggling people
whose search is never ended. No sooner did he undertake to show us a man who
has found himself and achieved tranquillity than he fell into fatal banalities. One

present story is ended."* We, as critical readers, cannot overmuch concern ourselves with such intimations of ultimate reconcilement and salvation. Our proper concern is with the present story, with the story as written.

Dostoevsky wrote the first of his four great novels in monthly install-ments for the *Russky Vestnik,* where it ran serially between January and December 1866. He was following his usual course of producing a long work under the immediate pressure of editors and printers. In this instance, however, he appears to have encountered very few diffi-culties in meeting the magazine's schedule. And the ease with which he accomplished the actual composition may have been partly due at least to the fact that the narrative mode he had adopted after con-siderable experimenting and much vacillation, the mode, that is, of telling the story from the standpoint of the "omniscient author," justi-fied itself in practice, allowing him to make the most of his material without strain or hindrance.

The strain had indeed told on him in the late months of 1865, when while living in Wiesbaden he had written an incomplete draft of the novel in the form both of a diary and of a murderer's confession. Those versions turned out to be so unsatisfactory, chiefly because of the cramping effects of the method of narration in the first person, that he was forced to scrap them. The economy of interest he had been trying to enforce by means of that method proved to be too much of a good thing, and he now took exactly the opposite tack, expand-ing the interest where formerly he had compressed it. Into the new expansive scheme he introduced the figures of Svidrigailov and Porfiry Petrovitch, who have nothing in common besides the fact that both represent possible attitudes toward Raskolnikov, viewpoints or per-spectives enabling us to see at once more clearly and more variously the significance of his case. Dostoevsky also introduced into his revised scheme the basic elements of a tale, entitled *The Drunkards,* which he had just sketched out in outline and in which he was proposing to enter into "all the ramifications" of the then rather topical subject of alcoholism rampant among the city poor, with the emphasis falling on "the picture of a family and the bringing up of children under such circumstances." It is in this somewhat fortuitous manner, or so it

---

thinks, for instance, of the elder Zossima's dreams of 'the coming wonderful union of men.' What is this 'wonderful union' if not another of those idyllic pictures of the future which even the socialists — so maliciously ridiculed in his cellar by the narrator of *Notes from Underground* — have by now learned to do without?" *Do-stoevskii i Nitsshe: filosofiya tragedii* (St. Petersburg, 1903).

would seem on the face of it, that the Marmeladov sequence, so reminiscent of the author's earlier vein in its pathos of indigence and harrowing exposition of the Petersburg misery, as the Russians are wont to call it, came to be included in the account of Raskolnikov's crime.

But the fortuitousness is more apparent than real. There is an inner logic, both of content and structure, in his combination of subject matter, from which the novel gains enormously — and this can be said even while conceding that the rather stagey woes of the Marmeladovs are inducive of some moments of weariness. A somewhat Dickensian family with deviations toward Russian intensity, they are of course the very embodiment of the Petersburg misery. But Raskolnikov is also a child of that misery, patently belonging to the world of the insulted and injured, though in him the humility and submissiveness of that world's human mixture are turned inside out. He is the first of its inhabitants to attempt its redemption by making a bid, in however futile and hideous a fashion, for freedom and power.

Intrinsically his figure is a composite of the typical protagonists of Dostoevsky's earlier and later fiction. Morbidly estranged as he is from life and ceaselessly brooding in his cupboard of a room, he at once brings to mind certain traits of the underground man as well as of the daydreaming recluse portrayed in such stories of the 1840s as "The Landlady" and "White Nights" — the recluse who, suffering from nearly pathological depression and nameless guilt feelings, keeps to himself and lives a life of wishful fantasy. At the same time Raskolnikov represents a startling departure from the recluse type in that, having overcome the latter's masochistic need for self-abasement, his aggression is no longer turned inward but outward. He is quite as much a fantast as the daydreaming recluse, but his fantasy has left behind it all *Schwärmerei* and noble aspiration *à la* Schiller: it has taken on the color of blood. A complete egoist on one side of his nature at least and a surprisingly candid one at that, he is filled with the wrath of outraged pride and a furious impatience to break out from his trapped existence even at the risk of self-destruction. Moreover, to see him from this angle of vision, as the Dostoevskyean hero in process of evolution, is to note another new element in him, namely, that he is an intellectual *pur sang*, recklessly yielding himself to the passion of thought and caught at last in the toils of an idea, mastered by it to the point of monomania. Thus the novel of which he is the protagonist has a double aspect. In virtue of its carryover of the theme of the Petersburg misery it brings to a close the series of so-called social narratives which, from *Poor Folk* to *The Insulted and Injured,* is dominated by a consistent motif that has been aptly defined as that of "the impotent protest of powerless people." In its second aspect, however, the novel throws off the limitations of the earlier theme, attaining the higher goals of its author's greater or ultimate period.

Raskolnikov's involvement with the Marmeladov clan enabled Dostoevsky to solve what must have been his main compositional problem: How to portray with entire cogency a hero who is a solitary and monomaniac acting throughout in a mood of "morbid irritability" verging on madness, without succumbing to him, that is to say, without letting him take the lead to the degree of making the world over in his image? This is but another way of formulating one of the principal difficulties which forced Dostoevsky to abandon the first versions of the book. For to have permitted Raskolnikov, as first-person narrator, to absorb the story unto himself would surely have resulted in its impoverishment, producing an impression of life closing in, a claustrophobic effect diminishing the hero's stature in our eyes and turning him into an altogether special case.* And this is where the Marmeladovs come in exactly, that for all the grimness of their situation and its grotesque features they still somehow exist within the bounds of the normal, whereas Raskolnikov is decidedly outside it; hence their presence adds considerably to the story's quota of circumstantial realism, helping to overcome the hazard implicit in Raskolnikov's malaise. For we must keep in mind that his story, which on one side is an account of a crime open to explanation on the seemingly objective grounds of material need and a sinister "nihilistic" theory, is converted on the subjective side into an analysis of an extreme pathological condition or soul-sickness, if you will.

The episodes dealing with Svidrigailov, the would-be seducer of Raskolnikov's sister Dounia, have an engrossing interest of their own, but they also serve the same functional purpose of reducing the protagonist's remoteness from the common human measure. In order to heighten the dramatic tension and explore to the end the complex meanings of Raskolnikov's plight, it was positively necessary to involve him in intimate human associations, notwithstanding the feeling of absolute aloneness, of "agonizing, everlasting solitude," into which he is plunged by his murderous act. It is a feeling brought on by the

---

* The special or clinical case is precisely what no master of the narrative medium will let himself in for. Dostoevsky did let himself in for it once, in the early nouvelle, *The Double*, which, for all its startling effects, cannot be rated otherwise than as a failure. He never repeated that youthful error. In lesser talents, however, this error becomes habitual, for in coping with the extremes of morbidity or irrationality they are frequently lured into betraying the shared sense of human reality.

guilt he refuses to acknowledge and strains every nerve to repress; and what better way was there of dramatizing the struggle within him between guilt and scornful pride than by showing him entering almost in spite of himself into relations with people who for reasons both good and bad are intent on penetrating his isolation? Sonia, his "chosen bride" and Christian mentor, is of course the chief agent of this turn of the plot, but so in his own paradoxical fashion is Svidrigailov. The latter, however, is so fascinating a character in his own right, exercising an appeal nearly matching that of the hero, that at times he threatens to run away with the story; certainly the scene of his suicide and of the dream-haunted night that precedes it are perfectly realized incidents and among the marvels of the book. It must have called for the nicest management on the author's part to hold him to his subordinate position. But that was only part of the task Dostoevsky set himself in undertaking to unify the three thematic elements at his disposal: the major theme of Raskolnikov's crime and its consequences and the strongly contrasted minor themes of the lowly and good Marmeladovs on the one hand and of the wealthy immoralist Svidrigailov on the other. And it is the achieved integration with its fine contrapuntal effects which makes for verisimilitude of a higher order, for novelistic truth and density, and for structural cohesion.

But though the Svidrigailov sequence is successfully integrated into the main action, there is no denying that he is invested with an originality and expressive power that invite comment. It will not do to see him, in the fashion of most critics of Dostoevsky, as being merely Raskolnikov's double, representing the pole of self-will in his character. The formal abstractness of this traditional approach to Svidrigailov cannot do him justice; and so far as the element of self-will is concerned, Raskolnikov, like all "the children of darkness" in Dostoevsky, has more than enough of it in himself and is in no need of Svidrigailov's services. No, the latter has an independent existence in the novel though his position in it is structurally subordinate; his function is not simply that of ministering to its hero. There is no innate relationship between the two, no affinity of the mystical order such as is posited in so many Dostoevsky studies. Actually Svidrigailov enters the novel by way of the external plot or intrigue (his pursuit of Dounia), yet once he is in it he provides the story not only with an additional perspective on Raskolnikov but also with the psychosexual vitality which it otherwise lacks, for both Raskolnikov and Sonia are singularly sexless. Svidrigailov exemplifies a distinct character type in Dostoevsky, the type of the nihilist in the realm of sensuality. He is a more elaborate and refined version of the rather coarse-grained libertine Valkovsky in *The Insulted and Injured* and he anticipates the figures of Stavrogin and the elder Karamazov in the later novels (like Stavrogin he is guilty of outraging a little girl). In this character type, sensuality becomes a flight from the vertiginous consciousness of freedom and from a kind of ennui which has gone beyond the psychological and has acquired a metaphysical status. Thus Svidrigailov believes in ghosts who "are as it were shreds and fragments of other worlds" and who appear only to people whose psyche is prepared to receive them. He rejects all dogma, including that of the atheists, as he is given to relativizing all possible ideas, whether of belief or unbelief. Whereas Raskolnikov does not believe in a future life, Svidrigailov speculates that perhaps the future life does exist but that there are only "spiders there or something of that sort."

> We always imagine eternity as something beyond our conception, something vast, vast! But why must it be vast? Instead of all that, what if it is one little room, like a bathhouse in the country, black and grimy and spiders in every corner, and that's all eternity is?

As for vice, he chides Raskolnikov for his moral prejudices, contending that in sexual vice

> there is at least something permanent, founded indeed upon nature and not dependent on fantasy, something present in the blood like an ever-burning ember, forever setting one on fire and maybe not to be quickly extinguished even with years. You agree that it's an occupation of a sort.

Admitting that it is a disease, like everything that exceeds moderation, he defends his indulgence in it by claiming that to give it up would mean that he would be forced to shoot himself. Clearly, his métier is not the simple-minded villainy of melodrama but a species of objective cruelty (as in his doing away with his wife and driving his footman to suicide), which is in a sense a form of meditation upon life beyond good and evil translated into practice. Therefore he is at the same time capable of acts of sympathy and kindness, as when he helps the Marmeladov orphans and lets Dounia go after cornering her. Good and evil are never ends to him but simply the available, even if sometimes redundant, means of convincing himself that it is possible to continue living. Hence the actions he performs strike one as transpiring somewhere outside himself, for they are at bottom experiments conducted by a self which is itself an experimental projection.

It has been observed often enough that every literary artist genuinely

an innovator creates his own audience. This is certainly true of Dostoevsky, in whose sphere we have now learned to move without undue
strain but who shocked his contemporaries by his open and bold reliance on melodrama and by the seeming fantasticality of his characters.
The Russian reader had learned by that time to identify the unhurried,
equable, lifelike realism of writers like Turgenev, Goncharov, and
Tolstoy with the higher norms of the novel; and what those writers
scrupulously avoided above all was the sensational and excessive. Dostoevsky was hard put to it to persuade the reader that he too, despite
his startling deviations from the newly established norms, was a realist.
Hence while writing *Crime and Punishment* he fretted over the
thought that his story would gain no credence from the public; and
since he had long been trying to defend himself against the charge of
insufficient regard for the real, he was pleased to note, shortly after
the appearance of the first installment of the novel, that a crime curiously similar to the one he was describing had been committed by a
Moscow student and reported in the newspapers. He at once seized
upon this item as confirming his own "special view" of the relation
between art and actuality.

> What the majority call fantastic and exceptional [he wrote to the critic
> Strakhov] sometimes signifies to me the very essence of reality. . . . In
> every issue of the newspapers you come upon accounts of the most real
> facts and amazing coincidences. For our writers, who are unconcerned
> with them, they are fantastic. But being facts they are reality none the
> less.

But this appeal to actual life — formless, disorderly, and inconse-
quent life with its "most real facts and amazing coincidences" — is
unworthy of the genius of Dostoevsky. In spite of his opposition to
such radical-minded simplifiers of the relation of art and life as
Chernishevsky, Dobroliubov, and Pisarev, critics exceedingly influential in their time, he was himself far from immune to the idea then
prevailing in his intellectual milieu that the work of art was useless
and perhaps even immoral in its inutility unless directly validated by
life or "reality," understood in the simplest empirical sense of these
terms. Dostoevsky was after all a Russian writer of his generation, a
generation ideologically inspired to exalt life over art and seeking to
justify the latter by citing the gifts of illumination and hopes of bet-
terment it ostensibly brings to life. Where Dostoevsky twisted that
common assumption to suit his creative practice was by claiming to
discern the essence of reality not in its typical everyday manifestations

but in the exceptional and fantastic. He was unable to go beyond that formula toward the assertion of a symbolic rather than literal correspondence between life and the fictive worlds of his own devising. Hence the speciousness of his argument from life in his literary apologetics, as in his pointing to life's "amazing coincidences" in the letter to Strakhov quoted above. The fact is that no coincidence copied from life can make in the least plausible the kind of coincidences, even the minor ones, you find in *Crime and Punishment,* such as the prosperous and respectable bourgeois Luzhin turning up in the same slum-lodging with the starving Marmeladov family or Svidrigailov, a rich man, finding no better place to stay in Petersburg than in the very same house where Sonia lives, a house in which his flat adjoins the room where she practices her trade and conducts those incredible conversations with Raskolnikov upon which he eavesdrops with the greatest relish. It is plain that Svidrigailov is situated where he is in order to make it possible for him to learn Raskolnikov's secret at the same time as he confides it to Sonia; an important turn of the plot depends on it. This is a calculated coincidence different in kind from those, however improbable, that life offers. It belongs to the stock-in-trade of melodrama, and Dostoevsky learned the use of it in his assiduous reading of Hoffmann, Dickens, Balzac, Sue, and a host of lesser authors of crime thrillers and adventure stories.

It is in literature rather than in unprocessed life that you find some of the sources of this novel, including its major plot element of a murder committed by someone who stands in no personal relation to the victim. Also, the Napoleon motif, on which so many changes are rung by Dostoevsky, is clearly transposed by him to a Petersburg setting from mid-nineteenth-century French fiction, Balzac and Stendhal in particular, both of whom glorified Napoleon (the former covertly and the latter overtly) and justified their ambitious plebeian heroes by appealing to his illustrious example. Thus Raskolnikov may be seen as a Russian version of Julien Sorel and Eugène de Rastignac — the young man on the make who comes to the capital from the provinces intent on a career and a conquest. It is especially Balzac's *Le Père Goriot* that suggests an influence in the design of Raskolnikov's story. In his essay on Dostoevsky* Georg Lukacs mentions the anecdote of the Chinese mandarin in Balzac's novel as containing the hint that the Russian writer might have developed. The relevant passage in the novel is worth citing in full. It occurs in a dialogue between Rastignac and his friend the medical student Bianchon:

* *Der russische Realismus in der Weltliteratur* (Berlin, 1949).

"What makes you look so serious?" asked the medical student taking his arm [Rastignac's] to walk up and down in front of the palace with him.

"I am bothered by troublesome thoughts."

"Of what kind are they? You know that thoughts can be cured."

"How?"

"By yielding to them."

"You are laughing at me, without knowing what I mean. Have you read Rousseau?"

"Do you remember the place where he asks the reader what he would do, if he could become rich by killing an old mandarin in China, by the sole act of his will, without stirring from Paris?"

"Yes."

"Well?"

"Pooh! I have already come to my thirty-third mandarin."

"Don't joke. Come, suppose you knew it were possible, and that a nod from you would do it, should you consent?"

"Is he a very old mandarin? But young or old, sick or well, my goodness — the deuce. No, I shouldn't."

And Bianchon concludes his argument in favor of sparing the Chinese by warning Rastignac against a rash solution of the problem posed at "the entrance of life," against the attempt to cut that Gordian knot with his sword. "If you mean to act thus," he says, "you must be an Alexander or else you will be sent to the gallows." Unlike Rastignac, however, Dostoevsky's hero confides in no one and sets out to cut the Gordian knot without in the least resembling an Alexander or a Napoleon, though hoping that his crime might possibly prove him to belong to their superior breed.

It seems to me, too, that Dostoevsky drew on *Le Père Goriot* for far more than a germinal anecdote of the Chinese mandarin. Svidrigailov's posture *vis-à-vis* Raskolnikov is in certain respects strongly reminiscent of Vautrin's relation to Rastignac in Balzac's novel. We know that Svidrigailov is missing from the early drafts of *Crime and Punishment,* and it is not improbable that when it came to composing the final version Dostoevsky decided to introduce a character playing Vautrin to his own Rastignac. Consider that both Vautrin and Svidrigailov are older men who assume the role of mentors in the ways of the world, that both have insinuating manners and appear cheerful and obliging when it suits them, that both are sexual deviants (the Frenchman is a homosexual and the Russian has very special tastes in underage girls), and that both are predatory types who make no secret of their immorality. Moreover, some of the ideas that Vautrin communicates to Rastignac turn up in Raskolnikov's thought virtually without modification, as if he had absorbed the lesson addressed to his French prototype. Vautrin declares, for instance, that there are but two courses open to a man, blind obedience or open revolt, and that he can make his way in the world either

> by the splendor of genius or the adroitness of corruption. He must burst like a cannon-ball into the ranks of his fellow-men, or he must move among them like the pestilence. Honesty is of no use. Men yield to the power of genius; they hate and calumniate it . . . but they yield to it if it persists, and kneel to it when they find that they cannot suppress it.

There is a remarkable parallel between this formulation and Raskolnikov's view, passionately expounded to Sonia, that

> whoever is strong in mind and spirit will have power over men. Anyone who is greatly daring is right in their eyes. . . . I divined that power is only vouchsafed to the man who dares to stoop and pick it up. There is only one thing, one thing needful: one has only to dare.

Clearly, Vautrin's genius who bursts like a cannon ball among his fellow men bears an uncommon resemblance to Raskolnikov's criminal of genius who dares assert the right inherent in his superiority and whose criminality is soon forgiven or forgotten as he becomes a lawgiver and leader among men. However, in constructing Raskolnikov's theory of the relation between power and genius, Dostoevsky borrowed from more than one source; Balzac is but one of them.

It is possible to speak if not of a school then surely of a Petersburgian genre in Russian literature, of which Dostoevsky is in fact the leading practitioner. Pushkin's "The Bronze Horseman" is doubtless the outstanding poem of that genre, as Gogol's "The Overcoat" is the outstanding story and *Crime and Punishment* the outstanding novel. One must be aware of its author's profound response to Petersburg and of the masterly way in which he appropriated it to imaginative purposes in order to perceive that as the scene of Raskolnikov's crime the city is one of the essential constituents of the story, more foreground than background, a unique urban setting charged with multiple meanings, of which one of the more urgent emerges from Dostoevsky's preoccupation with the Petersburg misery and his depiction of it in a manner demonstrating his solidarity with its victims. As a novelist of the modern metropolis he was of course in the line of Balzac and Dickens, by whom he was greatly influenced, though there is a marked difference in his representation of the city and theirs. Balzac's Paris, as Arnold Hauser has remarked, is still a romantic wilderness, "a theatrical setting painted in chiaroscuro contrasts, a fairyland in which dazzling riches and picturesque poverty live side by side," whereas Dostoevsky describes the metropolis in somber colors, taking us into its reeking taverns and coffinlike rooms, bringing to the fore its petty-bourgeois and proletarian types, its small shopkeepers and clerks, students, prostitutes, beggars, and derelicts. True as this is, there is also something else in Dostoevsky's vision of Petersburg, a sense not so much of romance as of poetic strangeness, a poetic emotion attached to objects in themselves desolate, a kind of exaltation in the very lostness, loneliness, and drabness which the big city imposes on its inhabitants, as is so poignantly brought out in the scene when in an evening hour Raskolnikov stops on a street corner to listen to a sentimental song ground out on a barrel organ and sung by a girl in a cracked and coarsened voice.

"Do you like street music?" said Raskolnikov, addressing a middle-aged man standing idly by him. The man looked at him, startled and wondering.

"I love to hear singing to a street organ," said Raskolnikov, and his manner seemed strangely out of keeping with the subject. "I like it on cold, dark, damp evenings — they must be damp — when all the passersby have pale green, sickly faces, or better still when the wet snow is falling straight down, where there's no wind — you know what I mean? and the street lamps shine through it. . . ."

"I don't know. . . . Excuse me. . . ." muttered the stranger, frightened by the question and Raskolnikov's strange manner. . . .

Catching Raskolnikov talking to himself on the street, Svidrigailov says to him: "This is a town of crazy people. . . . There are few places where there are so many gloomy, queer influences on the soul of man as in Petersburg." There is indeed something peculiarly Petersburgian about Raskolnikov, and not merely in the sense that he belongs to its

* The ambiguity of Petersburg in its odd blending of the real and the unreal is what Dostoevsky tried mainly to capture. In *A Raw Youth* there is an especially suggestive passage in which young Arkady speaks of a Petersburg morning as being at the same time infinitely prosaic and infinitely fantastic. "On such a wild Petersburg morning, foul, damp and foggy, the wild dream of some Hermann out of Pushkin's 'Queen of Spades' (a colossal figure, an extraordinary and regular Petersburg type . . . the type of the Petersburg period) might, I believe, strike one as a piece of solid reality. A hundred times over, in such a fog, I have been haunted by a strange and persistent fancy: 'What if this fog should part and float away? Would not all this rotten and slimy town go with it, rise up with the fog, and vanish like smoke, and the old Finnish marsh be left as before and in the midst of it, perhaps, to complete the picture, a bronze horseman on a panting, overdriven steed?' "

"proletariat of undergraduates." The crime he commits — in the idea of it, namely, which is so strange an amalgam of the abstract and artificial with the sheerly fantastic — corresponds intrinsically to the character of this city, frequently described in exactly such terms.* It is in the heat and stench of its slums, as he wanders endlessly through the streets, that Raskolnikov spawns his idea, which he himself likens to "a spell, a sorcery, an obsession." And afterward, having carried his idea to its terrible conclusion, though not at all in the bravura manner of a Napoleon but rather like a man deprived of reason and will power by mental illness, on the very next day he resumes his wanderings about the city in a state more often than not bordering on delirium.

St. Petersburg was far more the capital of the Russian empire than of the Russian land. It was erected on the Finnish marshland with cruel haste and at the cost of many lives by the edict of Peter the Great, who undertook, with the savage rationality typical of belated and alien converts to progress, to transform his backward domain all at once into an efficient state militarized along modern lines. The self-will and precipitate style of this operation brought into being a city without roots in the past or in the vast rural hinterland, the center of alienation and of everything novel and foreign violating the national traditions and the patriarchal mode of life. It was in Petersburg that in a fashion peculiar to it the imperial bureaucracy exerted itself to westernize the country from above while the turbulent and seditious "proletariat of undergraduates," impelled by other motives and a nobler vision, strove to effect the same end from below. Thus the material brutality of the caste pressing down upon society from the top met its counterpart in the tragic spiritual brutality of the dissident intelligentsia forcing the issue lower down.

No wonder the Slavophils hated Petersburg. Khomyakov, a leading ideologue of their faction, spoke of it as a city of dead beauty, where "all is stone, not only the houses but the trees and inhabitants as well." The Marquis de Custine, visiting the capital in 1839, could not believe that it would endure. "I have seen no place that is more penetrated with the instability of human beings," he wrote. Penetrated with the

---

The bronze horseman is Falconet's statue of Peter the Great, but implicitly the reference is of course to Pushkin's famous poem of that title. Hermann is the protagonist of Pushkin's story "The Queen of Spades," in whom some scholars have discerned an early model of Raskolnikov. For, like Dostoevsky's hero, Hermann is under the spell of Napoleon and he too, daring all on one throw, kills an old woman in an attempt to wrest from her the secret that will make his fortune. What the two characters share, basically, is the Petersburgian power-urge combined with the peculiar Petersburgian dreaminess.

instability of human beings — a marvelously apt phrase which we can apply to the Dostoevskyean world as a whole with but a slight shift of context. You will find this singular instability in Raskolnikov, to be sure, but you will also find in him more than a trace of that savage rationality characterizing the champions of the Petersburg period in Russian history and subsequently the revolutionary elite. He emerges from that "literate world of reckless youth," as Bakunin called it, in which the latter professed to see the hope of the Revolution, and he is the epitome of those traits of which Alexander Herzen gave an account of incomparable precision in his *Memoirs*.

> We are greatly given [he noted] to theoretical pedantry and argumentativeness. This German propensity is in us associated with a special national element — which we might call the Araktcheyev* element — a ruthlessness, a passionate rigidity, and an eagerness to dispatch their victims. To satisfy his grenadier ideal, Araktcheyev flogged living peasants to death; we flog to death ideas, arts, humanity, past leaders, anything you like. In dauntless array we advance step by step to the limit and overshoot it, never sinning against logic but only against *truth;* unaware, we go on further and further, forgetting that real sense and real understanding of life are shown precisely in stopping short before the extreme. . . .

In truth Raskolnikov is one of those young men whose coming was foreshadowed with fear by Joseph de Maistre, the author of *Soirées de St. Pétersbourg*, when he observed, in discussing the peasant uprisings of the eighteenth century, headed by such leaders as Emelian Pugachev, an obscure and illiterate Cossack, that if another such revolt ever took place in Russia it would be headed by a Pugachev "armed with a university degree." But the hour of the university Pugachevs had not quite struck when Raskolnikov set out entirely on his own, cut off from any social effort or collective historical action, to remove "certain obstacles." Proclaiming the necessity of breaking once and for all what must be broken, in other words, of killing not simply an old woman but the principle of authority bolstered by the moral law, he yet proceeds to commit not an act of political terror but another crime altogether that inevitably stamps him as no more than a common criminal, a criminal from egoism. He is a dissenter and rebel (*raskol*, the word from which his name derives, means schism or dissent), in essence the type of revolutionary terrorist of that period, whose act of terror is somehow displaced onto a private object. The terrorist

---

* Alexis Araktcheyev (1769–1834), a high official and trusted adviser of Alexander I in the closing years of his reign, put into effect such inordinately cruel administrative practices as to give rise to the dread term *Araktcheyevchina*.

is a political criminal, and if he is to be vindicated at all it is by an appeal to historical necessity; no such appeal is open to Raskolnikov.

Of course he has at his disposal a theory justifying his crime, and I have already indicated one source of it in Balzac. Another and more important source, to my mind, is Hegel's concept of the historic hero (the agent of the World-Spirit) and his victims. The enormous influence of the Hegelian philosophy in Russia during the late 1830s and the 1840s is well known; the period of this influence coincides with Dostoevsky's youth and it would have been impossible for him to escape it. But that he was in fact concerned with it is shown, moreover, by his letter (of February 22, 1854) from Siberia to his brother Mikhail asking that he send him, among other books, Hegel's *Philosophy of History.** It is strange that this source, far from esoteric, should have been overlooked. I imagine that scholars and critics have been so carried away by the apparent analogy between Raskolnikov (in his theory of himself, that is) and Nietzsche's Superman as to have missed a more substantial likeness, though one which is more in the nature of a caricature than an exact replica. It is only in the vulgarized popular version of the Superman that Raskolnikov's theory reminds us of him; so far as Nietzsche's actual idea of the Superman goes, as a product of a mutation of the human species, there is no resemblance. It is in Hegel rather that we discover a direct and obvious source of Raskolnikov's notion of inferior and superior men, the superior ones having the right to commit breaches of morality while their inferiors are obliged to mind their business, which is to stay put in the common rut. Now what Dostoevsky has done in devising Raskolnikov's justification is to convert into a theory of human nature what is in Hegel not a psychological theory at all but a theory of men as subjects and objects of history. Hegel's world-historical individual — such as Alexander or Caesar or Napoleon, the very names invoked by Dostoevsky's protagonist — performs the grandiose tasks set for him by the *Weltgeist,* irrespective of moral considerations; he can do no other, for, as Hegel puts it, "the history of the world moves on a higher level than that of morality." These heroes "treat other great and even sacred interests inconsiderately — a conduct which subjects them to moral reprehension. But so mighty a figure may trample down many an innocent flower, crush to pieces many things in its path." Thus as the subject of history he rides roughshod over its mere objects or victims. Dostoevsky gives us a parody version of

---

* "Send me the Koran, and Kant's *Critique of Pure Reason,* and if you have the chance of sending me anything not officially, then be sure to send Hegel, particularly Hegel's *Philosophy of History.* Upon that depends my whole future."

Hegel's theory of two types of men by abstracting it from its historical logic. This enables him to entangle Raskolnikov in what is in truth a comedy of mistaken identity: an obvious victim of the historical process — a small man in search of personal security and happiness — laughably taking himself for its hero. In this sense he is no better than a clown, and he does indeed laugh at himself from time to time.

> One sudden idea made him laugh. Napoleon, the pyramids, Waterloo, and a wretched skinny old woman, a pawnbroker with a red trunk under her bed. . . . It's too inartistic. A Napoleon creep under the old woman's bed! Ugh, how loathsome!

However, though Raskolnikov refuses the historical action of the political rebel, and, instead of throwing a bomb at a general or even the Czar himself, he crushes the skull of an old woman with an ax, there is still something in his deed, for all its weird abjectness and ugliness, which in some sense comes through to us as a protest against the Petersburg misery and the ethics justifying it. One cannot but agree with Alberto Moravia's statement in his essay "The Marx-Dostoevsky Duel" that though "Raskolnikov had not read Marx and regards himself as a superman beyond good and evil, he was already, in embryo, a people's commissar."* Moravia is one of the very few Western commentators on the novel who has not overlooked its aborted political meaning, which emerges again and again, as when Raskolnikov dissociates himself from his friend Razumihin's abuse of the socialists. He understands very well that rebellion can take another form, the collective form advocated by the socialists. After all, what the socialists want, he remarks to himself, is the happiness of all. As it happens, however, he is not the one "to put his little brick into the happiness of all," for what he wants is to live properly here and now. In his manuscript Dostoevsky inserted the following passage (later deleted) into a speech of Raskolnikov's: "What care I what will come to pass in the future. Is it possible to live at present? I cannot pass by with indifference all these horrors, this suffering and misery. I want power." Power for what purpose? Presumably to do good, to alleviate the suffering and misery. He is in a state of fatal self-contradiction, however, in that he attempts to further a common end of an altruistic character with egoistical and purely private means. In order to test his strength he needs more than anything else the support of a magistrate, Porfiry Petrovitch, who is the one figure in the story who can be said manifestly to speak for the author, and it is he who says to Raskolnikov:

* *Encounter,* November 1956.

You made up a theory and then were ashamed that it broke down and turned out to be not at all original! It turned out something base, that's true, but you are not hopelessly base! . . . How do I regard you? I regard you as one of those men who would stand and smile at their torturer while he cuts their entrails out, if only they have found faith or God.

It is significant that the phrase is "faith *or* God," not faith *in* God, as if to say that there are other faiths besides the traditional one.

That Raskolnikov stands in an inauthentic relation to his crime is thus confirmed by the author's spokesman in the novel. The crime does not truly belong to him, and that is the reason he affects us as being almost ludicrously inadequate to his deed, as when he faints in the police station the day right after the murder, even though there is as yet no suspicion attached to him, and calls attention to himself in other ways too. In spite of all his protestations to the contrary, he is prostrate with guilt and the yearning for punishment. It is not that he lacks the strength to kill and bear the responsibility for it to the end, but that he killed for himself alone, deranged by unconscious urges and overconscious theories, rather than for the common cause to which his "nihilistic" generation was dedicated; and that is also the secret of Sonia's hold on him. There is no social substance in his anarchic individualism, as there is none in Sonia's idea of Christian salvation.

Sonia, "the eternal victim so long as the world lasts," is a small thin girl of eighteen, every feature of whose face reflects "a sort of insatiable compassion." Raskolnikov turns to her in his need because, as he tells her: "We are both accursed, so let us go together." She is the very embodiment of meekness and humility (far more so than Myshkin or Alyosha), and only Dostoevsky, with his uncanny powers of representation, could have brought her to life without blundering into mawkish sentimentality. But though he so brilliantly persuades us of her reality as a novelistic creation, this in itself in no sense constitutes a "proof" of her idea of Christian salvation. She proves quite as much the Nietzschean negation of it. It appears to me that it is precisely in his characterization of Sonia, rather than of Raskolnikov, that Dostoevsky's insight coincides with that of Nietzsche; the fact that the Russian arrives at that insight by way of assent, and the German by way of dissent, is scarcely to the point here. Thus Nietzsche speaks in his *Antichrist* of "that queer and sick world into which the Gospels introduce us — as in a Russian novel, a world into which the scum of society, nervous disorders, and 'childlike' idiocy seem to be having a rendezvous." Sonia is truly an inhabitant of that world, and she has the stirring charm of the mixture it exhibits — "a mixture of the sublime, the sickly and the childlike." Nowhere in literature do we find so striking a confirmation of Nietzsche's idea of the evangelical type as in the figure of Sonia. What is that type? It is one in whom "the incapacity for resistance becomes morality," who experiences "any resistance, even any compulsion to resist, as unendurable *displeasure* . . . and finds blessedness (pleasure) only in no longer offering any resistance to anybody, neither to evil nor to him who is evil — love as the only, as the *last* possible way of life." Significantly, Sonia's faith is not one that has been attained through struggle. When Raskolnikov challenges her faith, she answers with simple pathos: "What should I be without God?" This is the kind of faith which, as Nietzsche said, "has been there from the beginning; it is as it were an infantilism that has receded into the spiritual."* Plainly, Sonia's faith is of a sort that offers no solution to Raskolnikov, whose spiritual existence is incommensurable with hers. No wonder that the epilogue to the novel, in which he finally seems to be preparing himself to accept her outlook, has struck many readers as implausible and out of key with the work as a whole.

A few weeks after Dostoevsky's death in January 1881 a terrorist of the People's Will party by the name of Andrey Zhelyabov took part in the successful attempt on the life of Alexander II. He was caught and brought to trial, and this is what he had to say to the court:

> I was baptized in the Orthodox Church but I reject Christianity, although I acknowledge the essential teaching of Jesus Christ. This essential teaching occupied an honored place among my moral incentives. I believe in the truth and righteousness of that teaching and I solemnly declare that faith without works is dead and that every true Christian ought to fight for the truth and for the rights of the oppressed and the weak, and even, if need be, to suffer for them. Such is my creed.

Evidently the blood he shed did not weigh on Zhelyabov's conscience, for he went to his death on the gallows calm and impenitent. Raskolnikov, cheated of Zhelyabov's fate, goes to a Siberian prison in the same state of perplexity and outrage with which he undertook to carry out his "loathsome scheme." But, then, it was a hideous old harpy he killed, not the Czar of all the Russias.

Whatever the manifest theme of the novel, its latent theme is not that of crime as such or the criminal's innate need of punishment but the right to violent rebellion. It was the violence that Dostoevsky condemned, even as he was secretly drawn to it, fearing that if let loose

---

* *The Portable Nietzsche,* edited by Walter Kaufmann (New York, 1954), p. 602 ff.

it would tear down the authority both of heaven and earth, and Raskolnikov goes down to defeat to prove his creator right.

In its aspect as a polemic against the radical generation of the 1860s — whose obscurantist rationalism and notion of enlightened self-interest as the motive force of human conduct Dostoevsky began satirizing in *Notes from Underground* — the novel depends on the sleight-of-hand of substituting a meaningless crime for a meaningful one. But if that were all, *Crime and Punishment* would not be the masterpiece it undoubtedly is. The very substitution of one type of crime for another set problems for Dostoevsky which he solved brilliantly by plunging his hero into a condition of pathology which ostensibly has nothing to do with the "heroic" theory by means of which he justifies himself. In his article, "On Crime," Raskolnikov wrote that the perpetration of a crime is always accompanied by illness, and that is an exact description of his own case, though he believes himself to be another kind of criminal altogether, one acting from rational calculation and in the interests of a higher idea; the irony of his self-deception is among the finest effects of the book. And it is astonishing how well Dostoevsky was able to preserve the unity of his protagonist's character, to present him as all of a piece in spite of the fact that we are dealing not with one but with several Raskolnikovs. There is Raskolnikov the altruist and there is Raskolnikov the egoist, "a despot by nature"; there is the crypto-revolutionary Raskolnikov and there is the self-styled genius who demands power as his right and as the guaranty of his freedom; then of course there is the neurotic who acts out his illness through a murder intellectually rationalized but inexplicable except in terms of an unconscious drive. After all, he conceives an "insurmountable repulsion" to Alyona Ivanovna, the old moneylender, weeks before he elaborates his murderous plan. Dostoevsky confronted the hazard of these contradictions with unequalled mastery. His capacity to combine them creatively in a single brain and a single psyche, while staving off the danger of incoherence at one end and of specious reconciliation at the other, is the measure of the victory scored in this novel by the imaginative artist in him over the ruthless polemicist.

Partisan Review, 1960

Dostoevsky:
Descent into the Underground

Je travaille dans l'absurde
VALÉRY

THERE IS VERY LITTLE in world literature which either in tone or substance reminds us of *Notes from Underground,* the short novel that marks Dostoevsky's breakthrough to his greater creative period. Perhaps the work that comes closest to it is *Rameau's Nephew,* though there is no evidence that the Russian novelist ever read Diderot's composition or even heard of it. Hence in comparing the two it seems more to the point to speak of an affinity rather than of influence or provenience in the accepted sense of these terms.

The affinity comes to mind in noting that the protagonists of both works share in the character-image of the "antihero," a new type destined to figure prominently in modern fiction, and that both are above all intent on expressing their feelings of *ressentiment* and malicious apprehension of men's motives and actions, not excluding their own. Both are bubbling over with "vicious spite," to use the undergroundling's insistent phrase, and what is even more scandalous is that they take so much pride in this spite as to flaunt it on every occasion. What is most original is not so much the "ideas" these works contain but precisely this spite, so openly and self-gratifyingly released, which recognizes no moral barriers and least of all the conventions of polite discourse because it is endemic to the wounded and cowed ego seeking to assert itself at all costs. One might speak of it as the spite long fermenting in human nature and finally inflaming it. Heretofore suppressed in the expression of culture and even in its consciousness, once let loose it cannot be dismissed as simply a manifestation of "sickness" or extreme morbidity. In its very extremity is comprised the essence of the plebeian self coming historically into its own at long last, identifying itself as indeed belonging to human reality, and in its despair, loathing, and paradoxical delight in its own shame and degradation, crying out: "I too exist!"

It is mainly in the tone of the two productions that a likeness is to be detected, particularly in the first part of Dostoevsky's novella, entitled "Underground," with its narrator's unrestrained, spluttering, hectoring speech, disconcerting interjections, verbal flare-ups, and gesturing that combine boastful defiance with wriggling self-abasement. But the similarity I have remarked upon peters out once Dostoevsky starts on the second part of his story, called "Apropos of the Wet Snow," in which the narrator, even while continuing his Thersites-like rant, recalls an especially shameful episode of his youth, the tale how, just for the "sport" of it as he himself observes, he first arouses the trust of the prostitute Liza only to abuse that trust and betray it in the most disgraceful manner. Stunned by the lowness of his behavior but, characteristically enough, not really astonished by it, he even attempts to rationalize it away by a fear of "deep" psychologizing.

The novella as a whole, in which it is very difficult to separate the ideological and psychological elements from the artistic conception, is in truth uniquely Dostoevskyean. Only in this sense can it be regarded as a kind of prologue to the great novels written during the remaining years of its author's creative career. Yet in another sense it is no prologue at all to the novels that follow it, for the later Dostoevsky's idealized Christian values of meekness and humility not only find no expression in it but are in fact alien to its very substance. Actually the stance adopted in it is in stark contradiction to the Christian hopes partly embodied in the later fiction. It is a work chiefly transitional in character, cutting off the novelist sharply and abruptly from his earlier humanitarianism and idealistic romanticism while propelling him, provisionally at least, towards a standpoint nowadays loosely called existentialist.

The man from underground, brooding in his "funkhole," cannot be counted among his creator's candidates for salvation. It is impossible to imagine him falling under the sway of such children of light as Sonia Marmeladov, Myshkin, and Alyosha Karamazov; his distempered state of mind is such that it is inconceivable that he could respond to them with anything but irritation and biting sarcasm. His psychology may be integrally a part of the syndrome the Russians call *dostoyevchina*, but it surely cannot enter in any coherent manner into a religious world-picture. Pluming himself on being "an educated man, a modern intellectual" while at the same doubting whether "a man of acute sensibility can respect himself at all," what he wants above all is recognition of his personality, restoration of his self-respect and proper dignity, or at least some alleviation of his sense of defeat and powerlessness. His hysterical behavior when dining with Zverkov and his friends because he feels ignored and looked down upon, his farcical attempt to force the six-foot-tall army officer (and himself "a short, thin little fellow") to take notice of him as a subject, not as a mere chance object, even his shamefully perverse treatment of Liza, yes, even his persistence in calling attention to his "unbounded vanity" — all are modes of extreme reaction to the painful sensation of his own insignificance and impotence.

The critics and interpreters of Dostoevsky whose principal interest is focused on his religiosity (a religiosity by no means fully developed as yet when the novella was being written) are hard put to explain away the undergroundling's basic attitude of cynical nihilism and somehow reconcile it with the Christian outlook. Their intercession is futile and can only lead to the falsification of the text, for what they are apt to do is to play down or even divert attention altogether from the rage of self-will by which Dostoevsky's paradoxist is possessed and which colors all his outbursts. In order to reinforce their implausible Christian reading of *Notes from Underground* they frequently have recourse to citing its author's letter to his brother Mikhail in which he complains that the censors had mangled the tenth chapter of the first part of his story: "Those swine of censors — where I mocked at everything and sometimes blasphemed for form's sake — they let pass, but where from all this I deduced the need of faith and Christ — that is suppressed." To a critic committed to Orthodoxy, like Konstantin Mochulsky, these words sufficiently prove the truth of his Christian interpretation. All that Mochulsky has succeeded in proving, however, is that he is capable of committing the "intentional fallacy" in the most obtrusive possible way. Intention is by no means equivalent to fulfillment, least of all an intention baldly stated in a letter rather than one that might be derived from the total effect of the text itself.

Moreover, the fact is that if we look closely at the disputed chapter (which comes to less than three pages) we fail to discover in it anything that even approaches blasphemy. What we chiefly find in it is mockery of the "Crystal Palace" with its "model flats." Surely the censors could not have been offended by the sarcasms heaped upon Chernishevsky's socialist Utopia or by the polemical thrusts at his influential novel *What Is To Be Done?* One can guess that if they were really offended it must have been by the nihilistic,* impudent, and "cruel" tone and spirit of the work in its entirety. It might even be said that for once, in removing from Chapter 10 the utterly unprepared for, *deus ex machina*–like interposition of an appeal to "faith and Christ," they were acting like genuine literary critics. They must have thought that in this specific context a sudden appeal of that sort was quite inappropriate, sounding as if the writer were merely playing with words or perhaps in some obscure way making fun of the church. Thus there is a coincidence of political and aesthetic judgment in the censors' decision not to let Chapter 10 stand as written. It is true that in a general sense an appeal to faith belongs to Dostoevsky's later phase, but it cannot belong without gross violation of the text to the nameless narrator of this particular novella, whose story is that of the worm turns; this turning, effected through an explosion of spiteful aggression and exposure of himself and others, excludes submission, even to some kind of mythic transcendent construct. In this connection it is worth stressing that when reissuing the novella in book form Dostoevsky chose *not* to replace the deleted passage affirming his protagonist's striving for "faith and Christ," even though the censorship at that time was much relaxed and there was no danger of renewed interference. One cannot but suppose that his conscience both as thinker and artist told him to leave the text alone, as his antihero was complete in himself and hardly the kind of figure able to bring off a sudden conversion with any degree of credibility.

There can be no doubt that the novelist put a good deal of himself into his nameless narrator, though only that part of himself streaked with "underground" traits and actuated by resentment and an excess of self-consciousness. The other side of his self, that which sought to be reconciled to authority both heavenly and earthly and find salvation in Christ and in the "Russian idea" of universal brotherhood, could not possibly have survived in the "underground." Hence it found no voice in the story. In truth, that voice was never to sound wholly triumphant in his creative work, which cannot be fully grasped without taking into account its dissonances, conflicts, and contradictions. Furthermore, in the early 1860s, as his novel *The Insulted and Injured* and his various articles in his magazines *Vremya* and *Epokha* show, he was not yet entirely prepared to commit himself with finality to the mystical Christian solution.

---

* "Nihilistic" in the Western sense of the term of course, not at all in its later nineteenth-century Russian usage where it serves mainly as a synonym of words like "revolutionary," "radical," or "subversive."

In the early months of 1864, as he was writing the *Notes*, all he was actually prepared to do was to descend into the "underground," where, rearming his intelligence with the venom it had long accumulated, he could cynically renounce his own past with its Schilleresque devotion to "the sublime and beautiful," its humanistic solidarity with "the humblest man" (presumably even so touchingly humble a figure as Devushkin, the hero of his first novel, *Poor Folk*). What he wanted was to break definitely with the radical doctrine of Belinsky and his circle (which on his own admission he had at one time accepted "entirely and fervently") and, in short, with all forms of utopian and romantic idealism as well as critical rationality. To confirm the rights of the underground man he was at last ready to kill the daydreaming recluse in himself embodied in the good but helpless protagonists of his earlier stories and to be done once and for all with the literary conventions and mannerisms of that initial period and its debilitating inhibitions. Now his antihero feels free to shout at Liza: "I had been humiliated, so I too wanted to humiliate someone; they wiped the floor with me, so I too wanted to show my power." So far as he is concerned, he adds, the whole world can go to hell so long as he has his cup of tea. As for Liza's compassionate love of him, there is nothing improbable in his inability to appreciate it. He is through with bookishness and "literary" notions and nothing can stop him from blurting out the truth so long prohibited by the conventions of literature:

> ... I could not possibly have loved anyone because, I repeat, to me love meant to tyrannize and to be morally superior. I have never in my life been able to imagine any other sort of love, and I have reached the point that sometimes I cannot help thinking even now that love only consists in the right to tyrannize over the woman you love, who grants you this right of her own free will. Even in most secret dreams I could not imagine love except as a struggle, and I always embarked upon it with hatred and ended it with moral subjugation, and afterwards I did not have the faintest idea what to do with the woman I had subjugated.

The first announced title of *Notes from Underground* was *A Confession,* and it is truly that (though not, to be sure, in a literal biographical sense), no matter how much certain contemporary Western critics, bemused by modern theories of "impersonal narration," try to detach the author from his technically contrived yet deeply felt account of his anguished inner life by converting it into some kind of ghostly contest of abstract ideas, such as scientific determinism versus free will. Critics of this type, mostly latecomers to Russian studies, fail to understand the Russian nineteenth century and the temperament of the great writers it produced. Though the great moral tension they lived in forced them to throw themselves passionately into ideological controversies, by the very same token they generally felt ill at ease in the cold climate of abstract speculation; and in this respect Dostoevsky is certainly no exception. Turgenev once described their situation very well when he wrote: "We were searching in philosophy for everything under the sun except pure thought."

To my mind, there is something small-minded and pusillanimous, too, in the decorous professorial attempts to depersonalize *Notes from Underground* in order to disengage the author from its deeply felt even if excruciating experience. How much more truthful were the older biographers and critics, now regarded as "old-fashioned" and lacking in "methodology," who spoke plainly of what is obvious. Thus Avrahm Yarmolinsky connected the undergroundling with his author without mincing words. "Plainly this tormented soul has much in common with his creator. If Dostoevsky did not necessarily share the undergroundling's experiences, his rebellion is his, their ideas are of a piece with his own thinking." In his view the story's narrator clearly embodies a potentiality of its writer's nature.* Leo Shestov identifies author and character even more directly:

> *Notes from Underground* is a public though not open renunciation of his own past. . . . Goodness and a life of self-sacrifice in the service of the Ideal can no longer inspire him. . . . Of course the story is not autobiographical in a literal sense . . . the episode with Liza is invented. . . . He needs the portrayal of Liza in order to spit at the Idea and to trample it in the mud. . . . He can no longer keep silent. Something elemental, gruesome and horrifying was born in his soul, and he was compelled to speak out. . . . A great desperation was needed before such thoughts could be generated in a human mind, and a superhuman audacity was needed to appear before people with such ideas. . . .

Scorched by the undergroundling's hot breath, by his shameless audacity in conferring upon his subjectivity, however base and low, a virtually ontological status, a certain type of critic or commentator, an antimanichean by nature whose pliancy is confined to the culture of ideas, immediately turns away with relief from the intemperate, unsightly, and outlandish figure before him in order to beat a retreat into the relatively innocuous sphere of theory and dialectics. It is only here that he feels truly at home and on this familiar safe ground he can proceed to divest the undergroundling of his existential reality by

---

* Cf., Avrahm Yarmolinsky, *Dostoevsky, a Life* (New York, 1934), p. 190.

transforming him into a philosopher or metaphysician.* But at what cost? At the cost of failing to notice that there are actually two voices that speak to us in the *Notes* — the voice of the nameless underground-ling, a novelized character representing no more than a certain po-tentiality of the author, whereas the other voice is that of the author in *person* who imitates the protagonist's agitated speech with the aim of discharging a ruthlessly polemical attack on the values of reason, progress, and enlightenment, that is to say, on the secular and socially radical values serving his ideological adversaries in the milieu of the Russian intelligentsia as the chief premise of their attachment to the program of reform and/or revolution.

What Dostoevsky had done, as was his wont in his later phase, was to incorporate an antinihilist pamphlet into the story of the under-groundling's desperate plight. Hence it is above all necessary to dis-tinguish between two types of ideas in the *Notes,* those issuing directly from the undergroundling's "situation," in the existential sense of this term, and those that do not in the least accord with his "situation," belonging exclusively to the author who, without overtly succumbing as yet to the mystical Christian alternative, is clearing the ground for his final commitment to it by engaging in a brilliant display of negative argumentation and dialectical derring-do. The actual mystico-religious commitment, though never achieved in a truly unqualified and con-clusive fashion, is to come later, in the novels that follow. In the mean-time all Dostoevsky is doing is borrowing the undergroundling's voice, cracked with hysteria, to denounce the quite concrete social and political freedoms demanded by his radical contemporaries in the name of an "absolute freedom" devoid of any experiential basis in the real life of man — a freedom whose absolute character is metaphysically con-trived, purely imaginary, abysmally utopian, and historically incon-ceivable.

Notes from Underground is a work that, though eliciting a great deal of admiration, has also given rise to a great deal of confusion. To clear up that confusion it is above all necessary to disentangle the two sets of ideas it contains in order to make sure that we do not at-tribute to the undergroundling proper the author's contumacious and highly sophistical arguments deriding his numerous opponents, such as Chernishevsky, Pisarev, and Saltykov-Schedrin, among the leading Rus-sian intellectuals of his time. Clearly, it is unmistakably the author's voice that comes through to us in the long ranting diatribe against

* As, for instance, in the following: "*Notes from Underground* inaugurated Do-stoevsky's superb dialetic. From being a psychologist he became a metaphysi-cian. . . ." Nicolas Berdyaev, *Dostoevsky* (New York, 1957), p. 28.

reason, progress, and enlightenment as well as in the portrayal of man as at once "stupid and phenomenally ungrateful" and "a frivolous, unaccountable creature" who nevertheless insists on "an absolutely free choice whatever the cost." This man, who regards two twice two makes four as "a piece of impudence" and who can always be counted on never to renounce "suffering, chaos and destruction," is obviously a clever provisional invention of the author, devised to fill a temporary need. In later years, having at long last completed his turn to "faith and Christ," Dostoevsky will depict man quite differently, in a very pessimistic vein in fact. The later version of Dostoevskyean man, unlike the earlier *homme absurde* projected in the *Notes,* is no longer the obdurate individualist demanding free choice at whatever cost. In his fantasy of absolute freedom *l'homme absurde* pokes fun at Chernishevsky's theory of "rational egoism,"* asserting that man is too irrational and unpredictable to act solely according to what is obviously to his advantage, whereas in his later incarnation it is precisely his advantage that he single-mindedly pursues in craving two things only:

* Critics who take an uncritical view of the *Notes,* that is those who take everything in it at face value, make far too much of the references in it to Chernishevsky's ideas and to his popular novel *What Is To Be Done?* These critics, in their scholastic fervor, at times discuss these references as if they were the key to the *Notes* and belong to its very essence. But this is hardly the case. To my mind, it is Dostoevsky in person (the second voice imitating and in fact interrupting the first and more authentic voice), rather than the undergroundling in his existential character, who engages in a polemic with Chernishevsky; and, as is well known, in his polemical moods Dostoevsky can be unconscionably malicious, and that he is grossly unfair to Chernishevsky goes without saying. For example, he jeers at Chernishevsky's theory of "rational egoism," professing to understand it in a manner all too literal. Yet this theory, borrowed from the British utilitarians, means something altogether different to Chernishevsky, a utopian socialist of the *narodnik* persuasion, than it meant to its British originators, ideologues of bourgeois individualism. Chernishevsky interpreted it in his own way, simply that if the Russian people, individually and collectively, ever reached a true understanding of what is good for them, they would undertake to overthrow the autocratic regime with its outmoded institutions and construct a society that suited them better. In other words, "rational egoism" in its Russian version is nothing less than a learned or Aesopian formula of revolution. Dostoevsky was far too intelligent to mistake its subversive meaning, and he could not possibly have confused Chernishevsky's understanding of it with those of Bentham or Buckle or Spencer. The explanation lies elsewhere. Carried away by polemical ardor, the author of the *Notes* resorted to literalism in order to ridicule his political adversary, not an unusual procedure on his part.

In Chernishevsky's novel a character named Vera Pavlovna makes a speech in praise of the Crystal Palace with its "model flats." What is in her mind is a kind of Fourierist phalanastery. This is naive on her part, to be sure, an excess of optimism, but nothing vicious or evil. Dostoevsky has no end of fun deriding the Crystal Palace, as if it represented an imminent reality, a direct sort of menace. But this is all too easy in its obvious tendentiousness. It is not the undergroundling who speaks here but the author venting his hatred of socialism.

"earthly bread" and "community of worship," for the sake of which he is ever ready to surrender his freedom to an authoritarian elite. Thus in the Legend of the Grand Inquisitor — which may be said to contain the novelist's last and most somber and severe assessment of man — his earlier and somewhat playful version of him as "a frivolous and unaccountable creature" is implicitly repudiated. In the later Dostoevsky the conception of the isolated self, proudly nursing his freedom to the extreme point of willing and desiring "even something stupid and injurious" to his own interests so long as it preserves his personality and liberty of action, has vanished without a trace.

Yet in the *Notes* we find another order of ideas that issue exclusively from the undergroundling's mode of life as an impoverished, lowly retired civil servant settled down in his "dark cellar" who spends his time reading "the sublime and beautiful" fantasies of romantic writers and endlessly brooding until in sickening revulsion at his "bookish" existence he darts out at intervals to plunge "into vile and petty vice." He is a sick, beaten, and spiteful man who longs for nothing so much as for a "positive definition" of himself, for he does not know how to become anything definite: "either a blackguard or an honest man, either a hero or an insect." If only he had been just a loafer! "Why, it's a title, a purpose in life. It's a career, gentlemen, a career!" He engages in acrimonious colloquies with the implied reader of his *Notes*, finally admitting that he himself does not believe in what he has written:

> Do you know what would be better? It would be better if I myself believed in anything I had just written. I assure you most solemnly, gentlemen, that there is not a word I've written I believe in! What I mean is perhaps I do believe, but at the same time I cannot help feeling and suspecting for some unknown reasons that I'm lying like a cobbler.
> Then why have you written all this?
> Well, suppose I put you in a dark cellar for forty years without anything to do and come to see you in your dark cellar after the forty years to find out what has become of you. Can a man be left for forty years with nothing to do?

Here we actually see the underground man *en situation*, as the French say, and only by examining it closely can we make any sense of his ravings and ranting. *Zapiski iz podpolia* (Notes from under the floor or floorboards), the Russian title of the story, no longer corresponds any too well to the word "underground" that Mrs. Constance Garnett chose for her English translation. By now the term "underground" has accumulated far too many implications, political and otherwise, that are quite foreign to Dostoevsky's intentions. For the undergroundling is no conspirator, no rebel; in his account of himself there is scarcely a hint that human existence has any kind of social or political dimension.

Who is he in fact? An idle intellectual who because of his persistent yet aimless cogitations turns "spiteful in his hole." At once proud and contemptuous of his own intelligence, he takes it to be the real cause of his failure to come to grips with life. In claiming that a man of the modern age (the nineteenth century, that is) "must be, is indeed morally bound to be a characterless person," he is referring solely to himself and his fellow intellectuals, for in the very same sentence he goes on to say that "a man of character, on the other hand, a man of action, is merely a fellow with a very circumscribed imagination." And there are plenty of those. So it appears that in modern times too there are enough men of action, though they belong to "the dull-witted" majority. The plain, normal man is stupid of course, yet he is not the one to butt his head against a stone wall; he knows how to go around it and to stand up for himself and take from life what he wants. Not so the undergroundling and his like, in whom civilization has developed that "manysidedness of sensations" that has converted them into the very antithesis of normality. And these are the strange specimens, the men of overwrought sensibility, who have sprung "*not* out of the lap of nature" but out of a test tube as it were. Nor is it by chance that the undergroundling, who complains that to be "acutely conscious is a disease, a real honest-to-goodness disease," is living in Petersburg, "the most abstract and premeditated city in the world." One can hardly imagine him dwelling in a more native, more organic place.

In the sense that they are both products of the Petersburgian genre of Russian literature, the undergroundling and Raskolnikov, the hero of the novel written right after the *Notes*, have certain turns of thought in common. For instance, they both divide humanity into two unequal parts, and this binary conception tends to command their imagination. For Raskolnikov the mass of men are ordinary people who cannot help but stay put in the common rut while a small number of superior and extraordinary men may permit themselves to overstep all barriers. The undergroundling, however, has an entirely different sort of division in mind: the normal and dull-witted men of character fully capable of action on the one hand, and, on the other, the isolated intellectuals who have lost touch with "real life" to the degree of actual disgust with it — "Why, we have gone so far as to look upon 'real life' as a sort of burden, and we are all agreed that life as we find it in books is much better.... Leave us alone without any books, and we shall at once get confused, lose ourselves in a maze, we shall not know ... what to love or to hate, what to respect or despise." So the undergroundling casts aside his habitual Schillerism, mocking his bookishness and literariness, and longs to find a way out of fantastication into vital existence.

And in the last paragraph of the *Notes* he proceeds from his own case to generalizations about the intelligentsia as a whole, thus justifying his attack on self-consciousness as a negative and life-denying element. In this connection Mochulsky is quite right in stating that here Dostoevsky is "posing the problem of contemporary Hamletism . . . in relation to the nature of consciousness." However, it is not consciousness in its character as a fundamental philosophical problem that Dostoevsky is concerned with but rather its particular use by the intelligentsia as a means of evasion of life or escape from it. It is in this sense that he subjects the intelligentsia, a special grouping thrown up by the modern division of labor, to a devastating criticism. The Russian intelligentsia, because of its position of extreme isolation from both the ruling upper strata and the people (the *narod*), is especially open to this criticism. It is among them, after all, that the idea of the superfluous man" acquired its intellectual subsistence. Yet in other countries too, where the intellectuals are somewhat less estranged from the social structure, they can still at least partly recognize themselves in the undergroundling's symptomatology: his clamor for consideration, mixed conceit and scorn of culture, and complaints of powerlessness. Indeed, there are not a few characters in modern Western fiction and drama who are directly or indirectly linked to him.

Where he is uniquely and exclusively himself is in the terrible spite eating away at him, for there is small chance that he will ever emerge from his dark cellar. It is hardly possible to conceive of him as succeeding in so circumscribing his imagination and sensibility as at last to turn into a man capable of self-assertive and positive activity. He will never be able to answer the question: *Chto lutche?* (which is better?) — "cheap happiness or exalted sufferings." Still, it is important to note that we leave him with an impression of immense vitality, of an unabashed and unabated love of life, of an unquenchable thirst for it. Hence we cannot but be swayed by the intransigent declaration with which he ends his confession:

> For my part, I have merely carried to extremes in my life what you have not dared to carry even half-way, and, in addition, you have mistaken your cowardice for common sense and have found comfort in that, deceiving yourselves. So that, as a matter of fact, I seem to be much more alive than you.

It is this veritable cult of life which stamps the man of the underground as a genuinely Dostoevskyean type. Despite their nasty "underground" and Karamazov-like traits, many of Dostoevsky's leading figures are tenaciously attached to life; and it is precisely their intuition of nothingness, barely hinted at by their author, which feeds their cult of life. Thus Raskolnikov, as he wanders through the streets of Petersburg in a state of despair verging on delirium, is nevertheless struck by the following thought:

> Where is it that I've read that someone condemned to death says or thinks, an hour before his death, that if he had to live on some high rock, on such a narrow ledge that he'd have room only to stand, and the ocean, everlasting darkness, everlasting tempest, around him, if he had to remain standing on a square yard of space all his life, a thousand years, an eternity, it were better to live than to die at once! Only to live and live! Life, whatever it may be! ... How true it is. Good God, how true! Man is a vile creature! ... And vile is he who calls him vile for that.

And Ivan Karamazov too, for all his intellectual extremism and experimentation with morally lethal ideas, such as "all is permitted," nonetheless admits to Alyosha that he has a longing for life and that he will go on living "in spite of logic." Many times he had asked himself

> whether there is in the world any despair that would overcome this frantic and perhaps unseemly thirst for life, and I have come to the conclusion that there isn't. ... Though I may not believe in the order of the universe, yet I love the sticky little leaves as they open in the spring. I love the blue sky, I love some people. ... I love some great deeds done by men, though I have long ceased to have faith in them.

Aware that this "frantic" thirst for life is "a feature of the Karamazovs," Ivan nevertheless insists that only "some consumptive moralists" would call it base — "The centripetal force of our planet is still fearfully strong." At bottom it was this feeling for the "centripetal force" and absolute identification with it that enabled Dostoevsky to alleviate, through the imaginative means he alone possessed, the undergroundling's cynical nihilism, to mitigate the impression conveyed by his ignoble and shameful remonstrances, thus redeeming him for literature conceived as an act of life.

Modern Occasions, 1972

The Other Dostoevsky

*Dostoevsky: the best and the worst, inseparable.
He really looks for the truth and fears to find it;
he often finds it all the same and then he is terrified . . . a poor great man. . . .*

VICTOR SERGE

THERE ARE TWO VISIONS in Dostoevsky, a major and a minor
one. The major one, expressing his passionate religiosity and nationalism, has been more than sufficiently written about, whereas the minor
one, atheistic in essence, has been noted hardly at all. Moreover, even
when interpreters have noted this vision they tend to distort it in the
attempt to assimilate it into Dostoevsky's more central and characteristic
concerns: he is thus credited with a unity of outlook that his work
cannot support.

In my view, Dostoevsky cannot be fully understood unless his anti-
thetic, or alternate, vision is taken into account — the dream of no less
than an earthly paradise to come, the age-old idea or myth of a golden
age no longer regretfully put in the distant past but hopefully projected into the future.

This alternate vision is cunningly dispersed in Dostoevsky's later
work and often formulated in a secretive, piecemeal, and even inverted
fashion. Hence one can scarcely present a coherent analysis of it
without first noting the essential vulnerability of his version of the
Christian world view. Very few of his numerous critics and expositors
have in fact been able to gauge the full measure of this vulnerability:
the reason for this is largely subjective, having to do chiefly with their
own religious or quasi-religious attachments.

Among these few, notably, is Prince D. D. Mirsky, who, in his highly
instructive *History of Russian Literature,* firmly rejects the unqualified
acceptance of Dostoevsky's work as "a revelation . . . in which ultimate
problems of good and evil are discussed and played out with ultimate

decisiveness and which, taken as a whole, gave a new doctrine of ... spiritual Christianity." Mirsky differs radically from the many interpreters adopting this approach in contending that the tragedies recounted by Dostoevsky are "irreducible tragedies that cannot be solved or pacified" and that his harmonies and solutions emerge "on a lower and shallower level than his conflicts." If his Christianity in particular strikes Mirsky as "of a very doubtful kind," the reason is that, in his opinion, it failed to reach the innermost recesses of the novelist's soul, being "a more or less superficial formation which it would be dangerous to identify with real Christianity."

Mirsky's *History* was first published in 1926, when he was very far indeed from his later conversion to political radicalism. In truth he was then not in the least interested in controverting the Christian doctrine on ideological or any other grounds. His criticism was if anything largely concerned with aesthetic valuations (though it was invariably linked to his acute understanding of the historical and psychological conditions associated with the rise of Russian literary expression). It is nevertheless typical of the direction that Dostoevsky studies have taken virtually since the novelist's death that an approach as disinterested as Mirsky's should not have been taken into account at all by what one might call the devout league of commentators, that is, those persuaded of Dostoevsky's exemplary Christianity. I have in mind, to mention only a few representative names, such men as Berdyaev, Mochulsky, Zenkovsky, and Vyacheslav Ivanov among the White Russian *émigrés*, R. P. Blackmur and Eliseo Vivas among the Americans, and, among the innumerable German studies, such a work as Reinhard Lauth's immensely long and ostensibly exhaustive *Die Philosophie Dostojewskis in systematischer Darstellung* (1950).

The aforementioned German work, which might be rendered into English as *Dostoevsky's Philosophy Systematically Presented*, is in itself a critical *gaffe* of the first order. For in Dostoevsky there is in fact no systematic philosophy, no consistent and logically shaped point of view, neither a stable outlook nor any kind of mental stasis. His speculatively charged, dynamic, spiritually and intellectually turbulent mode of thought breeds mostly insoluble contradictions, paradoxes at once stimulating and disruptive, as well as outright antinomies. The ponderous systematizing that Herr Lauth goes in for with such dogged persistence is a quality of his own intellectual temper, not of Dostoevsky's.

In truth, the Russian novelist can be spoken of as a philosopher only in a loose, analogical sense. Dostoevsky, whose thinking frequently proceeds in seeming unawareness of his contradictions, is no philosopher at all, in the strict sense of the term. Thus when Berdyaev remarks somewhere that Dostoevsky is to be regarded as Russia's greatest philosopher, all one can reply is that he must be using a definition of philosophy that most students of that discipline would find totally unacceptable. Or else that he is simply confusing the depth and acuteness of the Dostoevskyean consciousness with the specific kind of mental process that philosophers properly engage in.*

To my mind, Dostoevsky is best characterized as primarily a dramatic fabulist who happened to be intensely and singularly drawn to sheer thinking without regard to the rigors of method or logic. Always open to ideas, he converts them into highly dramatic (and quite as often melodramatic) forces in his fictive worlds, into the very particulars of emotions, action, purpose, and character, while at the same time mixing freely, almost casually, his scrutiny of the actual world with intuitions belonging essentially to the sphere of the numinous.

A number of scholarly works have been published in the Soviet Union that are of undoubted value in establishing the facts and circumstances of Dostoevsky's career; but in evaluating his work, the Soviet critics tend to follow the party line of denigrating the idea that Dostoevsky was a writer of world stature endowed with uncommon ideological and psychological powers. Instead, when not discrediting him altogether, they restrict his role to that of an antagonist of "bourgeois values" and champion of "the insulted and injured."

The attitude of Marxists not bound by the party line cannot be summed up so easily. In *Literature and Revolution* Trotsky, while by no means discounting Dostoevsky's importance as a great Russian creative figure, bluntly alludes to his Christianity as "perfidious." Georg Lukacs's essay in his book *Der russiche Realismus in der Weltliteratur* is

---

* That the Russians have never been very strong in philosophy is well known. In this sphere they are pupils, not teachers. No wonder that even as late as 1912 Trotsky, annoyed by the extravagant pretensions of the Russian intelligentsia, was able to taunt it for its sterility in philosophy. He asked: "What exactly have we given in the area of philosophy or social science?" His answer: "Nothing, a round zero. Vladimir Solovyov, who is usually remembered only on the anniversary of his death? His foggy metaphysics has not entered the history of world-thought; even in Russia his ideas failed to produce anything like a philosophical movement." Trotsky continues by holding up to scorn the philosophical small fry who are looking forward to the imminent appearance of "a Slavic Kant." "Where is he? He does not exist. Where is our Hegel? Where is one of equal importance in the history of thought? In philosophy we have none but third-rate disciples and faceless epigoni." (Cf., Trotsky's essay "Concerning the Intelligentsia," *Partisan Review*, Fall, 1968.)

illuminating, though too limited in scope to allow for anything like the full development of a Marxist perspective. It is precisely from such a perspective, however, that Arnold Hauser is able to present an elaborate, thoughtful, and highly plausible critical account in his *Social History of Art*.* In Hauser's view Dostoevsky owes the depth and refinement of his psychology

> . . . to the intensity with which he experiences the problematical nature of the modern intellectual, whereas the naiveté of his moral philosophy comes from his antirationalistic escapades, from his betrayal of reason and his inability to resist the temptations of romanticism and abstract idealism. His mystical nationalism, his religious orthodoxy, and his intuitive ethics form an intellectual unity, and obviously originate in the same experience, the same spiritual shock. . . . Only in later years Dostoevsky becomes the moralist, the mystic and the reactionary that he is often summarily described to be.

Still, having said all this Hauser proceeds to draw a distinction between the consciously held ideas of writers and their world view as shown in their creative practice. In the case of Dostoevsky, to be sure, this distinction is of particular significance. As Hauser puts it, "What decides the world-view of a writer is not so much whose side he supports as through whose eyes he looks at the world." When it comes to that one hardly needs to insist any longer that the author of *The Brothers Karamazov* looked at what is new in the world with far greater deliberateness, profundity, and agitation through the eyes of Ivan than through those of his nominal favorite, Alyosha, or through those of the laboriously wrought saintly Father Zossima. The same goes for *Crime and Punishment*, where it is not Sonia Marmeladov's pitiable situation and frenzy of faith that cast a spell over us but the restless spirit and conflict-ridden mind of the freethinker Raskolnikov.

On this theme it is well worth recalling the observation of an acute if somewhat casual American commentator that in order to account for Dostoevsky's numerous paradoxes one must first grasp the fact that he is a 99 percent atheist and therefore a 101 percent believer. Comments of this nature are hard to come by, however. Most writers on Dostoevsky, flinching from this sort of discriminating approach, prefer to repeat mechanically after him his overstated because only half-believed-in formulas of deliverance from evil, Christian renewal, and ultimate salvation.

Being at once an extreme skeptic and an extreme believer generated in Dostoevsky a chronically antinomic state of mind which he surrepti-

*Cf., pp. 142 ff. of *The Social History of Art*, Vol. 4 (Vintage Books).

tiously relished, I believe, even as he tried to conceal it from his
readers and especially from his patrons, including the renowned Pobe-
donstsev, who belonged to aristocratic and official circles. To ascribe
this to mere disingenuousness would be far too simple. It would mean
losing sight of his deep ambivalence, the complexity of his sensibility
and mind, as well as the extreme contradictions of the historical moment which in his own way he embodied.

The first thing to be considered is that Dostoevsky experienced in
his lifetime (even if only within the milieu of the newly formed intelligentsia) the heady and precipitate secularization of Russia, a process
aptly characterized by the critic E. Lampert (*Studies in Rebellion*,
London, 1957) as spelling "the end of a world created with the fixity
of the iconographic canon." It was at this immensely fateful juncture
in Russian history that Dostoevsky felt impelled to resist with frenetic
zeal the impact of Western thought, its radical social ideas no less
than its religious ones, whether Catholic or Protestant. Yet he never
really succeeded in extricating himself from the torture chamber of
doubt and unbelief that are part of the modern consciousness. In spite
of his ranting against the westernizing wing of the intelligentsia, he
could never really purge himself of the forbidden fruit of European
civilization.

It seems to me that a good many Western analysts of Russian culture and society err in making far too little of the suddenness with
which European ideas entered Russia. For the shock of the "illumination" brought by these ideas was virtually a mental and political revolution. To be sure, there are significant exceptions among Western
analysts. One such is Thomas Masaryk, who, in the second volume of
his book *The Spirit of Russia* (1919), has much that is pertinent to say
on this subject:

> Let the reader call to mind Tolstoy's *Confession,* where that writer de-
> scribes the revolution that took place within his mind when he learned,
> as a great novelty, that there was no God. In Europe, generations and
> centuries prepared the way for this novelty; medieval philosophy and
> theocratic organization had been transformed step by step. . . .
>
> But think of theocratic Russia, enter into the mind of the religiously
> trained Russian, and realize how there came to him, like a bolt from the
> blue, the message of Voltaire, Diderot, Comte, Kant, Hegel, Feuerbach,
> Stirner, Vogt, Straus and Marx. . . .
>
> But what must have been the effect of the sudden invasion of unbelief
> in Russia, a land where the church and its monasteries had hitherto been
> the highest and indeed the sole generally recognized spiritual author-
> ity. . . . In England Mill and Darwin were buried in Westminster Abbey;

in Russia, such men as Chernishevsky, adherents of Mill and Darwin, found their way to the penitentiary or to Siberia!

We know that in his youth Dostoevsky was captivated by illicit "messages" from Europe and that owing to his active involvement in the radical Petrashevsky circle he, too, soon "found his way" to a penitentiary in Siberia. This experience appears to have so unnerved him that upon his return from Siberia he gradually but decisively shifted his position and in his later work he no longer hesitated to adhere openly (and with the excessive zeal typical of converts) to Russian Orthodoxy and the more extreme forms of Slavophilism. It must be admitted, however, that this *volte-face* in no way weakened his creative powers. Perhaps this is so because in his apparent conversion there is more surface than substance, more willful rhetoric, seeming all the more intransigent for its willfulness, than positive conviction.

As a creative man of devastating intelligence, simultaneously visionary and subversive in temper, he harbored the radical suspicion that human beings are inherently incapable of ever fulfilling the Christian commandments of love and goodness. At times he was inclined to think that, contrary to Christian doctrine, man is altogether beyond redemption inasmuch as what has been built into him is "the faculty of cherishing in his soul the loftiest ideal side by side with his greatest baseness, and all quite sincerely."

This is said by Versilov, a principal character in *A Raw Youth*, but his is not an isolated case. You find different versions of the same idea in most of Dostoevsky's fiction. With which characters of his own creation does he identify most closely? According to Nikolay Strakhov, his intimate friend, Slavophile comrade-in-arms, and coauthor of the offical *Life and Letters*, "the characters who are most like him are the hero of *Notes from Underground*, Svidrigailov in *Crime and Punishment*, and Stavrogin in *The Possessed*." Note that these figures belong to the children of darkness, whom he condemns in his novels, not to his idealized children of light like Sonia Marmeladov, Prince Myshkin, Alyosha, and Father Zossima.

I think it is a grave error, however, to attribute Dostoevsky's very conspicuous "duality," as it is often called, to purely personal traits, to some kind of private psychogenic drama. He held it to be an incontrovertible truth that this duality is inherent in human consciousness, is tenaciously rooted in it. It is difficult to contest his keen insight in this matter. The point is that this insight does have conceptual consequences hardly compatible with his Christian faith; for surely the hope of ultimate Christian salvation is altogether futile if the split between good and evil in human nature is *never* to be overcome. This is not the least of the factors persuading one to call into question the role of saint and prophet he assumed in his later years.

As a writer he combined unbounded imagination and psychological intuition with an equally unbounded ideological striving so provocative and even lurid in its effects as to lay himself open to the charge of spiritual licentiousness and presumption. What else could Chekhov have had in mind when he expressed distaste for his work on account of its "spiritual immodesty"? In my view, Dostoevsky was neither "honest" nor "good." What he undoubtedly possessed, however, was greatness of soul.

His major fiction sufficiently attests to that greatness. Integral to his world is the paradoxical and highly original manner in which belief and unbelief are compounded in his work. To be sure, Dostoevsky delineated in various ways the unbelief of which he could not rid himself and which he covertly cherished. But it is worth stressing that the only well-formed and above all *affirmative* expression of his unbelief is comprised in his alternate vision of an earthly paradise marked out for the distant future when men, having abandoned their faith in God and immortality, nonetheless secrete from the very finality of their disenchantment, and from their absolute conviction of their forlorn situation in the universe, a new and as yet unheard of innocence leading to genuine peace and happiness.

The first hint of this vision is contained in *The Possessed,* in Stavrogin's dream of "a corner of the Greek archipelago as it was some three thousand years ago." The dream derives from Stavrogin's persistent memory of Claude Lorraine's painting *Acis and Galatea,* which he had once seen in the Dresden museum and which he chooses to call "The Golden Age." (According to his biographers, Dostoevsky had seen this picture several times and it made an indelible impression on him.)

In Stavrogin's version of the dream only the mythological past with its connotations of innocence and happiness is recalled, whereas in later works the past is displaced by the future. In a more elaborate form the vision is explored in *A Raw Youth* (1875). It receives further elaboration in "The Dream of a Ridiculous Man," published two years later, in which the vision of a golden age is transposed to a distant star whose inhabitants live harmoniously in their human and natural environment, as men might some day live on our own planet. Finally, in *The Brothers Karamazov* a recapitulation of this dream of an earthly paradise is mockingly recited by the devil, Ivan's alter ego and the product of his hallucination.

Admittedly this Dostoevskyean theme cannot be described as anything more than a minor vision expressed shamefacedly, with no end of equivocation. No wonder a good many of Dostoevsky's critics failed even to notice its presence. The major vision to which he continually and strenuously committed and recommitted himself he defined succinctly as "the Russian idea which will restore the world." With the utmost stubbornness he insisted on mixing his "Russian idea" with his passionate Christology. It seems that he was unable to hold on to Christ without his Russianism, or to his Russianism without Christ. Thus he wrote to Maykov in January 1867:

> Our people is immeasurably higher, nobler, more upright, more capable, and filled with a different, higher, Christian idea, which Europe with its dead carcass of Catholicism, and its stupidly self-contradictory Lutheranism, cannot even understand.

For someone as intelligent as Dostoevsky to make such brashly unconditional claims suggests that he was far from certain of their truth and was merely trying hard to convince himself. Yet, astonishingly enough, at the very same time he was constructing in his mind an alternate vision, devoid of either Russianism or religiosity. Like his major vision, his alternate minor vision is mystical as well as utopian even while radically negating "the sovereign idea," as he once called it, of immortality or any other survival of the belief in the supernatural.

The earthly paradise this vision projects is of course sheer heresy considered from the standpoint of Christian theology, but it does not have anything in common with what the Marxists call "scientific socialism." It is a conception entirely inspired by the abstract-idealist mode of thought, involving no material and political exertions, yet the edge of its idealism is sharp enough to cut through all notions of the religious renunciation of the world and man's rise to transcendent reality in the divine.

There is a dialectical twist in the way in which Dostoevsky distributes the dream among his characters. Thus Stavrogin himself, of whom we are told that he has lost all sense of the distinction between good and evil, first dreams of the "magic panorama" suggested by Claude Lorraine's painting *Acis and Galatea*. Of all the figures in *The Possessed* he is surely the one most desperately in need of it. For him the dream serves as therapy, even if the therapy finally fails when a small dot in the center of the light grows into the shape of a red spider, and the dream turns into a nightmare, reminding him of the spider he saw on a geranium leaf when Matryosha, the little girl he had violated, stood haggard and with feverish eyes on the threshold of his room lifting her tiny fist against him.

Yet if the dream is spoiled for Stavrogin, who is beyond saving, it already contains in embryo the characteristic scene that dominates all of the dreams in Dostoevsky's later works. The following is Stavrogin's account of the dream, preceded by the explanation that Claude Lorraine's picture appeared in it "yet not as a picture but as though it were an actual scene":

> As in the picture, I saw a corner of the Greek archipelago the way it was some three thousand years ago: caressing azure waves, rocks and islands, a shore in blossom, afar a magic panorama, a beckoning sunset — words fail one. European mankind remembers this place as its cradle. . . .
> Here was mankind's earthly paradise, gods descended from heaven and united with mortals. . . . Here lived beautiful men and women! They rose, they went to sleep, happy and innocent; the groves rang with their merry songs, the great overflow of unspent energies poured itself into love and simple-hearted joys. . . .
> Oh, how happy I was that my heart was shaken and at last I loved! The sun poured its rays upon these isles and this sea, rejoicing in its fair children. Oh, marvelous dream, lofty illusion! The most improbable of all visions, to which mankind throughout its existence has given its best energies . . . for which it has pined and been tormented, for which its prophets were crucified and killed. . . .
> All these sensations I lived through, as it were, in this dream. I do not know exactly what I dreamed about, my dream was only of sensation, but the cliffs, and the sea, and the slanting rays of the setting sun, all that I still seemed to see when I woke up and opened my eyes, for the first time in my life literally wet with tears. . . .
> A feeling of happiness, hitherto unknown to me, pierced my heart till it ached. . . . But suddenly I noticed a tiny dot in the center of the bright, bright light. . . .

Thus it is not given to Stavrogin, who leads "a life, so to speak, of mockery," and to whom good and evil are merely words without real substance, to see any more in the "marvelous dream" than the "lofty illusion" of a golden age that has passed beyond recall. It is only in his next novel, A Raw Youth, that Dostoevsky contrived to plant a more complete and ideologically explicit version of Stavrogin's painfully curtailed dream. Perhaps because this novel was first published serially in the progressive periodical National Notes, edited by the famous radical-populist poet Nekrasov, Dostoevsky could proceed freely to spin out and interpret his obsessive vision in a fashion that he might have thought inappropriate for the earlier novel, in fact as contradicting its national messianism. In the new novel he did permit himself, however, to let Versilov (who is actually, if not nominally, the chief figure) report on the dream in such a way as to disclose its true import, which now bears more on an idealized future than on the mythological past.

It is important to note that Versilov begins his account with almost exactly the same words used by Stavrogin. Again we hear of the picture *Acis and Galatea*, which Versilov too renames "The Golden Age," and again we are told of the vivid impression of a corner of the Greek archipelago, of its smiling waves, isles, and rocks, "a flowery shore, a view like fairyland in the distance, a setting sun with its slanting rays," in short, the scene of "an earthly paradise where gods come down from the skies" and where lives, happy and innocent, "a splendid race." In the rest of the passage he goes on to repeat almost verbatim Stavrogin's effusion:

> The Golden Age is the most unlikely of all the dreams that have been, but for it men have given up their life and all their strength, for the sake of it prophets have died and have been slain, without it the peoples will not live and cannot die, and the feeling of this I lived through, as it were, in that dream; rocks and sea, and the slanting rays — all this I seemed to see when I woke up and opened my eyes, literally wet with tears. I remember that I was glad, a sensation of happiness I had never known before thrilled my heart till it ached; it was the love of all humanity.

Versilov is a humanist, whose experience excludes Stavrogin's extreme desperation. His dream is not cut off by a tiny dot which turns into a red spider. The thoughts the dream suggests to him are animated by fervent hope, an auspicious view of the future in which the naive innocence of the golden age of the past is transcended in a new unity of mankind forged almost "on the last day of humanity" in spite of the absence of God. This absence is definitive, as Versilov makes clear to his son Arkady. Never again is Dostoevsky so outspoken about the larger implications of his secular vision. To understand these implications, it is necessary at this point to quote Versilov in full:

> I picture to myself, my boy... that war is at an end and strife has ceased. After curses, pelting with mud, and hisses, has come a lull, and men are left alone, according to their desire; the great idea of old has left

them; the great source of strength that till then had nourished and fostered them was vanishing like the majestic sun setting in Claude Lorraine's picture, but it was somehow the last day of humanity, and men suddenly understood that they were left quite alone, and at once felt terribly forlorn.

I have never, dear boy, been able to picture men ungrateful and grown stupid. Men left forlorn would begin to draw together more closely and more lovingly; they would clutch one another's hands, realizing that they were all that was left for one another! The great idea of immortality would have vanished, and they would have to fill its place; and all the wealth of love lavished upon Him, who was immortal, would be turned upon the whole of nature, on the world, on men, on every blade of grass. They would inevitably grow to love the earth and life as they gradually became aware of their transitory and finite nature, and with special love, not as of old, they would begin to observe and would discover in nature phenomena and secrets which they had not suspected before, for they would look at nature with new eyes, as a lover looking on his beloved.

On awakening they would hasten to kiss one another, eager to love, knowing that their days are short, and that is all that is left to them. They would work for one another, and each would give up all that he had to all, and by that only would be happy. Every child would know and feel that every one on earth was for him like a father and mother. "Tomorrow may be the last day," each one would think, looking at the setting sun; "but no matter, I shall die, but all they will remain and after them their children," and anxious over each other, would replace the thought of meeting beyond the tomb.

Oh, they would be in haste to love, to stifle the great sorrow in their hearts. They would be proud and brave for themselves, but would grow timid for one another; every one would tremble for the life and happiness of each; they would grow tender with one another, and would not be ashamed of it as now, and would be as caressing as children. Meeting, they would look at one another with deep and thoughtful eyes, and in their eyes would be love and sorrow.

How strange it is to hear a Dostoevskyean spokesman no longer predicting that following the loss of faith ("the great idea of old . . . the great source of strength") men will plunge into a terror of chaos but declaring instead that it is this very loss that will enable them finally to open a window to the sun — that is, to the whole of nature, to an affirmation of the sufficiency of the earthly life and to the tender even if sorrowful love binding them each to each that results from the knowledge of their absolute forlornness in the universe, a love, moreover, that will do away with war and strife.

Out of a heterodox anthropocentrism Dostoevsky thus constructs a veritable idyll of atheism; and this idyll, however visionary, calls into question and in a sense negates the final vision of chaos induced by unbelief which is evoked in his creation of such children of darkness as Raskolnikov and Stavrogin. This is a significant reversal of values. True, it is a purely hypothetical reversal; Dostoevsky does not indulge in it fully, or without equivocation. What holds him back is probably the fear of acknowledging (not least to himself) his variant conception of the future — that "the great idea of old" is bound to vanish in time, being no more than a historical "error" or "illusion," and that mankind will not only survive the loss but even finally achieve liberation from the vices of the past.

Such an admission on Dostoevsky's part might after all be read as in effect annulling his religious commitment; it is as if having reached this point in explicating his dream of an earthly paradise he is positively appalled by his own temerity. Thus he recklessly begins to maneuver to have it both ways. How? By imposing on Versilov's long speech — which, in its explicitness, cuts to the heart of the matter — an additional brief paragraph that appears to deny everything that has just been said. It is obvious to the critical reader that this paragraph is artificially tacked on. For here Versilov remarks with cavalier inconsequence that he cannot complete the picture of the future he has drawn without recalling Heine's vision of "Christ on the Baltic Sea." "I could not get on without Him. I could not help imagining Him, in fact, in the midst of his bereaved people. He comes to them . . . and then, as it were, the scales would fall from their eyes and there would break forth the great rapturous hymn of the new and last resurrection."

The Christ so suddenly and preposterously sprung upon us at the end of Versilov's speech strikes us as a strictly supposititious, or at best vestigial, figure — the phantom of a reluctant atheist. At this point Dostoevsky might well be accused of insincerity. However, I prefer to construe this hollow-sounding ending, which patently contravenes everything that Versilov had said before, as another instance of the Russian novelist's frequent practice of letting obdurate hope and irrational faith dissolve the imaginative logic as well as the intellectual coherence of even his most acute and original speculations.*

While Stavrogin's and Versilov's accounts of their dreams are no more than digressions, bearing no direct relation to the plotting of the novels

---

* It goes without saying that this tendency, bespeaking double-mindedness and irresolution, plays right into the hands of the devout believers among the Dostoevsky critics and scholars. In trying to overcome the dilemma that his alternate vision puts them in, they apply various methods. Some, not understanding what

in which they occur, the story of the "ridiculous man," on the other hand, is entirely centered on this theme, which is now developed to its maximum dramatic intensity and ideological value. Certain thematic variations of great complexity are also added. The elements in the story are fully rendered dramatically and psychologically, with no resort to "the banality of mere statement," as the Jamesian phrase has it. It is a truly superb fictional representation of its author's enduring vision of an earthly paradise. And his habitual fluctuation, his wavering between the two visions — the major Christian one and its antithetical alternate — are wholly embodied in it.

The "ridiculous man," the narrator-protagonist of the story, might as

---

they read, simply ignore it; others interpret it in such a way as utterly to distort its meaning.

For example the late Konstantin Mochulsky, a belated convert to Orthodoxy who served to the end of his life on the faculty of the St. Sergius Theological Seminary in Paris, literally turns handsprings to make us believe that Dostoevsky's minor alternate vision is merely a variant of his major Christian vision and is actually of a piece with it. He is quite aware that the three dreams — Stavrogin's, Versilov's, and that of the "ridiculous man" — form one whole, "a kind of triptych." But what is his interpretation? Basing himself entirely and with ludicrous solemnity on Versilov's appended last-minute appeal to Christ, while ignoring all that precedes it, he concludes that the triptych proves Dostoevsky's belief in "the resurrection and transfiguration of the flesh." Thus all ends happily for him with "the hymn of the last resurrection" (cf., p. 556 of *Dostoevsky: His Life and Work*, Princeton, 1967).

Nicolas Berdyaev, on the other hand, also a convert and a more prominent one, distorts Dostoevsky's text in a wholly different way. Unlike Mochulsky, he admits that what Versilov is saying is that all people will come to love each other and be at one "because the great idea of love and eternal life which used to sustain them had now been lost." Berdyaev goes even further in characterizing this "picture of love without God" as the "antithesis of Christian love." Where is the way out, then, for a commentator intent on making Dostoevsky out to be an exemplary Christian? The way out is blandly to assume, without bothering even to provide the slightest bit of textual evidence, that Dostoevsky is in no way implicated in Versilov's heretical vision. By thus denying the complicity that binds author to character, Berdyaev converts Versilov's speech into another Dostoevskyean dire warning that without immortality there can be no true love (cf., p. 128 ff. of *Dostoevsky*, Meridian Books, 1957).

This last claim may well be Berdyaev's most cherished belief, but to read it into Dostoevsky's alternate vision is a gross misrepresentation of the text. For one thing, Versilov is not an "adversary" character. For another, in the account he gives of his dream he is clearly being used by his author simply to voice a prescient, even if in some respects visionary, heretical-secularist speculation that other characters, who have nothing in common with Versilov, repeat in other contexts. In truth, Dostoevsky was never as simple-minded or narrow-minded as most of his dogmatic Orthodox commentators, of whatever Christian denomination, who set out to interpret him in such a homiletic fashion as to make certain of support for their truculent piety. Plainly, their main concern is to enlist the prestigious novelist as a "witness" in the service of their faith. In this biased procedure all literary-critical distinctions are invariably lost.

well be called the "absurd man," for in his singularly modern extremity he anticipates those figures of the "absurd" that haunt twentieth-century literature. At the very start the narrator tells us that he was "terribly disheartened" because of one circumstance beyond his power to control: "namely, the conviction which was gaining upon me that nothing in the whole world *made any difference*" (italics in the text).

Worse than that, he felt that it made no difference to him "whether the world existed or whether nothing existed anywhere at all." More-over, from the acute consciousness that nothing existed in his own life-time he gradually derives the idea that nothing existed in the past either, "only for some reason it had merely seemed to have been," so that inevitably, even if little by little, he becomes convinced that "there would be nothing in the future either." In so "absurd" a situation his indifference mounts to the point where he ceases being angry with people and almost stops noticing them. With the total disappearance of meaning, with existence following essence into the void, the "ridicu-lous man" has no option but to decide to shoot himself.

The only question left open is precisely when to pull the trigger. So he sits down at the table, draws the gun out of the drawer, and puts it in front of him, being certain that he will shoot himself that very night. The one thing he does not know is how much longer he will go on sitting at that table. While so sitting he falls asleep and dreams with-out being aware of it that he has already shot himself and is buried in the earth. But suddenly the grave is opened and he is "seized by some dark and unknown being" who carries him off into outer space, and after a long flight puts him down on another planet where he finds himself in the midst of the very earthly paradise that both Stavrogin and Versilov had dreamed of. The "ridiculous man" describes it in virtually identical words:

> I stood on this other earth in the bright light of a sunny day fair and beautiful as paradise. I believe I was standing on one of the islands which on our earth form the Greek archipelago. . . . Oh, everything was just as it is with us, except that everything seemed to be bathed in the radiance of some public festival and of some great and holy triumph attained at last. The gentle emerald sea softly lapped the shore and kissed it with manifest, visible, almost conscious love.

Once again the scene suggested by Claude Lorraine's *Acis and Galatea* is evoked. This third dreamer, "a modern Russian progressive and a despicable citizen of Petersburg," begins observing the life of the beau-tiful race that inhabits this earthly paradise. He is astonished to learn that these people "desired nothing and were at peace with themselves." Playful and high-spirited, they wander about their lovely woods and groves, living on simple food and conversing with the trees and with the animals that love them. They know sexual life and beget children, but the narrator never notices in them "those outbursts of *cruel* sensuality which overtake almost everybody on earth." Their idea of "life eternal" is so thoroughly pantheistic as to have nothing in common with the Christian conception of it:

> They found it almost impossible to understand me when I questioned them about life eternal, but apparently they were so convinced of it in their minds that for them it was no question at all. They had no places of worship, but they had a certain awareness of a constant, uninterrupted, and living union with the Universe at large. They had no specific religion, but instead they had a certain knowledge that when their earthly joy had reached the limits imposed upon it by nature, they — both the living and the dead — would reach a state of still closer communion with the Universe at large. They looked forward to that moment with joy, but without haste and without pining for it. . . .

Clearly, the Christian world view is not only unknown but also wholly superfluous to these dwellers in the earthly paradise who, as is expressly stated, have "no places of worship" or any "specific religion." Living as they do in close communion with "the Universe at large," they know nothing of the radical separation of man from nature (out of which grow the attendant notions of personal immortality and salvation) which is the deepest and most fundamental assumption underlying all of our "higher" religions.

There is no authorial comment or intrusion in the narrator's report on the happy mode of life he observes so exultingly. His acquiescence in it can be taken only as a form of identification. In his previous state of "absurdity" as in his later ecstasy — when "the sensation of the fullness of life" leaves him "breathless" as he "worships" the new life he has discovered — the narrator is at one with the writer, who in this way finds it possible to undercut his own ostensible Christian conviction without taking direct responsibility for secretly receding from it.

But what happens? As it turns out, the nameless narrator, the "despicable citizen of Petersburg" and a modern "Russian progressive" to boot, secretly suffers from a spiritual emptiness in his new-found paradise. As he puts it: "Surely my paltry heart and my vacillating and trivial mind could not have risen to such a revelation of truth!" At this point a different and horribly shocking truth is disclosed to us by the narrator — "I have been concealing it all the time, but . . . the fact is, I — corrupted them all."

This is the story's sudden reversal, the inevitable Fall into the hell of mankind's history as Dostoevsky realistically perceives it, which in other contexts he accepts or even, when overcome by his passionate Christianity, forgets. (He returns to it later in the story, at the very end, though unconvincingly, for it is much too late to effect another reversal.) In the very long passage that follows, however, he is again at one with the narrator, when, with a kind of analytic ferocity, he sums up what men are like and what they have done, without a hint of redemption. He appears to be telling us what happened on the other, the imaginary planet, after the Fall. It is all too clear that he is speaking about us, the inmates of our familiar and sadly exclusive earth. A short extract from this long passage will suggest its flavor and historical meaning:

> They learnt to lie, and they grew to appreciate the beauty of a lie. . . . Then voluptuousness was soon born, voluptuousness begot jealousy, and jealousy — cruelty. . . . Very soon the first blood was shed: they were shocked and horrified, and they began to separate and to shun one another. They formed alliances, but it was one against another. Recriminations began, reproaches. They came to know shame, and they made shame into a virtue. The conception of honor was born, and every alliance raised its own standard. . . .
> A struggle began for separation, for isolation, for personality, for mine and thine. They began talking in different languages. They came to know sorrow, and they loved sorrow. They thirsted for suffering, and they said that Truth could only be attained by suffering. It was then that science made its appearance among them. When they became wicked, they began talking of brotherhood and humanity and understood the meaning of those ideas. When they became guilty of crimes, they invented justice, and drew up whole codes of law, and to ensure the carrying out of their laws they erected a guillotine.
> They only vaguely remembered . . . that they ever were happy and innocent. They even laughed at the possibility of their former happiness and called it a dream . . . but the strange and wonderful thing was that though they had lost faith in their former state of happiness . . . they longed so much to be happy and innocent once more that, like children, they succumbed to the desire of their hearts, glorified this desire, built temples, and began offering up prayers to their own idea, their own "desire," and at the same time firmly believed that is could not be realized and brought about, though they still worshipped and adored it with tears.

Still, after this bitter résumé of history, in which all values, however supernal and glorified in religious tradition, have been ruthlessly exposed and traced to criminal sources, the "ridiculous man" awakes from his dream only to declare, in a mood of naive optimism, that now that he has "beheld the Truth," he knows that "people can be happy and beautiful without losing their ability to live on earth." It is really very simple; all that is necessary is "to love your neighbor as yourself."

It is plain that in this last page of his story Dostoevsky is back doing business at his old stand. The ending he has devised cannot be taken seriously. It lacks credibility. It is the product of Dostoevsky's attempt to have it both ways — to destroy the Christian version of history while at the same time recovering his belief and appeasing his conscience as a Christian. This ending can satisfy only the devout among his critics and expositors, who cannot accept the far-reaching exposure of values that precedes it.

It seems to me that this story perfectly exemplifies Victor Serge's observation that Dostoevsky "looks for the truth and fears to find it" and when he finds it "all the same . . . then he is terrified." Dostoevsky's truth is incorporated in the body of the story, his fear of it in the ending.

Let us then disregard the factitious ending. Indeed, the story's implicit logic prepares us for a different ending altogether. Upon awakening, should not the "ridiculous man," having been admitted to an earthly paradise only to act in it as the agent of corruption — "a horrible trichina, a germ of the plague" — finally carry out his initial resolve to kill himself? For now more than ever his design of suicide is fully motivated. After all, having "infected" the happy and innocent people, he has witnessed the rise, out of nothing less than their "wickedness," of consolatory but empty ideals, ideals that tease their "wickedness" without ever dislodging it.

Nor are the ideals that Dostoevsky cherished spared. Has he not repeatedly exalted suffering as heuristic and humanizing? Yet in the dream planet, which is really an analogue of our own, the corrupted people are shown to thirst for suffering, saying that "Truth can only be attained by suffering." But that is only another of the innumerable ways they have devised to rationalize away their "wickedness." Furthermore, we are told that precisely as they became "wicked they began talking of brotherhood and humanity. . . ." So much for Christian values!

But this is by no means all. Through the medium of his analytical dreamer Dostoevsky proceeds to tell us that having no real faith in their former state of happiness, these corrupted people "longed so much to be happy and innocent once more" that they yielded "to the desire of their hearts" and began building temples and offering prayers "to their own idea, their own desire." This insight into the essence of religion virtually corresponds to Feuerbach's idea that man abstracts the best in himself, alienates his ideal self by projecting it into a distant heaven as if it were an entity whose existence is outside himself. For Dostoevsky, the passionate Christian, to confess to that much is brutal heresy.

The form this parable takes is of great interest. Instead of projecting his earthly paradise into the future, as he usually did, Dostoevsky materializes it here and now by locating it on another planet. This permits him to describe a merely imaginary future as actually existing in the present while at the same time he shifts our own historical past to the future conceived as following rather than preceding the golden age. Thus he organizes the progress of the story so as to produce a kind of anamorphic image in which past, present, and future are made to coexist, like a distorted drawing that appears natural in a curved mirror.

In this way he accomplishes a double aim: he exhibits the splendors of the longed-for golden age while simultaneously exhibiting the innate evil of our nature which brings about its disintegration. This procedure fully expresses his own basic duality. In his own way he believes in his dream of the earthly paradise yet at the same time, because of his pessimism about human nature, he cannot fully commit himself to his vision but can only play with it.

Of course, according to Christian theology the idea proclaimed by the narrator upon awakening from his dream that "people can be happy and beautiful without losing their ability to live on earth" is wholly unacceptable. Theology teaches us that it is futile for man to seek to realize the divine in the earthly; he must aspire to a life in God. Here, in disdaining heavenly compensation, Dostoevsky is entirely abandoning orthodoxy, though without seeming to be aware of the implications of this abandonment. He wants the kingdom of God to be established in the here and now, and for this reason he constructs his earthly paradise, which is *the* kingdom. Yet the pressure of his ambivalence with its irrepressible iconoclasm is so great that he ends by destroying it.

Every time Dostoevsky embarked on the composition of a new work he was compelled at once to remake and unmake both the believer and unbeliever in himself. Toward the end of 1877, soon after publishing "The Dream of a Ridiculous Man," he began *The Brothers Karamazov*. In that great work the vision of an earthly paradise is again invoked, though under very ambiguous circumstances. This time the devil, appearing to Ivan in his delirium, recalls it as he repeats Ivan's innermost thoughts to mock them. Ivan's devil is an up-to-date one, sophisticated, a master ironist and sophist, a virtuoso of every nuance of malice.

Many critics of Dostoevsky have dealt with Ivan's session with the devil, but none that I can think of has ever referred to the particular passage in which the devil implicitly connects Ivan's unvoiced reflections on the theme of the earthly paradise with those of Versilov and the "ridiculous man." This internal reference, suggesting the author's preoccupation with this theme, cannot be properly understood unless it is read in the context of the devil's tactic of slyly denigrating Ivan's thought so as to deprive it of honor. What he is after is not only to exacerbate Ivan's guilt but also to make him feel that his thinking has been criminally foolish. It is a brilliant passage:

> ... Oh, I love the dreams of my ardent young friends, quivering with eagerness for life! ... Oh, blind race of men who have no understanding! As soon as men have all of them denied God — and I believe that period, analogous with geological periods, will come to pass — the old conception of the universe will fall of itself without cannibalism and what's more the old morality, and everything will begin anew. Men will unite to take from life all it can give, but only for joy and happiness in the present world. Man will be lifted up with a spirit of divine Titanic pride and the man-god will appear. From hour to hour extending his conquest of nature infinitely by his will and his science, man will feel such lofty joy from hour to hour in doing it that it will make up for all his old dreams of the joys of heaven. Every one will know that he is mortal and will accept death proudly and serenely like a God. His pride will teach him that it's useless for him to repine at life's being a moment, and he will love his brother without need of reward. Love will be sufficient only for a moment of life, but the very consciousness of its momentariness will intensify its fire, which now is dissipated in dreams of eternal love beyond the grave ... and so on and so forth in the same style. Charming!
>
> Ivan sat with his eyes on the floor, and his hands pressed to his ears, but he began trembling all over. The voice continued.
>
> The question now is, my young friend reflected, is it possible that such a period will ever come? If it does, everything is determined and humanity is settled for ever. But as, owing to man's inveterate stupidity, that cannot come about for at least a thousand years, every one who recognizes the truth even now may legitimately order his life as he

pleases, on the new principles. In that sense "all things are lawful" for him. . . .

This ironic devil is by no means an orthodox Christian. In fact, he is a pragmatist pure and simple. Instead of showing that Ivan's earthly paradise is an illusion, he confines his gibes to the consequences in the present of that sort of dream. He is saying that in the protracted intermission between the dream and its realization men like Ivan may "legitimately" act as they please, that "all things are lawful." In so far as he is a pragmatist, however, this devil has deserted his post and placed himself outside the religious sphere.

Yet, unlike some students of Dostoevsky, this devil understands perfectly well that there is no connection whatever between Ivan's dream (as that of Versilov and the "ridiculous man") and the story of the Garden of Eden in Genesis. Note that he does not accuse Ivan of plagiarism or even mention the lost paradise. That story tells of primal man's sin in falling from instinctual innocence into human consciousness, the knowledge of good and evil. In Dostoevsky's vision of an earthly paradise the consciousness of men, far from declining, is so heightened as to enable them to attain a new and radically different kind of innocence.

This idea was poetically anticipated by Heinrich von Kleist in his famous essay "On the Marionette Theater," where he states that now "that paradise is bolted shut, and the angel stands behind us, we must journey around the world and see whether perhaps it is open again somewhere on the yonder side." He surmises, though, that an opening is to be found after all, writing that "the last chapter in the history of the world" will begin when men "eat again of the tree of knowledge in order to fall back again into the state of innocence."

What is finally to be made of Dostoevsky's vision of earthly paradise? In my view, the important thing about it is not its rhapsodic utopianism, its dream of perfect concord, but rather the intensity of its rapture with the earthly, that is to say, its latent secularism and naturalism. Though in his last novel, *The Brothers Karamazov*, the vision is undermined by the devil's mockery, we cannot for that reason ignore it or assume that he repudiated it. It was a constant element in his thought and imagination, pointing toward the future — now the present — when literature, in Russia as earlier in the West, turned away from the question that obsessed him throughout his life: the question of the existence of God and immortality.

This alternate vision can thus be said to be a precursor of the his-

torical shift from the concern with what exists beyond the visible world
to the concern with the visible. As William James once phrased it,
"The earth of things, long thrown into shade by the glories of the
upper ether, must resume its rights."

With few exceptions, the greater poets of the present as of the past
century — from Wordsworth to Stevens — have been sufficiently inspired by this shift, even though with some nostalgia, to invest it with
positive feeling in their expression of it. The poetry of Wordsworth is
full of intimations of what some have called natural religion, as
M. H. Abrams persuasively argues in his recent book *Natural Super-
naturalism.* So he can ask:

> Paradise, and groves
> Elysian, Fortunate Fields — like those of old
> Sought in the Atlantic Main — why should they be
> A history only of departed things,
> Or a mere fiction of what never was?

Of his many answers to this question I will quote only one:

> For the discerning intellect of Man,
> When wedded to this goodly universe
> In love and holy passion, shall find these
> A simple produce of the common day.

In American literature the noblest statement on this theme was made
by Wallace Stevens. In his great poem "Sunday Morning" the issue
is undeviatingly faced in measured and subtle language. His musing
protagonist, the woman in her peignoir leisurely enjoying her "coffee
and oranges in a sunny chair," begins to dream a little and "feels the
dark / Encroachment of that old catastrophe." But "the green freedom
of a cockatoo" on her rug is more real to her. "The pungent oranges,
and bright, green wings / Seem things in some procession of the dead"
that winds its way "over the seas, to silent Palestine, / Dominion of the
blood and sepulchre." And now the poet addresses himself directly to
her unresolved doubts:

> Why should she give her bounty to the dead?
> What is divinity if it can come
> Only in silent shadows and in dreams?
> Shall she not find in comforts of the sun,
> In pungent fruit and bright, green wings, or else
> In any balm or beauty of the earth,
> Things to be cherished like the thought of heaven?

And the woman resumes:

> She says, "I am content when wakened birds,
> Before they fly, test the reality
> Of misty fields, by their sweet questionings;
> But when the birds are gone, and their warm fields
> Return no more, where, then, is paradise?
> There is not any haunt of prophecy,
> Nor any old chimera of the grave,
> Neither the golden underground, nor isle
> Melodious, where spirits gat them home,
> Nor visionary south, nor cloudy palm
> Remote on heaven's hill, that has endured
> As April's green endures; or will endure
> Like her remembrance of awakened birds
> Or her desire for June and evening, tipped
> By the consummation of the swallow's wings.

Unlike the modern poet, Dostoevsky could never put out of his mind the "dominion of the blood and sepulchre," but at times, however equivocally, he came close to discovering his paradise in the "balm or beauty of the earth."

New York Review of Books, 1972

Tolstoy: The Green Twig
and the Black Trunk

The critic's euphoria in the Tolstoyan weather. Tolstoy and literature. The green twig and the black trunk. The art of Tolstoy is of such irresistible simplicity and truth, is at once so intense and so transparent in all of its effects, that the need is seldom felt to analyze the means by which it becomes what it is, that is to say, its method or sum of techniques. In the bracing Tolstoyan air, the critic, however addicted to analysis, cannot help doubting his own task, sensing that there is something presumptuous and even unnatural, which requires an almost artificial deliberateness of intention, in the attempt to dissect an art so wonderfully integrated that, coming under its sway, we grasp it as a whole long before we are able to summon sufficient consciousness to examine the arrangement and interaction of its component parts.

Tolstoy is the exact opposite of those writers, typical of the modern age, whose works are to be understood only in terms of their creative strategies and design. The most self-observant of men, whose books are scarcely conceivable apart from the ceaseless introspection of which they are the embodiment, Tolstoy was the least self-conscious in his use of the literary medium. That is chiefly because in him the cleavage between art and life is of a minimal nature. In a Tolstoyan novel it is never the division but always the unity of art and life which makes for illumination. This novel, bristling with significant choices and crucial acts, teeming with dramatic motives, is not articulated through a plot as we commonly know it in fiction; one might say that in a sense there are no plots in Tolstoy but simply the unquestioned and unalterable

Written as an introduction to *The Great Short Novels of Tolstoy*, published in the Permanent Library series of The Dial Press in 1946.

process of life itself; such is the astonishing immediacy with which he possesses his characters that he can dispense with manipulative techniques, as he dispenses with the belletristic devices of exaggeration, distortion, and dissimulation. The fable, that specifically literary contrivance, or anything else which is merely invented or made up to suit the occasion, is very rarely found in his work. Nor is style an element of composition of which he is especially aware; he has no interest in language as such; he is the enemy of rhetoric and every kind of artifice and virtuosity. The conception of writing as of something calculated and constructed — a conception, first formulated explicitly in startlingly modern terms by Edgar Allan Poe, upon which literary culture has become more and more dependent — is entirely foreign to Tolstoy.

All that is of a piece, of course, with his unique attitude toward literature, that is, for a writer of modern times. For Tolstoy continually dissociated himself from literature whether considered matter-of-factly, as a profession like any other, or ideally as an autonomous way of life, a complete fate in the sense in which the French writers of Flaubert's generation conceived of it. In his youth a soldier who saw war at first hand, the proprietor and manager of Yasnaya Polyana, a husband and father not as other men are husbands and fathers but in what might be described as programmatic and even militant fashion, and subsequently a religious philosopher and the head of a sect, he was a writer through all the years — a writer, but never a *littérateur*, the very idea repelled him. The *littérateur* performs a function imposed by the social division of labor, and inevitably he pays the price of his specialization by accepting and even applauding his own one-sidedness and conceit, his noncommitted state as witness and observer, and the necessity under which he labors of preying upon life for the themes that it yields. It is with pride that Tolstoy exempted Lermontov and himself from the class of "men of letters" while commiserating with Turgenev and Goncharov for being so much of it; and in his *Reminiscences of Tolstoy* Gorky remarks that he spoke of literature but rarely and little, "as if it were something alien to him."

To account for that attitude by tracing it back to Tolstoy's aristocratic status, as if he disdained to identify himself with a plebeian profession, is to take much too simple a view of his personality. The point is, rather, that from the very first Tolstoy instinctively recognized the essential insufficiency and makeshift character of the narrowly aesthetic outlook, of the purely artistic appropriation of the world. His personality was built on too broad a frame to fit into an aesthetic mold, and he denied that art was anything more than the ornament and charm of life. He came of age at a time when the social group to

which he belonged had not yet been thoroughly exposed to the ravages
of the division of labor, when men of his stamp could still resist the
dubious consolations it brings in its train. Endowed with enormous
energies, possessed of boundless egotism and of an equally boundless
power of conscience, he was capable, in Leo Shestov's phrase, of destroying and creating worlds, and before he was quite twenty-seven
years old he had the audacity to declare his ambition, writing it all
solemnly down in his diary, of becoming the founder of "a new religion
corresponding with the present state of mankind; the religion of Christ
but purged of dogmas and mysticism — a practical religion, not promising future bliss but giving bliss on earth." No wonder, then, that
while approaching the task of mastering the literary medium with the
utmost seriousness, and prizing that mastery as a beautiful accomplish-
ment, he could not but dismiss the pieties of art as trivial compared
with the question he faced from the very beginning, the question he
so heroically sought to answer even in his most elemental creations, in
which he seems to us to move through the natural world with splendid
and miraculous ease, more fully at home there than any other literary
artist. Yet even in those creations the very same question appears now
in a manifest and now in a latent fashion, always the same question:
How to live, what to do?

In 1880, when Turgenev visited Yasnaya Polyana after a long estrangement, he wrote a letter bewailing Tolstoy's apparent desertion
of art. "I, for instance, am considered an artist," he said, "but what am
I compared with him? In contemporary European literature he has
no equal . . . But what is one to do with him. He has plunged headlong
into another sphere: he has surrounded himself with Bibles and
Gospels in all languages, and has written a whole heap of papers. He
has a trunk full of these mystical ethics and of various pseudo-interpre-
tations. He read me some of it, which I simply do not understand . . .
I told him, 'That is not the real thing'; but he replied: 'It is just the
real thing' . . . Very probably he will give nothing more to literature,
or if he reappears it will be with that trunk." Turgenev was wrong.
Tolstoy gave a great deal more to literature, and it is out of that same
trunk, so offensive in the eyes of the accomplished man of letters,
that he brought forth such masterpieces as *The Death of Ivan Ilyich*
and *Master and Man,* plays like *The Power of Darkness,* also many
popular tales which, stripped of all ornament, have an essential force
and grace of their own, and together with much that is abstract and
overrationalized, not a few expository works, like *What Then Must We
Do?,* which belong with the most powerful revolutionary writings of
the modern age. For it is not for nothing that Tolstoy was always

rummaging in that black trunk. At the bottom of it, underneath a heap of old papers, there lay a little mana-object, a little green twig which he carried with him through the years, a twig of which he was told at the age of five by his brother Nicholas — that it was buried by the road at the edge of a certain ravine and that on it was inscribed the secret by means of which "all men would cease suffering misfortunes, leave off quarreling and being angry, and become continuously happy." The legend of the green twig was part of a game played by the Tolstoy children, called the Ant-Brothers, which consisted of crawling under chairs screened off by shawls and cuddling together in the dark. Tolstoy asked to be buried on the very spot at the edge of the ravine at Yasnaya Polyana which he loved because of its association with the imaginary green twig and the ideal of human brotherhood. And when he was an old man he wrote that "the idea of ant-brothers lovingly clinging to one another, though not under two armchairs curtained by shawls but of all mankind under the wide dome of heaven, has remained unaltered in me. As I then believed that there existed a little green twig whereon was written the message which would destroy all evil in men and give them universal welfare, so I now believe that such truth exists and will be revealed to men and will give them all it promises." It is clear that the change in Tolstoy by which Turgenev was so appalled was entirely natural, was presupposed by all the conditions of his development and of his creative consciousness. In the total Tolstoyan perspective the black trunk of his old age represents exactly the same thing as the green twig of his childhood.

Even the crude heresies he expounded in *What Is Art?* lose much of their offensiveness in that perspective. In itself when examined without reference to the author's compelling grasp of the central and most fearful problems of human existence, the argument of that book strikes us as a willful inflation of the idea of moral utility at the expense of the values of the imagination. But actually the fault of the argument is not that it is wholly implausible — as a matter of fact, it is of long and reputable lineage in the history of culture — as that it is advanced recklessly and with a logic at once narrow and excessive; the Tolstoyan insight is here vitiated in the same way as the insight into sexual relations is vitiated in *The Kreutzer Sonata*. Still, both works, the onslaught on modern love and marriage as well as the onslaught on the fetishism of art to which the modern sensibility has succumbed, are significantly expressive of Tolstoy's spiritual crisis — a crisis badly understood by many people, who take it as a phenomenon disruptive of his creative power despite the fact that, in the last analysis, it is impossible to speak of two Tolstoys, the creative and the noncreative, for there is no real discontinuity in his career. Though there is a contradiction between the artist and the moralist in him, his personality retains its basic unity, transcending all contradictions. Boris Eichenbaum, one of the very best of Tolstoy's Russian critics, has observed that the spiritual crisis did not operate to disrupt his art because it was a crisis internally not externally determined, the prerequisite of a new act of cognition through which he sought to rearm his genius and to ascertain the possibility of new creative beginnings. Thus *My Confession*, with which Tolstoy's later period opens and which appeared immediately after *Anna Karenina*, is unmistakably a work of the imagination and at the same time a mighty feat of consciousness.

Six years after writing *What Is Art?* Tolstoy finished *Hadji Murad* (1904), one of the finest *nouvelles* in the Russian language and a model of narrative skill and objective artistry. Is not the song of the nightingales, that song of life and death which bursts into ecstasy at dawn on the day when Hadji Murad attempts to regain his freedom, the very same song which rises in that marvelous sensual scene in *Family Happiness*, a scene bathed in sunlight, when Masha, surprising Sergey Mikhaylych in the cherry orchard, enjoys for the first time the full savor of her youthful love? *Hadji Murad* was written not less than forty-five years after *Family Happiness*. It can be said of Tolstoy the man that he was a rationalist who was usually at odds with human beings; nor did he especially love them. As a novelist, however, he was not merely exceptionally aware of them but was capable of investing them with a heroic sympathy that broke the barriers to their inner being. In the portrait of Hadji Murad we at once sense the author's love of the warrior chieftain who is fated, by his tribal code and indeed the whole weight of the past, to be crushed like a lone thistle flower in a plowed field. The twin images that recur through the story — that of the nightingales' song of love and death and that of the crimson thistle plant tenaciously clinging to its bit of soil — serve both as a musical motif drawing together the narrative parts and as a symbol, wonderful in its aptness and simplicity, of the inviolable rhythm of nature and human destiny. Nature and human destiny! — that their rhythm is eternally one is the very essence of Tolstoy's vision of life. His religious conversion forced him to modify his central idea or intuition, and it is wholly appropriate that in *Hadji Murad*, a late work written many years after his renunciation of the objective art of his great novels, he should have reverted to the vision of his major creative period. To himself Tolstoy might have explained away the lapse by claiming that this work of his old age conformed to his notion of "good universal art," which he of course placed in a category below that of religious art; still it is worth noting that he refrained from publishing *Hadji Murad* and that it appeared in print only after his death.

And in *The Devil* — a moral tale, the product, like *The Kreutzer Sonata*, of Tolstoy's most sectarian period and extremest assertion of dogmatic asceticism — what we remember best is not Eugene Irtenev's torments of conscience, his efforts to subdue his passion, but precisely the description of his carnal meetings in the sun-drenched woods with Stephanida, the fresh and strong peasant girl with full breasts and bright black eyes. The truth is that in the struggle between the old moralist and the old magician in Tolstoy both gave as good as they got.

The rationalist and anti-Romantic in Tolstoy. Sources in the eighteenth century. Divergence from the intelligentsia. Creative method. Tolstoy has been described as the least neurotic of all the great Russians, and by the same token he can be said to be more committed than any of them to the rational understanding and ordering of life and to the throwing off of romantic illusions. Unlike Dostoevsky, he owes nothing either to the so-called natural school of Gogol or to the Romantic movement in Western literature. The school of Gogol is a school of morbidity, whereas Tolstoy is above all an artist of the normal — the normal, however, so intensified that it acquires a poetical truth and an emotional fullness which we are astounded to discover in the ordinary situations of life. Analysis is always at the center of the Tolstoyan creation. It is the sort of analysis, however, which has little in common with the analytical modes of such novelists as Dostoevsky and Proust, for example, both characteristically modern though in entirely different ways. While in their work analysis is precipitated mainly by deviations from the norm, from the broad standard of human conduct, in Tolstoy the analysis remains in line with that standard, is in fact inconceivable apart from it. Dostoevsky's "underground" man, who is a bundle of plebeian resentments, is unimaginable in a Tolstoyan novel. Even in Tolstoy's treatment of death there is nothing actually morbid — certainly not in the description of the death of Prince Andrey in *War and Peace* and of Nikolay Levin in *Anna Karenina*. As for *The Death of Ivan Ilyich*, that story would be utterly pointless if we were to see Ivan Ilyich as a special type and what happened to him as anything out of the ordinary. Ivan Ilyich is Everyman, and the state of absolute solitude into which he falls as his life ebbs away is the existential norm, the inescapable realization of mortality. Nothing could be more mistaken than the idea that Tolstoy's concern with death is an abnormal trait. On the contrary, if anything it is a supernormal trait, for the intensity of his concern with death is proportionate to the intensity of his concern with life. Of Tolstoy it can be said that he truly lived his life, and for that very reason he was so tormented by the thought of dying. It was a literal thought, physical through and through, a vital manifestation of the simplicity with which he grasped man's life in the world. This simplicity is of a metaphysical nature, and in it, as one Russian critic has remarked, you find the essence of Tolstoy's world-view, the energizing and generalizing formula that served him as the means unifying the diverse motives of his intellectual and literary experience. It is due to this metaphysical simplicity that he was unable to come to terms with any system of dogmatic theology and that in the end, despite all his efforts to retain it, he was compelled to exclude even the idea of God from his own system of rationalized religion. Thus all notions of immortality seemed absurd to Tolstoy, and his scheme of salvation was entirely calculated to make men happy here and now. It is reported of Thoreau that when he lay dying his answer to all talk of the hereafter was "one world at a time." That is the sort of answer with which Tolstoy's mentality is wholly in accord.

The way in which his rationalism enters his art is shown in his analysis of character, an analysis which leaves nothing undefined, nothing unexplained. That systematization of ambiguity which marks the modern novel is organically alien to Tolstoy. Given the framework in which his characters move we are told everything that we need to know or want to know about them. The tangled intimate life, the underside of their consciousness, their author is not concerned with: he sets them up in the known world and sees them through their predicaments, however irksome and baffling, without ever depriving them of the rationality which supports their existence. For just as in Tolstoy's religiosity there is no element of mysticism, so in his creative art there is no element of mystery.

Unlike most of his contemporaries, Tolstoy did not pass through the school of Romanticism, and perhaps that is the reason he never hesitated to strike out the dark areas in the place in which he outlined his leading figures. He has few links with the literary culture evolved in Russia after 1820; the fact is that he has more in common with his literary grandfathers than with his literary fathers. Insofar as he has any literary affiliations at all they go back to the eighteenth century, to Rousseau, to Sterne, to the French classical writers, and in Russia to the period of Karamzin, Zhukovsky, Novikov, and Radichev. He has their robustness and skepticism. His quarrels with Turgenev, his inability to get on with the liberal and radical writers grouped around the *Contemporary*, a Petersburg periodical edited by the poet Nekrasov in which Tolstoy's first stories were published, are explained not so much by personal factors, such as his intractability of temper, as by the extreme differences between the conditions of his development and those of the Russian intelligentsia, whose rise coincides with the appearance of the plebeian on the literary scene. Tolstoy's family background was archaistic, not in the sense of provincial backwardness, but in the sense of the deliberate and even stylized attempt made by his family — more particularly his father — to preserve at Yasnaya Polyana the patriarchal traditions of the Russian nobility of the eighteenth century. It was a conscious and militant archaism directed against the "new" civilization of Petersburg, with its state bureaucracy and merchant princes. The young Tolstoy was scornful of the "theories" and "convictions" held by the writers he met in Petersburg in the 1850s; instead of putting his trust in "theories" and "convictions" he relied on those Franklinesque rules and precepts of conduct with which he filled his diaries — rules and precepts he deduced from his idea of unalterable "moral instincts." In Nekrasov's circle he was regarded as a "wild man," a "troglodyte"; and in the early 1860s, when he set out on his second European tour, Nekrasov and his friends hoped that he would return in a mood of agreement with their notions of education and historical progress. Nothing came of it, of course, for he returned armed with more of those "simplifications" that cut under their assumptions. But if the westernizers found no comfort in Tolstoy, neither did the Slavophils. The latters' ideology, with its forced and artificial doctrine of superiority to the West, was also aligned with plebeian social tasks; at bottom it represented the discomfiture of a small and weak plebeian class in a semifeudal society, a discomfiture idealized through national messianism. It was an obscurantist ideology incompatible with Tolstoy's belief in self-improvement and in the possibility of human perfection. Moreover, in Tolstoy's approach to Western culture there was no distress, no anger, no hostility. He was never put off by it, for he considered European culture to be a natural sphere the products of which he could appropriate at will, and in any order he pleased, without in the least committing himself to its inner logic. He felt no more committed by his use of Western ideas than the French-speaking gentry in *War and Peace* feel obligated to import the social institutions of France along with its language. Thus Tolstoy was able to sort out Western tendencies to suit himself, as in *War and Peace,* where he is to some extent indebted for his conception of Napoleon to certain French publicists of the 1850s and sixties, who in their endeavor to deflate the pretensions of Napoleon III went so far in their polemics as also to blot out the image of his illustrious ancestor. Again, in that

novel he is partly indebted for his so-called organic idea of war to
Proudhon's book *La Guerre et la Paix,* which came out in a Russian
translation in 1864. (Tolstoy had met Proudhon in Brussels in March
1861.) And the arbitrary way in which he helped himself to the ideas of
Western thinkers is shown by the fact that he entirely ignored Proudhon's enthusiastic affirmation of Napoleon's historical role. The West
was the realm of the city, a realm so strange to Tolstoy that he could
regard it as neutral territory. The city was essentially unreal to him;
he believed in the existence solely of the landowners and of the peasants. The contrast between Dostoevsky and Tolstoy, which Merezhkovsky and after him Thomas Mann have presented in terms of the
abstract typology of the "man of spirit" as against the "man of nature,"
is more relevantly analyzed in terms of the contradiction between city
and country, between the alienated intellectual proletariat of the city
and the unalienated patriciate-peasantry of the country.

Much has been written concerning the influence of Rousseau on
Tolstoy, but here again it is necessary to keep in mind that in Western
literature we perceive the Rousseauist ideas through the colored screen
of Romanticism while in Tolstoy Rousseau survives through his rationalism no less than through his sensibility. In point of fact, the Rousseauist
cult of nature is operative in Tolstoy in a manner that leads toward realism, as is seen in his Caucasian tales, for instance. If these tales now
seem romantic to us, it is largely because of the picturesque material of
which they are composed. A narrative like *The Cossacks* is actually
turned in a tendentious way against the tradition of "Caucasian
romanticism" in Russian literature — the tradition of Pushkin, Lermontov, and Marlinsky. Olenin, the protagonist of *The Cossacks,* is so
little of a Romantic hero that he is incapable of dominating even his
own story; the impression of his personality is dissipated as the attention shifts to the Cossack-led Lukashka, to Daddy Eroshka, and to the
girl Marianka. Think what Chateaubriand would have made of a
heroine like Marianka. In Tolstoy, however, she is portrayed in an au-
thentically natural style, with all the calm strength, unawareness of
subjective values, and indifference of a primitive human being.
Though she is a "child of nature" and therefore an object of poetical
associations, she is seen much too soberly to arouse those high-flown
sentiments which "nature" inspires in Romantic poets like Novalis or
even the Goethe of *Werther.* Where the Romantics convert nature
into a solace for the trials of civilization, into a theater of lyrical idleness and noble pleasures, Tolstoy identifies nature with work, independence, self-possession.

Compared with Pierre, Prince Andrey, or Levin, Olenin is a weak hero, but he is important in that in his reflections he sums up everything which went into the making of the early Tolstoy and which was in later years given a religious twist and offered as a doctrine of world salvation. The primacy which the issue of happiness assumes in Olenin's thoughts is the key to his Tolstoyan nature. "Happiness is this," he said to himself, "happiness lies in living for others. That is evident. The desire for happiness is innate in every man; therefore it is legitimate. When trying to satisfy it selfishly — that is, by seeking for oneself riches, fame, comforts, or love — it may happen that circumstances arise which make it impossible to satisfy these desires. It follows that it is these desires which are illegitimate, but not the need for happiness. But what desires can always be satisfied despite external circumstances? What are they? Love, self-sacrifice." In these few sentences we get the quintessence of the Tolstoyan mentality: the belief that ultimate truth can be arrived at through common-sense reasoning, the utilitarian justification of the values of love and self-sacrifice and their release from all other-worldly sanctions, the striving for the simplification of existence which takes the form of a return to a life closer to nature — a return, however, involving a self-consciousness and a constant recourse to reason that augurs ill for the success of any such experiment.

Tolstoy's art is so frequently spoken of as "organic" that one is likely to overlook the rationalistic structure on which it is based. This structure consists of successive layers of concrete details, physical and psychological, driven into place and held together by a generalization or dogma. Thus in *The Cossacks* the generalization is the idea of the return to nature; in *Two Hussars* it is the superiority of the older Turbin to the younger, that is to say, of the more naive times of the past to the "modern" period. (The original title of the story was *Father and Son.*) The binding dogma in *Family Happiness* is the instability and deceptiveness of love as compared with a sound family life and the rearing of children in insuring the happiness of a married couple. Yet the didacticism of such ideas seldom interferes with our enjoyment of the Tolstoyan fiction. For the wonderful thing about it is its tissue of detail, the tenacious way in which it holds together, as if it were a glutinous substance, and its incomparable rightness and truthfulness.

Parallelism of construction is another leading characteristic of the Tolstoyan method. In *War and Peace,* in the chronicle of the lives of the Bolkonsky and Rostov families, this parallelism is not devised dramatically, as a deliberate contrast, but in other narratives it is driven toward a stark comparison, as between Anna and Vronsky on the one hand and Kitty and Levin on the other in *Anna Karenina,* or between two generations in *Two Hussars,* or between Lukashka and Olenin in *The Cossacks.* One writer on Tolstoy put it very well when he said that in the Tolstoyan novel all ideas and phenomena exist in pairs. Comparison is inherent in his method.

His early *nouvelles* can certainly be read and appreciated without reference to their historical context, to the ideological differences between him and his contemporaries which set him off to confound them with more proofs of his disdain for their "progressive" opinions. Still, the origin of *Family Happiness* in the quarrels of the period is worth recalling. At that time (in the 1850s) public opinion was much exercised over the question of free love and the emancipation of women; George Sand was a novelist widely read in intellectual circles, and of course most advanced people agreed with George Sand's libertarian solution of the question. Not so Tolstoy, who opposed all such tendencies, for he regarded marriage and family life as the foundations of society. Thus *Family Happiness,* with its denigration of love and of equal rights for women, was conceived, quite apart from its personal genesis in Tolstoy's affair with Valerya Arsenev, as a polemical rejoinder to George Sand, then adored by virtually all the Petersburg writers, including Dostoevsky.

The faith in family life is integral of Tolstoy. It has the deepest psychological roots in his private history, and socially it exemplifies his championship of patriarchal relations. It is a necessary part of his archaistic outlook, which in later life was transformed into a special kind of radicalism, genuinely revolutionary in some of its aspects and thoroughly archaistic in others. *War and Peace* is as much a chronicle of certain families as a historical novel. The historical sense is not really native to Tolstoy. His interest in the period of 1812 is peculiarly his own, derived from his interest in the story of his own family. He began work on *Anna Karenina* after failing in the attempt to write another historical novel, a sequel to *War and Peace.* And *Anna Karenina* is of course the novel in which his inordinate concern with marriage and family life receives its fullest expression.

The existential center of the Tolstoyan art. Tolstoy as the last of the unalienated artists. So much has been made here of the rationalism of Tolstoy that it becomes necessary to explain how his art is saved from the ill effects of it. Art and reason are not naturally congruous with one another, and many a work of the imagination has miscarried because of an excess of logic. "There may be a system of logic; a system of being there can never be," said Kierkegaard. And art is above all a re-creation of individual being; the system maker must perforce abstract from the real world while the artist, if he is true to his medium, recoils from the process of abstraction because it is precisely the irreducible quality of life, its multiple divulgements in all their uniqueness and singularity, which provoke his imagination.

Now there is only one novel of Tolstoy's that might be described as a casualty of his rationalism, and that is *Resurrection.* The greater part of his fiction is existentially centered in a concrete inwardness and subjectivity by which it gains its quality of genius. In this sense it becomes possible to say that Tolstoy is much more a novelist of life and death than he is of good and evil — good and evil are not categories of existence but of moral analysis. And the binding dogmas or ideas of Tolstoy's fiction are not in contradiction with its existential sense; on the contrary, their interaction is a triumph of creative tact and proof of the essential wholeness of Tolstoy's nature. The Tolstoyan characters grasp their lives through their total personalities, not merely through their intellects. Their experience is full of moments of shock, of radical choice and decision, when they confront themselves in the terrible and inevitable aloneness of their being. To mention but one of innumerable instances of such spiritual confrontation, there is the moment in *Anna Karenina* when Anna's husband begins to suspect her relation to Vronsky. That is the moment when the accepted and taken-for-granted falls to pieces, when the carefully built-up credibility of the world is torn apart by a revelation of its underlying irrationality. For according to Alexey Alexandrovitch's ideas one ought to have confidence in one's wife because jealousy was insulting to oneself as well as to her. He had never really asked himself why his wife deserved such confidence and why he believed that she would always love him. But now, though he still felt that jealousy was a bad and shameful state,

> he also felt that he was standing face to face with something illogical and irrational, and did not know what was to be done. Alexey Alexandrovitch was standing face to face with life, with the possibility of his wife's loving someone other than himself, and this seemed to him very irrational and incomprehensible because it was life itself. All his life Alexey Alexandrovitch had lived and worked in official spheres, having to do with the reflection of life. And every time he stumbled against life itself he had shrunk away from it. Now he experienced a feeling akin to that of a man who, while calmly crossing a precipice by a bridge, should suddenly discover that the bridge is broken, and that there is a chasm below. That chasm was life itself, the bridge that artificial life in which Alexey

Alexandrovitch had lived. For the first time the question presented itself to him of the possibility of his wife's loving someone else, and he was horrified at it.

It is exactly this "standing face to face with life," and the realization that there are things in it that are irreducible and incomprehensible, which drew Tolstoy toward the theme of death. Again and again he returned to this theme, out of a fear of death which is really the highest form of courage. Most people put death out of their minds because they cannot bear to think of it. Gorky reports that Tolstoy once said to him that "if a man has learned to think, no matter what he may think about, he is always thinking of his own death. All philosophers were like that. And what truths can there be, if there is death?" That is a statement of despair and nihilism the paradox of which is that it springs from the depths of Tolstoy's existential feeling of life; and this is because the despair and nihilism spring not from the renunciation but from the affirmation of life; Tolstoy never gave up the search for an all-embracing truth, for a rational justification of man's existence on the earth.

The fact is that Tolstoy was at bottom so sure in his mastery of life and so firm in his inner feeling of security that he could afford to deal intimately with death. Consider the difference in this respect between him and Franz Kafka, another novelist of the existential mode. In Kafka the theme of death is absent, not because of strength but rather because of neurotic weakness. He was ridden by a conviction, as he himself defined it, of "complete helplessness," and baffled by the seeming impossibility of solving even the most elementary problems of living, he could not look beyond life into the face of death. He wrote: "Without ancestors, without marriage, without progeny, with an unbridled desire for ancestors, marriage, and progeny. All stretch out their hands towards me: ancestors, marriage, and progeny, but from a point far too remote from me." That is the complaint of an utterly alienated man, without a past and without a future. Tolstoy, on the other hand, was attached with the strongest bonds to the patrician-peasant life of Yasnaya Polyana, he was in possession of the world and of his own humanity. His secret is that he is the last of the unalienated artists. Hence it is necessary to insist on the differences not so much between him and other artists generally as between him and the modern breed of alienated artists. It is thanks to this unalienated condition that he is capable of moving us powerfully when describing the simplest, the most ordinary, and therefore in their own way also the gravest, occasions of life — occasions that the alienated artist can approach only from a distance, through flat naturalistic techniques, or through immense subtleties of analysis, or through the transportation of his subject onto the plane of myth and fantasy.

But, of course, even Tolstoy, being a man of the nineteenth century, could not finally escape the blight of alienation. In his lifetime Russian society disintegrated; he witnessed the passing of the old society of status and its replacement by a cruelly impersonal system of bourgeois relations. Tolstoy resisted the catastrophic ruin of the traditional order by straining all the powers of his reason to discover a way out. His so-called conversion is the most dramatic and desperate episode in his stubborn and protracted struggle against alienation. His attack on civilization is essentially an attack on the conditions that make for alienation. The doctrine of Christian anarchism, developed after his conversion, reflects, as Lenin put it, "the accumulated hate, the ripened aspiration for a better life, the desire to throw off the past — and also the immaturity, the dreamy contemplativeness, the political inexperience, and the revolutionary flabbiness of the villages." Still, the point of that doctrine lies not in its religious content, which is very small indeed, but rather in its formulation of a social ideal and of a utopian social program.

Partisan Review, 1946

Gogol As a Modern Instance*

In reflecting about Gogol while preparing my remarks for this commemorative occasion I found myself thinking of him first of all as a peculiarly modern instance of the literary artist. This may surprise those who see him entirely in terms of the Russian background, placing him all too securely within a nearly self-sufficient national tradition. There is no denying, to be sure, that the Russian background is of primary importance for the understanding of Gogol's creative course. He crosses the frontiers of language far less easily than writers like Turgenev and Dostoevsky and Tolstoy and Chekhov, whose creations exercise an appeal unconfined by differences of nationality and cultural setting. Gogol's work, with the possible exception of his story "The Overcoat" cannot be said to have become an intimate possession of the Western world; only in the Russian milieu is it an indispensable part of a literary education. But the reason for that is quite simple. Gogol's characters, like Chichikov and Khlestakov, are no less universal than the characters of Tolstoy and Dostoevsky. What hinders us in our appropriation of them is the fact that Gogol is so great a master of style and verbal orchestration that his power to move us is virtually indissoluble from his language.

Another approach to Gogol is by way of his creative psychology, in which one recognizes certain traits that recall us to the fate of modern literature. It is above all our sense of the deeply problematic character of this literature that impels us to conceive of Gogol as our contemporary. His creative psychology is so tortuous and obsessive, so given over to moods of self-estrangement and self-loathing, so marked by abrupt turns from levity to despair, that one cannot but see it as a tissue of contradictions from top to bottom. These contra-

* Text of a talk at a public meeting in Columbia University commemorating the one-hundredth anniversary of Gogol's death.

dictions are at once the secret of his poetic power and the cause of his ruin as a man — his tragic renunciation of the creative life in mid-career and the frightful end that came to him under the stress of a spiritual crisis of a surpassingly primitive and even savage nature. It is easy enough to expatiate on the neurotic components in his make-up, or, to put it more precisely, on the unmistakable pathology of his life experience. Let us keep in mind, however, that in the case of great artists neuroticism is never in itself a sufficient explanation. For the. neuroticism of such artists tend to assume a symbolic meaning, taking on the suprapersonal significance of a general state of mind or of a radical change in consciousness. In this sense it becomes possible to relate the discontinuities and discords in Gogol to the problematical character of the modern artist as a type. Gogol's dilemma was that he was incapable of reconciling the meaning of his art with the meaning of his life. This discord, to which the artists of the modern epoch are peculiarly open, was scarcely operative in the classic ages of literature when life and art were not at war but integrated by common presuppositions and a common faith.

The problem of the separation of art and life has an objective historical import that is not to be grasped if analyzed solely from the standpoint of the artist's personal character and disposition. It is exactly from this point of view that Arnold Hauser discusses, in the second volume of his *Social History of Art,* the struggles and sufferings of Flaubert. Hauser attributes Flaubert's lack of a direct relationship to life, his dogmatic aestheticism and his turning away with disdain from human existence as a symptom of "the gulf that has opened up in the modern artistic career between the possession of life and the expression of it." Gogol, too, wanted to possess his life in a manner quite incompatible with his expression of it; and there is still another way in which we might link these two novelists in spite of the obvious differences between them. Both are leading protagonists in the extremely complex and perilous passage of European literature from Romanticism to realism. Like Flaubert, Gogol is an inverted Romantic trying to resolve the tension between actuality and romance, between the deflation and inflation of life's vital illusions, by the most rigorous application of rhetorical and stylistic force, by exploiting the necromantic properties of language so as to establish some kind of psychic control and a measure of moral poise, however precarious. In wholly different ways both of these literary artists used language as a shield against chaos and as a therapeutic resource; and both were compelled to create prodigious images of negation even as they inwardly yearned to utter the saving, the positive, the loving word. Thus Flaubert, who began as a Romantic, was inclined from the outset to idealize love; yet what he actually wrote is novels about the destructive effects of love and its power to entangle us in fatal illusions. The theme of love was of course closed to Gogol by his prohibitive fear of sexuality, but in his own chosen themes he too was compulsively driven to expose precisely that which he would have liked to portray in glowing colors. Starting from the invulnerably naive premise that it was his task to idealize the feudal-bureaucratic order of imperial Russia and to paint an idyllic picture of the rural squires, what he in fact produced is a picture so grotesquely satiric that it could easily be made to serve as an instrument of social disruption. Flaubert found his ideal enemy in the bourgeois, whom he tirelessly berated, while Gogol, inasmuch as in his time the Russian bourgeois existed as more than an embryo in the body politic, seized on the government official and on the parasitic landlord as types whom he could paralyze with his satiric virus and then fix forever in the monstrous tableau his imagination constructed. Even Flaubert's statement, *Madame Bovary, c'est moi,* has its parallel in Gogol's remark that in laughing at his characters the reader was really laughing at their author, for he had impregnated them with his own looseness and "nastiness."

It is not difficult to recognize in Gogol some of the features of Dostoevsky's underground man, in particular the split between sickly, spiteful vanity on the one hand and aspirations toward truth and goodness on the other. Some Russian scholars have surmised that Dostoevsky had Gogol in mind in his portrayal of Foma Fomich, the buffoonlike protagonist of his long story "The Friend of the Family." Whether this surmise is correct or not, there is indeed something in Foma Fomich's insufferably didactic tone, in his outrageous preaching of virtue and uplift that reminds us irresistibly of Gogol's vainglorious and clownish bombast in that incredible book, *Selected Passages from the Correspondence with Friends,* probably the most implausible work ever produced by a writer of genius.

The truth is that Gogol was quite aware of his own "underground" traits, and he spoke more than once of "the terrible mixture of contradictions" of which his nature was composed. This master of language, the first truly important artist of Russian prose, strove with might and main to overcome what he regarded as the morbid negativism of his relationship to life, a striving pitiful in its futility; for as he himself admitted in "The Author's Confession," his real predilection was "for bringing out the trivialities of life, describing the vulgarity of mediocrity . . . and all those small things which generally remain unobserved." What is missing, however, in this self-analysis of Gogol's is any hint of the astonishing comic sense that enabled him to invest mediocrity and smallness of soul with a superreal quality that ultimately acts to liberate us and restore us to our humanity. The one thing that Gogol failed to believe in is that laughter cures. His conviction of guilt and unworthiness forced him to hold out obstinately against that catharsis of laughter for which his readers are immensely grateful to him.

Gogol was in no sense a cultivated man of letters. He appeared on the literary scene like an utterly unexpected and rude guest after whose departure life at home could never again be the same. It does not matter that the rude guest's performance was not quite understood for what it was, that a critic like Belinsky, for instance, could cite this performance as an overriding example of the writer's assumption of responsibility to society, of his civic consciousness and fidelity to the factually real. What was then chiefly overlooked in Gogol was the fantastic gratuity of his humor and his transcendence of the limited social motive through the unearthly and well-nigh metaphysical pathos of a supreme creation like "The Overcoat." For in truth Baschmatskin, the little copying clerk who is the hero of that story, attains a stature far greater than that of any mere victim of an unjust social system. He is a timeless apparition of humanity *in extremis,* of man homeless not only in his society but in the universe. There is one story in American literature, Melville's "Bartleby the Scrivener," which has a spiritual affinity with "The Overcoat." But it is no more than affinity. Melville's story, for all its profound overtones, lacks the inner coherence, the resonance, and marvelous stylization of Gogol's masterpiece.

But having allowed for the period prejudices of a critic like Belinsky and discounted the narrowly sociological approach to Gogol, I still cannot accept the aesthetic-modernist reading of his work that we get in Vladimir Nabokov's critical study of him. Brilliantly appreciative as Nabokov is of the grotesque side of Gogol and, indeed, of all that side of him relating to the poetry of the irrational and the spirit of incongruity and mystification, he has no eye whatever for his subject's place in literary history and social and national peculiarities. Nabokov seems to suffer from something like a phobic fear of all interpretive techniques not strictly literary in reference — a fear driving him toward the extremely one-sided emphasis which takes the literary act to be a phenomenon solely "of language and not of ideas." And Nabokov reduces his formalist bias to sheer absurdity when he goes so far as to state that "Gogol's heroes happen to be Russian squires and officials; their imagined surroundings and social conditions are perfectly unimportant." He is equally vehement in denying that Gogol can in any way be characterized as a realist. It is true, of course, that Gogol never deliberately set out to describe his social environment; but the fact is that his subjective method of exaggeration, of caricature and farce, produced an imagery of sloth, ugliness, and self-satisfied inferiority which, if not directly reflective, is none the less fully expressive of the realities of life in czarist Russia. Moreover, Nabokov ignores the dynamic plebeianism of Gogol's genius. For that is what enabled him to make a radically new selection of material and to assimilate to his medium elements of everyday existence, with their lowlife and vulgar details, heretofore excluded by the aristocratic conventions of literature in Russia as elsewhere. Even if the creatures of his imagination are not so much "real people" as caricatures, he none the less contributed greatly to the development of realism by opening up the lower reaches and underside of life to literary portraiture.

It is impossible to abstract Gogol from his historical moment and to dissociate the necessary and contingent elements of his creative personality so as to arrive at the pure substance of Gogolism. Nabokov's rite of purification converts Gogol into the ghost of his own work. I do not object to Nabokov's Gogol because he bears so little resemblance to the Gogol of Belinsky and Dobroliubov but rather because Nabokov's Gogol is too pure to be true, too literary and abstract to be genuine. The poet who inserted into *Dead Souls* epic apostrophes to Holy Russia — apostrophes infused with messianic hope in which love and despair are inextricably mingled — was not a purist writing in a vein of exclusive subjectivity and dedicated to the tormenting refinements of his solitary dreams. He, too, like all of Russia's great writers, suffered with his country and his people.

1952

The Education
of Anton Chekhov

THE UNDERSTANDING of Chekhov's background and personality is greatly enhanced by a reading of his *Selected Letters,* edited by Lillian Hellman and translated by Sidonie K. Lederer. From first to last the impression conveyed is that of astounding courage and of heroic manliness and self-possession. Dead at the age of forty-four, apparently Chekhov knew well enough even before reaching his mid-twenties that his life would be short and racked with hurt and pain; and he resolutely kept that knowledge from his family and friends. The severe and repeated pulmonary hemorrhages and other afflictions he suffered would surely have laid low anyone more self-indulgent or open to the not inconsiderable spiritual temptations of disease and physical debility. Another exacerbating circumstance was the material pressure he was under since early youth when he had first undertaken the major responsibility for the support of his large family, mostly made up of weaklings and ne'er-do-wells. All in all he had little time for imaginative self-realization, and a good part of the time he did have was consumed in the study and practice of medicine as well as in the frequent travels and changes of abode forced upon him by the state of his health.

Thus what comes through to us most vividly in his letters is a sense of the enormous odds against which Chekhov pitted himself in striving to achieve those rare qualities of his narrative and dramatic art that make it so uniquely his own. This art is at once astringent and poetic, circumstantially exact in a prose-sense yet structurally allied to the lyric mode. It is an art of unmistakable originality, though not of the very first order; and if it is known above all for fixing imperishably conditions of human staleness, futility, torpor, and ennui, the explanation is not to be sought in any hidden enervation of the author or covert sympathy for negative states of being — he was no Baudelairean bell with a crack in it — but rather in the passionate, even if undemonstrative, integrity with which he resisted the denial of life's richer and finer possibilities.

A late child of the fatally belated Russian Enlightenment and the last important figure in the great nineteenth-century line of the masters of Russian prose, he believed that life could be lived with intelligence and love, without coercion and falsehood, at the same time that he concentrated on showing that life as actually lived was sad and boring. But in his expression of this sadness and boredom there is no finality (of acceptance or complicity or mean pleasure in exposure and reduction), such as we find in many similar evocations of negative states in Western literature of the modern period. The petty decadence inherent in such evocations is entirely alien to Chekhov. He is not attacking human nature, saying that this is the way things are and always will be, while calling for some impossible transcendence which is no more than a metaphysical coda to positive despair. The pessimism commonly ascribed to him is one of mood and temperament perhaps, and it no doubt reflects the stalemate reached by Russian society at the time of his emergence on the literary scene; but it never is a pessimism of ultimate belief and vision. The voice that cries out "No, one cannot go on living like that!" at the end of one of his typical anecdotes of wasted existence ("The Man in a Shell") is indubitably that of the writer; and in that somber masterpiece "Ward No. 6" he identifies himself most lucidly and credibly with the standpoint of the madman Gromov, whose madness is of a piece with his refusal to come to terms with "human baseness and oppression trampling up truth" and to renounce his faith that "a splendid life will in time prevail upon the earth." The source of the powerful emotion embodied in this tale is the felt idea that however forlorn the world of men may be it nevertheless contains within itself the promise of release and change. It is the wonder and triumph of Chekhov that the animating principle of his pathos of "lives clipped and wingless" is resistance to slackness and inertia — the seepage of the psyche epitomized in the term Oblomovism. Let us keep in mind, though, that only one form of Oblomovism is represented in Goncharov's famous novel. Chekhov's insight penetrated to other and more complicated forms of it that are perhaps not so easily determinable; and Oblomovism, after all, is a state not merely of Russia but of the soul.

These letters, if read in conjunction with any fairly adequate biography, enforce the conviction of a productive life whose end is for once not in its beginnings but is marked throughout by change, growth, increasing self-development and self-mastery, *Bildung* and *Selbstbildung* in the classic sense. It can justly be said of Chekhov that the sum of what happened to him is that he achieved an education toward freedom. "The sense of personal freedom," he wrote, "is the chief constituent of creative genius," and the freedom he thus invokes is scarcely to be understood without reference to his beginnings, his ancestry, his childhood, the formative years. The grandson of a serf and the son of a petty tradesman, he suffered in his childhood and early youth the ravages of that backwardness, cruelty, and servility which were as much a family as a national inheritance. If all his life he remained immune to the appeal of the Russian versions of traditionalism, if he remained an agnostic and a radical, a resolute friend of the West and advocate of science and the secular intelligence, it is largely because of the lessons absorbed in those formative years. It is with irresistible concreteness that he put his case to a correspondent: "From childhood I have believed in progress and cannot help believing, as the difference between the time when I got whipped and the time when the whippings ceased was terrific."

The perception of this difference is ineluctably one of the great points of the arduous educational process through which he strove to attain his freedom. He literally had to make himself over to undo the stultification brought on by the early influences that played upon him, influences in no way fortuitous but imbedded in Russian life. In this respect the *locus classicus,* from the standpoint of the biographer and the literary critic alike, is the passage in his letter to Suvorin of January 7, 1889, in which he explains why plebeian writers must buy at the price of their youth what the writers of the gentry have been endowed with by nature. "Go ahead," he tells Suvorin, "and write a story about a young man, the son of a serf, an ex-small shopkeeper, a choir boy, high-school and university student, brought up on respect for rank, kissing priests' hands, and the worship of others' ideas, offering thanks for every mouthful of bread, often whipped, going to school without shoes, fighting, torturing animals, fond of dining with rich relatives, playing the hypocrite before God and people without any cause, except that of a consciousness of his own insignificance — then tell how this young man squeezes the slave out of himself one drop at a time and how he wakes one fine morning to feel that in his veins flows not the blood of a slave but real human blood. . . ." Here we come upon the essence of Chekhov's story and upon the basic Chekhovian theme. In this effort to squeeze the slave out of himself we confront the actuality of his education, the ordeal of it, the struggle, the relapses, the price paid, and the victory scored. The meaning of this education, in the sense of its absolute necessity and the consequences of failure to undertake it, forms the sum and substance of the criticism of life contained in his plays and fictions.

Chekhov was intrinsically too modest in his spiritual make-up and too much of a wry realist (no wonder he objected to Dostoevsky's novels on the ground of their "immodesty") to be capable of engaging in momentous affirmations carrying him beyond the experience provided by his time and environment. For this and related reasons it is far from difficult to make out, as some commentators have done, that generally all he leaves us with is a mood of "delicious depression." Such a view is wholly erroneous, to my mind. We cannot gain anything like a full recovery of the import of his work unless we grasp the one surpassing moral intuition controlling it — that man can hope to realize the promise of his humanity only if he succeeds in overcoming the slave within himself in all his guises and disguises. The Rilkean dictum "You must change your life!" is implicit in the entire Chekhovian statement. But to interpret this one fundamental intuition in a bare political sense, as the Soviet critics are instructing their readers to do to the benefit of the official dogma, is patently a gross oversimplification. A slave is not transformed into a man by changing masters. Moreover, the slave in man is a cunning animal that knows not only how to survive changes, however radical, in social institutions but also how to adapt such changes to suit his nature. "People must never be humiliated — that is the main thing," Chekhov wrote in an early letter; and in a later one he wrote: "God's earth is good. It is only we on it who are bad.... The important thing is that we must be just, and all the rest will be added unto us." It is in the light of such precepts that he is best understood. To take him simply as a critic of Russian society at a certain stage of its development is to limit him intolerably.

In one of her engaging and perceptive introductory notes to the text of this volume, Miss Hellman remarks that Chekhov was without "that final spiritual violence which the very great creative artist has always had. And he knew it as he knew most things about himself." To this I would assent, though with some uneasiness about the use of the word violence as the clincher in her formulation. Ultimate imaginative power need not necessarily be equated with the shock tactics of frenzied and eruptive geniuses. One agrees, none the less, that such ultimate power is wanting in Chekhov. Perhaps the crux of the matter is that he expended so much vitality on his exemplary education that what was left could not suffice to carry him beyond the lessons that engrossed him. This too is of course among the lessons he learned, as is implied in his rueful saying that he was forced to buy at the price of his youth what others are endowed with by nature. He was certainly aware that he never really got all he bargained for. Still, taking everything into account, the stricken life and the fashioned work, the price was well worth paying. For his effort to redeem the age he lived in he deserves to be ranked as nearly the equal of his great predecessors in Russian letters.

New Republic, 1955

Two Subversive Russians

I

One Day in the Life of Ivan Denisovich (translated by Max Hayward and Ronald Hingley) is a significant book, perhaps the most significant that has come out of Russia in many years. A completely authentic account of life in the forced-labor camps under Stalin, it is cast in a fictional form superbly adapted to its subject. Its narrative tone and method, relying on the selective accumulation of minute factual particulars, finely controls the powerful emotional content, never getting out of hand, never descending to rhetorical presentation or to any sort of preaching and moralizing.

The author, Alexander Solzhenitsyn, who is at present teaching physics and mathematics in a secondary school, served with distinction in the Red Army during the war but was arrested in 1945 on what is now officially admitted to be a "baseless political charge," and was sentenced to eight years' imprisonment. The experience recorded in *One Day* no doubt parallels his own, but he is not the novel's protagonist. That role, from first page to last, is reserved for the simple village workman, Ivan Denisovich Shukhov, who has no head for politics or any kind of "learned conversation." He is a wonderful creation, exhibiting certain traits that are new as well as traits deeply rooted in the Russian literary tradition. The figure in that tradition he most reminds me of is Tolstoy's Platon Karatayev. But there is also a significant difference between them. For Karatayev, standing somewhat apart from the other characters in *War and Peace*, who are portrayed with surpassing realism, is in the main a mythic figure, an abstraction of Christian goodness, while Shukhov, in no way dependent on religious doctrine or precept, is invested with a goodness that is altogether credible, altogether imbedded in the actual. He fills in every crevice of his own nature, without appeal to higher powers or utopian and ambiguous dreams of saintliness.

As all ideologies are alien to Shukhov, so none can ruin him. Neither hero nor saint, existing in an environment where the only time the prisoners are not marched out to work in the early mornings is when the thermometer goes down to forty-two degrees below zero, he yields neither to hope nor despair but depends for survival on his own largely unconscious and invulnerable humanity. Though in no way exceptional, he is the unbeatable human being whom the regime can at any time destroy but never convert nor make over in its own image, thus giving the lie to Orwell's nightmare of total demoralization in 1984. Humble yet extremely resourceful in small ways, a man whose self-respect demands that he do his work properly and even joyfully, Shukhov has been "walking this earth for forty years. He'd lost half his teeth and was getting bald. He'd never given or taken a bribe from anybody, and he hadn't learned that trick in the camp either." He knows that the authorities twisted the law any way they wanted. "You finished a ten-year stretch and they gave you another one. Or if not, they still wouldn't let you go home. ... So you just went on living like this, with your eyes on the ground, and you had no time to think about how you got in and when you'd get out." And why was Shukhov put in a concentration camp? He had escaped from a German prisoners-of-war cage and upon returning to his own lines found himself accused of treason. Though guiltless, he was forced to give evidence against himself: "The way he figured, it was very simple. If he didn't sign, he was as good as buried. But if he did, he'd still go on living for a while. So he signed." Shukhov's fate is the essence of the Stalinist terror-system.

However, the way in which the author chiefly succeeds in his characterization of Shukhov is not by harping on his innocence or putting any kind of political gloss on his ordeal but by depicting him throughout as a person in his own right — not merely a victim and least of all a symptom but always a person, even when ill, starving, and freezing. The secondary characters, such as Alyoshka the Baptist and Tuyrin the boss of the work squad, are portrayed with equal responsiveness to their personal qualities. Now it is precisely this newly won and truly existential personalization of vision, so long outlawed in the Communist theory and practice of literature, which surprises and impresses us most in *One Day*. As a novel it is not, in my view, the "great work of art" that some people say it is; its scale is too small for that. But it is a very fine book in which not a false note is struck. Its theme, the nature of man under extreme conditions of inhumanity, is treated unpretentiously, without despair or overt bitterness, and, above all, without the distempers and consolations of ideology. It is the same theme that Dostoevsky developed, though in a manner quite different, in his *House of the Dead,* another account of life in a Siberian prison, published almost exactly a hundred years ago. Dostoevsky, too, was a political criminal, sentenced by the Czar to penal servitude. How greatly the Russian people have suffered that their writers thus tragically echo each other across a century!

One Day first appeared in the Moscow literary monthly *Novy Mir* for November in 1962 in an edition of 95,000 copies that was at once sold out. Its publication in Russia thus clearly marks some kind of breakthrough toward freedom in Soviet writing. Thank God, the world is still unpredictable after all. No one, not even the most astute Kremlinologist among us, could possibly have foreseen that the party hierarchs would be prevailed upon to permit the publication of a work so devastating in its implications. It's all very well to say that its subject fits in with Khrushchev's renewed campaign against Stalin. That is true only in an immediate and narrowly political sense.

The novel's meaning, in its broader aspects, is scarcely open to political manipulation. It is senseless to see its meaning serving the partisan interests of any faction in the Soviet power structure. No, the integrity of this story of an ordinary winter day, from reveille to lights out, in the life of Prisoner No. S-854 is inviolable. In the long run it cannot conceivably benefit any authoritarian elite, whether Communist or anti-Communist. The lessons it enforces — such as "How can you expect a man who's warm to understand a man who's cold?" — are of a down-to-earth simplicity that should make any ideologue of power quail. And in the one "learned conversation" in the book, overheard on the run by the protagonist, we come upon the following words in a very brief discussion of Eisenstein's famous film *Ivan The Terrible*: "The politics of it is *utterly* vile — vindication of a one-man tyranny. An insult to the memory of three generations of Russian intellectuals . . . Don't call Eisenstein a genius! Call him a toady, say he carried out orders like a dog. A genius doesn't adapt his treatment to the taste of tyrants!" If Khrushchev can turn such sentiments to his own use, he is by all means welcome to them.

New York Review of Books, 1964

II

The paperback edition of this book, containing *The Trial Begins* (translated by Max Hayward) and *On Socialist Realism* (translated by George Dennis), appears at an opportune moment. We know now, of course, that Abram Tertz, a name the mysterious anonymity of which has long intrigued us, is the pseudonym of the Russian author Andrei D. Sinyavsky, recently tried in a Soviet court, along with Yuli M. Daniel, and sentenced to seven years of hard labor on charges of smuggling anti-Soviet writings to be published abroad. This trial has had international repercussions and was protested even by some foreign Communist newspapers and leading personalities, such as Louis Aragon.

Smuggled out of the Soviet Union in the late 1950s, *The Trial Begins,* a short novel, was originally printed in *Encounter,* and the long, exceedingly brilliant as well as highly informative essay on socialist realism originally appeared in *Dissent.* What these two works demonstrate, above all, is a very considerable talent that functions with ease both in the creative and critical spheres. There is uncommon wit, irony, and immense cleverness in Mr. Sinyavsky's fiction, while his criticism is distinguished by the same qualities as well as an astonishingly agile historical imagination.

The Trial Begins is a satirical account of Soviet society in the last years of Stalin's life, when ever-newer and more monstrous purges were in the works and the atmosphere in Moscow was very gloomy indeed. But the tone of the story, written some years after Stalin's death, clearly reflects the new mood prevailing among Soviet intellectuals — a mood, if not necessarily of hope, then certainly of relief and some measure of relaxation. It is a tone essentially light-hearted, mocking, even laughter-provoking, and is oriented, in my opinion, toward Western models in matters of style and technique. There are no "lacerations" here à la Dostoevsky or that impression of "depth" that we usually associate with the Russian novel.

Nor is this work simply a satire on conditions in the Soviet Union, which it surely is, and very successfully at that. Its satirical thrust goes beyond its political specifics toward the actualities of the human state everywhere, as in the enticing portrait of Marina, the married woman intent on making a career out of being irresistibly beautiful. To be beautiful is to her in itself "a worthy and sufficient end, and all the rest — men, money, clothes, apartments, cars — were only a means to serve it." Perhaps the funniest thing in the story is a dialogue concerning the sexual act in which a character named Karlinsky attempts to seduce Marina by means of a display of verbal fireworks. Almost intolerably brilliant, Karlinsky goes so far as to describe the brain as "only a cognitive adjunct of the sexual organs," but when Marina finally succumbs, the occasion turns into a fiasco — in his case an all-too-active brain evidently nullifies the sexual impulse. The spoofing dialogue about sex is among the wittiest in fiction and should prove an eye-opener to the increasing number of writers in America who approach the same subject with pious solemnity and are even disposed to regard pornography as no less than a literary genre on a par with tragedy and comedy.

There is very little plot in this story, and what there is of it has a look of improvisation. But plot is not its point, for its appeal is mainly in the dialogue and in the narrator's droll comment. As for the Communist bureaucrats that appear in it, they are surely more grotesque than menacing. They are characters out of Gogol brought up to date. Even when Seryozha, a charming boy, is accused of being "an unconscious Trotskyite" and packed off to a concentration camp, the effect is more gently sardonic than sorrowful. And in terms of political interest, the passage I found most impressive is that describing Stalin's funeral: "The Master was dead. The town seemed empty as a desert. You felt like sitting on your haunches, lifting up your head, and howling like a homeless dog." I suspect that this passage, from which I have quoted only the first two sentences, is historically more authentic than most accounts of that event which have reached us. Yet the principal impression one gathers from this short novel is that ideology plays a very small part in the author's scheme of values. I suppose that from his point of view both the petrified ideology of official communism and our own rabid variety of crusading anticommunism are equally obsessive forms of mental enslavement. He writes with the kind of inspired frivolity (or appearance of it) that reminds one of the early Evelyn Waugh, and with the energy of a fine literary intelligence at long last released from the confinement of officially "permitted" publication. No wonder he took his chances in transmitting his manuscripts abroad.

On Socialist Realism is in its analytic way as witty and ironic as *The Trial Begins*. What is socialist realism? It is the literary and artistic wing of a culture that is "teleological" through and through, that is to say, subject "to a higher destiny, from which it gains its title of nobility. In the final reckoning we live only to speed the coming of Communism." It is art with a Purpose. Works produced by socialist realists vary, of course, in style and content, but "in all of them the Purpose is present, whether directly or indirectly, open or veiled. They are panegyrics on Communism, satires on some of its many enemies, or descriptions of life in its revolutionary development, i.e., life moving towards Communism." Hence the inevitable appearance in this literature of a cast of "universally respected" and "privileged" characters called "positive heroes." "This is the Holy of Holies of socialist realism, its cornerstone and main achievement."

But the trouble is that these "positive heroes" are cardboard figures, mere dummies of ideology, in whom no one but the very stupid can believe.

Now, as Mr. Sinyavsky sees it, what kills socialist realism as a form of art is not that it presents what should be as what actually is but rather that it is not consistent enough or bold enough to erect its own classical canons in the manner of the religious cultures of the past. For no matter what we hear to the contrary in the West, art is not really "afraid of dictatorship, severity, repressions, or even conservatism and clichés. When necessary, art can be narrowly religious, dumbly governmental, devoid of individuality — and yet good. We go into aesthetic raptures over the stereotypes of Egyptian art, Russian icons and folklore. Art is elastic enough to fit into any Procrustes bed that history presents to it. But there is one thing it cannot stand — eclecticism." And the misfortune of Soviet writers is that they are socialist realists with insufficient conviction. They went to school, are well-read in all sorts of literature, and know only too well that there were great writers before them — "Balzac, Maupassant, Tolstoy, and yes, what's his name? — Chekhov. This is what has undone us. We wanted to become famous and write like Chekhov. This unnatural liaison has produced . . . a loathsome literary salad." Who was the most orthodox of socialist realists, even before the term was invented? According to Mr. Sinyavsky, the most orthodox as well as the most successful artistically was none other than Mayakovsky; and the reason is that he was thoroughly consistent, setting out to glorify the Revolution without looking back to the Russian nineteenth century — a century of "searchings, of ardent or calm aspirations . . . torn by uncertainties and doubts."

Mr. Sinyavsky holds out little hope for socialist realism, though not for the reasons usually given in the West. For my part, I believe that its vogue in Russia will prove to be short-lived and that the state will gradually if reluctantly withdraw its support of it. In a society dominated by rapid technological change and with a political system devoid of stability, there is no room for a new kind of classicism — "that most stable of styles." Communist society is real but its ideology is ossified. Under such conditions a new kind of dynamic realism can be expected to emerge.

Book Week, 1966

In Dubious Battle

ALTHOUGH *August 1914* is a long novel, it is only the first volume of a work of many parts. In his brief foreword the author tells us that the whole work "may take as long as twenty years" to write and that he probably "will not live to finish it." We are obviously dealing here with an extremely ambitious project, an account in epical novelistic form of the events, including the October Revolution and its aftermath, that have shaped Russia's destiny in the twentieth century.

Clearly, Solzhenitsyn has for many years been haunted by the question of how Russia had come to find itself in its present disheartening condition. A long inquiry into history was required to discover the answer, and he decided to start with the Russian defeat in the battle of Tannenberg, which occurred during the first month of World War I, and specifically with the encirclement and destruction of General Samsonov's Second Army, which invaded East Prussia at the beginning of August. Solzhenitsyn evidently regards this initial defeat as momentous, the decisive portent of the repeated Russian failure to halt the German advance, signifying the beginning of the disintegration of the Russian army, if not of the regime itself.

The defeat is the subject of this first volume which, freely mixing fictitious with historical characters, attempts at once to represent the battle in full detail and to elucidate the causes of its catastrophic outcome. Of course no complete judgment of Solzhenitsyn's immense undertaking can be formed until the novel as a whole becomes available. Still, this first volume does provide us with some indications (even if only provisional ones) of the novelist's approach to his material, his characteristic literary devices as well as his ideological position and outlook.

In spite of the efforts of the Soviet regime to stifle him we have for some time now been reading quite a bit of Solzhenitsyn, and this new novel only reinforces our conviction that he is by far the most gifted of living Russian writers and that he has the moral and intellectual stamina to continue to write powerfully in defiance of malevolent political persecution. The regime may yet kill him but so far it has been unable to silence him.

Critics have often compared him to Tolstoy, and rightly, for his manner is on the whole Tolstoyan. Yet his relationship with Tolstoy is complex and contradictory. Thus inevitably this new epic, even though unfinished, invites comparison with *War and Peace*; and, on the basis of my first impressions, I might as well say that Solzhenitsyn strikes me as superior to Tolstoy in his understanding of military strategy and tactics, quite as good as Tolstoy in his scenes of actual battle, but altogether inferior to him in his representation of private life (the theme of peace). Solzhenitsyn's students, young ladies, businessmen, and "deep thinkers" are not particularly memorable when measured against such Tolstoyan characters as Natasha, Sonya, Pierre Bezukhov, Prince Andrey and his father. In their private and inner lives Solzhenitsyn's people remain types whom he has not succeeded in converting into individuals. But the greater part of his novel and certainly his most masterful scenes, of which there are many, pertain to war rather than to peace.

Solzhenitsyn's narrative of the war tells us what happens both from the viewpoint of the rank-and-file and from that of the higher-ups, the commanders in the field as well as the staff officers in the rear. The result is a highly comprehensive view of war, and in this respect he truly reminds us of Tolstoy, who also endeavored to understand war from the vantage point both of the commanders and of the common soldiers.

However, at a crucial point the paths of the two novelists diverge very sharply. Whereas Tolstoy made every effort to idealize both the personality and the strategy of his commander-in-chief, General Kutuzov, Solzhenitsyn exposes nearly all of his generals, each of them based on the actual leaders of the Russian army, as incompetents and time-servers. His "ponderous and baffled" General Samsonov, who commits suicide after losing his troops, is treated sympathetically and is shown as the victim of the confusion and disorganization that prevail at General Headquarters.

Solzhenitsyn takes great pains to expose and analyze in depth the course of the catastrophe. Though undersupplied and underequipped, the Russian soldiers are shown to be brave enough, but time and again betrayed by the corruption, ineptness, and sheer lack of know-how of the military leadership. Because of outmoded methods of communication and confusing and contradictory orders, many divisions are needlessly sacrificed. Even as the Russian generals vainly seek to ascertain the disposition of the enemy forces, they are so stupidly incautious that they send uncoded wireless messages, which are of course regularly intercepted by the Germans. Sukhomlinov, the minister of war, is a military ignoramus who owes his high position to intrigue and his flattery of the Czar. Some of the younger graduates of the military academy, known as the "Young Turks," have been preparing themselves for years to introduce military reform only to be frustrated and put down by their seniors, whose smugness and conceit are boundless.

For Solzhenitsyn, the inefficiency of the Russian command is in no sense a historical accident. It is a major symptom of the backwardness and incompetence of the czarist regime, which "granted no power or influence to anyone not fortunate enough to be close to the throne." Furthermore, as Solzhenitsyn sees it, the Russian invasion of East Prussia only a few weeks after the declaration of war was a grave strategic error, for the Russian army was ill prepared to carry through such a bold undertaking, the advance was much too precipitous and badly coordinated. Solzhenitsyn for the most part does not use generalizations to show what happened. In clear and vigorous narrative prose he describes dozens of vivid scenes taking place throughout the battlefield as the Russians stumble into the German trap, scenes that obviously have affinities with those in *War and Peace*.

But it soon becomes clear that the mentality of Kutuzov is anathema to Solzhenitsyn, and because of this he enters into a direct polemic against Tolstoy in passages of commentary as well as in the fiction itself. For example, in writing of the Russian defeat, he remarks that "there might appear to be some consolation in Tolstoy's conviction that it is not generals who lead armies.... not presidents or leaders who run states or political parties — were it not that all too often the twentieth century has proved to us that it *is* such men who do these things." And further on the polemic is continued in the sardonic portrait of General Blagoveshchensky, who "had read about Kutuzov in Tolstoy's *War and Peace* and at sixty years of age, grayhaired, fat, and stiff, he felt himself to be just like Kutuzov...."

> Like Kutuzov he was wary, cautious, and cunning. And like Tolstoy's Kutuzov he realized that one should never issue sharp, decisive instructions; that "nothing but confusion could result from a battle started against

one's will"; that "military matters go their own way, which they are fated to follow whether or not it corresponds to what men propose"; that "there is an inevitable course of events"; and that the best general is the one who "declines to participate in these events." His long military service had convinced the general of the correctness of Tolstoy's views; there was nothing worse than sticking one's neck out by using one's initiative — people who did so always got into trouble.

This is clear enough, and of course Blagoveshchensky's "wise" Tolstoyan passivity, his determination not to stick his neck out, contributes to the catastrophe at Tannenberg. In fact throughout the book Solzhenitsyn seizes every opportunity to expose Kutuzovism, the very qualities of mind and character of which Tolstoy was so enamored and into which he read the essence of Russianism. Solzhenitsyn, on the other hand, is a military activist, an exponent of intelligence, skill, organization, and modernization. He advocates a kind of technocratic efficiency in military as well as civilian affairs. Hence, if the novel can be said to have a single hero, it is surely Colonel Vorotyntsev, a staff officer who turns up at every important juncture of the action, who admires modern German military methodology, and who refuses "to sit at General Headquarters as a pen-pusher ... at a time when a hazardous maneuver of the utmost boldness was being put into effect in Prussia."

Unlike the generals, Vorotyntsev appears to be Solzhenitsyn's own creation and he is the intelligence of the novel. Perfectly aware of the stodginess and sloth of the Russian generals, he is nevertheless a patriot who believes that Russia is "immeasurably strong, even if she is governed by a pack of fools." Convinced of that strength, the consciousness of defeat, far from demoralizing him, compels him openly to denounce his superiors at a conference presided over by the Grand Duke Nikolai Nikolaevich himself, with the result that his career is cut short when he is ordered by the grand duke to leave the room for overstepping "the bounds of what is permissible." It is plain that this clear-headed colonel speaks for the author and that he will reappear in later volumes. Whether he will eventually join the Bolsheviks remains to be seen.

However, there is another side to the novel which, in contrast to its bias toward the technocratic and the instrumental, is traditionally Russian and patently indebted to the Tolstoyan model. The peasant-soldier Blagodaryov, whom Vorotyntsev chooses from the trenches as his orderly and who accompanies him on some of his most dangerous missions, is directly reminiscent of Platon Karatayev, the peasant-soldier in *War and Peace* whom Pierre encounters in a French prison and from whom he absorbs the teaching that the supreme values of life are simplicity, truthfulness, and goodness. The very surname Blagodaryov (the root-word is *blaga,* which might be translated as gratitude or even beneficence) speaks for itself. He is cheerful, modest, and good, even when undergoing the worst trials. There is in him, we are told, "a great fund of simple humanity, a goodness that had nothing to do with rank, class, or politics but was the unspoiled simplicity of Nature herself."

Moreover, the sturdy ideal qualities of Karatayev Blagodaryov are associated with Solzhenitsyn's admiration for another very Russian trait, as when he exultingly observes that "no disaster, no amount of bloodshed, is ever enough to galvanize Russians out of their passive endurance." In this admiration of suffering in passive endurance Solzhenitsyn is clearly at one with both Tolstoy and Dostoevsky. He fails to perceive the extreme ambiguity of this conspicuous Russian trait. It is by no means the purely positive quality that Solzhenitsyn, like his great predecessors, takes it to be. There is something about it which one can only regard as insidious. For, after all, did not this Russian compliance and acquiescence in passive suffering make possible the emergence of both the czarist and Stalinist autocracy?

Another Russian writer, Vasily Grossman, debates this question in his recent novel *Forever Flowing.** He ponders the paradox that runs throughout Russian history, the paradox that there exists in the same people a "meekness and readiness to endure suffering ... unequaled since the epoch of the first Christians" together with a "contempt for and disregard of human suffering" as well as a certain subservience to abstract theories on human welfare. He contends that the great Russian writers, the radicals no less than the reactionaries, idealized Karatayevism as singularly Russian and noble and therefore vastly to be preferred to the mushy liberalism of the West.

Grossman concludes that in "the Russian fascination with Byzantine, ascetic purity, with Christian meekness, lives the unwitting admission of the permanence of Russian slavery. The sources of this Christian meekness and gentleness, of this Byzantine "ascetic purity" are also discernible in the "Leninist passion, fanaticism, and intolerance." It is clear that this trend of thought is completely alien to Solzhenitsyn, who sometimes seems to accept uncritically the Russian tradition even while contradicting it in advocating efficiency and

* Harper and Row, 1972.

modernization so forcefully. Looked at purely as a novelistic character, Blagodaryov is truly admirable, but what he represents is a profound attachment to the Russian past, which is obviously at odds with the technocratic and practical bias that pervades the novel.

August 1914 makes plain that its author is above all a Russian rather than a Soviet patriot. His Russianism, as I have mentioned, is of a very traditional sort, so much so that at times one feels that his position might be described as quasi-Slavophile. In this sense he has really more in common with Dostoevsky than with Tolstoy. His manner and tone in this novel are Tolstoyan, to be sure; he in no way shares Dostoevsky's obsession with pathological and criminal states of mind, nor is he drawn to the famous Dostoevskyan "lacerations." Yet ideologically, mainly because of his mystical, religious populism, he is closer to Dostoevsky than to Tolstoy, who, after all, was a staunch pacifist and whose version of the Christian doctrine transcended every form of nationalism. Solzhenitsyn is a Christian believer of the Orthodox variety but he is no pacifist. He is also a passionate nationalist. This fact emerges in many passages of the novel, as, for example, in the following speech of the engineer Ilya Isakovich to a group of revolutionary young people:

> "The country one lives in is in trouble. So which is right: to say, 'Go to hell, I'll have none of you,' or to say, 'I want to help you, I belong here'? Living in this country, one must make up one's mind once and for all and stick to one's decision. Do I really belong to it heart and soul? Or don't I? If I don't, then I can smash it or leave it, it makes no difference which I do. . . . But if I *do* belong to it, then I must adapt myself to the slow process of history, by work, by persuasion and gradual change. . . ."

Ilya Isakovich and his guest the engineer Obodovsky are the civilian counterparts of Colonel Vorotyntsev, and they are rather more explicit than he is in declaring their contempt for the radical traditions of the intelligentsia. Obodovsky argues that

> " . . . anyone who has created something with his own hands knows that production is neither capitalist nor socialist but *one* thing only: it is what creates national wealth. . . . Along come a bunch of arts students and they explain to the workers that they are earning too little, and that that little engineer over there in spectacles is earning God knows how much, and that it's sheer bribery. And these simple, uneducated people believe it and they are indignant. . . ."

"I believe," Obodovsky says, "the Union of Engineers could easily become one of the leading forces in Russia. It's more important and more constructive than any political party." He promises, "Give us ten years of peaceful development and you won't recognize Russian industry, or Russian agriculture for that matter." This technocratic mystique is one of the dominant motifs of the novel, and it is clear that the author is fully in sympathy with it.

To my mind there is something profoundly unpolitical in this mystique of technocracy. Where, in what country, have engineers ever seized power or even aspired to do so? In the United States as in all other Western countries of high technology the corporate elite is firmly in control and the engineers they employ knuckle under. They invariably carry out the decisions of their bosses, who are far more interested in financial manipulation than in the specific skills their engineers possess. After all, it is the Communists who finally succeeded in industrializing Russia, while the Russian engineers worked under Lenin, Stalin, and now Brezhnev and Kosygin with the same docility that their Western counterparts exhibit in servicing the big corporations. His new book shows that Solzhenitsyn is in no sense a Marxist: he is a nationalist and a patriot, a belated *narodnik* whose mystic-religious populism oddly accords with his technological and pragmatic inclinations. There is an inherent contradiction, and a rather bizarre one at that, in trying to combine the two positions of which, surprisingly enough, Solzhenitsyn appears to be quite unaware, at least in the first volume.

In addition to Vorotyntsev and the two engineers, there is another fictional character in the novel, Varsonofiev, who is presented as a "deep thinker" and whose sole function seems to be that of voicing the author's philosophical views. In an argument with two radical students Varsonofiev expresses approval of the war, for, as he puts it, "When the trumpet sounds, a man must be a man, even if merely for his own self-respect." Russia's backbone must not be broken, "and for that, young men must go to war." So much for Lenin's program of revolutionary defeatism! Varsonofiev asserts, "Do not be so arrogant as to imagine that you can invent an ideal social order, because with that invention you may destroy your beloved 'people.'" In his view "history is *irrational* . . . It has its own, and to us perhaps incomprehensible, organic structure." The worst mistake one can make is to believe that history is "governed by reason."

The ideas expounded by Varsonofiev, who is allotted only one scene in the novel, are crucial to Solzhenitsyn's view of the world. Once the premise that history is irrational is accepted, then not only

Marxism but all other theories of history as well cease to make sense. Or does Solzhenitsyn suppose that only small, limited segments of history are open to rational analysis? Surely he must assume this, for otherwise I cannot see how he can reconcile the strenuous efforts of his hero Vorotyntsev to discover the causes of Russia's defeat with the assumption, which he seems to endorse, that the historical process is wholly irrational and incomprehensible. If that assumption were correct, it would be futile for Solzhenitsyn to concern himself so deeply and seriously with Russia's destiny, which, after all, cannot be exempted from the forces of history.

There is only one convinced Marxist among the many soldiers portrayed in this novel, and he is the young ensign Sasha Lenartovich, who is prepared to lay down his life any moment for the great cause of the Revolution, and can think of nothing worse than "to die at the age of twenty-four defending autocracy." He looks forward to Russia's defeat, believing as he does in the Leninist policy of "the worse, the better." Lenartovich seeks to escape the war by surrendering to the Germans and in that aim he fails. He will probably turn up in later volumes as an officer in the Red Army. It is to Solzhenitsyn's credit that he manages to be scrupulously fair in his fictional rendering of this revolutionary type. But that he finds Lenartovich no hero is clear. The characters with whom he does seem to identify — Vorotyntsev, the engineers, and Varsonofiev — are patriotic to the core.

Solzhenitsyn is a hero of Russian intellectual resistance to the vicious cultural policies of the present Soviet regime. He is also a very fine writer of fiction whose work will surely become a part of the canon of Russian literature. I do not think that the impression of confusion and turbidity conveyed by his more general ideas should count much against him. Tolstoy's ideas of history, presented so insistently in *War and Peace*, are equally open to criticism, yet we do not hesitate to accord that novel the very highest stature; nor does Dostoevsky's reactionary obscurantism prevent us from appreciating his great importance as an imaginative creator. I for one have never been prepared to judge works of fiction by subjecting them to a political-ideological test, for to do so is inevitably to lose oneself in a maze of considerations that are beside the point of literature. To be sure, ideological awareness and political attention are by no means to be eschewed by the literary critic, but in the last analysis he cannot afford to permit his own bias, whether radical or conservative, to overpower his judgment and perceptions.

In my opinion, *August 1914* is not Solzhenitsyn's *chef-d'oeuvre*. However, let us keep in mind the fact that it is only the first volume of a much longer work. When complete, it may indeed turn out to be the masterpiece we have every reason to expect of him.

New York Review of Books, 1972

Mrs. Woolf and Mrs. Brown

In her wonderfully high-spirited essay "Mr. Bennett and Mrs. Brown," written in 1924, Virginia Woolf came out for scrapping the conventional realism of the Edwardian generation, the generation of Wells, Galsworthy, and Bennett. The new course for English fiction, she declared, is being set by novelists like Joyce and Forster and Lawrence and herself, who were discarding the old outworn methods. Confident that they could be relied on to make good the promise of the age, she boldly predicted that it would prove to be "one of the great ages of English literature." But in conclusion she warned that it could be reached only "if we are determined never, never to desert Mrs. Brown."

Mrs. Brown, the old lady in the railway carriage, served Mrs. Woolf as the symbol of reality — of reality as we think we know it and of the human character as we live it daily and hourly. It was Mrs. Woolf's idea, in other words, that no adequate substitute for Mrs. Brown can be found but that it is possible to devise new ways of coping with the rather stodgy yet ever so obstinate old lady. Now, however, in evaluating the actual literary practice that followed and by some years even preceded the theoretical flights of her manifesto against the Edwardians, the questions that need to be asked are these: What really happened between Mrs. Woolf and Mrs. Brown? Did Mrs. Woolf succeed in holding on to Mrs. Brown or was she finally forced to desert her? And if she deserted her, as I think she did, what were the consequences of this act? Did it reduce or increase her powers as a novelist who was also one of the leading innovators in modern writing? Our judgment not only of Mrs. Woolf's fiction but of contemporary fiction in general is affected by whatever answers can be given to such questions.

E. M. Forster is among the critics who have applauded Mrs.

Woolf's creative efforts; and he appears to snub Mrs. Brown when speaking of *The Waves,* surely the most abstract of Mrs. Woolf's novels, as her best work. But in another passage of the same essay he implicitly modifies his estimate of her achievement. There are two kinds of life in fiction, he observes, "life on the page and life eternal," and it is only the first kind of life that Mrs. Woolf was able to master. "Her characters never seem unreal, however slight or fantastic their lineaments, and they can be trusted to behave appropriately. Life eternal she could seldom give; she could seldom so portray a character that it was remembered afterwards on its own account." Mrs. Woolf no doubt made a very brave attempt to break through conventional realism and to create new forms for the novel. *Mrs. Dalloway* and *To the Lighthouse* are minor successes and unique in their way, but on the whole she failed. Some years ago William Troy outlined the full extent of this failure in a brilliant essay, in which he demonstrated that Mrs. Woolf's style is the product of a "facile traditionalism," that the unity of her novels is "merely superficial or decorative, corresponding to no fundamental organization of the experience," and that her characters are "unable to function anywhere but on the plane of the sensibility."

Mr. Troy's definitive analysis may be supplemented by several observations. There is the fact, for example, that at one time Mrs. Woolf thought of herself as an associate of Joyce, whereas actually there is little kinship between them. Consider to what totally different uses they put such a device as the interior monologue. While in Joyce the interior monologue is a means of bringing us closer to the characters, of telling us *more* about them than we could learn from a purely objective account of their behavior, in Mrs. Woolf it becomes a means of telling us *less* about them, of disengaging their ego from concrete situations in life and converting it into a vehicle of poetic memory. Her tendency is to drain the interior monologue of its modern content and turn it back to the habitual forms of lyrical expression — and reverie. Where Joyce performs a radically new act of aesthetic selection, Mrs. Woolf performs what is in the main an act of exclusion; for she retains no more fictional material than will suffice to identify the scene and its human inhabitants; beyond that all is sensation and impression of a volatile kind. And it is so volatile because only on the surface does it flow from the actual experience of the characters — its real source is the general tradition of English poetry and of the poetic sensibility. However, there is a crucial fault in Mrs. Woolf's grasp even of this tradition, for she comprehends it one-sidedly, and perhaps in much too feminine a fashion, not as a complete order but first and foremost as an order of sentiments.

In *Between the Acts,* Mrs. Woolf's last and most unhappy book, the following complaint is sounded time and again: "None speaks with a single voice. None with a voice free from the old vibrations. Always I hear corrupt murmurs; the chink of gold and metal. Mad music . . ." One feels that this is the author's requiem for a lost art, that here she is pronouncing judgment against herself. But it is by no means the final judgment. Something remains that is deeply moving, an expiatory tenderness, the soul's searching of its own roots. To read her closely is to catch the strains of that "mad music" that sometimes possessed her, a music which breaks through the "old vibrations," the used-up words and disembodied imagery of such "poetic" abstractions as Time and Change, Life and Death. It is the deranged song of Septimus Smith, who is Mrs. Dalloway's double and who dies that she may live. Septimus is the mysterious stranger, the marked man, the poet upon whom an outrage had been committed; he is at once the sacrificial goat and a veritable "lord of creation." This apparition haunted Mrs. Woolf, but always she strove to escape from it. She felt more at home with Mrs. Dalloway.

The ultimate failure of Virginia Woolf's experiments might perhaps be explained by going back to her initial conception of reality as an old lady in a railway carriage called Mrs. Brown. For what is Mrs. Brown if not the product of the traditional realism of the English novel? What is she if not the dominant figure of that world so scorned by Mrs. Woolf — the world of Messrs. Wells, Galsworthy, and Bennett? The truth is that she tacitly accepted, even as she revolted against her elders, their innermost vision of reality. Hence all she could do is turn their vices inside out — since they had materialized the novel, she was to devote herself to spiritualizing it. Forgotten was the pledge "never, never to desert Mrs. Brown." But Mrs. Woolf was profoundly mistaken in her belief that she had seen through Mrs. Brown and was now free to dismiss her. If literature can be said to have a permanent theme, that theme is precisely The Mystery of Mrs. Brown, who is a creature of many paradoxes and truly unfathomable. She is not to be encompassed either by the materialist or by the idealist approach and she lets the novelists make what they can of her. To some she appears as a commonplace old lady; to others as a tiger in the night.

Mrs. Woolf's idea of Mrs. Brown is expressive of all the assumptions she was born to, of the safety and domestication of that upper-class British culture to which she was so perfectly adjusted. Now the breach between poetry and prose, conceived as opposed to each other in the same absolute way (but is it absolute?) that pleasure is opposed to pain, is one of the most secure assumptions of that culture; and Mrs. Woolf carried its traditional dualism to its furthest extreme. Therefore she was forced to invent a definition of what is real, of what life is, quite as artificial as the one she repudiated. "Life," she declaimed in her essay "Modern Fiction," "is not a series of gig lamps symmetrically arranged; life is a luminous halo, a semi-transparent envelope surrounding us from the beginning of consciousness to the end." That is the essence of idealism, of that other, that sacrosanct reality in which Mrs. Woolf luxuriates but from which Mrs. Brown is excluded.

Yet if Mrs. Woolf was not a great literary artist, she was surely a great woman of letters. "She liked writing," as Mr. Forster says, "with an intensity that few writers have attained, or even desired." *The Death of the Moth,* her last collection of essays and reviews, while not quite so impressive as the two volumes of *The Common Reader,* contains at least a half dozen pieces that are first rate. Never a systematic critic, she was a master of such neglected forms as the literary portrait and the familiar essay. And it is her enthusiasm and the purity and passion of her devotion to writing, rather than the poetic code which she endeavored to impose on the fictional medium, that will in the end secure a place for her, even though of the secondary order, in the history of English letters.

Kenyon Review, 1942

An Introduction to Kafka

FRANZ KAFKA is today firmly linked in the literary mind to such names as Joyce and Proust and Yeats and Rilke and Eliot — the sacred untouchables, as they have been rightly called, of the modern creative line. Among them he is exceptional in that he enjoyed no public recognition of consequence in his lifetime, for he withheld his longer narratives from publication and was scarcely known beyond a narrow circle of German writers. His posthumous world fame came to him only in the past two decades.

The first translation of one of his books appeared in this country in 1930, six years after his death. That book was *The Castle,* a novel that ranks high in the Kafka canon. Few readers were then able to gauge its true worth, and even as late as 1937, when *The Trial* was brought out here, it was chiefly Kafka's apparent mystifications rather than his pattern of meaning and basic motives that aroused interest. Readers were astonished by his work but hardly convinced of its importance. Since then his idiosyncratic but powerful sensibility has entered into the blood stream of twentieth-century literature. He has been made the subject of numerous citical studies in many languages; and everywhere the more sensitive younger writers, conscious of the static condition of the prevailing fictional techniques and seeking creative renewal, have taken his example to heart. There can be little doubt any longer of his stature as an artist in the metaphysical mode, whose concern is with the ultimate structure of human existence, or of his surpassing originality as an innovator in creative method. Like Rilke in the *Duino Elegies* he asked the supreme question: *Was war wirklich im All?* (What was real in the world?)

A master of narrative tone, of a subtle, judicious, and ironically

Written as an introduction to the *Selected Tales of Franz Kafka* in the Modern Library edition.

conservative style, Kafka combines in his fiction the real and the unreal, extreme subjectivity of content with forms rigorously objective, a lovingly exact portrayal of the factual world with dreamlike dissolution of it. By unifying these contrary elements he was able to achieve a fundamentally new appropriation of the resources of the prose medium. This much can be said, I think, without attempting to give an integrated critical estimate of his work, which may well be premature even now. The analysis and description of its qualities will suffice. Thus it is clear that if Kafka so compellingly arouses in us a sense of immediate relatedness, of strong even if uneasy identification, it is because of the profound quality of his feeling for the experience of human loss, estrangement, guilt, and anxiety — an experience increasingly dominant in the modern age.

That Kafka is among the most neurotic of literary artists goes without saying. It accounts, mainly, for the felt menace of his fantastic symbolism and for his drastic departure from the well-defined norms of the literary imagination. For all its obviousness, however, the fact of Kafka's neuroticism presents a danger, if not a vulgar temptation, to the unliterary mind, which tends to confuse a fact so patent with critical judgment and appraisal. No greater error is possible in our approach to literary art. To avoid that common error it is above all necessary to perceive that Kafka is something more than a neurotic artist; he is also an artist of neurosis, that is to say, he succeeds in objectifying through imaginative means the states of mind typical of neurosis and hence in incorporating his private world into the public world we all live in. Once that is accomplished, the creative writer has performed the essential operation which is the secret of his triumph as an artist, if not as a man; he has exorcised his demon, freed himself of his personal burden, converting us into his accomplices. And we, as good readers, as willing accomplices, have no real reason to complain. Neurosis may be the occasion but literature is the consequence. Moreover, the creative writer is the last person we may look to if our concern is with drawing a line between the normal and the abnormal. For whatever the practicing psychologist may make of that crude though useful distinction, the artist cannot attend to it without inhibiting his sense of life in its full concreteness and complexity.

The novelist Graham Greene has remarked that "every creative writer worth our consideration, every writer who can be called in the wide sense of the term a poet, is a victim: a man given over to an obsession." Kafka's obsession was an inordinate sense of inadequacy, failure, and sinfulness — a sinfulness corresponding to nothing he had actually done or left undone, but lodged in the innermost recesses of his being. "The state in which we find ourselves is sinful, quite independently of guilt," he wrote in his notebook. The clue to *The Trial* is the reflection that "only our concept of time makes it possible for us to speak of the Day of Judgment by that name; in reality it is a summary court in perpetual session." And in the same sequence of reflections we find the perfectly typical sentence: "The hunting dogs are playing in the courtyard, but the hare will not escape them, no matter how fast it may be flying already through the woods." The identification here is plainly with the hare; and with the hunting dogs, too, insofar as they represent the hare's longing for self-punishment, his inner wish to be cornered, to be hurt and torn to pieces so as to atone for the guilt that fills him from top to bottom. In this one short sentence about the hare and the dogs you have the gist of the typical Kafkan narrative, the obsessive theme, the nuclear fable concerning the victim of an unappeasable power to which he returns again and again, varying and complicating its structure with astonishing resourcefulness, and erecting on so slender a foundation such marvelous superstructures as that of the myth of the Old Commander in "In the Penal Colony," the myth of the Law in *The Trial,* and of the celestial bureaucracy in *The Castle.*

The simplicity of the nuclear fable in Kafka should not lead us, however, to disregard the qualities that make him one of the most enigmatic figures in world literature. It does no good to speak of him as an author of religious allegories. Unlike such religious allegorists as Dante or Bunyan he does not depend on the definitive logic of a generally known system of theology; his creative mode presupposes no body of knowledge external to itself; he is not allegorical in any accepted sense but rather an innovator so deeply individualistic as to fit none of the familiar categories. Also, the difficulty of understanding him is on a different plane from that encountered in reading a novelist like James Joyce, for example. Whereas the obscurities of the latter are inherent in the elaborate stylization of his material and in his complex structural designs, in Kafka's case it is the meaning alone that baffles us. Both in language and construction he is elementary compared to Joyce, yet many readers have been mystified by his fictions. But the mystification is gradually cleared up once we learn to listen attentively to his tone and become accustomed to the complete freedom with which he suspends certain conventions of storytelling when it suits his symbolic purpose. Thus when we read in the first sentence of "The

Metamorphosis" that the clerk Gregor Samsa awoke one morning to find himself changed into a gigantic insect, it is a mistake to think that by means of this bold stroke Kafka intends to call into question the laws of nature. What he calls into question, rather, is the convention that the laws of nature are at all times to be observed in fiction; and having suspended that convention in the very first paragraph of the story, from that point on he develops it in a logical and realistic manner. The clerk's metamorphosis is a multiple symbol of his alienation from the human state, of his "awakening" to the full horror of his dull, spiritless existence, and of the desperate self-disgust of his unconscious fantasy-life, in which the wish to displace the father and take over his authority in the family is annulled by the guilt-need to suffer a revolting punishment for his presumption.

Another type of symbolism, far less psychologically charged, is found in stories like "The Great Wall of China." What is the Great Wall? It is likewise a multiple symbol — of human solidarity, of earthly fulfillment, and of mankind's effort to obtain supernatural guidance. But why was the wall built in a piecemeal fashion, thus permitting the nomads of the North to slip through the gaps? The reply is that it is in the nature of man to achieve only limited ends. He cannot comprehend the Whole; his vision is discontinuous, his security always incomplete; his aims he can realize only in fragmentary fashion. No doubt the "high command" is ultimately responsible for the apparently inexpedient method of the wall's construction; yet it would never do to question its decrees. Not that such questioning is blasphemous in itself but rather that in the long run it is useless. Logic can bring us only to a certain point. Beyond that an answer of a sort is given by the beautiful parable of the river in spring. And as the story continues, the theme of the wall is dialectically converted into a series of poetic speculations concerning the relationship between the Chinese and the imperial court at Pekin, that is between God and man. While in "Investigations of a Dog" the remoteness of God is represented as a remoteness in time, in this story the imagery is chiefly spatial. Pekin is so far away from the villagers of the South that they can hardly imagine its existence. They worship dynasties long since dead; news arriving from the imperial court is obsolete by the time it reaches them. This inability of the "Chinese" to possess their Emperor in his vital contemporaneity appears to be a reflection on the idea of God as known to modern man — an idea ill-defined, nebulous and, above all, archaic. Man is now unaware of the real powers that govern his life; insofar as he has any knowledge of divinity it is as of something purely historical.

The quarrel between the religious and the psychoanalytic interpreters of Kafka is of no great moment, as his work is sufficiently meaningful to support some of the "truths" of both schools. Thus the father who condemns his son to death by drowning (in "The Judgment") can be understood as the tyrannical father of Freudian lore and at the same time as the God of Judgment rising in His wrath to destroy man's illusion of self-sufficiency in the world. At bottom there is no conflict between the two interpretations. For one thing, they are not mutually exclusive; for another, the reading we give the story depends as much on our own outlook — within certain limits of course — as on that of the author. There was in Kafka's character an element of radical humility not permitting him to set out to "prove" any given attitude toward life or idea about it. This he plainly tells us in some of the aphorisms that he wrote about himself in the third person: "He proves nothing but himself, his sole proof is himself, all his opponents overcome him at once, not by refuting him (he is irrefutable) but by proving themselves."

That Kafka was a man of religious temper I have no doubt. Though the creator of a surpassing imagery of human failure and frustration, inclined to feel imprisoned on this earth, afflicted with "the melancholy, the impotence, the sicknesses, the feverish fancies of the captive," he never abandons his trust in the spirituality of existence, in the "indestructible," and is disheartened by his literary effort because he wants his writing to attain the power of lifting the world into the realm of "the pure, the true, the immutable." Yet there is nothing either in his private papers or in his fiction to warrant the claim that he was a believer in a personal God who gave his assent to any of the dogmatic systems associated with institutional religion. Even original sin, the dogma closest to the thematic center of his work, he interprets speculatively as "consisting of the complaint, which man makes and never ceases making, that a wrong had been done to him, that the original sin was committed upon him." From the standpoint of the theologian that is sheer heresy, gentle, self-incriminating heresy, to be sure, but heresy nevertheless. The German critic Franz Blei, who was personally acquainted with Kafka, speaks of him as "the servant of a God not believed in." A piety so paradoxical, so immune to categorical definition, so removed from the fixed and traditional, refusing the consolation of revealed religion yet intent on winning through to "a faith like a guillotine, as heavy, as light," could never have found expression in general ideas or logical thought but only in the language of art, the one language capable of offering everything while claiming nothing, asserting nothing, proving nothing.

Born in 1883 of middle-class Jewish parents, Kafka appears to have lost his self-confidence early in life, exchanging for it, as he himself put it, "a boundless sense of guilt." Moods of loss and failure, and the idea of the insolubility even of the most ordinary human problems, depressed his youth and later inspired his art. In the center of his life stands the father, a figure fully corresponding to that Freudian terror, the Primal Sire. Energetic, overbearing, capricious, successful, respectable, the father, not so much by malicious intention as by being simply what he was, exposed to ridicule his son's impractical inclinations and spiritual wanderings. The mother, though solicitous for her son, was far too much absorbed in her husband to play an independent role; and young Franz was thus driven to extremes of loneliness and introspection that continually negated themselves in the idea of integration through marriage, children, and the practice of an honorable profession ("a true calling . . . the right vocation"). The effect on him of his father was such that though he usually talked exceedingly well, in the presence of the formidable parent he took to stuttering. "For me," he wrote to his father in later life, "you began to have that mysterious quality which all tyrants have, whose privilege is based on their personality, not on reason." It is clear that the source of the principle of authority so characteristic of his art is to be traced to his ambivalent attitude to his father, an attitude of strong repulsion as well as identification. Constructed out of elements of his own personality, the protagonist of his major fictions is coerced by extranatural powers who are continually justified and exalted even as they are made to manifest themselves in the guise of a menacing and arbitrary bureaucracy. Max Brod, Kafka's lifelong friend, biographer, and editor of his posthumous writings, relates that in many talks he attempted to demonstrate to him the foolishness of his self-contempt and chronic overestimation of his father. These talks were useless, for Kafka produced a "torrent of arguments" that shattered and repelled his friend, who soon realized that only from the standpoint of an outsider could it be asked: "What difference could his father's approval make to Kafka?" His need for that approval was obviously "an innate, irrefutable feeling" that lasted to the end of his life.

In 1906 he took his degree in law at the German University in Prague and soon afterwards obtained a post in an accident insurance office. But his real interest was in writing, which he approached with the utmost moral earnestness, regarding it as a sacred expenditure of energy, an effort at communion with one's fellow men, the reflected splendor of religious perception. However, it could never serve as his means of livelihood; aside from his objection in principle to turning literary talent into a source of material benefits, there were other obstacles. He wrote at a pace altogether his own, filled with a raging discontent; at the same time there was the drastic need to stand on his own feet, to win immediate independence from the family. Yet the work at the insurance office disintegrated him; the two occupations were incompatible.

In his letters he writes of literature as his only hope for happiness and fulfillment; and telling of trancelike states when he felt himself at the boundary of the human, he adds that they lacked the serenity of inspiration and were not conducive to the best writing. He speaks of himself as having been on the way to create "a new secret doctrine, a Kabala," but his replies as to the meaning of that doctrine are as diverse as they are contradictory. (His precision, Brod rightly says, was moral, not intellectual.) "I represent," we read in his diary, "the negative elements of my age . . . Unlike Kierkegaard, I was not guided in life by the new heavily sinking hand of Christianity, nor have I caught hold, like the Zionists, of one of the ends of the flying prayer-shawl of the Jews." The one break in his relationship with Brod seems to have been caused by his coolness to Zionism. "What have I in common with the Jews," he wrote, "when I have scarely anything in common with myself?" In later years, however, he developed a lively interest in the aspirations of the Zionists, studied Jewish folk literature, the Hebrew language, and read the Talmud (to which his style, by the way, in its reasoning, argumentative quality, in its movement through assertion and contradiction, statement and refutation, bears some resemblance).

It was in 1912 — a fateful year in his life — that he met Felice B., the young woman from Berlin whom he wanted to marry but was forced to renounce, suffering terrible anguish in twice breaking off his engagement to her. He felt that for a man in his uprooted condition, lacking independent status and a secure orientation in life, marriage was an impossible task. But that was the year, too, in which his literary intentions and continual probing of his own predicament came together in a way enabling him to forge decisively ahead in his work. Compared to what he wrote in the fall of that year everything he had previously written seems sketchy and unfinished. On the night of September 22 of that seminal fall he wrote "The Judgment" in one sitting, remarking afterwards that during that long stretch between ten o'clock in the evening and six o'clock the next morning he more than once carried his weight on his own back. "The Judgment" is the first Kafkan story which is all of a piece and the first in which the characteristic theme of the struggle between father and son is sounded to the depths. That same month and the next he wrote the long opening chapter of *Amerika,* his first novel, and in November he completed "The Metamorphosis," certainly his greatest story, in which he achieves an overpowering effect through his consummate handling of the factual detail that supports and actualizes the somber fantasy of the plot. This story is the very embodiment of that quality of the exigent and the extreme, that sense of a human being hemmed in by his own existence and absolutely committed to it, which touches us so deeply in Kafka because it is at once method and content, entreaty and response, the goal and the way. It is mainly through this "existential" quality that Kafka *substantiates* his world for us, imparting the unmistakable appeal of reality to those elements in it that might otherwise appear to be little more than the products of a bizarre or erratic imagination. In "The Metamorphosis," I would say, Kafka for the first time fully realized his own innermost conception of writing — a conception of inexpressible urgency and inwardness. Long before the composition of the story, he attempted to explain what writing meant to him when he said, in a letter to his friend Oskar Pollak, that "the books we need are of the kind that act upon us like a misfortune, that make us suffer like the death of someone we love more than ourselves, that make us feel as though we were on the verge of suicide, or lost in a forest remote from all human habitation — a book should serve as the ax for the frozen sea within us."

In October of the same year Max Brod notes in his diary: "Kafka in ecstasy. Writes all night long..." And again: "Kafka in incredible ecstasy." There is something more to this ecstatic state than elation and the sense of freedom a writer normally experiences when making visible progress in his work. The patently compulsive nature of "The Judgment" and "The Metamorphosis," no less than Kafka's own comment upon them in his diaries, suggest that these stories served as "the ax for the frozen sea" within him — in other words, that the process of their creation involved a breakthrough to layers of repressed material which had heretofore proven inaccessible. It is as if in these psychodynamic fictions the neurotic sufferer in Kafka and the artist in him locked hands and held on for dear life. Precisely of works such as these one can say with Yeats that "the more unconscious the creation the more powerful."

The novel *Amerika,* begun in that period, stands somewhat apart from the bulk of Kafka's work. The extranatural plays no part in it; there is no evocation of mysterious powers or any derangement of the known and recognizable world for the sake of injecting into it the menace of the irrational and unfathomable. It is the only one of Kafka's longer narratives in which he fully indulged his flair for comedy. The intention behind it, however, is not the exposure of specific foibles but the portrayal of the typical human condition. "If sufficiently systematized, comedy turns into reality," he wrote in his notebooks. And this statement can stand as the motto of this pica-resque tale of the adventures of the sixteen-year-old boy Karl Ross-mann, a native of Prague, in the mechanized cities of the United States, a country which Kafka had never seen but of which he had a definite image in his mind.

Steeped as he was in moods of loss and failure, he tended to re-gard with astonishment and inordinate admiration all examples of constructive will, of the ability of men to discover their true calling and achieve that integration in the community, in which he attached the highest value but which he believed to be beyond his own reach. His constant plaint was the same as that of the character in Haw-thorne's story "The Intelligence Office," who never ceases to cry out: "I want my place, my own place, my proper sphere, my thing to do, which nature intended me to perform when she fashioned me thus awry, and which I have vainly sought all my lifetime!" For this reason Benjamin Franklin, who was singularly successful in all his undertakings, was among Kafka's favorite historical figures; and Franklin's *Autobiography* is one of the sources of *Amerika.* Let no one think, however, that Kafka was charmed by Poor Richard's opin-ion of himself or by his general philosophy; what interested him in this exemplary American career was its inexplicable element of fate, which in this case had manifested itself in a positive guise. He probably read Poor Richard's recommendations of virtue, his list of proverbs on frugality, temperance, moderation, tranquility, and the like, as one reads a work on strategy, interpreting those dismally sagacious sayings as so many moves in the complicated game of ingratiating oneself with the nameless authorities whose law, though its intent and meaning are unknown and unknowable, prevails none-theless. It was the Ulysses-like aspect of Franklin that attracted Kafka, and he conceived of America as his Mediterranean. Ameri-cans, he thought, wore perpetual smiles on their faces, for somehow they had managed, perhaps through the protection afforded them by the extraordinary dimensions of the New World, to beat fate to the draw.

Karl Rossmann is truly innocent, and in this respect he differs radically from K., the protagonist of *The Trial* and *The Castle*. Whereas K., who is thoroughly impregnated with rationality, approaches the problem of guilt largely in a legalistic fashion, reacting vindictively to the misfortunes that befall him and seeking to prove by logical processes that he has committed no crime and should therefore be let alone, Karl suffers persecution without dreaming of vengeance or unduly dwelling on the wrongs that have been done him. When his rich uncle willfully turns him out of his house for virtually no reason at all, he utters no word of protest but calmly goes about the business of adjusting himself to his new situation. He is not a subjective character; his energy is of that benign kind which flows congenially even into the narrowest channels of reality.

The Kafkan irony expends itself on Karl by entangling him in a series of accidents, errors, and misunderstandings that are as circumstantially precise as they are magical in arrangement. His first steps in America — whose bewildering and immense bureaucratic mechanisms he dare not examine too closely — are attended by good fortune; but after a few months he is suddenly overtaken by disaster and compelled to take to the road in search of work in the company of the unemployed and thievish mechanics Delamarche and Robinson. After many trials he is befriended by a woman, a kind of Athene in the shape of a hotel manager. But this position too is soon lost to him, when he is abducted by the thievish mechanics with the design of forcing him into the service of Brunelda, a great slob of a Circe who had transformed them both into swinish lechers. (The seventh chapter, called "The Refuge," describing the Chaplinesque chase of Karl by a policeman, his encounter with the incomparable Brunelda, the election parade, and his conversation with the coffee-nourished student, is to my mind one of the finest single pieces of writing in modern fiction.) In the end he escapes from Brunelda's household to find work in the "Nature Theatre of Oklahoma," a beneficent and fantastic enterprise miraculously welcoming the unemployed into its almost limitless spaces, where they are provided with jobs and reconciled to the inscrutable purposes of the powers ruling the life of man.

Kafka makes no attempt to give a realistic account of America. He is quite inaccurate in every detail, yet the picture as a whole has uncanny symbolic truth. And if on its existential side this story is a sort of good-humored parody of the career of Poor Richard, on its literary side it derives from Dickens. David Copperfield, who is also a good boy with the wit to make the most of his virtue in his trials and tribulations, is Karl's prototype. But this "imitation" of Dickens' novel is in its way a burlesque treatment of it and is analogous to Joyce's use of Homer in his *Ulysses*.

One misses in *Amerika* the profound implications of Kafka's other work. Plainly his imagination did not wholly support this one effort to guide the life of a human being to a happy outcome. He was more at home in the dread castles and courts where K. wanders in search of justice, only to discover at the very last that justice is as meaningless at it is inescapable. *Amerika* belongs to what one might call the psychological phase of Kafka's art. The movement of this art is from psychology to experimental mythology, from the immediate appropriation of personal states to their projection into the world at large. Thus the principle of authority on which his work is grounded is at the outset, as in "The Judgment" and "The Metamorphosis," represented in the figure of a "real" father, a father whom it is not very difficult to identify in terms of the Freudian "family romance," while in the later and longer fictions the father is no longer recognizable as a figure in the world we know. He has been removed from the family circle and generalized into an institutional power — hierarchic, remote, mysterious — such as the Law, the Court, and the order of officials that reside in the Castle.

In respect to this line of development "In the Penal Colony" can be regarded as a transitional story. It was written in November 1914, when Kafka had already begun working on *The Trial*. Perhaps because it shows the influence of Kierkegaard, upon whom Kafka first came in 1913, the religious analogues of this story are clearer than in the earlier tales. The Old Commander, whose dread memory is invoked in "In the Penal Colony," retains some of the individual traits of the "real" father, at the same time as he is mythicized in the manner of the images of authority projected in the later novels.

But in the long run the early breakthrough in his writing to the deeper layers of his psychic life failed to free Kafka of his nerve-destroying fears and sense of unworthiness. He continued to quarrel with himself, plotting self-punishment, thinking even of suicide. "Balzac carried a cane on which was carved the legend: I smash every obstacle; my legend reads: Every obstacle smashes me." The constant seesaw between writing and his job affected his health. He suffered from headaches and insomnia, finally tuberculosis set in and he was compelled to spend years in sanitariums. His illness he considered to be psychically determined — "My head conspired with my lung behind my back." It was not until 1923, when he met Dora Dymant, a girl brought up in an orthodox Jewish family in Poland, and he found himself well enough to move with her to Berlin, that he at long last realized his longing for independence. But, as it turned out, it was already too late to obtain the restitution he sought for the lost years of sickness and misery. In June 1924, at the age of forty-one, he died in a hospital near Vienna of laryngeal tuberculosis.

During his lifetime he published only some of his shorter works, and he never quite finished any of his three novels. Before his death he wrote to Max Brod requesting him to burn all the manuscripts he was leaving behind. Fortunately, his friend took upon himself the honorable responsibility of disregarding that desperate last instruction.

1952

On F. R. Leavis

and D. H. Lawrence

 THAT F. R. LEAVIS is a first-rate critical personality is certain, but that is by no means the same thing as saying that he is a first-rate literary critic. No doubt he has at times achieved that stature; at other times not at all. I am here primarily concerned with him as a critic, not with his reputation as a formidable teacher, nor with his educational theories, nor with his standing as the charismatic head of the sectarian *Scrutiny* group, consisting in the later years of that periodical mostly of epigones who have for some years now acquired positions of influence in the British schools. In the America of the late 1940s and early 1950s the New Critics tried to annex him by gratuitously referring to him as one of their own, a comrade-in-arms. That was a mistaken assessment, if not something worse.

Actually, the peculiar combination of formalism and traditionalist ideology (*à la* Eliot), characteristic of the "New Criticism," has always been foreign to Leavis. He has never committed himself to any kind of religiosity (covert or overt) and he has explicitly repudiated the formalist position. Typical of him is the following remark, repeated throughout his career in different critical contexts: "Questions of technique — versification, convention, relation of diction to the spoken language, and so on — cannot be isolated from considerations of fundamental purpose, essential ethos, and quality of life." In his view, a "serious interest in literature" cannot be limited to the kind of local analysis, however intensive, associated with "practical criticism" — the effects of linguistic strategy, metaphor, symbol, etc. "A real literary interest is an interest in man, society and civilization, and its boundaries cannot be drawn." Clearly, this position is wholly at odds with the circumscriptions imposed upon the theory and function of

literary criticism by the "New Critics." Happily, their dominance of
the American literary scene in the immediate postwar period is a thing
of the past now and virtually forgotten; and my aim in recalling them in
this discussion of Leavis is simply to set the record straight.

What I chiefly like about Leavis' work are its Johnsonian qualities:
the robustness, the firmness, the downrightness. He is not one to beat
around the bush, to play the diplomat, to cultivate ambiguity, or to
shun controversy. A critic in the Arnoldian tradition, he aspires, in his
own words, "to the highest critical standards and the observance of
the most scrupulous critical discipline" — an admirable aspiration in
the attainment of which, however, he has, to my mind, failed quite as
often as he has succeeded. For he is plagued by all the defects of his
virtues. What I have in mind is not his plain speaking, of course, but
rather the *esprit de sérieux* animating many of his critical pronouncements. It expresses itself in a kind of provincial moralism (by no
means to be equated with the "marked moral intensity" he so esteems
in his literary preferences), a Protestant narrowness of sensibility,
basically puritan, resulting in what seems to me the thoroughly un-
justified rejection of Flaubert, Joyce, and other important literary
artists of the modern line, a tendency to elevate "English studies" to
the status of a major force in the shaping of culture if not of society
itself, and his endless and tiresome fulminations against Bloomsbury,
the "London literary establishment," the system of "personal and institutional relations" that appears to him to dominate the British literary
world and to obstruct the free play of the critical mind.

It is not my intention to defend the literary establishment, whether
of London or of New York, or to question Leavis' all-too-strenuous
distaste for such literary figures — of unequal stature, to be sure —
as Lytton Strachey, Clive Bell, Virginia Woolf, and Lord David Cecil.
The trouble is that his clamorous and prolonged campaign against the
establishment has all the marks of an obsession. It is common knowledge that every major capital has one, and that it is usually lacking in
the seriousness and discrimination that Leavis demands. It is quite
possible to dissent from established opinion without going on and on
about it in a compulsive manner. After all, Bloomsbury, which no
longer exists, is at present merely a footnote in literary history. A class
struggle in literature is one thing, even if of doubtful value, as in the
1930s we saw in this country, because the partisanship involved easily
gets out of hand; but the conversion of a petty social antagonism into
a full-scale crusade is something else again.

In truth, what Leavis is waging can in no sense be described as a
Kulturkampf, which invariably deals with basic values, the clash of

opposing world-views, not merely literary issues and personalities. Leavis' obsession cannot be regarded otherwise than as a symptom. Of what? I am afraid there is no other way to characterize it than as a symptom of class *ressentiment,* and that very condition also sufficiently explains his uncritical identification with his supreme paragon among modern writers, D. H. Lawrence, upon whom he heaps panegyrics in his regrettably influential book, *D. H. Lawrence: Novelist* (1955). But more about that book (and even earlier critical studies) later. First one wants to take a close look at his new collection of essays and reviews.

In his new book, *Anna Karenina and Other Essays,* the lead essay is excellent. Its interest lies not so much in any new insights it offers — in that respect John Bayley's recent *Tolstoy and the Novel* is certainly superior — but rather in the angle from which Leavis approaches the novel. Given his age, critical background, and past allegiances, he was bound to confront openly certain animadversions on *Anna Karenina* expressed by Arnold, James, and, surprisingly enough, D. H. Lawrence. Admiring as he is of all three of these figures, especially Lawrence, he could not conceivably have arrived at his major conclusion, that *Anna Karenina* is not only one of the great European novels but "surely *the* European novel," without first challenging their negative views. A younger commentator on Tolstoy might well have ignored these views as being manifestly irrelevant. Leavis, however, immersed as he is in "English studies," is constrained to deal with them.

Arnold, though immensely struck by Tolstoy's novel, nevertheless characterized it as "not a work of art but a piece of life." Leavis demonstrates what hardly needs demonstrating today, that everything in the novel is fully rendered, fully "enacted," and that only of *a work of art* of such validity and force can one authoritatively say: "This is life." The antithesis of these formulas — "a piece of life" and "this is life" — is very apt, very neat. As for Henry James, his view was substantially the same as Arnold's. And given his peculiarly subjective conception of the art of the novel, what could he do, when faced with the Russian novel's centrality of experience and sheer comprehensiveness, but stress its alleged deficiency in "composition" and utter the phrase "fluid pudding"? One therefore welcomes Leavis' comment on James's "narrowly provident economy" in novel writing, for it is about time that a critic of Leavis' stature should come right out with this sort of objection, thus implicitly calling into question the portentous, self-justifying, and self-loving mystifications that play no small part in his famous prefaces. Leavis rightly insists that the creativity possessed by Tolstoy is of the highest kind — "a higher kind than James's." One might add that the Jamesian type of creativity, particularly as displayed in his later phase, is so idiosyncratic as to preclude his becoming a model for others. Moreover, it provides scarcely sufficient grounds for generalizing about the medium of narrative prose.

But in the case of Lawrence — whose opinion of *Anna Karenina* is thoughtless, to say the least — Leavis has a different problem on his hands. For, long before writing his book on him, he committed himself to the estimate of Lawrence as "the finest literary critic of our time — a great literary critic if ever there was one." So Leavis treats Lawrence's opinion of Tolstoy as a mere momentary aberration. But such an approach is evasive; it simply won't do. Just listen to Lawrence:

> Why, when you look at it, all the tragedy comes from Vronsky's and Anna's fear of society . . . They couldn't live in the pride of their sincere passion, and spit in Mother Grundy's eye. And that, that cowardice, was the real "sin." The novel makes it obvious, and knocks all old Leo's teeth out.

The novel makes obvious nothing of the sort. The impact of its cumulative episodes convinces us that it was impossible for Anna and Vronsky to live for long "in the pride of their sincere passion." Leavis goes into great detail to show how adverse conditions (of personality and environment) defeated them; thus the charge of cowardice amounts to no less than "a refusal to take what, with all the force of specificity and subtle truth to life, the novel actually gives." The implied comparison with Frieda and himself (which Lawrence alludes to in a letter) is fatuous. Being the kind of man he was, Vronsky could not live just by devoting himself to being Anna's lover — his attempts to become an artist and later a landed magistrate are pathetic and come to nothing — while Lawrence had his work cut out for him even before he met Frieda: he could wander from country to country and still do his writing with unparalleled ease. As for Frieda, though the loss of her children made her suffer, she was, as Leavis observes, "an amoral German aristocrat" who finally attained "a floating indolence of well-being," remaining "placidly undomesticated." Anna, however, could not be reconciled to the loss of her son. And from all the evidence concerning Frieda that we have, adds Leavis, "we can see that what Tolstoy makes present to us in Anna is certainly something finer."

❋

Still, in this very essay Leavis again praises Lawrence as a "marvelously perceptive critic." Is such high praise deserved? I think not. Lawrence made some very percipient remarks about the relation of the truth of "art-speech" to the novel as a genre. But such remarks are merely fine generalities; when it comes to specifics he is nearly always wrong-headed, absurdly doctrinaire. Thus in a letter he refers to Chekhov as "a second-rate writer and a willy wet-leg." Dostoevsky enrages him: he is "foul," presumably for "mixing sadism and God." About the characters in *The Possessed* he says: "They bore me, these squirming sorts of people; they teem like insects." So much for Verhovensky *père*, Stavrogin, Kirillov, Shatov, Captain Lebyadkin, and his sister! And again about Dostoevsky:

> He is . . . like the rat, slithering along in hate, in the shadows . . . His will is fixed and gripped like a trap. He is not nice.

To be sure. Dostoevsky is far from "nice," but if niceness is to be our criterion, then Lawrence's fiction, in which emotions of cruelty, anger, and hatred so frequently dominate, is positively malignant. Reviewing Thomas Mann's *Death in Venice,* Lawrence finds its author "somewhat banal," suffering from the same complaint as Flaubert, whose *Madame Bovary* seems to him "dead." Nor does he in the least appreciate either Proust or Joyce.

The truth is that as a critic Lawrence is wholly lacking in disinterestedness and even a minimum of objectivity. Violently prejudiced, he is a contemner of many works of great formal beauty, as well as psychological and dialectical power, simply because their contents fail to correspond to his own new gospel of life, or "metaphysic," as he sometimes called it. Even his *Studies in Classic American Literature* is not the masterpiece it is reputed to be. It contains one basic insight which has influenced some American critics, and I too have been affected by it. He detects in "moral duplicity" the "fatal flaw" of nineteenth-century American writers, excepting Whitman, and in this insight he appears to me to be right. Hawthorne, for instance, gives "tight mental allegiance to a morality which the passional self repudiates." Yet in his essay "Hawthorne and The Scarlet Letter," having made his point about that "blue-eyed *Wunderkind* of a Nathaniel" he soon wanders off into sheer rant about matters irrelevant to the text. Page after page of the essay is given up to a furious denunciation of Hester Prynne as "a demon, a devil when she was so meekly going around as a sick-nurse . . . the great nemesis of woman." What Lawrence is doing is simply exploiting his ostensible subject in order to indulge himself in a fit of characteristic misogyny, damning a certain type of modern woman whom he loathed. Whether such a type is more than a figment of Lawrence's imagination is doubtful, but that she is not the Hester of Hawthorne's novel, in either a latent or a manifest sense, is certain.

The essay about Cooper opens well, only to turn into a romance. Nor does Lawrence even begin to understand Poe, to see through his neurotic rationality (his famous bent for ratiocination) and recognize it for what it really is — a shield against the murderous fantasies that threaten to unhinge his mind. All that he notes in Poe is "the pride of human conceit in knowledge," with Ligeia, Berenice, and the rest as victims of his "obscene" will to know. Here Lawrence is again riding his favorite hobbyhorse, the execration of knowledge or "mental consciousness," his *bête noire* of which he cannot rid himself either in his discursive prose or in his fiction. Moreover, the Poe essay is entirely lacking in specific literary or critical interest, being a piece of amateur psychologism pure and simple, and offensively preachy at that. Yet even as psychology it is useless. One has only to compare it to Marie Bonaparte's psychoanalytic study of Poe — not to be classified as literary criticism either — to realize how wide of the mark it is.

But though the Lawrence question still haunts Leavis' new volume, there are essays in it deserving commendation, such as the two very satisfactory pieces on Conrad, the fine analysis of "Johnson as Critic," and the truly enlightening review of *The Letters of Ezra Pound*, in which he sums up with admirable economy and persuasiveness all that he previously said about him. Though paying generous tribute to Pound's beneficent influence on Yeats and Eliot (among others) at "crucial moments," of their creative careers, he nonetheless contends that his limitations are overwhelming. *Mauberley* is his only valid claim to significance as a poet, while "the spectacle of his degeneration is a terrible one." It is apparent in the "barren and monotonous" *Cantos*, as in his hapless politics, in which there is "something repellently brutal, a certain naive, tough and truculent insensitiveness turning into a positive vice."

In this fully supported judgment Leavis is at his best, and it should suffice to shatter the Pound cult, were it not for the fact that the cultists and their leading hierophant, Hugh Kenner, in their highly suspect, devious ideological bias and vain exegetical ardor had not already proven themselves immune to critical argument. I wonder how they will now react to the startling revelation by Daniel Cory (*Encounter*, May 1968), a reliable witness and a friend of Pound's of long standing, that the poet had but recently admitted to him in Italy that he had in fact "botched" the *Cantos*. ("I knew too little about so many things ... I picked out this and that thing that interested me, and then jumbled them into a bag. But that's not the way to make a work of art.") There is much pathos in this belated confession, bringing a melancholy end to a long and remarkable career.

Pound's admission also makes fools of the cultists who have for a long time dominated the criticism of Pound. Even the late R. P. Blackmur, in an essay of the 1950s, in effect retracted his shrewd earlier reservations about Pound. And T. S. Eliot certainly lent a hand in promoting the cult in a variety of cordial and (perhaps) propitiatory remarks about Pound, finally announcing that his interest is not in what the latter had to say but only in the way he said it. Leavis comes down hard on this equivocal statement, in which form is so drastically isolated from substance as to convert it into a sheer abstraction.

In the last essay of this new collection, "The Orthodoxy of Enlightenment," we are again embroiled in the Lawrence question. Reviewing the Penguin documentary record of the trial of *Lady Chatterley's Lover*, he strains to show, though without any recognition of the irony involved, that his backing of Lawrence had been misconceived and misused in the trial by persons of a type that would have been inevitably hostile to Lawrence during his lifetime and who are now, to put it bluntly, kowtowing to him because of the new "enlightenment" of sex. It should be observed that even in his extravagant book about Lawrence (1955), Leavis excised *Lady Chatterley*, as well as *The Plumed Serpent*, from the canon. Now he speaks of it as "a bad novel," arguing that his distaste for it is something "that the normal Lawrence would have shared and justified," if the "abnormal state" he was in when writing the novel had not "violated his wholeness." What a way of putting it! This new evocation of a Lawrence split into normality and abnormality flagrantly contradicts the insistence in *D. H. Lawrence: Novelist* that there is "no profound emotional disturbance in Lawrence, no obdurate major disharmony; intelligence in him can be, as it is, the servant of the whole integrated psyche."

Plainly, there is something deeply wrong here, a tortuous, willed self-deception, on account of which this critic's reputation for integrity and independence of judgment incurs a damaging loss. No doubt there are stages to be noted in Lawrence's development as a thinker and artist, but the novels that Leavis disowns — including *Sons and Lovers*, which he manages to dismiss, without seeming to do so, as little more than a case history — embody the essential Lawrence just as much as those Leavis acclaims as supreme masterpieces. (To my mind, *Sons and Lovers* remains Lawrence's best novel, by far the most convincing, fully enveloping its Oedipal theme, which cannot be reduced to mere clinical material, and free of the patently compensatory overassertiveness and arbitrariness, that in no small degree mar his later work.)

Leavis' emphasis on "health" and "sanity" and his mandatory distinction between what "makes for life" and what does not are singularly inappropriate to "placing" Lawrence. Terms like "health," "sanity," and even "life" are at once too vague and too inclusive, too invertebrate as it were, for use in any precise analysis, and, above all, too moralistic to make much sense in literary discourse. As criteria they are in constant peril of toppling over — though Leavis would hardly countenance such a fall — into the popular ·cure-all of "the power of positive thinking." Evidently there is no getting away from the Lawrence question in examining Leavis' contribution to contemporary criticism.

The truth is that by radically separating his art from his doctrine without fully acknowledging what he is up to, Leavis has been able to create a Lawrence who never really existed. Hence the stress on the word *novelist* in his book on him. But this procedure is misleading in Lawrence's case. For as E. M. Forster has observed, he was "both preacher and poet ... though without the preaching the poetry could not exist. With some writers one can disentangle the two, with him they were inseparable." It is this very "inseparability," which cannot be said to affect in the same drastic manner Dostoevsky and other novelists of intense ideological animus, which calls into question Lawrence's status as an artist. Furthermore, as Forster adds, as he grew older he became "more and more mannered and didactic." None of that is recognized by Leavis. Nor does the concept of neoprimitivism, of which Lawrence is the most extreme exponent in modern literature, ever engage Leavis' attention, though that concept is far more cogently deployed in appraising Lawrence than the meager literary notions Leavis brings to bear in his apotheosis of him as before all else an artist, "a creative writer of the greatest kind," as well as "an incomparable critic," and "one of the greatest masters of comedy." His determination to endow his *bel idéal* with every possible virtue is appalling.

I have already dealt to some extent with Lawrence's criticism. To attribute to him a mastery of the comic mode is equally spurious, for a kind of archness, even cuteness, was the only result of his occasional attempts to be amusing. Historically, Lawrence represents, as I see it, "the return of the repressed" (to use Freudian terminology) to English literary expression after the long Victorian epoch of inhibition and repression of the sensual life. Such a return, however, exalting the pleasure principle above the reality principle, cannot but take, under inauspicious social and historical conditions, a form at once anarchic and compulsive. Nor is this return, as embodied in Lawrence, in any sense complete, involving as it does frequent relapses and more than incidental backsliding. Thus even while protesting the repression of sexuality by civilization, he at the same time turns away from any real orgiastic freedom and actually *disincarnates* sexuality by preaching the continuance of traditional male domination, by envisaging marriage as "ultimate" and "final" (a lapse into the very idealism he otherwise repudiated), and by denying (emphatically in *The Plumed Serpent*) the orgasm to women.

Such obscurantist predications are not what I would call creative contradictions but rather a set of corrosive inconsistencies that add to his disabilities precisely in his role as novelist. He is not what Leavis says he is: he is not an up-to-date version of George Eliot, nor is he a realist, except superficially and only intermittently. Leavis maintains that modern civilization found in Lawrence "a student and analyst of incomparable range and insight." But he was not so much a student or analyst of civilization as its outright and rigorous opponent. He rejected culture, intellect, consciousness, knowledge — the values that Leavis is above all attached to. Lawrence wrote:

> My great religion is a belief in the blood, the flesh. We can go wrong in our minds. But what our blood feels . . . is always true. The intellect is only a bit and a bridle. What do I care about knowledge? All I want is to answer to my blood, direct, without the fribbling intervention of mind, or moral, or what not.

This is no abstraction but a solemn and programmatic avowal, the essential "message" informing most of his work, in the interest of which he was all too prone to disregard the modifications, reservations, and strategic reversals imposed by the discipline of novelistic art. Can Leavis honestly claim that he shares this "message" or faith? One can imagine a critic — though not much of one — who might find this faith acceptable, but my point is that Leavis' assertion of his own beliefs positively *disallows* his solidarity with Lawrence. The visionary neo-primitivism, the regression to an animistic and archaic mode of apprehending the world, which dissolves the distinction between the human and the inhuman and between nature and culture, are wholly alien to Leavis. The latter frequently affirms Lawrence's "intelligence"; and I for one have no doubt that he was very intelligent; at the same time I have no doubt that after *Sons and Lovers,* ever alert to the threatening inroads of the so abominated "mental consciousness," he more often than not refused to use his intelligence.

Psychic disorder is just as noticeable in Lawrence as it is in literary artists like Baudelaire or Dostoevsky or Kafka. But from a literary standpoint the significant difference is that, in Baudelaire, Dostoevsky, or Kafka, art is for the most part the consequence, even if neurosis is the occasion. This is only contingently and even at times fortuitously true in Lawrence. The conscientious critic, however, cannot adopt the psychiatrist's crude though useful distinctions between the normal and the abnormal without undercutting the fullness and complexity of his response to the manifold if contradictory "truths of art-speech." The many quarrels Leavis picks with T. S. Eliot seem to be chiefly motivated by the latter's disparagement of Lawrence. One of these concerns Eliot's "over-insistence" on Lawrence's "sexual morbidity," which Leavis finds very odd in a writer whose own attitudes "to sex have been, in prose and poetry, almost uniformly negative — attitudes of distaste, disgust, and rejection." This is as good an example as any of Leavis' tendency to circumscribe the literary medium by setting up preconceived and obligatory values for it.

For my part, I cannot see why an attitude of sexual disgust is not as valid a theme for poetic expression as an attitude of affirmation, of "health and sanity." The value of literary art cannot be judged by the bias of its ideology or world-view, but rather by its rendering of felt experience, the intensity of its existential commitment, and above all the incontrovertible force of its concrete enactment. Eliot's awareness of this is shown by the unremitting attention he gave to the problem of "belief" in poetry. There is something irksome in Leavis' polemic against Eliot, to whom his best books, *New Bearings in English Poetry* and *Revaluations* are heavily indebted. Aside from the discord relating to Lawrence, Eliot is accused of endorsing Wyndham Lewis, not to mention Djuna Barnes' *Nightwood* and Miller's *Tropic of Cancer,* of being too close to Bloomsbury, of printing Auden and Spender in *The Criterion,* etc., etc. But all this is trivial. What is really vulnerable in Eliot — his collapse into Anglo-Catholicism in the late twenties and his embrace of the dogma of original sin — Leavis leaves strictly alone. In other words, he fails to perceive that given Eliot's militant new adherence to institutional Christianity, it was only logical for him to attack Lawrence as a dangerous "heretic" in *After Strange Gods,* which is a primer of heresy. There existed in Eliot an empirical critic of genius, usually prevailing in his prose, as well as a fretful and conscience-ridden Christian perceptor. The former produced his important literary essays; the latter produced such nebulous tracts as *Notes toward the Definition of Culture* and *The Idea of a Christian Society*. His derogation of Lawrence as a writer "incapable of what is ordinarily called thinking" is far from unjust, if we stress, that is, the word "ordinarily." But Eliot in his moods of Christian fervor strikes me as equally incapable of that kind of thinking, and so does Leavis, who so plumes himself on his critical rigor, when he flaunts his identification with Lawrence.

I think that Lawrence was a unique and original writer, perhaps the most "natural" writer in English literature by virtue of his innate gift of fluidity and spontaneous free flow of expression. But this is by no means the same thing as saying that he was a great novelist. In that respect his disabilities are irreducible. His most persistent fault is the unabashed eagerness with which he nearly always subordinates art to prophecy and his ruthless manipulation of scene, act, and character to justify his new gospel of life at all costs.

While describing himself as "a fearfully religious man," he was unable, all the same, to believe in any religious tenet except in a purely symbolical manner; and his nostalgia for remote pre-Christian modes of relatedness to the world expresses nothing more than a desire to give his intuition free play, to escape the limiting and probing articulations of historical consciousness. As Philip Rieff has aptly observed, what he wanted to preserve was "the dynamic of religion" as form without any specific content. Thus he was a "literary Methodist," proposing attitudes of prayer "without mentioning anyone to whom to pray." And in the political sphere, into which he sometimes ventured, he was a fantast pure and simple. He understood neither socialism nor liberal democracy, invariably confusing political theory with individual psychology. However, the charges of protofascism, of having developed, as Bertrand Russell put it, "the whole philosophy of fascism before the politicians thought of it," seem to me almost grotesquely unfair. His preaching of "blood-consciousness" has nothing whatever to do with racial or national purity of blood, or the assertion of superiority of one race over another. (The notion of "blood-consciousness," if at all meaningful, can only be taken as the equivalent, and a very muddled one at that, or Freud's Unconscious or Id.) Moreover, Lawrence's fundamental rejection of industrialism places him in diametrical opposition to the fascists, who, glorifying the martial virtues, are the least ready to scrap the industrial machine.

The paradox is that, for all his denunciations of "the modern cult of personality," and his attack on the ego as "a vile entity," our interest in him as an artist is primarily called forth precisely by his personality. All the people who knew him, whether friend or enemy, invariably recalled "the strange and marvelous radiance" emanating from him, the "spritelike, electric, elemental" quality. That is what surely comes through in his writing, particularly in the passionate tenderness of his evocations of nature — "birds, beasts, and flowers." But the other side of his personality — the acrimony, the fits of jeering and hectoring — also comes through. His general ideas about the novel are unimpeachable, and very fine indeed. Let me cite some of my favorite dicta:

> Never trust the artist. Trust the tale. The proper function of a critic is to save the tale from the artist who created it.
>
> If you try to nail anything down in the novel, either it kills the novel, or the novel gets up and walks away with the nail.
>
> The novel is the highest example of subtle inter-relatedness that man has discovered. Everything is true in its own time, place, circumstance, and untrue outside of its own place, time, circumstance . . . Morality in the novel is the trembling instability of the balance. When the novelist puts his thumb in the scale, to pull down the balance to his own predilection, that is immorality.

Unfortunately, his practice belies his theory. In the very novels and tales Leavis regards as masterpieces he seldom hesitates to put his thumb in the scales, "to pull down the balance to his own predilection." This is exactly what Dostoevsky never did, even in *The Possessed*, where a subtle balance is maintained in spite of its national and religious prepossessions. For he was able to identify not only with such children of light as Sonia Marmeladov and Prince Myshkin but also with the characters ostensibly set up for ideological rebuttal — Raskolnikov, Stavrogin, the elder Vorhovensky, Ivan Karamazov — all children of darkness whom he nonetheless absorbed creatively without depriving them of their essential humanity. And the secret of that is complicity, that is to say, the indispensable process of identification with the creatures of one's own imagination without regard to positiveness or negativeness of ultimate judgment. In this sense, Flaubert identified with Charles Bovary and M. Homais no less than with Emma. Not so Lawrence, who identified the people who speak for him, like Ursula in *The Rainbow* and Birkin in *Women in Love*, with himself, thus turning them into mere mouthpieces; while he treated his adversary characters, like Skrebensky and Gerald Crich, with punitive harshness, and he proceeded in the same manner against Clifford in *Lady Chatterley* and against Rico in *St. Mawr* — a novella rated very highly by Leavis but shown up, by both Eliseo Vivas and Graham Hough in their respective books on Lawrence, as the shabby performance it actually is. Even *The Fox*, a novella beautifully articulated and rendered in convincing detail, is spoiled in the last few pages when the young protagonist, having won the girl March after the willed death of her friend Jill, suddenly steps out of his role in order to assume as his own some of Lawrence's dogmatic notions. It is gratuitous as well as out of character for him to demand of March that she submerge herself in him. "He wanted to make her submit, yield, blindly pass away out of all her strenuous consciousness." This is no longer the simple farmer boy we have been reading about but Lawrence conducting his continuous struggle with Frieda for dominance.*

What we are up against in Lawrence's fiction is a kind of "credibility gap" of his own making, the result of the excessive and willful intrusion of a personality inebriated with doctrinal salvationism.

In *The Rainbow*, as Graham Hough notes, Ursula loves Skrebensky physically while finding him inadequate spiritually, and that is "intelligible enough, but that she found him inadequate in both respects makes their love wholly unintelligible, merely makes one wonder what the basis of their affair can ever have been." This is even more true, I think, of the Gudrun-Gerald relationship in *Women in Love*, so bafflingly implausible in connecting motive and action. For much of the novel, despite occasional outbursts of hostility to Gerald, Gudrun is presented as standing apart and not as a mere mouthpiece for the author, as Birkin is. But in the last chapters, when she is with her lover in the Tyrolese Alps, she is suddenly bursting with Lawrentian ideas that make her want to destroy Gerald. What is wrong? Gerald is immersed in the "ethics of productivity," he is an industrial magnate concerned solely with efficiency and deriving his values from the established social order. Then, through some kind of typical Lawrentian legerdemain, she links these external traits, external, I mean, to his sexual being, with sexual defectiveness. Hence her fury and determination to do him in. It is as if a Marxist novelist were to deduce sexual characteristics of any given bourgeois protagonist from the propositions of *Das Kapital*. So Lawrence simplifies in the most ludicrous fashion the connection between quite different aspects of life. The

---

* See his letter to Katherine Mansfield (December 1918): "In a way, Frieda is the devouring mother. It is awfully hard, once the sex relation has gone this way, to recover. If we don't recover, we die. But Frieda says I am antediluvian in my positive attitude. I do think a woman must yield some sort of precedence to a man, and he must take this precedence. I do think men must go ahead absolutely in front of their women, without turning around for permission or approval from their women. Consequently the women must follow as it were unquestioningly. I can't help it, I believe this. Frieda doesn't. Hence our fight."

trouble is, as Hough observes, that Lawrence came to assume that "sexual compatibility and compatibility of mind and spirit are indissolubly linked." But existence is marked by startling incongruities, and human love is only very rarely so rounded and complete. Individuality is no more cut of the whole cloth than historical reality.

And for all of Lawrence's desire to adjust consciousness "to the basic physical realities" and his warm approval of "sex stimulus" in art, he was quite unable to achieve in his favored female characters the sensual reality, the sense of desirability and carnal attraction that we find so affecting in Emma Bovary, Anna Karenina, or even in Kate Croy and Charlotte Stant — heroines of Henry James, who is so frequently dismissed as a eunuch. Lawrence repeatedly tells us that Ursula and Gudrun are very alluring but he cannot make us feel it. Sometimes I think that Lawrence was much too overwrought, too morbidly sensitive to physical experience to cope with the sexual theme. William H. Gass was surely right, in a recent essay, in characterizing Lawrence's attempts to describe directly sexual feelings and sensations as "moments of disaster":

> ... When Lawrence wishes to render these [sexual] feelings, he turns to an abstract, incantational shorthand, often full of biblical overtones and antique simplicities, phrases which are used like formulas, reiterated until they become meaningless: hearts grow bitter and black and cold, souls melt or swoon, bodies freeze or burn, people are rapt or blind, they utter strange blind cries, their feelings ebb and flow ... they "go mad with voluptuous delight," they overmaster or submit, bowels move poignantly ... and their eyes sing, laugh, dance, stab, harden, burn, flash, seize, subside, cool, dim and die. One lust could do for another, angers are peas, nothing is clearly envisaged, nothing is precise, and we pass through them soon in a daze. *

Lawrence is in essence very far removed from the "life-enhancing elements" that Leavis likes to celebrate in his favorite writers. The "obliteration of personality" that Mellors, for instance, demands from Connie, the radical ambition, that is, to "de-create" the self in its social aspects, is essentially hostile to the quite different form that Leavis' search for "life" has taken. The obsession with Lawrence is the incubus that weighs his criticism down, which, despite its Protestant moralism, is nonetheless among the more heroic efforts in English of this century. He was at his best in his earlier work, but even in *The Common Pursuit* (1952), as in his latest volume, you find many excellent things. And in comparison with the sorry state of criticism

* *New York Review,* August 1, 1968.

today — when the older critics (Wilson, Tate, Trilling) are silent about contemporary writing, and the field has been pre-empted by younger men, swinging reviewers rather than critics in any proper sense of the term, who, in the name of a trivialized aestheticism and sophistication, welcome every whim of fad and fashion as a creative "breakthrough" and a "new" conquest of imaginative experience — Leavis looms large as a force and as a surpassing example. He may be too moralistic and exclusive in his approach, but the currently modish idea that morality has nothing to do with literature is a sheer perversion, an accommodation to the indulgence of degeneracy that marks the arts in our age — an indulgence that on no account will deny artistic status even to obvious pornography.* Of course, there are exceptions among the younger critics; their influence, however, hardly counts against that of the promoters of a phony avant-gardism who draw no distinction between integral talent and the crude products of the celebrity-machine.

Ours is a consumers' society, in which culture has been transformed into another provider of goodies, to be processed, consumed, digested, and eliminated to make room for more. In a situation of this kind, the appearance of another Leavis, or Eliot, or critics of like caliber, is no longer to be expected. No wonder that the more intelligent young people are turning away from literature to politics, where sensitivity of conscience and moral feeling can still find expression, even if only within a minority movement, and where cynical calculation masquerading as worldly sophistication can still be seen through for what it actually is.

New York Review of Books, 1968

---

* The literary cheerleaders of the new porno-aesthetics are much inclined to embellish their lineage by including Lawrence among their precursors. To claim descent from De Sade is one thing, but to try appropriating Lawrence is something else again and is nothing less than falsification. For despite the spill of four-letter words in *Lady Chatterley,* Lawrence despised pornography and wanted it banned. Thus he wrote: "Then what is pornography? Not sex appeal or sex stimulus in art. But even I would censor genuine pornography, rigorously. It would not be very difficult . . . you recognize it by the insult it offers, invariably, to sex, and to the human spirit . . . The insult to the human body, the insult to a vital human relationship! Ugly and cheap they make the human nudity, ugly and degraded they make the sexual act, trivial and cheap and nasty."

And in a letter of 1929 about *Lady Chatterley,* he remarked: "You mustn't think I advocate perpetual sex. Far from it. Nothing nauseates me more than promiscuous sex in and out of season. But I want, with *Lady Chatterley,* to make an adjustment in consciousness to the basic physical realities." Surely this attitude has nothing in common with the kind of freaky excitement about sex fomented by our contemporary porno-aesthetes.

III
POLITICS, RELIGION, AND CULTURE

Excerpts from
"The Literary Class War"

... THE GREEK IDEA of katharsis in art is one of the most fertile conceptions ever devised. However, its classic formulation by Aristotle as a process effecting a proper purgation of the emotions through pity and terror, is a static, passive conception quite in line with the needs of a slave-owning class endowed with cultural tastes and appreciative of the great art of tragedy, but unwilling to permit the even tenor of its parasitic existence to be disturbed by gruesome realities. Thus the "significant change" effected in the reader or spectator by the katharsis leaves him limp and reconciled to the "immutable laws of life." After the grand spectacle of a Sophoclean tragedy, the Greek gentleman went home to his slaves, stimulated indeed, but resigned to the whims of the gods and "human nature." This form of katharsis is merely a sort of transcendental mental laxative for a cultured leisure class.

Nevertheless, a consistent examination of the qualitative properties of artistic creation leaves one with the conviction that without katharsis that creation loses all significance, loses that high gravity which is the most characteristic function of art. Within proletarian literature one can discern the implicit form of a new katharsis, likewise a purgation of the emotions, a cleansing, but altogether of a different genus: *a cleansing through fire*. Applying the dynamic viewpoint of dialectics, a synthesizing third factor is added to the Aristotelean pity and terror — and that is militancy, combativeness. The proletarian katharsis is a release through action — something diametrically opposed to the philosophical resignation of the older idea. Audaciously breaking through the wall that separates literature from life, it impels the reader to a course of action, of militant struggle; it objectifies art to such a degree that it becomes instrumental in aiding to change the world. A proletarian drama, for instance, inspires the spectator with pity as he identifies himself with the characters on the stage; he is terror-stricken by the horror of workers' existence under capitalism; but these two emotions are finally fused in the white heat of battle into a revolutionary deed, with the weapon of proletarian class-will in the hands of the masses. This is the vital katharsis by means of which the proletarian writer fecundates his art.

. . . Since the expulsion of the economic romanticism prevailing in America till the crash in the autumn of the year 1929, American writers have increasingly shown a tendency to think in social terms, turning to the Left for ideational substance. It would, however, be the sheerest wish-thinking to suppose that this can be taken at face value as an indication of a fundamental trend. It is quite certain that following the economic interests of their class, most bourgeois writers will swing toward fascism, while only a few, the most honest, the least dominated by delusions, will join the proletariat.

If it weren't for the object lesson of proletarian class-rule in Russia and the resurgence of Marxism all along the front, those writers who did take the final step would have probably sought an outlet from the confusion attendant upon the collapse of prosperity in mysticism or some type of neoreligion. It is precisely the iron dynamic of the Marxian philosophy that effected the apostasy of such writers as Edmund Wilson, Newton Arvin, and Granville Hicks. I believe it is a mistake to think that it is the widespread misery and economic chaos that is the chief cause of these writers' espousal of collectivism. The widespread misery and the economic chaos merely impelled them to approach Marxism for a way out; without Marxism this misery and chaos would have simply thrown them into the arms of Mr. Eliot and M. Maritain.

With regard to fellow travelers a lenient attitude is more or less in order. They cannot be expected to accept completely the proletarian viewpoint in one bound, but caution is necessary. If they make the Marxian world-view their own and evidence a comprehensive understanding of it, they can be counted on to integrate themselves into the proletariat. If they fail to do so, it is almost certain that sooner or later they will desert and rejoin the bourgeoisie, as many socialists did during the war. The emotional, romantic approach to communism is a paper bridge for anyone who wants to cross over into the camp of revolution. Lenin once censured Upton Sinclair for his pacifism, describing him as an "emotional Socialist without theoretical grounding." Only their ability and *willingness* to master Marxian theory will insure their loyalty. The view on the Russian Revolution they adhere to is a good test. Thus we find some fellow travelers persisting in a pseudo-liberal attitude to the Soviet Union, perpetually deploring "the lack of freedom in Russia." Is it really so difficult to understand that the concept of freedom under the capitalist regime is merely formal? "Freedom is the recognition of necessity." (Engels) Everything should of course be done to facilitate a fellow traveler's assimilation, but once it becomes clear that his bourgeois class-roots are too strong, he should be neatly and rapidly dispatched on the road back, because he will only bring confusion into the ranks of the real militants.

In his essay *The Class Point-of-View* Lenin left us some good advice as to tactics in this respect. "The party of the proletariat," he wrote, "must learn to catch every liberal just at the moment when he is prepared to move forward an inch, and compel him to move forward a yard. If he is obstinate and won't, we shall go forward without him, and over his body."

New Masses, 1932

Trials of the Mind

After such knowledge, what forgiveness?

Oᴜʀ ᴅᴀʏs are ceasing to be. We are beginning to live from hour to hour, awaiting the change of headlines. History has seized time in a brutal embrace. We dread the Apocalypse.

The newspapers recite their tidings: AUSTRIANS KNEEL BE-FORE HITLER; NAZIS FLOG LABORERS INTO LINE. And in Moscow the state continues to massacre the firstborn of October. What an inexhaustible repertoire of shame and catastrophe!

The First World War ended two decades ago, and its end was preceded by the first workers' revolution. Ninety years have passed since the most subversive document of all times, *The Communist Manifesto,* injected its directive images into the nascent consciousness of the proletariat. We were not prepared for defeat. The future had our confidence, which we granted freely, sustained by the tradition of Marxism. In that tradition we saw the marriage of science and humanism. But now, amidst all these ferocious surprises, who has the strength to reaffirm his beliefs, to transcend the feeling that he had been duped? One is afraid of one's fear. Will it soon become so precise as to exclude hope?

Moscow, the capital of revolution, acclaimed by the oppressed of all nations. The acclaim is turning to revulsion, but many still cling to their faith — perhaps out of desperate need for some kind of certainty. At the third trial, as at the first and second, the leaders of Bolshevism confessed to crimes and perfidies without number. The picture they gave of themselves was so indescribably vile as to constitute the absolute of evil. But let us beware of absolutes: all too often they are but masks of the fabulous. "The monstrosity of my crime is immeasurable!" cried Bukharin. If he told the truth then our original conception of socialism was only a romantic dream. If he and the other accused told the truth then all that remains for us to do is bow our heads and listen meekly as capitalism — once again, if only in contrast, secure in its ethics — makes haste to preach its sermon over the grave of the Revolution.

The lessons, however, that the capitalist moralizers draw from the trials are in the last analysis summed up in the doctrine of original sin. We are eternally depraved; not even communism can save us. And in the Soviet press also the end-terms of the thunderous denunciations finally merge into the concepts of theology. No social analysis can explain such diabolic crimes: every attempted explanation exhausts the resources of the rational. For despite all the falsifications of historical facts, the transformation of the old Bolsheviks into fascists remains materially, psychologically, and politically unmotivated. Hence it is not really political criminals who are being tried, but sinners, evildoers, perhaps sorcerers. Thus we learn that it is in Moscow, the fountainhead of progress and the center of atheism, that the black arts flourish and conjurers have made politicians their bedfellows.

But it is not only the old Bolsheviks who are on trial — we too, all of us, are in the prisoners' dock. These are trials of the mind and of the human spirit. Their meanings encompass the age. Much is being said and written about the "moral collapse of Bolshevism," but how little about the moral collapse of the intellectuals. Among them smugness has become the pseudonym of panic, and the more rapidly they abandon the values of culture the more sonorous their speeches in its defence. Everywhere they submit to the accomplished fact, everywhere they place themselves under the surveillance of authority, they rationalize, they explain away. Within such narrow mind-space revolves the thought of those who trade in the mind's beauties and powers.

War and revolution are the most crucial events in the history of humanity; they are the supreme tests of character, of political integrity, of moral fortitude. The trials present the problem of revolution negatively, as counterrevolution. We are on the verge of a new war, and already hostilities have broken out in several parts of the world. If to be a "friend of culture" means something more than merely being a friend of books, it is by subjecting the behavior of the intellectuals to these supreme tests that we can best judge not only their politics, but their morality — in fact their culture itself.

After the last war the intellectuals repented, vowing they would never again be deceived — but now they are once more clamoring for blood. And always in the name of the most lofty ideals! They want to guarantee the survival of culture by guaranteeing the victory of the "democratic" imperialist powers in the coming struggle. The perpetuation of "democratic" capitalism is their sole perspective. In other words, they will fight to save culture from being put to a violent death at the hands of fascism, but they are perfectly willing to let it expire peacefully in the bed of bourgeois democracy.

The Moscow trials dramatized the agony of the Russian Revolution. What was the response of the intellectuals? As a group they permitted themselves to be taken in by the professional illusionists of the Comintern. Some became outright defenders of the official versions; others are silent, not ashamed to be spiritually terrorized; only a small minority, mostly of the older generation of intellectuals, dared to speak out. The attitude the liberal journals have taken to the trials, despite occasional retractions, can be summarized in the following formula: "Some people will believe the trials are frame-ups; some people will believe the trials are not frame-ups. However, both sides are partisan. As for ourselves, we prefer to view them *sub specie aeternitatis*. Perhaps in a hundred years we shall know the truth." All other issues they measure with the inch-ruler of reformist empiricism; but for their editorials on the trials they hold in reserve a philosophical world-outlook. The truth or falsity of the evidence they consider irrelevant — they refuse to examine it. Besides, they argue, the matter doesn't really concern us. It's a factional question. To these people the struggle between revolution and counterrevolution within the labor movement is just a *factional* question!

Given such logic, even the term "liberal" becomes a liability. Recently the editors of *The New Republic* purged themselves publicly of liberalism by declaring that only the designation "progressive" suits them, as indeed it does. For in its peculiarly modern sense, a "progressive" is a person who will successively or simultaneously adopt every point of view, every alternative — except one. By thus expelling the revolutionary method of fighting fascism from the area of choice, the "progressive" conceives of himself as the only genuine realist. Actually, however, bourgeois antifascism is merely another quixotic attempt of the middle-class ego to surmount historic finalities. To the drastic solutions of the crisis which fascism and communism offer to society, the "progressive" antifascist replies by exhibiting his miserable assortment of plagiarisms from the ideologies of the two principal classes. His "realism" thus turns out to be nothing else than the sublimation of his inability ever to be original.

The masters of property, on the other hand, arrive at their immutable decisions on the basis of economic necessity. They know that the "intellectual" of the family has no talent for practical affairs. He is outraged because the firm no longer treats its employees with the decency and kindliness that prevailed when business was flourishing. He has failed to understand that in order to avoid bankruptcy serious measures must be taken. But they are quite sure that in the end he will "come around," accept a minor post, and occupy himself with keeping the firm's books in order.

"I am not what I am." It is Iago speaking, as he dissects the means of mystification. The problem is to make sure of identities. Your interlocutor, your correspondent, your confidant — who are they? And he who is pressing your hand, is he wearing a disguise? The idea too is capable of blackmail; likewise the theory, it will soon disown itself. Ideology has its subconscious, its secret corridors. Its neuroses contrive amalgams.

At the trials the collaborators of Lenin declare themselves to have labored for years to bring about the restoration of capitalism. The accuser is Stalin. Is he the savior of the Revolution or its destroyer? And Trotsky? He, of course, is the great dragon, the old serpent, he that is called Satan, the deceiver of the whole world, the universal demon. But the judges and criminals alike are Marxists, accustomed to think in terms of social forces and economic determinants. What forces and determinants conditioned the betrayal of Bolshevism by its organizers and theoreticians? The answer, again, is Trotsky, who seems to lead both a worldly and other-worldly existence. But he himself, powerful as he is, is only a tool in the hands of the Gestapo. Whose disciples are the defendants — his or Stalin's? They plotted to kill Stalin, but now they proclaim their love of him. In confessing are they being loyal to the national state, which Stalin embodies, or to the Revolution? Remember Iago:

> Another of his fathom they have none,
> To lead their business: in which regard,
> Though I do hate him as I do hell-pains,
> Yet for necessity of present life,
> I must show out a flag and sign of love.

But the mystification goes even deeper. We have been told that only a planned, collectivized economy, such as the Soviet Union has, is rational. But the paradox is that it is precisely Soviet economy which is today the most opaque, whose laws of development are the least known and least understood by social and economic science. If it's socialism that is being built there, why the monocratic method of construction, in the "Egyptian style," with everyone except the administrators reduced to the conditions of fellaheen? Legally the workers own the means of production, but the control is monopolized by the bureaucratic caste. In reality, however, control means ownership — or rather ownership serves as the theory, and control as the practice. Is it possible that all these years radicals the world over have been imposed upon, ensnared by an elementary plot of mistaken identity? Formally this new exploitative society does not resemble the exploitations that are historically known. Can it be that it is taken for socialism simply because it represents itself as such and because it seems *different?* If this hypothesis is true, it matters not in the least with what particular kind of ideology the new exploiters are operating. What they do is important, not what their ideology leads them to think they are doing. Ideology, when at odds with the facts, is merely false consciousness, though a deep contradiction between the ideology and the facts gives birth to social and cultural neuroses, frustrations, and crimes.

In the Soviet Union the *organization* — which concentrates within itself the state and the party — exhausts the totality of social and property relations. Everything revolves around the organization, it dominates every aspect of life, it is society's prose as well as its poetry. "It is a huge machine," wrote Bukharin in 1934, "such as has never been seen in the existence of humanity." In the tyrannies of the ancient world and of the East, in medieval Europe, and in the modern bourgeois countries (including the fascist states), the members of certain classes, and sometimes even the members of all classes, possessed, and still possess, some means, some mediating quantity, that won them a measure of security from the demands of the organization. If private property did not bolster them up, they sought to take advantage of the divisions in authority, such as between church and state. On this objective basis a morality of independence, of resistance to the pressure of the social power, could form. But in the Soviet Union, for the first time in history, the individual has been deprived of every conceivable means of resistance. Authority is monolithic: property and politics are one. Under such circumstances it becomes impossible to defy the organization, to set one's will against it. One cannot escape it: not only does it absorb the whole of life but it also seeks to model the shapes of death.

Regardless of the specific reasons that may be advanced to explain the confessions of the old Bolsheviks, to my mind it is this state of affairs within the country which provides the most *generalized* explanation of their conduct. The trials are juridical metaphors of counterrevolution; but it is necessary to analyse them in such a way as to disclose their broad historical content. Quite a few books, pamphlets, and newspaper articles have been published which refute factually the evidence of the defendants. Nevertheless, there is no having done with their larger meanings. The ordeals of Marxism in its Russian captivity are subject matter for the philosophy of history, not for the philosophy of the criminal code.

It is in its particular use of history that Marxism distinguishes itself from all other doctrines. In Marxism history becomes reverberant; it is both its science and its rhetoric. It was inevitable that the counter-revolution should strike at Marxism by reaching out to confound its central source of value. Not only were the universally known, the plain facts of the Russian Revolution falsified at the trials; the historic orientation, the objectives of the leaders as well as their identity were perverted. By compelling the makers of the Revolution to confess that they betrayed it, Stalin was attempting to justify his own betrayal. His plot to assassinate the history of Leninism dictates the implication of his victims in a plot to assassinate Lenin. In thus forcing history to undo its deeds, to rewrite its past, Stalin is subjectively undertaking to free himself of its necessity.

But the trials are also performances, plays, dramatic fictions. If literature reflects life, then their reality or unreality as literature ought to affect our judgment. It might be useful to examine them from the point of view of literary criticism. Are they tragedies or comedies? What perceptions, what psychological insights do they contain? What do they make of human nature? Considered as closed imaginative wholes, what is their inner consistency — what coherence obtains in them between act, motive, and character?

Various interpreters of the trials have mentioned Dostoevsky, and, in truth, the confession was one of Dostoevsky's major modes of creation. But the poles of Dostoevsky's world were pride and humility. In these plays, however, the characters show themselves to be destitute of pride; as for their humility, it is banal, mechanized, automatic: the author seems to have filched whole columns from the *Pravda* to put in the mouth of his creatures. Moreover, they are completely lacking in individuation; the psychology of each is equal to the psychology of all the others. There is no conflict: their speeches assist the very forces with whom they are contending. These are people of will and stature, yet their motives are unworthy of them and their acts are shadowy, seldom emerging from the realm of intention and inept scheming. Finally, the quality of the sentiments expressed, the root-and-branch philistinism of every remark, removes the last shred of dramatic plausibility, of emotional conviction. Is it possible that human beings who have lived so intensely, who admit to such monstrous crimes and who are nearing death, could fail to rise to the level of eloquence? Manifestly no imaginative artist could have composed such plays; only a policeman can write so badly.

No, these are not dramas, they are predramas, magical rites. Both tragedy and comedy have their origin in rites whose purpose was to produce fertility. Such ritualistic performances were believed to be effective in casting out the Old Year with its burden of sins and pollution. By expelling Pharmakos — the scapegoat, the sin-bearer — the community cleansed itself symbolically of evil. Tragedy, art — that is a later growth. In the Soviet Union the tragic is still in its embryonic phase; the state is barren, and to cure itself it practices exorcisms and conjures up spirits. Pharmakos-Trotsky is cast out into the wilderness, while the people and the government unite in a death-celebration.

In what sense can we speak of the treason of the intellectuals? Marxism has taught us that the intellectuals are a special grouping within the middle class, as much infected with its unrest and ambition as with its fright and fantasies. This definition implies that when the working class is apparently beaten, the intellectuals veer back to their old positions, each time of course under cover of a new set of rationalizations. The events of recent years have fully confirmed this definition; only, in this period it is Stalinism which provides both the rationalizations and a portion of the profits. There is, therefore, nothing very astonishing in what has happened.

One must keep in mind, however, that within the social division of labor the intellectuals are assigned the sphere of technical and spiritual culture: hence culture is their only real property. They are the guardians of values, on the one hand their cultivators and on the other their exploiters. They watch over the hidden manna even as they consume it. And while it might be naive to expect them to cleave to revolutionary ideas at a time when the proletariat is in rout, it should be pointed out that in their own mad flight they are trampling on the very values they depend on for permanent sustenance.

It does not require a revolutionary to be repelled by lies. It is not necessary to be a Marxist to be opposed to the perversion of historical facts. Never has the lie been so omnipotent, so blatant, as it is today; but the intellectuals, instead of pitting themselves against the power of the lie, are intent on selecting that version of it which appears respectable. The defense of culture has become their official program, but unofficially they acquiesce in the mutilation of all the elements that are the most vital source of culture. In this period one cannot accept degrading techniques and procedures in politics without degrading one's own intellectual discipline, without impairing its worth.

To the man of intellect, pride is a primary necessity. But this pride is being subverted by the strategy of the lesser evil in which so many have gotten entangled. The strategy of the lesser evil is the mind's education in opportunism. It creates the conditions for the disorientation of thought and the decay of its morality. The effects of this process are now palpable. On all sides today human beings are emptying themselves of individuality, finding it safer to become *tools*. No matter what question is asked, the stooge raises his hand. Literature, for example, after the bohemian roar of the twenties and the "proletarian" gnashing of teeth of the early thirties, is gradually subsiding into the gentility of accommodation. It would seem that for an intellectual it is far less pernicious to be indifferent to politics than to lose himself in its labyrinths.

Never have so many *fascinating* terms from the *obsolete* past, to borrow a phrase of Lenin's, been forced back into our consciousness as at present. We had assumed that all the justifications for supporting a war for "democracy" had been exploded by the experience of the living generations of men. Nevertheless the intellectuals are again rushing to staff the propaganda agencies of the war makers. The exigencies of imperialist rivalry makes a new world war inevitable, especially since, with the degeneration of the Comintern, the threat of revolutionary action has been definitely withdrawn. Is it the business of the radical intellectual to take sides in this contest of national imperialisms? It is true that fascism is "infinitely worse" than democratic capitalism. What reason, however, is there to believe that democratic capitalism can conduct a major war without at the same time coordinating its human and industrial resources along fascist lines? And who will annihilate the potential German revolution, if not the French and British imperialists — once they have removed Hitler? The quarrel between the advocates of collective security and the isolationists is essentially a quarrel within the ruling class. Collective security is the formula of those who want to go to war at once, but the isolationists are equally committed to uphold bourgeois interests. The war, even if the "democrats" win, will not solve a single fundamental problem of society. The new Versailles, which all the devout essays and speeches of the intellectuals will fail to avert, will prepare the ground for forms of social retrogression even more frightful than fascism — if such are imaginable. To assent to the war plans of one's own ruling class means to assent to "civil peace" at home — the *Union Sacrée* — which the politics of the class struggle defines as "the highest form of the conspiracy of the rulers against the ruled." And this is the "future" for which Stalinism and liberalism demand of us that we abandon the principles of classic Marxism, its knowledge and foresight. Their demands must be rejected. Only unalterable opposition to capitalism, only the utilization of the imperialist war for revolutionary ends, opens any prospects to humanity and its culture.

The historic process must be conceived on the plane of tragedy. To regard it as melodrama is to believe that it yields to accident, cunning, and heroics. On a provisional scale such yielding may occur; none the less, within the final implacable summation the impurities are dissolved and the interventions repulsed. In acting, man takes liberties; but only in recognizing as he acts the tragic nature of the forces that involve him does he gain freedom. To endeavor to become the authors of the tragedy of history is utopian — all we can do is identify ourselves as its characters.

Engels transposed Hegel's definition of tragedy as the struggle between two rights into the statement that it is the struggle between old and new values. The class war, insofar as it encompasses the historic process, is essentially tragic. Both sides are right — yet in different ways. One class defends its acquisitions, its "right" not to be uprooted and destroyed. The other fights for its future, as only through strife can it realize its metamorphosis into "the human race." The intellectual, if his values are not to petrify, must join with the new, and in that very union he will redeem the old.

What is this new apotheosis of "democratic hope," this artificial optimism and fraternity of the people's front if not a vain effort to escape the tragic? Being unreal, it is but the inversion of despair. The trials in Moscow, staged by the party of fraternity and hope, disclosed the mechanism of the inversion; and the intellectual sterility of the age belies its optimism. In attempting to crawl out from the cave of national socialism the Stalinist party will discover that peasant guile is no substitute for those qualities which only the international action of the class can create. To the liberal, "progressive," and machine-Communist alike history is an obstruction to be circumvented rather than the mode and temper of social existence. The petty bourgeois makes the happy ending of melodrama his condition for participating in a tragedy. Such a gross misreading of the text of historic experience can end only in defeat, and to the defeated, as a modern poet has written, history

May say Alas but cannot help nor pardon.

Partisan Review, 1938

Proletarian Literature:

A Political Autopsy

THERE IS HARDLY a literary critic in America who has not at one time or another taken a hand in the controversy concerning proletarian literature. Few of the contributors to this historic controversy, however, were aware of its concrete political background and perspectives. What was new about the proletarian literary movement was its emphasis on political and social relations; and in approaching this movement the critics, it is true, discussed the connection between art and politics and between art and society. But they failed to notice that it is not these general and abstract connections but primarily its specific political history which explained proletarian literature.

Like other types of literary creation, this literature undoubtedly reflected class interests, needs, and attitudes; yet unlike other types, it reflected such interests, needs, and attitudes through the coordinated medium of a political party. That party is the Communist Party, which alone of all parties in the labor movement displayed any solicitude for proletarian literature — a solicitude, needless to say, in full measure returned by its recipient.

It is impossible, in my opinion, to understand the development of this literature, its rise and fall, without understanding its relation to the Communist Party. There are other factors, of course, but all of them have been modified by this one fundamental relation. Thus the Marxist doctrine, for example, whose existence antedates that of the Communist International but in whose name the Communist literary critics habitually speak, has been generally taken as the theoretical basis of proletarian literature and its source of values. In identifying their own views — that is, the views of their party — with those of Marxism, these critics constructed a strategic mystification which had important consequences. One can place most of the books and essays dealing with Marxism and literature under the heading of this mystification, for what they actually deal with is literature and the particular interpretation of Marxism held by the official party. As such it is a perfectly legitimate subject, but the writers who use it should be aware of its real nature and hence of its limitations. Another result has been that it is the Marxist philosophy and not specifically the Communist Party which has been held responsible for the excesses and crudities of proletarian literature and which has drawn the fire of its opponents; and yet there are Marxist thinkers of reputation who believe that the theory behind this literature has nothing in common with revolutionary thought. Manifestly, a subject as intricate and contradictory as proletarian literature needs more than a purely theoretical analysis. Let us look first to its political history.

To revolutionary optimists the triumph of the left wing in American literature seemed inevitable in the early 1930s. And, on the whole, in looking back at those years, the expectation of this triumph appears to have been based on plausible enough grounds. At face value most of the factors entering into the situation were indeed favorable to a realignment of letters along radical lines.

The suffering imposed on the bulk of the population by the economic crisis elevated the "common man" to a martyrdom that almost overnight integrated him into the sympathies of the literary artist. Humanized by the calamities that befell him, the "common man" now began figuring in the imaginative scheme with positive force. Notwithstanding the contempt heaped upon him for many years as a mobster and a boob, he now emerged as the ideal-carrier of fictions, invocations in verse, and critical manifestoes. In the part of petty beneficiary of a prosperous and soulless materialism he had long typified the negation of values; cast in the role of at once a piteous victim and militant rebel he typified their revival. And his apotheosis was consummated when writers made a practice of detaching him from his ordinary human environment in order to place him within "the glorious collectivity of the embattled proletariat."

A further causative factor was provided, of course, by the exhaustion of the literary modes current in the twenties. Being for the most part expressions of disillusionment with society, these modes could not cope with the demands for its reconstruction. The various regional programs, designed as they were for local uses, appeared inconsequential in the face of a national crisis involving profound spiritual and material transformations. The proletarian program, on the other hand, invoking history in all its tenses to confirm its ambitions, laid claim to a universality and radicalism of outlook poles asunder from the restricted and polite values of the past.

Furthermore, a political party existed in America, the Communist Party, which made haste to identify this literary program as a part of its own larger perspective and which welcomed into its political home all writers wishing to realize in practice their conversion to the revolutionary cause. This party, at that time virtually in sole occupation of the Marxist arena, thus became the organizer of proletarian literature and its ultimate court of appeal. The Left literary magazines were published under its auspices or edited by its members. It appointed political commissars to supervise the public relations of the new literary movement and to minister to its doctrinal health. It furnished it with an initial audience and with an organizational base; and, finally, it conditioned the writers that had come under its control to conceive of the Soviet Union, its own source of strength and seat of highest authority, as the living embodiment of their hopes for socialism.

Nominally, despite the elaborate and often weirdly sectarian theories proclaimed by individual members, the program of this literary movement was quite simple and so broad in its appeal as to attract hundreds of writers in all countries. It can be reduced to the following formula: *the writer should ally himself with the working class and recognize the class struggle as the central fact of modern life.* Beyond that he was promised the freedom to choose his own subjects, deal with any characters, and work in any style he pleased. The Communist Party was seldom mentioned directly in connection with this formula of conversion. Granville Hicks's book, *The Great Tradition,* was in effect nothing more than a historical argument for the realization of this formula by American literature, whose liberation from "confusion, superficiality, and despair" was predicted as the reward of compliance.

This formula, however, despite its deceptive simplicity, is actually a complicated political mechanism. Its abstract political meaning conceals multiple confusions that proved to be as beneficial to the fortunes of the Communist Party as they were pernicious in their consequences for literature. In the first place, it should be noted that this formula is empty of aesthetic principle and advocates no particular aesthetic direction; second, it establishes no defensible frontiers, so to speak, between art and politics — it merges them; third, it draws no distinctions between the politics of writing in a *generic and normative sense* and the politics of an individual writer in a particular historical period; and lastly, it fails to define in what way a writer's alliance with the working class is or is not an alliance with any particular political party of that class. Through this formula the writer was actually offered a contract of an unprecedented character, but all the specific stipulations were left to be written in after he had attached his signature to it. The principal mystification involved in this transaction consisted of the fact that while the writer thought he was allying himself with the working class, in reality he was surrendering his independence to the Communist Party, which for its own convenience had fused the concepts of party and class.

The Communist critics, sometimes deliberately and sometimes through ignorance, cultivated these mystifications, for it is with their aid that they succeeded in stuffing the creativity of the Left into the sack of political orthodoxy. In their criticism, opinions as to the literary merit of a work of art were by no means ruled out, but the fundamental criteria concerned themselves with the author's loyalty to the working class and his interpretation of the class struggle. And it is exactly at that point, of course, that the literary critic resigned in favor of his party. Loyalty to the working class? Interpretation of the class struggle? What are these if not political matters, and who is better versed in political matters than the party under whose patronage proletarian literature was developing? No critic, regardless how learned in Marxism, could possibly presume to pit his own judgment against the party's political sway and reputed infallibility in the reading of the law and the prophets. To impugn the party's political authority meant to court excommunication. Thus it turned out that a novel or a play was certificated "revolutionary" only when its political ideas — existing or latent — corresponded to those of the party. And since the party had long ago awarded itself a monopoly of *correct* politics, the seemingly liberal formula that had enticed so many recruits was soon filled with a content altogether at variance with its manifest meaning. If not in origin then in function it became no more than an administrative tool, a political contrivance for imposing party views on critical and creative writing. What we were witnessing was a miniature version of the process which in Russia had resulted in the replacement of the dictatorship of the proletariat by the dictatorship of the Communist Party. Within the brief space of a few years the term "proletarian literature" was transformed into a euphemism for a Communist Party literature which tenaciously upheld a fanatical faith identifying the party with the working class, Stalinism with Marxism, and the Soviet Union with socialism. The "literary movement" droned these beliefs into its members with the result that instead of revolutionary writing — which may mean a thousand and one things depending upon time, place, and individual bias — an internationally uniform literature was created whose main service was the carrying out of party assignments. For strategic purposes, of course, the official spokesmen found it advisable to conceal their essentially factional inspiration and narrow standards under a variety of pseudonyms designed to give the appearance of flexibility, objectivity, freedom from control, etc. However (and I think I can allow myself the dogmatism of saying this), unless we understand the relation of these pseudonyms to their referents we can learn very little about Left writing in America, or, for that matter, in any other country.

It is essential to understand the difference between the literature of a class and the literature of a party. Whereas the literature of a class represents an enormous diversity of levels, groupings, and interests, the literature of a party is in its very nature limited by utilitarian objectives. It cannot properly be called literature, for it tends to become a vehicle for the dissemination of special policies and views; a party is too small a unit of social life to serve as the base for the formation of a spiritual and artistic superstructure. Expressing the historic being and consciousness of an entire sector of society, the literature of a class accumulates organic traditions and norms. Confident of its past and frequently of its future as well, it permits a free exchange and conflict of feelings and ideas. A true class literature constantly strives and partially succeeds in overcoming and transcending its given social limitations; its aim is the all-human pattern and image, though this aim may be frustrated by historical needs of the opposite character. A party, however, being merely the political instrument of a class and usually of only one of several groupings in that class, must necessarily reproduce itself in literature in all its narrowness and rigidity.

But there are classes and classes, as there are parties and parties. Not all classes are capable of producing an art and literature of their own. The conception of a proletarian literature relies for its defense on abstract and formal analogies between the proletariat and the bourgeoisie. Literature is the outgrowth of a whole culture, one of its inseparable parts and manifestations. A class which has no culture of its own can have no literature either. Now in all class societies it is the ruling class alone which possesses both the material means and the self-consciousness — independent, firmly rooted, and elaborated — that are the prerequisites of cultural creation. As an oppressed class, the proletariat, insofar as it is a cultural consumer, lives on the leavings of the bourgeoisie. It has neither the means nor the consciousness necessary for cultural self-differentiation. Its conditions of existence allow it to produce certain limited and minor cultural forms, such as urban folklore, language variations, etc.; but it is powerless to intervene in science, philosophy, art, and literature. Neither is it admissible, for the purpose of proving the possibility of a proletarian culture, to compare the proletariat of today to the bourgeoisie of yesterday, when the latter was itself oppressed. While the oppression of the bourgeoisie by the feudal regime was chiefly political, the modern property relations dominate the proletariat in a *total* fashion. Because it was already an owning class, disposing of considerable wealth and leisure, the third estate could begin creating cultural values even before its political emancipation. The proletariat, on the other hand, before it can achieve the freedom that participation in culture requires, must first institute changes in society which includes its own abolition. And if that historic task is ever accomplished, it will not be the proletariat — which will then no longer exist — but a classless and stateless humanity that will shape the new culture in its own image.

Virtually all the theorists of proletarian culture are fetishists of ideology, which they naively equate with and substitute for culture. And since they believe that in Marxism the proletariat possesses a distinct and separate ideology of its own, they conclude that all that is lacking for the creation of an art and literature of the working class is a plan and the will to carry it into effect. But the truth is that Marxism is not an ideology *of* the working class — it is an ideology *for* the working class brought to it from without. "The history of all countries," Lenin wrote in *What Is To Be Done?*, "bears witness that the working class is capable of developing only a trade-unionist consciousness ... that is, the conviction of the necessity of joining together in unions, of conducting a struggle against the employer, of demanding from the government this or that legislative measure in the interests of the workers, etc. The socialist doctrine (Marxism), however, has proceeded from the philosophical, historical, and economic theories which originated with educated representatives of the owning classes, the intellectuals." Now inasmuch as proletarian literature, by the innumerable definitions* of it given by its own

---

* In his *The Novel and the People,* the British Communist critic, Ralph Fox, states that "Marxism gives to the creative artist the key to reality ..." "He [the proletarian writer] will be unable to make his picture a true one unless he is truly a Marxist, a dialectician with a finished philosophical outlook." The Soviet Rus-

theorists, is nothing more than the socialist doctrine transferred to
the creative sphere, it follows that it is a literature produced outside
the proletariat and brought to it from without. But it is impossible to
conceive of a literature issuing full-blown from a doctrine — it must
also have some kind of concrete political basis. That political basis
is none other than the Communist Party, which conceives of itself as
the guardian of the socialist doctrine and its organizational embodiment.

This analysis is confirmed by an examination of the works which
the official critics have accepted as proletarian. Whether we choose
Soviet novels by orthodox authors like Gladkov, Fadeyev, and Sholo-
khov; or recent "militant" works by the Frenchmen Aragon and
Malraux; or the revolutionary* prose and verse of American writers
like Robert Cantwell, Fielding Burke, Michael Gold, Clifford Odets,
John Howard Lawson, Albert Maltz, Jack Conroy, Ben Field, Isidor
Schneider, Josephine Herbst, Kenneth Fearing, Muriel Rukeyser,
Edwin Rolfe, etc. — in none of them shall we find an imagination or
sensibility which is not of a piece with some variety — either plebeian
or aristocratic but mostly the former — of the bourgeois creative
mode. It is purely in a doctrinal-political fashion that these works
differ from "the literature of another class." But even the doctrine,
the one distinctive element in it, is not proletarian in any real sense;
into literature as into the proletariat it is imported via a political
party by "educated representatives of the owning classes" (Lenin)
— the Marxist intellectuals.

It is clear that proletarian literature is the literature of a party dis-

---

sian, Sergey Dinamov, speaks of the writer's "Party and class evaluation of life."
The German, Otto Biha, contends that the "proletarian writer can view the world
only from a consistent Marxian standpoint..." The American, Edwin Seaver,
defines the proletarian novel by its "acceptance and use of the Marxian interpretation"; another American, Edwin Berry Burgum, defines it similarly, as "a novel
written under the influence of dialectic materialism from the point of view of the
class-conscious proletariat."

* Throughout this article, in conformity with the practice of the international
Communist press, the terms "proletarian literature" and "revolutionary literature"
are used as synonyms. That this usage is still current is shown by Joshua Kunitz's
article, *In Defence of a Term*, in the *New Masses* (July 12, 1938). There have
been attempts to define "proletarian literature" as writing by people of proletarian
origin about the life of their class. This definition, however, is purely formal and
politically neutral. Obviously, a writer, though of proletarian origin and proletarian
in his subject matter, might at the same time be fascist in his political allegiance.
As a matter of fact, there are such literary types in Nazi Germany. Hence Communist critics have always insisted that the "proletarianism" of a work should be
defined in relation to its political outlook rather than by its author's choice of
themes or class origin.

guised as the literature of a class. This fact explains both the speed
of its development and the speed of its disintegration. Its peculiar
artificiality, the devious and volatile nature of its critical principles,
its artistic chaos plus its political homogeneity and discipline, its uses
as a cover for organizational activities — all these are explained by
the periodic shifts and changes of the "party line." The growth of
proletarian literature in this country between 1930 and 1935 is precisely coincident with the growth of the party during that period,
when its policy was ultra-Left and opposed to any united or people's
fronts. At that time the party saw the revolution as an immediate
possibility, and its literature was extreme in its Leftism, aggressive,
declamatory, prophetic. It was intolerant of all other schools of
writing and proclaimed itself to be the sole heir of the literary creations of the ages. Its practitioners were persuaded by the party
critics to turn out sentimental idealizations of the worker-types they
were describing in their stories and plays. These works, most of
which were quite crude as literary art, presented a silly and distorted
picture of America. Despite good revolutionary intentions, their
political content was schematic. Instead of giving a realistic and
individualized portrayal of social experience, their authors *inferred*
its characteristics by speculative methods from the theses of the
Comintern about the "world situation"; and since the Comintern had
declared at that time that the workers of all countries were ready to
seize power and establish socialism, they endeavored to demonstrate
that the Comintern was right by showing "reality" behaving according to its directives. The better writers, of course, such as Josephine
Herbst, Grace Lumpkin, Robert Cantwell, and Kenneth Fearing,
avoided these fantasies by sticking to what they knew. But proletarian literature as a whole, here and abroad, followed the party in
predicting and celebrating the victory of the revolution in a period
when it was actually losing every battle.

At present this literature is withering away because the party no
longer needs it. Since 1935 the party has acquired respectability by
reconstructing itself on a reformist and patriotic basis. Having
abandoned its revolutionary position and allied itself with liberal capitalism, its cultural requirements are altogether different from what
they were in the past. Everything within its orbit, including the proletarian literary movement which separates it from other reformist
and Left-bourgeois tendencies is being done away with in order to
expedite the "building of a democratic front." That the political
party which fathered proletarian literature should now be devouring
it is no cause for astonishment. A certain type of internal cannibalism

— witness the Moscow trials — is intrinsic to its history and necessary for the fulfillment of its peculiar tasks.

The period of the proletarian mystification of American letters is now definitely over. To say this, however, is by no means equivalent to saying that in recent years the official Left has declined in size and in influence. On the contrary, there are more writers today extending active political support to the Communist Party than ever in the past. To read the long and diversified lists of names signed to some of the appeals or petitions issued by the League of American Writers, an organization controlled by members and sympathizers of that party, is to realize that in such centers as New York, Chicago, and Hollywood a large sector of literary opinion is in substantial agreement with the policies of the American section of the Comintern. Nothing could be more naive, however, than to equate the popularity of these policies among writers with the triumph of the proletarian literary program. The actual process is in the opposite direction.

The official Left is now engaged in re-establishing that dichotomy between the writer as citizen and the writer as artist which it once decried as a source of bourgeois infection. It has discovered how to take advantage of a dualism between art and life that in the past it pretended to find intolerable. Why examine what a writer puts into his books when the real profit is derived from regulating his political conduct as an individual to conform with that of the Communist Party? The official Left is today primarily interested not in literature but in *authors;* from them it seeks to obtain public statements approving its political program on current issues — a favor which it is only too glad to reciprocate by guaranteeing to the works of the obliging literary men immunity from its "Marxist" criticism. (In the case of the more prominent literary personalities the rate of reciprocation is, of course, much higher. Eulogies, such as have been provided for a recent novel by Ernest Hemingway, are expected and delivered.) Thus the narrow, one-sided truism of Granville Hicks and his colleagues' defining *art* as a weapon becomes in practice the many-sided opportunism of converting the *artist* into one. This takes the form of extracting from him surplus publicity value by putting his public reputation to work in political testimonials which directly or indirectly refer back to the Communist Party or any of its agencies. Such political habits are in themselves sufficient to render insincere the attempt to introduce a radical content into literature, but in the present surreptitious abandonment of this attempt these habits are only of minor importance. If at present proletarian writing in this country is in the last stages of dissolution, it is largely because it is under political orders to commit suicide.

The experienced literary politicians who once acted as the apostles of proletarian literature would doubtless vehemently deny that they are in the midst of abolishing it. But that is exactly how their party code requires them to behave. It is now no longer news, except to fanatical Stalinists and reactionaries bent on maintaining a Red scare, that the Comintern has put away its revolutionary aims and embarked on national-reformist policies; and it is no friendlier to revolutionary ideas in the cultural than in the political sphere. Its literary adherents are, of course, lagging behind the "party line." A cultural lag is to be expected. All sorts of amusing inconsistencies and atavisms are to be observed in the pages of the Stalinist literary periodicals. In a purely academic way the small fry are still permitted to play with Marxist notions. The literary movement as a whole, however, is being quickly dissolved in the body of American writing. It is a long time since we have read a programmatic article on proletarian "aesthetics" in the *New Masses,* which has replaced its former standards of evaluation with the abstract categories of "progress" and "reaction." This year only one novel and two volumes of verse were published in America that follow in any appreciable degree the accepted patterns of the proletarian literary mode.

In fiction the themes of unemployment and union organization have persisted. Being objectively present in the material of the social-minded writer, they cannot be arbitrarily cast aside; and neither does the politics of reformism make such a casting aside necessary. The question relates entirely to the political treatment such themes receive. If once, in following the official perspective, the proletarian writer transformed his positive characters — who invariably were either unemployed or on strike — into revolutionaries performing some act that symbolized the overthrow of the system of private property, today he would have to resolve their problems by attaching them to some activity of the New Deal. The new Communist orthodoxy having decreed that peace, progress, and prosperity are possible under capitalism, the writer is unable to revolutionize his characters in any concrete sense without violating the precepts of the political faith of which, presumably, he is a loyal adherent. To be really logical, the unfortunate practitioner of the "party line" in fiction would have to substitute one of the President's fireside chats or a resolution for an immediate declaration of war on Japan for those visions of proletarian upheaval and the ultra-future of the classless society which nourished his inspiration in the past.

There are certain forms of demagogy, however, which a medium as palpable as fiction — unless it degenerates to the level of pulp propaganda — excludes by its very nature. Thus the media of art, if only by that fact alone, prove their superior humanity to the media of politics. The kind of casuistry which may easily pass for truth within the pseudocontext of a political speech or editorial, will be exposed in all its emptiness once it is injected into the real context of a living experience, such as the art of fiction strives to represent. The novel is the pre-eminent example of an experiential art; and to falsify the experiential terms in which it realizes itself is infinitely more difficult than to falsify abstract reasoning. Whereas politics summarizes social experience, the novel subjects it to an empiric analysis. Hence the test of the novel is more rigorous, less at the mercy of manipulation and rhetorical depravity. Proletarian fiction cannot *maintain its identity* while following its political leadership into an alliance with capitalist democracy. The only alternative for a school of writing that finds itself in such extraordinary straits is to abdicate. As citizens the members of that school are still moving within the orbit of their party, but what they write is increasingly becoming a matter that concerns no one but themselves — and the individual reader and critic, of course. The orientation toward capitalist democracy has deprived the proletarian writers of those political values which alone distinguished them from the nonproletarians. If historically American literature can be said to possess an ideology that generalizes it socially, it is none other than the ideology of capitalist democracy; and it is hardly necessary to develop a proletarian literature so that it may practice ideologically what American literature has been practicing virtually since its inception.

The other wings of cultural expression dominated by the Stalinist party are in a similar state of disintegration. That the revolutionary theater is dead no one doubts. As for Marxist criticism, it finds itself with less and less work on its hands. All that the Marxist critics can do is write conventional pieces with a slight social edge or else compose political polemics against the "counterrevolutionary fascist-aiding Trotskyites." These trenchant compositions, however, have as little in common with an analysis of art or letters as Trotskyism has with fascism. It is the absence of enemies, of course, which determines this Marxist idleness. If your critical sphere is American writing — in which there are as yet very few traces of fascism — and you have accepted the notion that your only real enemies are the fascists and that with everyone else it is necessary to cooperate, then to all intents and purposes your function as a Marxist critic has been abolished. What is left, of course, is the party-task of misrepresenting and assaulting the work of those Left writers who have repudiated Russian "socialism" and the Comintern. Michael Gold, for instance, has recently arraigned John Dos Passos before the bar of "progress" and convicted him of writing nothing but *merde*.* But such critical activities are exercises in the art of abuse rather than in the art of criticism.

In the last chapter of *The Great Tradition*, revised in 1935, Granville Hicks wrote that "if revolutionary writers should become convinced, on adequate or inadequate grounds, that capitalism could survive, that revolution is unnecessary or impossible, they would cease to be revolutionary writers." Given the political milieu in which Mr. Hicks works, it was rash of him to commit himself to so definite a formula, which has the virtue of proving the statement that revolutionary literature, at least as Mr. Hicks conceived it in 1935, is no longer in existence. But it passed away without the benefit of any kind of convictions, either "on adequate or inadequate grounds," on the part of Mr. Hicks's "revolutionary writers." An episode in the history of totalitarian communism, it will be remembered as a comedy of mistaken identities and the tragedy of a frustrated social impulse in contemporary letters.

Southern Review, 1939

* In the *Daily Worker*, Feb. 28, 1938, Gold wrote: "On rereading his trilogy, one cannot help seeing how important the merde is in his psychology, and how, after a brief, futile effort, he has sunk back into it, as into a native element," etc. etc. Hailed as late as 1936 as the foremost representative of the revolutionary novel in America, he is now condemned as a hater of humanity and a decadent. This "critical" revaluation is based, to be sure, not on a "rereading" of the trilogy as Gold pretends, but on the fact that since 1936 Dos Passos has emphatically expressed in disagreement with Stalinist policies in Spain and elsewhere.

Twilight of the Thirties:
Passage from an Editorial

To SPEAK OF MODERN LITERATURE is to speak of that peculiar social grouping, the intelligentsia, to whom it belongs. The intelligentsia, too, is a modern product, created by the drastic division of labor that prevails under capitalism. Restricted to the realm of technical and spiritual culture, which is their only real property, the intellectuals make their livelihood by preserving the old and by producing the new forms of consciousness. Now Marxist criticism, in discussing the social base of literature, has always laid too much stress on such terms as "bourgeois" and "proletarian." This is an error, I think, because literature is not linked directly to the polar classes, but associates itself with (or dissociates itself from) the life of society as a whole as well as the different classes within it by giving expression to the given bias, the given moods and ideas of the intellectuals. An examination of the special role and changing status of the intelligentsia is, therefore, essential to any social examination of modern literature.

Trotsky is, I believe, the only Marxist critic who develops his analysis of writers and literary trends largely around this concept. Thus he connects the symbolist schools that flourished in Russia before the October Revolution with the growing self-determination, in that period, of the intelligentsia, which proclaimed that "it had its own value, regardless of its relation to the people." But Trotsky does not credit this factor with sufficient power. This self-determination occurred also in other countries and it was directed not only against the masses but against the ruling strata as well. Materially and politically it was an illusion, of course, since the intellectuals remained at bottom as dependent as ever; yet in other respects it encouraged the creation of moral and aesthetic values running counter to and often violently critical of the bourgeois spirit.

Regardless of their specific historical meanings, most of the typically modern literary tendencies, such as romanticism, naturalism, symbolism, expressionism, surrealism, etc., could not have become articulate save through the support, through the necessary social framework, provided by this relative detachment of the intellectuals from a society intrinsically hostile, and at best indifferent, to the rights of the human personality and to everything imaginative, gratuitous, natural, and commercially devoid of advantages. In American literature, for instance, the typically modern did not appear until late, until the years before the First World War in fact; and the reason seems to be that in America, because of the concentration on the physical mastery of the continent, it was not until the twentieth century that a separate intellectual class emerged conscious of itself as standing apart from society and as possessing special and superior interests and ideals.

The modern artist has been rebuked time and again by social-minded critics both of the Right and of the Left for his obsessive introversion, his jealously maintained privacy, his aesthetic mysticism, his bent toward the obscure and the morbid. Yet without such qualities, given the boundaries of the bourgeois world, he could not have survived. These qualities are not derived from a limitless confidence that this artist has in himself (the opposite is often the case) but from the group ethos, from the proud self-imposed isolation of a cultivated minority. It is this isolation which was translated ideologically into various doctrines — the theory of art for art's sake is a striking example — that could simultaneously be put to aristocratic and bohemian uses. For a long time it enabled the art object to resist being drawn into the web of commodity relations. Being an impersonal exchange value, a commodity is a product that dominates its producer; and whereas in almost every other sphere the conversion of products into commodities robbed the producers of their individuality, in the sphere of art many producers still found it possible — through a valiant effort, certainly, and at the cost of much suffering — to remain the masters instead of the victims of their products.

But the contradiction in this is that it is precisely its integrity which is to a large extent synonymous with the "antisocial" character of so much of modern art. Inevitably so, for during the greater part of the bourgeois epoch not to conform meant to repel the social, and rather than pay the price of being at one with society, the artist chose to be alone with his art: he preferred alienation from the community to alienation from himself. "Anywhere out of the world," said Baudelaire: and Flaubert formulated the belief of a whole race of artists in claiming that "now that the bourgeoisie is all humanity" art had become particularly valuable, since in art, at least, "all is liberty in a world of fictions." "When there is no encouragement to be derived from one's fellows," he wrote, "when the exterior world is disgusting, enervating, corruptive, and brutalizing, honest and sensitive people are forced to seek within themselves a more suitable place to live ... The soul, made to overflow, will be concentrated in itself."

Flaubert and the other protestants of art and thought did not so much retire into themselves, however, as into their group lives and group cultures. They immersed themselves in the "destructive element," which has been defined as the awareness of "a void in the present." Moreover, in their desire to recover the lost unity of consciousness, they created a whole range of what might be called idealized negations of the society they scorned: some made a religion of art, some denied the reality of ideas in order to gain freedom in a life of sensations, some embarked on expeditions into the past in search of ancient mythologies and the old religions. From *René* to *The Waste Land*, what is modern literature if not a vindictive, neurotic, and continually renewed dispute with the modern world?

But the effect of the crisis of our time has been to undermine this tradition, so that at present it is fast breaking up. In the first place its social equilibrium was destroyed as soon as the weakened capitalist system withdrew the privilege of limited self-determination hitherto granted to its intellectuals. Once the very existence of this system was threatened, it could no longer afford to "keep" its intelligentsia in a state of even semi-independence; nor could the latter, now that it was compelled to think seriously of its future, afford any longer to belittle and neglect political creeds and political action. Despite all their postures of objectivity, it is the law of social gravitation toward the ruling class which, in the last analysis, determines the behavior of the intellectuals. Still, their problem was not simple, for the actual location of the ruling class was not at all obvious anymore. The question was: Who is the real ruler? Is he the benighted and visibly decaying bourgeois or is he that enlightened and mighty proletarian who, as they were assured, was successfully building socialism in Russia as well as preparing the revolution the world over? And many decided to throw in their lot with the youthful contender for power.

The modern literature of individualism was then belabored on all sides by the new converts to the socialist cause. Those of its critics who remained friendly admired its past splendors while insisting that it put political teeth into its abstract-spiritual dissent from bourgeois values. On the other hand the whole-hog Leftists, led by the impassioned party-liners, attacked it outright for projecting its ideals back into history instead of forward into the classless society, for being self-centered, pessimistic, obscurantist, and so on and so forth.

But now that this movement has abandoned its social goal, it can be seen that in reality it was not to the revolution that so many writers were converted but simply to politics. Yet politics — ordinary reformist and parliamentary politics — has nothing to offer to the literary artist. It was one thing to criticize the individualist tradition from a revolutionary standpoint, but it is something else again to criticize it from the standpoint of Stalinist social-mindedness. In view of what has happened, is it not clear that the older tradition was a thousand times more "progressive" — if that is to be our criterion — was infinitely more disinterested, infinitely more sensitive to the actual conditions of human existence, than the shallow political writing of our latter days?

Is a new tendency in literature possible today? Is there a basis for a new vanguard group whose members, not frightened by isolation, know how to swim against the current? After all, not all writers have reverted to some safe-and-sane way of thinking, and among those who consider themselves liberals and even Marxists not all are held on a leash by some pseudoradical organization. The revolution may have sunk out of sight and the intelligentsia may be sticking close to its paymaster-mentors, but the impulse to represent experience truthfully persists. The impulse persists, even though the job of judgment and representation has seldom been so arduous, so perplexing, so enmeshed in ambiguous claims and counterclaims. Yet part of the job is to evaluate these claims. If one is to be equal to the contemporary subject matter, one cannot shut one's eyes to the unruly presences that beset it.

I do not believe that a new avant-garde movement, in the proper historical sense of the term, can be formed in this prewar situation. For obituaries, however, the time is not yet; despite multiple pressures a literary minority can still maintain its identity. And even if it cannot look forward to an expansive career, still what it can do is to warn. We should remember the fateful words of Wilfred Owen, spoken during the last war: "All a poet can do today is to warn. That is why the true poets must be truthful."

For this minority, which has learned how to resist the reactionary

Zeitgeist, there is surely no turning back to prepolitical modes of expression; but neither should it bind itself to some closed and definitive political doctrine. For it is in becoming a mouthpiece that the writer defeats himself. His work is vitiated not so much by the errors he commits in his own right, not so much by the errors he has actually *lived,* as by the seemingly impersonal errors which are for that very reason all the more abjectly mindless, by the errors that he imitates out of cowardice and the servile desire to ingratiate himself.

Moreover, even the best of doctrines is thick with prohibitions. It is much too remote and narrow a base for literature, which relates itself to life through experience and only secondarily through ideas. If a sufficiently organic, active, and broad revolutionary movement existed, it might assimilate the artist by opening to him its own avenue to experience; but in the absence of such a movement all he can do is to utilize the possibilities of individual and group secession from, and protest against, the dominant values of our time. Needless to say, this does not imply a return to a philosophy of individualism. It means that all we have left to go on now is individual integrity — the probing conscience, the will to repulse and to assail the forces released by a disintegrated society.

The dissident artist, if he understands the extremity of the age and voices what it tries to stifle, will thus be saved from its sterility and delivered from its corruption. Instead of deceiving himself and others — either by playing with bureaucratized visions of the shining cities of the future or by turning his art into a shrine for things that are dead and gone — he would be faithful to the metamorphosis of the present. And every metamorphosis, as Marx wrote, "is partly a swan song and partly a prelude to a great new poem."

Partisan Review, 1939

Religion and the Intellectuals*

THE BACK-TO-RELIGION MOVEMENT among the intellectuals is scarcely to be understood without reference to the permutations of the *Zeitgeist* — and the *Zeitgeist* makes fools of us all. In the 1930s the key term was "revolution" while now it is "tradition." And it is tradition which provides the leading motive, not belief in God.

There are currently but two positions among us worth talking about: that of the secular radicals at one pole and that of the traditionalists at the other. Secular radicalism, in its multiple variations, is in a state of extreme crisis brought on by the cumulative historical frustrations and calamities of the twentieth century. Having lost confidence in the doctrine of progress, it is now more than ever exposed to the criticism of its opponents. The traditionalists, who attempted very little on the plane of historical action and who mostly stayed put in their dusty corners, have now come forward to speak their piece, with "I told you so" as the leitmotif of their quite unoriginal presentation. This is their privileged moment, and they are bound to make the most of it. And why not? Still, if it is the new religiosity that we are to discuss, then the first thing to be remarked about it is that it is hardly distinguishable from the world-view of traditionalism, with which it is far more deeply involved than with the primary and crucial commitments of genuine belief.

What, concretely, does it mean to believe? When Stephen Dedalus, in *Ulysses,* is asked whether he believes in "creation from nothing and miracles and a personal God," that is to say, whether he believes "in the narrow sense of the word," his reply is that there is only one sense of the word. It might be said of Stephen that he is a casuist in everything but the essential: in all essential matters his sincerity is unconditional. Unable to accept what is required of all

* A contribution to the *Partisan Review* symposium of 1950 on the growth of religiosity among American intellectuals.

true believers, i.e., required in no strict sense perhaps by all the established churches, though surely both by the mind of conscience and the conscience of mind, Stephen confesses to being "a horrible example of free thought."

Of course, some modern thinkers tell us that one can be religious without believing, so to speak, in anything in particular, certainly not in the particulars of dogmatic theology. All that is necessary is to reinterpret the concept of the divine as pure transcendence, or as the absolute ground of existence (an absolute of which nothing, however, can be demonstrably known), or, more mildly still, as a perspective uniting the real and the ideal. All such notions are wretched substitutes for the *mysterium tremendum* of a dying and rising god. Though notions of that kind may serve the modernizing dialectician bent on saving something of religion by cutting its losses, they starve the religious imagination by depriving it of its major assets in ritual, myth, and dogma. It seems to me that Stephen Dedalus, in his stubborn innocence, is aware of the ineluctable facts of religion in a way that eludes the subtle dialecticians; and I have no doubt that in this respect Stephen is wholly at one with his author. Another "horrible example of free thought" in modern fiction is Kirillov, of *The Possessed,* who commits suicide because he will settle for nothing less than God's actual existence. All his life long, the author of *The Possessed* said of himself, he was tormented by the problem of the existence of God.

Such stubborn innocence is alien, however, to the partisans of tradition, who have learned not only how to by-pass Dostoevsky's "problem" but also how to make it appear that the very formulation of it is somehow in bad taste. Their way is simply to restore God to His heaven by means of a mental operation speciously pragmatic so as to secure for tradition its indispensable metaphysical basis. In other words, if they believe in God it is mainly because such belief is logically implicit in their traditionalist alignment. One further step in this analysis and we discover that it is not they, as individuals, in the aloneness of their existential subjectivity, who have come to have faith in God but, rather, that it is the tradition which is possessed of that faith. The tradition does everything; they merely feed on its heavenly manna.

What this suggests is that at bottom traditionalism is really a form of perverted historicism, in the sense that it is fixated on some period of the past idealized through the medium of the historical imagination, that uniquely modern product. (The neoclassicist and traditionalist school of Maurras was fixated on the period of Louis XIV, for instance.) Whitehead once remarked that there are two ways of reading history, backwards and forwards, and that thinking requires both methods. The traditionalists, however, are committed to reading history only backwards, for they tend to regard nearly everything that has happened since the elected period to be part of a process of degeneration, as nothing less, in fact, than a falling away from grace.

But is it actually possible to believe traditionally while living in an untraditional society dominated by secular forces? Belief of that kind is vulnerable both on objective and subjective grounds. It neither offers new and challenging motives for effecting the reconciliation of faith and knowledge; nor does it yield itself to immediacy and the inescapable hazards of unqualified subjectivity as did the faith of a rebel Christian like Kierkegaard, who, differentiating radically between the Christianity of the New Testament and that of Christendom, sought to anchor his desperate and paradoxical belief not in tradition, hierarchy, and authority but in God and the revelation in Christ. Piety toward the past is what traditionalism offers instead. Christendom is its all, while of Christianity it conceives in a formal and remote fashion as an unattainable ideal, an ideal so strictly divorced from all natural and historical processes that it can be safely tucked away in eternity.

The center of gravity of traditionalism is seldom in religious experience. Its center, clearly, is in the attachment to the social and cultural order of some past age in which religion, in a highly developed institutionalized form, played an integral part. Thus the locus of value is displaced from the sacred or supernatural object to the institutional factor. One might put it another way by saying that to the traditionalists, whether of the Anglo-American school of Eliot or the French school of Maurras, religion is merely the theory of which certain social and ecclesiastical institutions are the practice.* But long ago it was written that "he who cometh to God must believe that He is"; and the proposition that "He is" is scarcely to be deduced from the plain historical fact, which no one has ever questioned, that the men of past societies have believed in Him.

---

* It is necessary to distinguish here between Eliot the poet and Eliot the ideologue of tradition in such prose writings as *Notes toward the Definition of Culture*. In Eliot's later poetry there is a strain of mystical religion the actuality of which is not open to question. As an ideologue, however, he inclines toward socio-historical formulations that bring him close to the position of Maurras. It is particularly among the followers of Eliot, some of whom have performed the remarkable feat of taking over his ideas on culture and society without an equivalent commitment to religious belief, that the archaistic social attitudes of traditionalism become the center of value.

Since nobody has gone so far as to claim that a new revelation is at hand, or that a prophetic *pneuma* is sweeping the world, as it swept the Christian world in the era of the Reformation or the Jewish world with the rise of Hasidism, one is perhaps justified in summing up the so-called religious revival as the high talk of literary men and journalists about the necessity of returning to traditional Christianity. (Here again one is struck by the fact that the emphasis in all this talk is not so much on the truth of traditional Christianity as on the allegedly beneficent consequences of its restoration. The argument from consequences, so grossly pragmatic, is thus inevitably laid hold of by the very same people who ostensibly reject the pragmatic mode of thought as philosophically vulgar and spiritually inadmissible.) There have also been a number of conversions — a fact not very important as a sign of cultural change if it were not for the attitudes of ingratiation and appeasement toward the converts and the entire phenomenon of conversion now manifest in intellectual circles. Not so long ago this phenomenon was generally regarded with amused bafflement or unconcern. That is a difference worth noting, as it is exactly the *Zeitgeist* which accounts for it. It is noteworthy, too, that among the new converts there is no exigent religious individualism à la Tolstoy, no prophets or visionaries, no grand and courageous reformation of ethical demands. Nothing of that sort is to be expected, for nearly all the converts have reached their present state through a process of historical retrospection which has apparently brought home to them the power and sublimity of the traditions and institutions of Christendom.

As usual, it is the literary men who are in the vanguard of the movement. In certain literary quarters the idea of tradition has lately taken on an honorific meaning that empties it of all empirical content. Thus *"the* tradition" — as it is spoken of in some of our literary reviews, with the definite article stressing an exclusiveness staggering in its presumption and historical naiveté — has been transmogrified into a patent ideological construction. It has come to stand for a special kind of higher reality, no less, bristling with magico-religious associations on the one hand and promises of aristocratic investiture on the other. Of course, the number of intellectuals now taking up tradition is much smaller than the number that took up revolution in the thirties. Still the trend is unmistakable, particularly among the intellectuals migrating into the academy, who easily discern a desirable connection between tradition, in its purely ideological aspects to be sure, and their newly acquired social function and status.

The pity of it is that not a few gifted writers are plunging from one debauch of ideology into another without giving themselves time to sober up. Actually, what they need is not more of the same medicine but a dose of skepticism so strong as to make them stand fast against the solicitations of ideologies whose chief function is that of mythicizing the world — the essential prerequisite of subjecting the mind to some form of authoritarian discipline. The intellectual converts to myth and dogma, some of whom formerly adhered to a social-revolutionary position, fondly imagine that they have undergone a total change of outlook. That is the typical error of abstract unhistorical thinking.

What was it, in fact, that disillusioned those people with Soviet communism, for so long the dominant version of the secular-revolutionary outlook? It was the discovery that Soviet communism had nothing in common with the classic socialist ideals but that, like fascism, it was a form of revolutionary reaction, that is, a form of reaction devoid of norms and standards, arbitrary in its violence and boundless in its hankering for power and mastery. Yet this discovery, however painful, has not led them to reject the authoritarian approach, no matter what its source. To accomplish such a rejection is beyond either their need or desire, for what they want above all is to be possessed by the spirit of consolation and to be lured by the promise of metaphysical certainty and social stability. Hence if they abjured revolutionary reaction it was only to go over to the traditional reaction of ideologies much older than communism, a reaction richly endowed with norms and standards, embellished with the achievements, real or imaginary, of past generations, and institutionalized in the Roman Church and other conservative organizations. The difference between the two types of reaction must appear to them like the difference noted by Hegel between the shockingly bare and matter-of-fact social relationships of modern society and those of the ancient city-states, where "the iron bond of necessity was still garlanded with roses." But Hegel's insight is not applicable to the realities of our epoch. The iron bond of necessity is what we must think of, not the withered roses; and for that it is essential that we introduce into our thought, to quote Hegel again, "the seriousness, the suffering, the patience and the labor of the negative." Then we shall realize soon enough that in reality there is no Chinese wall separating the two types of reaction. They share a common secret, in that the appeal of both is to "miracle, mystery, and authority" — the three forces that Dostoevsky's Grand Inquisitor found indispensable for holding captive the conscience and loyalty of mankind.

The reactionary implications of traditionalism in the social and political sphere are of course inevitably lost on the majority of its partisans, who tend to think in high-falutin' romantic-literary categories that fall short of any possibility of application in the real world. In those circles a high tone is invariably taken toward the disciplines of the political mind, as if politics, denoting those facts of power from which there is no longer any escape and by which our fate is increasingly determined, comprised some inferior form of reality with which no person of really fine sensibilities would seriously concern himself.

It is curious, too, that those people, who in literature urge upon us the adoption of a neoclassicist aesthetic to replace the muddle of Romanticism, should remain so strangely unaware of the extent to which they are indebted for their leading ideas to Romanticism, particularly the German brand of Romanticism, with its strivings to re-enchant the world, its idealization of Christendom, its nostalgic remembrance of the feudal-agrarian past, its archaizing social attitudes generally, and the conversion of its chief spokesmen to Catholicism. In Novalis' essay "Die Christenheit oder Europa" you will find most of the generative ideas of traditionalism, expressed with a beautiful poetic abandon inconceivable in our time, which has produced texts belonging to the same order of thought, such as Eliot's *Idea of a Christian Society* and *Notes towards the Definition of Culture*, that are marked by a painful though futile effort to achieve precision and relevance.

I may be overstating the case but it seems to me that there is a connection between the present slump in creative writing and the ascendancy of traditionalist ideas in this decade. It is a fact that in the forties writing fell far below the level attained in the twenties or even in the thirties. And literary discourse has again become cluttered with a modish phraseology nearly as obnoxious as the class-struggle phraseology of the thirties. There is the term "original sin," for instance, which has lately taken on a flavor definitely avant-gardist, like the word "marvelous" in the lingo of the surrealists. Altogether there is far too much manipulation of the notions of guilt, evil, and sin, notions drawn from theological sources at second or third hand and converted, under cover of the religious revival, into a kind of aesthetic demonology which is really little more than a mid-century version of the "Satanism" that prevailed in the advanced literary circles of Paris at the time of Baudelaire's youth.

All that is but a symptom of the appalling disinclination on the part of the new literary converts to make anything more of the Christian ethic of love and goodness than the world will allow. What they make much more of is the orthodox doctrine of evil — a doctrine the ambiguities of which have baffled many a theologian but which for that very reason perhaps suits the literary faculty in its present state of privation. It is a doctrine that can be worked with facility both as a mystification of magical import and as a prefabricated motive to be pressed into service wherever concrete and specific insight into human nature and conduct is missing. To be sure, there is no denying the reality of evil. But it is precisely its reality which is obscured and dissipated when turned into an all-sufficing explanation and then made the object of aesthetic play-acting with modern ideas of the irrational and the demonic, ideas as ubiquitous as they are indeterminate. One recalls that in *Faust* Mephistopheles observes with his characteristic shrewdness that

> Auch die Kultur, die alle Welt beleckt,
> Hat auf den Teufel sich erstreckt.

Since that verse was written Faust has been virtually eclipsed by Mephistopheles in the role of protagonist of the higher productions of *Kultur*; and being exceedingly practiced in beating the high-minded at their own game, Mephistopheles is no doubt far from displeased by his rise to a position of glamor in the cultural hierarchy.

Moreover, the free play now given to the doctrine of evil and sin has more than an aesthetic resonance. The moral implications are not to be overlooked. If the utopians on the Left (the futurists, as Toynbee calls them) disastrously assume the innate goodness of man in their social schemes, the utopians on the Right (the archaists, in Toynbee's phrase) are ever inclined to assume a fixed human nature that is innately evil, an assumption which has always served as one of the principal justifications of man's inhumanity to man. It is the permanent alibi of those unconcerned with justice. Futurism and archaism are a pair of alternative reactions produced by the schism in the soul of the members of a disintegrating society. Insofar as the American intellectuals are abandoning futurism in favor of archaism they are once more choosing an easy alternative and engaging themselves in a pursuit of Utopia that will again end in frustration and disillusion.

1950

The Sense and Nonsense
of Whittaker Chambers

WHAT CHIEFLY CAUGHT my interest when I first encountered Whittaker Chambers, back in the early thirties not long before the "underground" claimed him, was something in his talk and manner, a vibration, an accent, that I can only describe as Dostoevskyean in essence. I thought at the time that he was far from unconscious of the effect he produced. He had the air of a man who took more pleasure in the stylized than in the natural qualities of his personality. Still, whether aware or not, it was distinctly the Dostoevskyean note that he struck — that peculiar note of personal intensity and spiritual truculence, of commitment to the "Idea" so absolute as to suggest that life had no meaning apart from it, all oddly combined with a flair for mystification and melodrama. That early impression, since confirmed by other people, is now reaffirmed in his book.

Witness is in the main a fully convincing account of the role its author played in the Hiss case. It is also a heady mixture of auto-biography, politics, and apocalyptic prophecy; and it contains a good many of the characteristic elements of a production à la Dostoevsky, above all the atmosphere of scandal and monstrous imputation, the furtive meetings and the secret agents, the spies, informers, and police-men, desperate collisions, extreme ideas, suffering, pity, and remorse, the entire action moving inexorably toward the typical *dénouement* of a judicial trial, in the course of which heroes and victims alike are exposed as living prey to the crowds and all the secrets come tumbling out.

The influence of the Russian novelist is literally everywhere in the book, in the action as in the moral import, in the plot no less than in the ideology. And Chambers goes in for ideology without stint or limit. Even his Maryland farm, of which he writes at great length, is at once a real place and a piece of ideology pure and simple. And the ideology is fashioned in accordance with the precepts of the Russian master, from whom he borrows some of his key terms and characteristic turns of thought. Thus Chambers seems to have appropriated, lock, stock, and barrel, the entire Dostoevskyean polemic against socialism as the culminating movement of Western rationalism and secularism, leading through the rejection of God to the deification of man. He accuses the radicals of worshiping "Almighty man," just as the creator of Ivan Karamazov accused them of worshiping the "man-god," and refuses to distinguish in principle between liberals, socialists, and party-line Communists, whatever the divergences among them. Regardless of their political practice at any given time, in theory they are all equally committed to unbelief, to the elevation of man above God — the supreme act of rebellion converting man into a monster.

That is exactly the approach of Dostoevsky, who also saw no reason to discriminate among the varieties of free thought. (He did not hesitate, for instance, to lay the blame for the criminal acts of Nechayev — the model for the sinister figure of Pyotr Verhovensky in *The Possessed* — not only upon such revolutionary theorists as Belinsky and Herzen but also upon the far more moderate liberal idealists of the type of Granovsky, a Moscow professor who taught his students scarcely anything more virulent than that man was a creature endowed with a mind and that it was his duty to use it.) Science and reason are the enemy. And what is socialism? According to Dostoevsky it is "not merely the labor question, it is before all else the atheistic question, the question of the form taken by atheism today, the question of the Tower of Babel built without God, not to mount from earth to Heaven, but to set up Heaven on earth." This, indeed, is the *locus classicus*. It is the pivotal thought of Chambers' book. But there are other ideas in Dostoevsky which he entirely ignores; and with good reason, for they emphatically call into question his view of religion as the one secure basis of freedom. Perhaps he would not be so certain of their "indivisible" union if he had been more attentive to the important historical lesson contained in the legend of the Grand Inquisitor — a lesson which belies the national-religious thesis of Dostoevsky's work as a whole and which is a deadly critique of the shallow doctrine that if men but believed they would soon enter the promised spiritual kingdom. In that legend Dostoevsky tells us that religion too, yes, even the religion of Christ, can be transformed into an instrument of power in the hands of a self-chosen elite bent on depriving men of their freedom and organizing a "universal human antheap." And it is precisely men's readiness to believe and their irresistible craving for "community of worship," the principal source of bigotry and intolerance, that induces them to accept the total claims of their rulers.

The Russian writer's influence on Chambers is one-sided but very real. In the biographical chapters, too, the story is sometimes given a Dostoevskyean twist. Consider the following brief passage in which, while recalling his student days at Columbia, Chambers portrays himself for all the world as if he were writing not about a boy from Long Island but a blood brother of Shatov or Raskolnikov, brooding in the Russian cold about the ultimate problems of existence. "One day, early in 1925, I sat down on a concrete bench on the Columbia campus, facing a little Greek shrine and the statue of my old political hero, Alexander Hamilton. The sun was shining, but it was chilly, and I sat huddled in my overcoat. I was there to answer once for all two questions: Can a man go on living in a world that is dying? If he can, what should he do in the crisis of the twentieth century?" The "huddled in my overcoat" is a good touch; but the peremptory "to answer *once for all* two questions" (and what questions!) is really priceless. Here, histrionics aside, it is not only the inflection of the narrative line which reminds us of the author of *Crime and Punishment*; even more suggestive is the thoroughly *ideologized* conceptions of life it reveals. Essentially it is the idea that in order to live at all one must first ascertain the answer to the ultimate questions — an idea so utterly unpragmatic that one is almost tempted to call it "un-American."

However, in spite of Chambers' wonderful aptitude for turning ideas into dramatic motives, in its lack of humor and irony his book is anything but Dostoevskyean. His seriousness is of that portentous kind which in a novelist we would at once recognize as a failure of sensibility. For Chambers eliminates from his account anything that might conceivably be taken as ambiguous or incongruous in his own motives and convictions, and this permits him to bear down all the more heavily on those of his opponents. No sense of humor or irony can survive that sort of attack. He is a splendid satirist; the mordant phrase, manipulated with ease and perfect timing, is ever at his disposal; but of that true irony, which implicates the person writing no less than other people, the subject as well as the object, there is not a trace in his pages. This deficiency makes it hard for him both to modulate his ideas and to relate himself to them without pomposity and self-conceit. Perhaps that will explain the occasional lapses in taste and the tone of heroic self-dramatization which is sometimes indistinguishable from sheer bathos, as when he writes that at issue in the Hiss case was "the question whether this sick society, which we call Western civilization, could in its extremity still cast up a man whose faith in it was so great that he would voluntarily abandon those things which men hold good, including life, to defend it."

And his prose is open to criticism on related grounds. He is a born writer, greatly accomplished in a technical sense. Yet his prose, for all its unusual merit, is not very adaptable to confessional writing. Tightly organized and controlled, even streamlined, though in the best sense of that much-abused word, it is hardly an appropriate medium for the expression of intimate personal truth or the exploration of inner life. It shuns the spontaneous and repels subjectivity.

The fact is that when we are through reading this enormously long book, with its masses of detail, we are still left with very little knowledge of the author as a person. We have been instructed in his politics and in his philosophy; we have learned much about his childhood years, so fearfully depressing and ill-making; and we have learned to know him in his successive adult roles — Communist Party member, Soviet agent, editor of *Time*, Maryland farmer, convert, and witness. None the less he remains shielded from us to the very end, encased in his "character-armor." We communicate almost exclusively with the externalized Chambers, a man apparently bent on transforming his life into a public destiny, incapable of projecting himself on any level but that of objectified meaning, and possessed by a lust for the Absolute (the ultimate and unqualified pledge of objective Being). He is certain of its existence; and he finds it — invariably. First History, now God. For he repented of his unbelief even before he openly emerged from the Communist underground, thus insuring himself of uninterrupted contact with the Absolute.

One wishes that Chambers had absorbed less of Dostoevsky's political ideology — a sphere in which he is assuredly a false guide — and had instead absorbed more of his insight into unconscious motivation and the cunning maneuvers of the battered ego in reaching out for self-esteem, pleasure, and power. He might then not be quite so intent on dissolving the concrete existence of men in their specific conditions of life into the abstractions of the impersonal Idea, whether in its idealist or materialist version. (The difference between the two versions is not half so great as the devotees of metaphysics imagine.) Nor would he take it for granted, as he now does, that behavior can be directly deduced from ideology, thus overlooking the fact that the relation between them is frequently not only indirect but devious and thoroughly distorted.

But to Chambers the Idea is everything; men nothing. The role of personality in history is abolished. For instance, he absolves Stalin of responsibility for any and all of the evils of communism, and even goes so far as to characterize him as a "revolutionary statesman" for carrying through the Great Purge. ("From the Communist viewpoint, Stalin could have taken no other course, so long as he believed he was right.... That was the horror of the Purge — that acting as a Communist, Stalin had acted rightly.") This is sheer fantasy. What evidence is there that the Purge advanced the cause of communism, that it was in any sense "objectively necessary," or that Stalin was under any illusions as to its effect? It should be obvious that the Purge strengthened Stalin's personal dictatorship at the cost of considerably weakening the Communist movement the world over. It shook the faith of millions in the Soviet myth. (For that matter, Chambers himself might still be numbered among the faithful if not for the Purge, the direct cause of his break.) After all, no policy that Stalin promulgated *after* the Purge could have been seriously resisted, let alone blocked, by the abject and beaten Old Guard of the Revolution. Not the necessities, real or imaginary, of the revolutionary cause but the drive for unlimited power on the part of Stalin and his faction, who have never hesitated to sacrifice the good of the cause for their own advantage, is the one plausible explanation of the Purge.

Chambers appears to have quit the Communist Party cherishing some of the same illusions with which he entered it. He was certainly close enough to the Stalinist oligarchy to have learned that it has long ago ceased to regard power merely as a means — least of all as a means of bringing to realization "the vision of man," as he calls it — but as an end in itself. The present Stalinist elite, which raised its leader to the supreme heights and which he, in turn, organized and disciplined in his own inimitable fashion, no longer cares to remember the socialist idealism of the generation that made the Revolution. It has been taught to despise that idealism; and Chambers' portrait of Colonel Bykov, his Russian superior in the "apparatus," is perfectly illustrative of this psychology. Whatever the nature of their rationalizations, those people now act more and more like the totalitarians in George Orwell's novel, *1984*, whose program comes to only one thing: power entirely for its own sake. "Power is not a means; it is an end.... The object of persecution is persecution. The object of torture is torture. The object of power is power."

The original idea of communism accounts for the behavior of real live Communists no more and no less than the original idea of Christianity can account for the behavior of real live Christians in the centuries when they wielded temporal power; the Great Purge, the slave-labor camps and the other horrors of the Soviet system can no more be deduced from the classic texts of socialism than the murderous Albigensian Crusade and the practices of the Holy Inquisition can be deduced from the Sermon on the Mount. Chambers denies that there is any phase or single event in the history of Bolshevism, like the Kronstadt rebellion for example, that can be taken as a turning point in its degeneration. Its fascist character, he writes, was "inherent in it from the beginning." That is true in a sense, but scarcely in a meaningful way. It is equally true that besides the totalitarian potential a good many other things were inherent in the Revolution which came to nothing by reason of the power in the hands of certain men and the irreducibly tragic nature of the circumstances under which they exercised it, such as Russia's isolation and ruinous poverty and the fusion of the absolutist element in the Marxist dialectic with the caesaro-papist heritage of the Russian mind. Chambers is so obsessed with the "atheistic question" that he is willing to absolve the very worst men of responsibility for their crimes in order all the more justifiably to implicate the values and ideas they profess. He forgets that men in general, not only the worst among them, tend to honor such values and ideas more in the breach than in the observance. At one time Lenin warned his followers that there is no idea or movement that cannot be turned into its exact opposite. If that is true, it is because ideas and movements have no reality except insofar as they derive it from living men. No ideology, whether secular or religious, exists in some ghostlike fashion apart from the men who believe in it or merely use it for their own ends; and since its one lodging place is in the power-mongering human mind, it can never be immune to corruption.

Though disappointing in its character as a work of ideas, *Witness* is still of the first importance as an authentic expression of historical crisis and as a presentation of crucial facts. And by far the most crucial is the fact that the Soviet military intelligence, by winning to its service men of the type of Harry Dexter White and Alger Hiss, came very close to penetrating the top headquarters of the U.S. Government: "It was not yet in the Cabinet room, but it was not far outside the door." The stealing of secret documents was, of course, of little consequence compared to the power that the infiltrators acquired to influence policy. This infiltration was not simply the exploit of clever spies; the spy-thriller aspect of their performance is of negligible interest. What is of commanding interest is the lesson it enforces; and that lesson is that the infiltration, which was more extensive, probably, than we shall ever know, was intrinsically the result of the political attitudes that prevailed in this country for a whole decade, if not longer, at the very least between 1938 and 1948.

Chambers may be exaggerating in saying that in those years it was the Popular Front mind that dominated American life, but he is hardly exaggerating when he specifies that it was that mind which then dominated most "avenues of communication between the intellectuals and the nation. It told the nation what it should believe; it made up the nation's mind for it. The Popular Fronters had made themselves the 'experts.' They controlled the narrows of news and opinion.... The nation ... could not grasp or believe that a conspiracy on the scale of communism was possible or that it had already made so deep a penetration...." And the fierce resistance which Chambers encountered when he finally broke through with his testimony to the nation at large was essentially a symptom of the anguish of the Popular Front mind and its unreasoning anger at being made to confront the facts of political life. The importance of the Hiss case was precisely that it dramatized that mind's struggle for survival and its vindictiveness under attack. That mind is above all terrified of the disorder and evil of history, and it flees the harsh choices which history so often imposes. It fought to save Hiss in order to safeguard its own illusions and to escape the knowledge of its gullibility and chronic refusal of reality.

Where Chambers goes wrong, I think, is in his attempt to implicate that mind in the revolutionary ethos. Hence his distorted picture of the New Deal as a "genuine revolution, whose deepest purpose was not simply reform within existing conditions, but a basic change in the social and, above all, the power relationships within the nation." The proof? The New Deal was bent on replacing the power of business with that of politics. But this notion is altogether too narrow, too one-sided. Of course the New Deal was bound to increase the power of government in its effort to pull the economy out of depression and to save business from its own follies. The New Deal is unrecognizable in Chambers' description of it. Here again he proceeds in accordance with the method of pure ideological deduction, this time deducing the New Deal from the revolutionary intention he imputes to the Popular Front mind. He is in error, it seems to me, in his evaluation of that mind. I see that mind not only as unrevolutionary but as profoundly bourgeois in its political amorphousness, evasion of historical choice, and search for formulas of empty reassurance. It is the bourgeois mind in its mood of good will and vague liberal aspiration, the mind of degenerated humanism glowing with the false militancy of universal political uplift. It wishes to maintain its loyalty to free institutions and at the same time to accommodate itself to the Communists, particularly so when the latter oblige by playing the game of not being "real Communists" at all but democrats of the extreme Left. It wanted to be and was duly sold on the theory of Chinese Stalinism as a movement of agrarian reform; and it never wanted to know the truth about Soviet Russia, even though for many years now, certainly since the Great Purge in the mid-thirties, it has not been very difficult to discover what that truth was. The Communist mind, on the other hand, while utopian in its faith in the "science of history" and the materialist dogmas, is crassly realistic to the point of cynicism in its grasping sense of power and in the choice of means to attain it; its will is always armed and, whenever feasible, it prefers constraint to compromise in settling issues. If the New Dealers, insofar as they can be identified with the Popular Front mind (and the identification is by no means complete), failed to recognize the Communists in their midst, it was not, as Chambers asserts, because they lived in the same mental world with them but because at bottom they had almost nothing in common with the agents of the police state.

The dynamism of the New Deal in its early years should not mislead us as to its objectives, which were in reality very limited. Chambers invests that indigenous reform movement with sinister qualities, thus justifying his present allegiance to the far Right. I do not believe that the explanation for his political behavior is to be sought in any love he has of late acquired for laissez-faire economics and the division of society into warring classes. It must be his dread and hatred of communism that impel him to reject precipitantly all ideas of social reform and innovation. But if communism is so overwhelming an issue, what does the far Right actually offer by way of leadership in the struggle against it? As I see it, it provides neither a fundamental understanding of communism nor the moral, intellectual, or political weapons with which to conduct that struggle to a successful conclusion. That withered conservatism, which invariably mistakes all social adjustments, however necessary and belated, for wild plunges into the sinful economics of "statism," and which looks to a reduction in taxes and a balanced budget for salvation, has simply ceased to count in the world of today. It is really another form of nihilism, by far the most mediocre and boring of all. Whatever the material force which this withered conservatism may still command in some countries, the Stalinist aggressors know well that it presents no serious obstacle to their worldwide sweep. Chambers, who can hardly be called an optimist, surely understands that this is the case, as he virtually despairs of "the world outside Communism, which lacks a faith and a vision." What, then, is the answer? His answer is religion.

It is at this juncture that Chambers ceases to think politically, giving in entirely to his mystic proclivities. One doubts that he has ever been really at home in politics, if we take politics to be a delimited form of social thought and action. It was in the course of his search for wholeness and identity that he joined the Communists, reading a transcendent meaning into their political passions. He admits that while in the party he avoided reading all "books critical of Communism" and also that he had never sought to influence policy. Nor did his activity as spy-courier in the party's secret apparatus make any urgent claims upon his political sense. Unconcerned with politics in its hard empirical aspects, he is essentially a mystic swept into the world of parties and movements by the crazy pressures of the age.

What he is unable to see in his present mood is that the appeal to religion, however valid in its own sphere, turns into the merest surrogate when made to do the work of politics. It is well known that the religious consciousness is reconcilable to so many contradictory and even antagonistic concepts of society that the attempt to hold it to any particular social or political orientation is nearly useless. There is no substitute for politics, just as for those who must have it there is no substitute for religion. It is true that religious believers have every reason to be hostile to communism; yet the motive of belief forms but one strand in a complex of motives. Believers, like all men, live in the real world of varied and pressing needs and interests, of which the material interest is surely the last that we can afford to underrate; and all too frequently the predominant concerns of men are such that the acknowledged duty to their faith is easily thrust aside. In 1917 the Russian peasants, though traditionally far from irreligious, backed the Bolsheviks despite all churchly admonition — the petitions of Orthodoxy counted as nothing against the promise of peace, bread, and land. Clearly, Lenin's professed atheism in no way deterred the peasants in their support of the Revolution; and now large sections of the peasantry of Italy and other countries show the same lack of inhibition in voting the Communist ticket. The breakup of traditional societies is a salient feature of our time, and no impromptu summons can recall these societies to the ancient faith. Of what relevance are the propositions of Christian theology in China or India, or in areas

like the Middle East, where the crumbling of the social order un-
looses the rage of masses and Stalinist ambition feeds on hunger and
despair?

It is futile to expect religion to undertake the radical task of re-
organizing the world. Its institutional practices are remote from such
aims, and its doctrines have hardened in the mold of otherworldliness.
In truth, we have nothing to go on but the rational disciplines of the
secular mind as, alone and imperiled, it confronts its freedom in a
universe stripped of supernatural sanctions. Chambers' melodramatic
formula — God or Stalin? — is of no help to us in our modern predicament. He reproaches Western civilization for its "three centuries of
rationalism." Now rationalism has its fallacies, to be sure, but is it
fair to hold it to account for the horrors of the Russian police state,
which has behind it not even one, much less three centuries, of
rationalism? Soviet society bears the indelible stamp of the long
Russian past of feudal-bureaucratic rule, an absolutist rule of the
mind as of the body. Of course, the Marxist teaching is not exempt
from censure for the consequences of the Revolution. It should be
added, however, that this teaching, Western in its main origins and
holding a heavy charge of Judaeo-Christian ethics, has suffered a
strange metamorphosis in its Muscovite captivity. And now, in its
movement deeper into the East, it is seized upon, with all the fervor
of native absolutism, by the backward, semimendicant intelligentsia
of the Asian countries. This intelligentsia, untrained in habits of
social responsibility and unformed in the traditions of humanist and
rationalist thought, has converted Marxism into a dogma of nothing
less than incendiary content. Its detachment from the West is virtually
complete.

Chambers allows for no modulations in his attacks on the rationalist
and naturalist trends in Western culture. For him the only issue is
atheism, even where the disorder is patently economic and social. His
religious-political plea is made unconvincing by the very terms it is
cast in, terms belonging to that type of religious conservatism which
ordinarily finds its complement in political reaction. It may well be
that the religious mind has a significant part to play in "the crisis of
history," but the intervention of that mind will do religion no good if
the Christian credentials are used to no better purpose than to conse-
crate, as the late Emmanuel Mounier put it, "the appeal to pre-existing
ideas and established powers."

Mounier, a French Catholic thinker of radical tendency, saw with
uncommon lucidity the dangers that threaten the religious mind in
its turn to political projects. He protested against the idealist habit of

thought by which the activity of men in nature and society is reduced to no more than a reflection of the spirit, and he warned against enlisting the religious tradition in defense of the conservative cult of the past — a defense by prestige which sooner or later exposes the defenders to vengeful blows. Not at all alarmed by the fact that his analysis of the present crisis coincided in some respects with that of the secular radicals, he kept a tight hold on the obvious truth which religionists generally appear to have great difficulty in keeping in mind — the inescapable truth that economic and social ills can only be cured by economic and social means, even if not by those means exclusively. "Christianity no longer holds the field," he wrote in his last book, *Personalism.* "There are other massive realities; undeniable values are emerging apparently without its help, arousing moral forces, heroisms, and even kinds of saintliness. It does not seem, for its own part, able to combine with the modern world . . . in a marriage such as it consummated with the medieval world. Is it, indeed, approaching its end? . . . Perhaps the decomposing hulk of a world that Christianity built, that has now slipped its moorings, is drifting away, and leaving behind it the pioneers of a new Christianity. . . ."

Whether Mounier's hope for a "new Christianity" will be historically justified or not we do not know, but that he had a deep understanding of the discords experienced by the modern consciousness in relating itself to religious life there can be no doubt. He corrects the excesses of a writer like Chambers, whose illusion it is that he is serving religion by pulling down the image of man.

Partisan Review, 1952

American Intellectuals
in the Postwar Situation*

IT IS TRUE of course that of late American artists and intellectuals have largely come to terms with the realities of the national life. Hence, if they no longer feel "disinherited" and "astray," neither for that matter are they attached any longer to the attitudes of dissidence and revolt that prevailed among them for some decades. As their mood has gradually shifted from opposition to acceptance, they have grown unreceptive to extreme ideas, less exacting and "pure" in ideological commitment, more open to the persuasions of actuality. This far-reaching change has by no means run its course. It is of a complexity not to be grasped by a simple approach, whether positive or negative; and it is easy to fall into one-sided constructions in discussing it.

Among the factors entering into the change, the principal one, to my mind, is the exposure of the Soviet myth and the consequent resolve (shared by nearly all but the few remaining fellow travelers) to be done with utopian illusions and heady expectations. In their chastened mood American democracy looks like the real thing to the intellectuals. Its incontestable virtue is that, for all its distortions and contradictions, it actually exists. It is not a mere theory or a deduction from some textbook on world salvation. Whether capitalist or not, it has so far sustained that freedom of expression and experiment without which the survival of the intelligence is inconceivable in a modern society — a society lacking any organic basis, social or religious, for unity of belief or uniformity of conduct. In the palmy days when it was possible to take democracy for granted — that is,

* A contribution to the *Partisan Review* symposium, "Our Country and Our Culture," May–June 1952.

before the rise to global power of Hitlerism and then of Stalinism — the intellectuals were hardly aware of the very tangible benefits they derived from it. Now, however, only the most doctrinaire types would be disposed to trade in those benefits for some imaginary perfection of good in the remote future.

This change of perspective has inevitably made for a greater degree of identification with American life, with its traditions and prospects; and to suppose that this is simply a regression to nationalism is a mistake. (The nationalist motive is in fact far more strongly operative among European than among American intellectuals.) What has happened, rather, is that we have gained a sense of immediate related-ness to the national environment, a sense of what is concretely, even if minimally, our own. In these terms one can indeed speak of a "recon-ciliation" of the intellectuals.

Another factor, relating to the arts proper, is that the passage of time has considerably blunted the edge of the old Jamesian complaint as to the barrenness of the native scene. James was surely right in drawing the moral that "the flower of art blooms only where the soil is deep, that it takes a great deal of history to produce a little litera-ture, that it needs a complex social machinery to set a writer in motion." But since 1879, when that severe sentence was written, much has happened to modify the conditions James deplored. For one thing, the time is past when "business alone was respectable" in America and when many of its artists were therefore forced into a state of dreary and dreamy isolation. The businessman, though still a most formidable figure, is no longer looked up to as the one and only culture-hero of the country: not since the debacle of 1929, at any rate. Moreover, the national literature has now accumulated a substantial tradition and the dynamism of our historical life in this century has brought into existence a social machinery more than sufficiently complex for literary purposes. This is not to say that this machinery works beneficently; there is no necessary relation between beneficence and literary purpose. If anything, the machinery has now become so prodigious, so vast in operation and prodigal in per-formance, that the writer is just as likely to be thrown back as to be set into motion by it.

As for the Jamesian vision of Europe as the "rich, deep, dark Old World," its appeal has been markedly reduced by a series of social upheavals, revolutions, and two world wars. The historical richness is still there, though what it comes to at present is hardly more than a combination of décor and recollection; it is the depths and the darkness of the Old World that are almost intolerably actual at present, and in that oppressive atmosphere the Jamesian vision pales and dissolves. It is hard to believe that Western Europe has lost its cultural priority for good, even if for the time being the social and political strains are too great to permit the exercise of leadership. Its past is not in question here, since we cannot but appropriate it as our past too. What is in question is the effort of contemporaries, and that effort is of a scale and intensity insufficient to compel our attention or to provoke meaningful reactions in American culture. Existentialism was, I suppose, the last consequential movement to engage our interest, but the literary work that it produced turned out to be of small consequence. Moreover, the impression is that much of the culture-building energy of Europe's intellectuals is now dissipated in political adventurism; that in their thinking both of their position and ours they are apt to fall into disastrous oversimplifications. And some have plunged into the abyss of Stalin's Utopia.

But if among us that fatal temptation has been largely overcome, it is scarcely because we have been especially endowed with good sense or idealism. The difference lies in the more fortunate, more spacious American environment. Thus it is imperative not to overlook so direct and concrete a factor as the long spell of prosperity that America has enjoyed since the war. It has at long last effected the absorption of the intellectuals into the institutional life of the country. The prosperity that followed the First World War had no such result, the game being strictly business and the intellectuals remaining mostly on the outside looking in, while this time their status has been strikingly improved by the phenomenal expansion of the economy. Writers and artists have succeeded in breaking down the scholastic barriers that kept them out of university teaching, and many economists and sociologists have made their way into government bureaus. In particular it has been the many-sided extension of the educational system which has furnished the greater opportunity. Consider that the intellectual bohemian or proletarian has turned into a marginal figure nowadays, reminding us in his rather quixotic aloneness of the ardors and truancies of the past. We are witnessing a process that might well be described as that of the *embourgeoisement* of the American intelligentsia. In the main, it accounts for the fact that the idea of socialism, whether in its revolutionary or democratic reference, has virtually ceased to figure in current intellectual discussion.

Yet the material security so newly gained must be seen as an achievement of the American system not under normal conditions but under the stress of war and preparation for war. We have been drawn, as Reinhold Niebuhr recently put it, into "an historic situation in which the paradise of our domestic security is suspended in a hell of global insecurity." "Suspended" is the key word, for a good many other satisfactions of American life similarly exist in a state of insecure suspension. The fact is that the Cold War has reduced social tensions within the nation even as it has increased international tension. The war-geared economy has made for conditions of prosperity which again are typically taken to mean that "good Americanism" contains within itself the secret of overcoming the hazards of history. The illusion that our society is in its very nature immune to tragic social conflicts and collisions has been revived, and once more it is assumed that the more acute problems of the modern epoch are unreal so far as we are concerned. And in their recoil from radicalism certain intellectuals have now made that easy asssumption their own. Not that they say so openly, but their complacence and spiritual torpor quite give them away.

Especially vulnerable in this respect are some of the ex-radicals and ex-Marxists, who have gone so far in smoothly readapting themselves, in unlearning the old and learning the new lessons, as to be scarcely distinguishable from the common run of philistines. In their narrow world anti-Stalinism has become almost a professional stance. It has come to mean so much that it excludes nearly all other concerns and ideas, with the result that they are trying to turn anti-Stalinism into something which it can never be: a total outlook on life, no less, or even a philosophy of history. Apparently some of them find it altogether easy to put up with the vicious antics of a political bum like Senator McCarthy, even as they grow more and more intolerant of any basic criticism of existing social arrangements.

The old anti-Stalinism of the independent Left had the true pathos and conviction of a minority fighting under its own banner for its own ends; but that was back in the thirties and early forties. Its function then was to warn — and though the warning was not heeded the anti-Stalinists of that period played a vanguard role in that they were the first to discern the totalitarian essence of the Soviet myth. Since then, however, that minority political grouping has lost its bearings, continuing to denounce the evils of communism with deadly sameness and in apparent obliviousness of the fact that in the past few years anti-Stalinism has virtually become the official creed of our entire society. What is needed is not more and more demonstrations of the badness of Stalinism but some workable ideas as to how to go about its defeat. The locus of political action has shifted to the sphere of foreign policy, and it is precisely in the formulation and discussion

of foreign policy that the deconverted radicals, with very few exceptions, have displayed no special aptitude or initiative or grasp of the
immensely perplexing problems that will have to be solved before
American leadership of the "free world" can be made to yield positive
results.*

"It is difficult to change gods," says Shatov to Stavrogin in *The
Possessed.* Shatov, who turns from "nihilism" to Orthodoxy and
national messianism, knows whereof he is speaking. One wishes that
more people among us confessed to the difficulty, instead of engaging
themselves with unseemly haste to positions so safe and sound as
to be devoid of all moral or intellectual content. There is the
emergent group of parvenu conservatives, for instance, who, having
but lately discovered the pleasures of conformity, are now aggressively
intent on combating all dissent from the bourgeois outlook and
devaluating the critical traditions of modern thought. Thus it has
become fashionable to dismiss ideas of cultural or social insurgence
by relating them, with a facility all too suspect, to the Russian
experience, while at the same time all sorts of heretofore unsuspected
plausibilities — if not profundities — are read into the standard notions of the ideologues of reaction; and a new magazine like *The
Freeman,* with its boosting of laissez faire and hero worship of Taft
and McCarthy, is by no means an untypical phenomenon.

In our literary culture there is a more complicated play of forces.
The rout of the left-wing movement has depoliticalized literature —
which is not necessarily a bad thing in itself if the political motive
had been not simply abandoned but creatively displaced by a root-

---

* Characteristic of the petrified anti-Stalinists is their inability to distinguish
between communism as an external and as an internal danger. For communism,
though surely a grave danger *to* America — perhaps the gravest that the nation
has had to cope with since the Civil War — is hardly so grave a danger *in*
America. The local party has lost its power in the trade unions, it has been
deserted by nearly half its membership, and it has only a residual hold on some
sections of liberal opinion. The Kremlin's postwar strategy has all but destroyed
the influence of the American Communists, an influence almost wholly due to
their success in deceiving people as to their real allegiance and intention. In the
period of the People's Front and later of the war alliance with Russia, conditions
were extremely favorable to the Stalinist strategy of deception and infiltration.
These conditions no longer exist in this country, and the nation as a whole has
now been able to take the measure of the party-liners and their assorted dupes
and stooges. No doubt they still have a nuisance value to the Kremlin, but to
regard them on that account as the main danger *inside* the U.S. is to escape from
actualities into the shadow-world of political sectarianism and sheer obsession.
Of course, so long as the Soviet power exists its propagandists and spies will
circulate among us, and it is up to the intelligence agencies of the government
to deal with them. It is scarcely the function of political-minded intellectuals,
however, to serve as an adjunct to the F.B.I.

idea of a different order. No such idea has emerged so far; what is
to be observed now is a kind of detachment from principle and frag-
mentation of the literary life. Also to be observed is the rise of a
neophilistine tendency, an oddly belated growth of the mood of
acceptance and of the defensive reaction to communism, which, if
unchecked by the revival of the critical spirit, threatens to submerge
the tradition of dissent in American writing.

The neophilistines make an opportune kind of optimism their
credo; they are impatient to assume the unchallengeable reality of
the "world," and while reconciled to mass-culture they are inclined
to deprecate the traditional attitudes of the literary and artistic
avant-garde — attitudes said to arise out of negativism pure and
simple and willful indulgence in "alienation." Now the avant-garde
is of course open to criticism. It has the typical faults of its incongruous position in a mass-society, such as snobbery and pride of
caste. It is disposed to take a much too solemn and devotional view
of the artist's vocation. Its distortions of perspective result from its
aloofness and somewhat inflexible morality of opposition. But to
accuse it of having invented alienation is ludicrous. For what the
avant-garde actually represents historically, from its very beginnings
in the early nineteenth century, is the effort to preserve the integrity
of art and the intellect amidst the conditions of alienation brought
on by the major social forces of the modern era. The avant-garde
has attempted to ward off the ravages of alienation in a number of
ways: by means of developing a tradition of its own and cultivating
its own group norms and standards, by resisting the bourgeois incen-
tives to accommodation and perforce making a virtue of its separate-
ness from the mass. That this strategy has in the main been successful
is demonstrated by the only test that really counts — the test of
creative achievement. After all, it is chiefly the avant-garde which
must be given credit for the production of most of the literary masterpieces of the past hundred years, from *Madame Bovary* to the *Four
Quartets*; and the other arts are equally indebted to its venturesome
spirit.

If the artists of the avant-garde are alienated, as it is said, then
at least they are free to convert their consciousness of that unhappy
state into an imaginative resource. This cannot be claimed for the
artists in mass-culture, whose function literally depends on their
capacity to cultivate a kind of strategic unawareness of meaning and
consequence. Of course, there are certain elements in mass-culture,
some types of jazz and the folklore of sport for instance, that have a
positive value. On the whole, though, the proliferation of kitsch in

this country under the leveling stimulus of the profitmotive is a liability of our society which is not to be wished away by pious appeals to democracy and the rights of the "common man." But if under present conditions we cannot stop the ruthless expansion of mass-culture, the least we can do is to keep apart and refuse its favors.

Partisan Review, 1952

The Great Outsider

Wʜᴇɴ, ᴏɴ Aᴜɢᴜꜱᴛ 30, 1940, an agent of Stalin's drove an ice ax into Trotsky's skull, the news scarcely caused a ripple of interest among intellectuals of the American Left. Except for the small group of Trotskyites — a group even then in the process of dissolution — most of them cared nothing for Trotsky and his ideas. Power is what they respected and Trotsky had none. His unique intellectual genius and his greatness as Marxist leader and strategist of revolution was of no interest to them; nor were they moved by his past achievements as the principal organizer of the October insurrection and victorious commander of the Red Army in the Civil War. They had attached their loyalty to the Soviet Union, and in no sense to Marxism. Insofar as they took Marxism into account at all, it meant merely what, at any given moment, Stalin said it meant.

This is what is not properly understood about the thirties nowadays, and, by failing to stress it, most of the writing dealing with that decade is positively misleading. Consider the following almost unbelievable fact: in 1937, when the John Dewey Commission of Inquiry into the Soviet charges against Trotsky was being organized, a considerable number of prominent American intellectuals published a manifesto warning "all men of good will" against assisting the commission and declaring that critics of the Moscow trials were slandering the Soviet Union and "dealing a blow to the forces of progress." The manifesto was signed by Theodore Dreiser, Granville Hicks, Corliss Lamont, Max Lerner, Anna Louise Strong, Paul Sweezy, and many other writers, artists, and professors. This statement — with its attempt to justify the blood-purges and its assertion of Stalin's "integrity" — is to my mind far more revealing of the political atmosphere prevailing in the "radical" thirties than most of the documents cited by historians and authors of memoirs.

The thirties was a period of radicalization, to be sure, but it was mainly a radicalization controlled and manipulated by the Stalinist party-machine. Hence one can scarcely discuss this decade without also characterizing it as a period of ideological vulgarity and opportunism, of double-think and power-worship, sustained throughout by a mean and crude and unthinking kind of secular religiosity. No wonder that some of its survivors (joined, perhaps not too surprisingly, by a few ex-Trotskyites) have now turned into Cold Warriors of the "hard-nosed" variety whose endless exposures of communism and the Soviet state, so simplemindedly Manichaean in political content, can hardly be said to serve any purpose except incitement to war.

How the radical intellectuals in the United States as well as in other Western countries accepted and spread the Stalinist mythology is one of the many themes Isaac Deutscher explores in this third and concluding volume of *The Prophet Outcast*, his biography of Trotsky. This volume, which comprises the years between 1929 and 1940, describes the critical social and political events of the period — the devastating effects of industrialization, collectivization and the Great Purges in Russia, the collapse of the socialist and Communist movements in Europe under the onslaught of nazism and the initial stage of the Second World War. During this time, Trotsky's own dramatic life was moving towards its catastrophic *dénouement* — just as his mind was working at its highest pitch to define with theoretical precision and the insight gained from his singular experience, the causes and meaning of Communist degeneration and Russia's decline into a totalitarian state.

But perhaps the word "biography" is quite inaccurate to describe Deutscher's trilogy, for, though Trotsky was certainly a great personality, in a sense there was really nothing "personal" about his life. The idea of "the private life," with all the perhaps extravagant values which we are accustomed to attach to it and in which our literature has long been steeped, was radically alien to him. Everything Trotsky did, everything he wrote, was politically motivated and had political consequences. To think of him, however, as a politician in the usual sense, that is, as a man above all involved in a power game, is utterly to misconceive his role. With his devotion to principles and ideas, he could not but regard power in the sense of personal advantage and display as a vulgar temptation; to Trotsky politics was the conscious making of history for the highest ends. Therein lies his historic dignity and strength, even though in pragmatic terms his fidelity to principles and ideas weakened him considerably in his struggle against Stalin, whose cunning, toughness, and ruthlessness he always tended to underestimate.

Yet now that Stalin too is dead and his reputation as Lenin's true heir is demolished, who is to say that Trotsky is not finally emerging as the victor whose apparently utopian faith in history is at last being vindicated? It is precisely to this possibility that Deutscher devotes the last pages of his book: in a postscript entitled "Victory in Defeat" he makes a statement of the utmost interest, even if it may strike a good many people as giving much too free a rein to his Marxist hopes. The fact is that we have a long way to go before the calumniation of Trotsky ceases to be standard practice in the Soviet Union. Deutscher remarks that when Trotsky's "rehabilitation" comes, it will be carried out in a manner "free from cult, ritual and primitive magic." If that time ever comes, however, it certainly won't be during the ascendancy of Khrushchev and his generation who, even if they no longer conduct themselves as old-style Stalinists, are still quite unable to hold on to power without appealing to cult, ritual, and primitive magic. Even if they consider this appeal next in importance to police-terror, the ultimate resource, which they hold in reserve, it is none the less indispensable to them.

It is only when the historians of the Revolution and its aftermath are liberated from the fetters of the party line — or, to put it another way, when the party has been deprived of its monopoly of power — that the true role of Trotsky and the real nature of his political creed will become known to the people living under communism. In the long run Trotsky — at times in spite of himself — stands for the Western and libertarian and internationalist trend in the Communist movement. Thus the logic of his position impelled him, in the last years of his life, to call for a *political* revolution in Russia against bureaucratic absolutism, a revolution inspired by democratic aims which would at the same time preserve and strengthen the basically social character of the Soviet state and the collective, planned nature of the economy. The need for such a revolution has by no means been nullified by Khrushchev's wavering and contradictory attempts to reform Soviet society from above. If Trotsky is still regarded in the East as the supreme heretic (even though the grotesque charges of spy and traitor have been tacitly withdrawn), it is plainly because his programmatic ideas represent even now the greatest possible threat to the ruling bureaucracy, a far greater threat in fact than that represented by the capitalist West.

These are some of the issues, of far more than merely theoretical value, in which this concluding volume of Deutscher's trilogy involves us. The trilogy as a whole is a work of enormous scope, written in a language at once lucid and eloquent, and it is scrupulously based on primary sources. Deutscher's study is an extremely fine example of historical narration at its best, and of political analysis which is as percipient as it is comprehensive. I say this without necessarily agreeing with all its theses or judgments; in any case, sheer agreement or disagreement is not so important a test of value as the intellectual level on which it takes place — and in Deutscher's trilogy the level is very high indeed.

One can nonetheless predict that *The Prophet Outcast*, like the two volumes that preceded it, will be read by few and given little serious attention. The reason for this is that Deutscher is an unrepentant Marxist whose approach acts abrasively on the sensibilities of most political intellectuals. Some of our ex-Stalinists and ex-Trotskyites still enjoy a privileged status: their *expertise* is drawn upon and they are praised for their repudiation of left-wing ideals. Having abandoned not only the theory of socialism but even the very notion of its desirability, they naturally have no use whatever for someone so stubbornly against the Left's collapse into vague middle-class "liberalism" or an outright alignment with the status quo — if not worse. From their point of view Deutscher has committed the unpardonable sin of writing about Trotsky with admiration and not with the intention of exposing and degrading him. Moreover, he has compounded his sin by openly adopting the conviction which Trotsky held all his life and which caused him to lose a good many of his followers, that it is necessary to distinguish in principle between the "socialist-progressive" and "bureaucratic-retrograde" trends in the Soviet Union. Ex-radicals find this position unacceptable. Thus both Trotsky and his gifted biographer are consigned to the outer darkness.

To this day Trotsky remains the great outsider that he became when he was deported from Russia in 1929. Deutscher's explanation of this phenomenon is inherently plausible:

> His ideas and methods were those of classical Marxism and were bound up with the prospect of revolution in the "advanced" West. His political character had been formed in the atmosphere of revolution from below and proletarian democracy, in which Russian and international Marxism had been nurtured. Yet in the period between the two world wars, despite the intense class struggles, international revolution stagnated. The staying power of Western capitalism proved far greater than classical Marxism had expected; and it was further enhanced as Social Democratic reformism and Stalinism disarmed the labor movement, politically and

morally. Only in the aftermath of the Second World War was international revolution to resume its course; but then its main arena was to be in the underdeveloped East, and its forms, partly also its content, were to be very different from those predicted by classical Marxism. To eastern Europe revolution was to be brought, in the main, from "above and from outside" . . . In any case, the years of Trotsky's exile were, from the Marxist viewpoint, a time out of joint . . . and the ground crumbled under the champion of classical Marxism. In the stormy events of the 1930s . . . Trotsky was to remain the great outsider.

In *The Basic Writings of Trotsky* Irving Howe has edited a sufficiently representative collection preceded by what is for the most part an excellent introduction. The book contains selections from Trotsky's work before and after the Revolution, and the subject matter is not limited to politics alone. The essay on Céline is a masterpiece of brilliant insight and formulation. Of particular interest are Trotsky's writings on the German situation in the immediate pre-Hitler years, in which he urged upon the Communist movement the only possible strategy that might have prevented the Nazi assumption of power. Howe is right in remarking that "had his advice been followed (the Stalinists attacked him for 'capitulating' to Social Democracy!), the world might have been spared some of the horrors of our century; at the very least the German working class would have gone down in battle rather than allowing the Nazi thugs to take power without resistance." (Deutscher is equally impressed with Trotsky's diagnosis of the situation in Germany. He considers his attempt to arouse the workers of that country to the danger of Hitlerism to be "his greatest deed in exile," observing that "like no one else and much earlier than anyone, he grasped the destructive delirium with which National Socialism was to burst upon the world.")

Howe's criticism of Trotsky's ideas in his introductory essay is for the most part cogent enough. It is true, for instance, that Trotsky's "class-analysis" of bourgeois democracy is insufficient, and even dangerous in its undervaluation of the meaningfulness of political freedom, however formal and limited such freedom may be under a system of class-domination. But I cannot see that anything is gained by stating that in terms of Trotsky's theory of Hitlerism the murder of six million Jews in Europe cannot be "adequately explained." If Trotsky's theory does not explain this monstrous phenomenon, neither does any other theory that I know of. Perhaps the word "explain" is at fault here, for it assumes a rational structure in human reality which we have no grounds for assuming. Evil on so huge a scale is inexplicable, except perhaps by an appeal to the age-old mystification of "original sin," which precisely by undertaking to explain everything that happens in human affairs ends up by explaining nothing. But there is nonetheless a significant difference between Trotsky's theory of nazism (formulated before the Nazis came to power) and that of competing theories. If Trotsky's theory had been translated into practice, that is, into actual political action, the crime of genocide would surely have been averted. One cannot say as much for the other theories, which are chiefly *ex post facto* constructions, theories pure and simple, involving no commitment to action and therefore powerless to produce operative procedures of prevention. The authors of such theories are still in the stage of those "philosophers" whom Marx once dismissed as merely interpreting the world differently, the real point being to change it.

New York Review of Books, 1964

Liberal Anticommunism
Revisited*

I WAS NEVER a liberal anti-Communist or, for that matter, any other kind of liberal. When a very small group of us broke away from the Communist movement in the late 1930s we did so because of our fundamental allegiance to democratic socialism; and substantially that is still my position today. Needless to say, democratic socialism, in our understanding of it, was fully consonant with freedom of thought and expression, in the arts no less than in science and philosophy. Though by no means "orthodox" in our approach to Marxism, we did not think of ourselves as abandoning its basic program and ideals; least of all did we think of ourselves as errant sons returning to the "bourgeois" fold. For it was not communism, in its doctrinal formulations by Marx or even by Lenin, that we broke away from, but the Soviet embodiment of it known as Stalinism, then in total command not only of the Russian Communists but of the entire Communist apparatus abroad, which, under cover now of a revolutionary and now of a populist-democratic phraseology, was functioning as an instrument of Soviet policy pure and simple.

In that period the American liberals — and I mean the liberals of the *Nation–New Republic* variety — supported Roosevelt in domestic policy, and Stalin, whom they saw as a bulwark of antifascism, in foreign policy. Hence inevitably we identified many of the most vocal and influential liberals as fellow travelers, and we could not possibly have associated ourselves with them politically. And it must be emphasized again and again that in those years what is now called the anticommunism of the Left was almost exclusively an anti-Stalinist movement, not at all incompatible with adherence to dissident forms

* A contribution to the *Commentary* symposium of 1967 in which participants were asked whether they would still call themselves anti-Communist in one sense or another.

of communism, such as that formulated in exile by Trotsky and other heresiarchs of lesser fame. Nor did our anti-Stalinism in any way commit us to supporting the prevailing socio-economic system in America. We thought of capitalism not as a uniquely American and uniquely successful phenomenon validating "freedom" and "democracy" — such a notion, in vogue for almost two decades now, would have seemed to us ridiculous then — but as a historically determined system of world economic power. Our hostility to that power was so obvious that we mostly took it for granted while concentrating on the exposure of Stalinist terror, duplicity, and mendacity. To pursue such a course was far from easy, for at that time the climate of opinion among intellectuals was decidedly against us as more and more of them found in the threat of Nazi aggression the perfect rationalization for their backing of the Stalinists.

Clearly, the history of radical anti-Stalinism as I have very briefly and sketchily outlined it above has very little to do with the Cold War anticommunism of our latter days, though not a few intellectuals who belonged to the movement of those early years have done their best to distort that history in the interest of creating an impression of continuity and consistency in their own political careers, thus absolving themselves of the guilt of any involvement with the by now abhorred Marxist doctrines. Such people, having equated their Marxist past with the U.S. version of original sin, have turned into sophists and sycophants of the American ruling elite. Of course, they still pretend that they are fighting Stalinism, as in the old days, even as it has become all too plain, except to those who profess to take seriously the cant of our native "democratic" rhetoric, that what official America really finds objectionable at bottom is not the Stalinist aspect of communism but communism as such, authoritarian or not. In writing of the relation of American power to the underdeveloped countries, Robert L. Heilbroner has recently and with exemplary lucidity put his whole matter in the proper perspective in these pages ("Counterrevolutionary America," April 1967). What is official America's fear?

> There is a threat in the specter of a Communist or near-Communist supremacy in the underdeveloped world. It is that the rise of Communism would signal the end of capitalism as the dominant world order, and would force the acknowledgement that America no longer constituted the model on which the future of world civilization would be mainly based. In this way . . . the existence of Communism frightens American capitalism as the rise of Protestantism frightened the Catholic Church or the French Revolution the English aristocracy.

It is, I think, the fear of losing our place in the sun, of finding ourselves at bay, that motivates a great deal of the anti-Communism on which so much of our foreign policy seems to be founded.

Mr. Heilbroner is well aware that this is not a complete account of America's side in the Cold War, since it leaves out the element of Great Power rivalry, which would be the same even if Russia were non-Communist. But he has put his finger on the main factor — exactly that factor which most authors of Cold War studies have so far studiously evaded. Hence his analysis, which explains why for official America the main danger is always located on the Left, is by far more coherent and historically plausible than the myths spread by the official propagandists, including the former anti-Stalinists turned anti-Communists *tout court*. For anticommunism in the present-day meaning of the term, equivalent as it is to opposition to authentic socialism in whatever form, has no doubt helped to provide the ideological fuel needed by the policymakers in Washington (and the mass media at their service) for heating up the Cold War whenever it suits their extremely narrow-minded, class-oriented conception of the national interest. And certainly, in that sense precisely, the responsibility for our disastrous involvement in Vietnam rests with the anti-Communists of the Left (in this context the word "Left" can be used only in a Pickwickian sense) as much as with anyone else.

However, I do not agree with Mr. Christopher Lasch's recent assertion that "things would be different if the American Left had not long ago committed itself to outdo the Right in its anti-Communist zeal."* I doubt whether, on an all-national scale, things would be very much different; Mr. Lasch seems to be overestimating the power of resistance which the intellectuals as a social formation can exert against the gravitational pull of a ruling elite when it appears to be firmly entrenched in positions of authority. The old American Left he has in mind has for some years now consisted of exiguously small groups of intellectuals, divided among themselves, and the percentage of staffers it has contributed to the Pentagon's think-factories and the various Cold War institutes masquerading as centers of "Russian studies" is correspondingly sparse. But I do agree with Mr. Lasch's argument that "once the Left itself accepted anti-Communism as the *sine qua non* of political respectability, it became a prisoner of its own immediate success...." The old American Left has paid a steep price for its attainment of political respectability, and that price is self-betrayal.

* *Teach-ins: U.S.A.*, edited by Louis Menashe and Ronald Radosh (Praeger), p. 308.

Insofar as Cold War anticommunism implies implicit or explicit support of our society's present social and economic set-up — and, in my opinion, it implies no less than that — I cannot be counted among its partisans. Nor am I a supporter of the present regime in Moscow, which, though it has done away with the worst features of Stalinism, is still far from fulfilling the original promise of the Russian Revolution. The present Soviet leadership, while fulfilling certain elementary requirements of socialism, is at the same time pursuing a course of cynical *Realpolitik* abroad in the mode traditionally associated with Great Power behavior throughout history. For instance, it is playing the Arab card in the Middle East, just as the British did in the 1930s and 1940s, though the latter played the game with more restraint and finesse than the Russian latecomers. But only naifs and "true believers" have failed to note that the State Department, though inhibited by certain domestic forces and unequivocal past commitments, is itching to play the same card, in the hope of outbidding the Russian "competition." The Arabs are the overwhelming majority in the Middle East, and that is the sufficient justification of policy for all the powers, great or not so great, including de Gaulle's France. Witness the very mild, "soft" response to the Arabs' severing of relations with the U.S. in the wake of the Big Lie that America and Britain intervened militarily in favor of Israel. Witness, also, the covert wooing of King Hussein, another "bulwark of anticommunism," though undoubtedly not so steady a bulwark as King Constantine of Greece. In Washington, as in Moscow, Cold War considerations are paramount, and from that vantage point the national interests of Israel, which is not really a part of the Cold War and which cannot but resist being dragged into it as a pawn of one or another superpower, are merely an annoying distraction.

What Soviet society is badly in need of is a fundamental *political* reform that would once and for all eliminate the one-party monopoly of power and the arbitrary rule of the bureaucracy. But this is a long-term prospect. It cannot be accomplished from the outside but only by the Russian people themselves as education and full-scale modernization in the economic sphere gradually promote among them more libertarian perspectives. Cold War anticommunism, Washington-style, can only obstruct their gaining of such perspectives, and a nuclear war would surely bury them for good. And so it would bury us.

In the days when communism was a monolithic world-structure, ruled by an iron hand in the Kremlin, it was possible for a democratic socialist to support, even if only on tactical grounds, what the editor of

Commentary calls a "policy of containing the spread of Communism";
and I am still opposed to the Communists being allowed to take over
countries by force and against the will of the majority of their population. But this is no longer the question today, when monolithic totalitarian world communism has ceased to exist. Least of all is it the
question in Vietnam, where American power has all along prevented
even a moderately honest election and is actually shoring up obsolete
social institutions and reactionary, corrupt governing classes. The Or-
wellian language in which the administration is defending its war in
Vietnam is absolutely insufferable. Perhaps democracy, even in the
restricted American sense of the term, is impossible in a backward
area like Vietnam. But if that is the case, surely Generals Thieu and
Ky, as well as any future puppets in Saigon, are the last people in the
world one can trust to undertake even a minimum program of political
democratization and economic modernization.

The recent revelations concerning covert CIA backing of certain
intellectual and cultural projects, which have for years pretended to
be free of Washington control, came as no surprise to me. It is inherent in the logic of anticommunism as currently defined, for in terms
of that logic the means are irrelevant and only the Cold War ends are
important. (Our crusade in Vietnam is ruled by the very same logic.)
The people who accepted secret CIA subsidies without being clear in
their own minds as to what was involved are in many ways to be compared to the "fellow travelers" and "stooges" of the 1930s, who supported Stalin's reading of Marxism and his murderous policies even as
they spoke of the Russia he despotically ruled as a "workers' paradise"
and as a "classless society." But in contrast to the "stooges" of yesterday, the "stooges" of today are paid cash on the line for their pious
declarations.

1967

The Princess

THE TOTALLY UNEXPECTED appearance among us of Stalin's daughter as a leading exponent of anticommunism, as a living witness, that is, of the horrors of the system of which her father was the chief architect, is surely one of the weirdest incidents of the Cold War. Still, there is something fishy about this entire incident and the resultant worldwide publicity it has called forth. It strikes one as being more like a *coup de théâtre* than as a political event of genuine substance.

The fact is that save for a few valuable personal details about her mother and father, as well as about the life at home of her father's principal cronies like Voroshilov, Molotov, and Mikoyan, her exposure of the Soviet regime in *Only One Year* offers virtually nothing that has not been known to many of us for a long, long time. Thus for her to set out at this late date to persuade us of the vileness of this regime is supererogatory, to say the least; and if any new documentation is still needed, a novel like Alexander Solzhenitsyn's *The First Circle* is far more engrossing, far and away a superior work. The truth is that Svetlana merely aspires to be a writer, while Solzhenitsyn actually is one, and infinitely more stirring and eloquent than she can ever be. In the matter of sensibility, courage, and tenacity of mind and spirit, she nowhere comes near the impression that Solzhenitsyn has made on us. Svetlana is lavish with words, to be sure, but her level of culture strikes me as being about that of a steady reader of the *Reader's Digest* — a periodical she has probably never laid eyes on.

So Svetlana's latest work, being devoid of the quality of personal exigency or authentic political content, is, to my mind, strictly redundant. It is plain that the fanfare with which she has been greeted and the acclaim with which her writings are published are solely due to the fact that she is Stalin's daughter. For years she was the princess of the Kremlin, and at present she is the princess of Harper & Row and of the media. So Svetlana is still a princess, though now pressed into service on "our" side of the Cold War. I confess that I find this entire episode somewhat disconcerting, if not actually unseemly. It appears to me that if I were a child of Stalin's, I would take care to retire into some quiet backwater or else seek release from this awful misfortune in some other equally drastic manner. True enough, it is not her fault that she is the daughter of "a moral and spiritual monster," as she now speaks of her father. (In *Twenty Letters* her tone was quite different, with Beria cast in the role of the chief culprit.) There are situations in life, however, that are wholly irredeemable and irreparable. For Svetlana to push herself forward and play the role of a celebrity after all that her vicious father had wrought is nothing more than blatant self-indulgence, a piece of inordinate egotism, sheer *chutzpah* in fact.

In reviewing this book for the *New Yorker* Edmund Wilson characterized it as "a unique document" that will take its place "among the great Russian autobiographical works: Herzen, Kropotkin, Tolstoy's *My Confession*." This is a statement so fatuous as to leave one fairly gasping. Surely Mr. Wilson, an outstandingly gifted critic, has come a cropper here. As I read Svetlana's book it contains not one iota of Herzen's brilliant wit and world-historical perspectives. As for Tolstoy, his *My Confession* is unequaled as the work of a powerful imagination and at the same time as a mighty feat of consciousness. In my view Svetlana's laborious production has nothing whatever in common with the great Russian autobiographies that Mr. Wilson mentions with such astonishing facility of reference. Not so very long ago I praised Mr. Wilson for the *esprit voltairien* that animated him in resisting the flopover to religiosity of some of our leading intellectuals in the late 1940s and early 1950s. How, then, can he accept without demur Svetlana's mawkish religiosity and schoolgirlish obeisances to "the Lord." Altogether she seems to regard herself as a regular subscriber to the Lord's services, without whose "special assistance," as she claims, she could not have taken the "decisive step" of putting herself under the protection of the American embassy in Delhi. "Of importance to me," she writes, "were not the dogmas of Christianity, nor the ritual, but the eternal Life, the eternal Good." And again: "All the great religions of the earth have a high moral teaching in common." Yes, but what about their practice? When one thinks of the innumerable wars, massacres, and pogroms perpetrated in the name of one religion or another one cannot but be appalled by her innocence. Or is it innocence? No wonder Pimen, the metropolitan of Orthodoxy in Moscow, was able to say: "She is not a Christian, she is interested in all religions at once." As a young girl she was a devout Communist, which, after all, is a secular religion of a sort. Now she prefers religions otherworldly in essence. She cannot do without dreams of salvation, but all such dreams imply an absolute; and her present absolute is "the Supreme Mind" which "governs the world." Even Tolstoy was not at all sure of this last proposition, but Svetlana is no skeptic. She luxuriates in certainties.

Moreover, she writes about America as if it were Utopia achieved, a veritable paradise on earth. Everywhere she finds the same "homey atmosphere of informality, mutual trust, and simplicity." "How they love to smile," she exclaims in looking at Americans. It does not even occur to her that this perpetual smile conceals a nervous tic, a radical uncertainty about their real identity. The only Americans exempted from her general benedictions are the hippies she saw during a stroll through Greenwich Village. "Hippies are nothing but froth, nothing but trash in the streets of large cities." The real America she locates in the small towns and farms — "the epitome of health." It may be news to her but the majority of Americans now live in the big cities. No doubt much can be said against the hippies; on the other hand, to say that they are nothing but trash is an absurd and arrogant statement. The fact is that Svetlana's response to the United States is mere witless idealization. The only Americans she has met are a few very well-to-do people who have treated her with special consideration since she is the daughter of you know who and "a hot property" besides. And from this extremely restricted experience she draws large generalizations. That the cities are decaying, that the blacks are in revolt, that millions don't get enough to eat, and that millions are protesting the senseless war in Vietnam — all this she shuts out from her consciousness. To recognize such disagreeable facts would after all dispel her dream of the promised land.

Furthermore, she tells her story with less than complete candor. I, for one, am far from convinced that she went to India for the sole purpose of scattering her Indian husband's ashes in the Ganges. This husband, Brajesh Sing, is quoted as telling her that the Ganges does not really matter, for all rivers are alike in flowing into the sea. She persisted nonetheless, and her request got very special attention, first from Khrushchev and later from Kosygin and Suslov. And when she finally arrived in the village of Kalakandar, the home of her husband's family, she was told that only men could perform the religious rite of scattering the ashes in the sacred river. At this point she no longer cared, for her eyes were already riveted on distant America, so big and so glamorous. To me it appears far more likely that her reason for going to India was the manuscript of *Twenty Letters* ("that ticket to another life") which she had previously sent off to Delhi by diplomatic pouch. And so far as her idea of America is concerned, she seems to have absorbed it from special showings of American movies in the Kremlin. Thus she gradually built up a fancy-picture of America staggering in its naiveté and to which she still holds fast.

She writes that she "loved and respected" her father until she grew up. But now that she knows the horrid truth about him, she has found another cult-object she can worship, and this time it is nothing less than a whole country, very large, extremely various, and extremely contradictory in many of its aspects. This woman seems to be bent on wasting herself in postures of adoration. The term "democratic socialism" is not mentioned in her book; nor is the term "capitalism." The only choice her limited mind can comprehend is between the Soviet Union as it is today and America as it is. Clearly, Svetlana is not a woman capable of communing with history. She is merely its victim.

Commentary, 1970

What and Where Is
the New Left?

THE NEW LEFT is a very elusive term, to say the least, though to judge from the enormous publicity it has received in the past few years from the media generally as well as from the frequent and persistently rancorous attacks on it in such reputable intellectual magazines as *Dissent* and *Commentary*, one might easily gain the impression that it represents a substantial organization armed with a systematic theory of American society and a practical mode of action designed to put that theory to the test. Actually, nothing of the sort is true. More than a half a decade after its full emergence on the political scene, it remains what it has been since its inception — an unstable mood of new-fledged radicalism and a fermentation of leftist rhetoric rather than a real movement. The fact is that it still lacks a relevant theory of revolutionary change and a strategy of action. It has no generally recognized leadership nor even a single newspaper or journal that can legitimately speak in its name. If anyone should want to question the New Left as to its precise program and perspectives for the future there is no address he can write to nor is there a single spokesman available empowered to state its position in an authoritative fashion.

No wonder that the term New Left lends itself to all kinds of sophistical uses by self-serving rightist politicians and journalists. Only the other day I heard a nationally prominent Republican governor proclaim on TV that major elements of the Democratic party have gone over to the New Left. That such outright propaganda lies can conceivably be uttered is at least partly due to the New Left's failure to find its own organizational form and a clearly defined ideological and political platform on which it can take its stand. So where is the New Left and what is it? At present it seems to me to be strictly nowhere, and one cannot but agree with one of its politically more sophisticated adversaries, namely Zbigniew Brzenzinski, who writes that it consists of no more than "a rather fluid combination of individual sympathisers ... and a scattering of new organizations, of which the SDS has become the best known." In his view it is basically the expression of "a more extensive restlessness among American middle-class university youth," and in its extreme wing he sees the phenomenon of "middle-class rebellion against middle-class society." Yet even Mr. Brzenzinski's stringent account is already out of date, for the SDS, whose dues-paying membership is estimated never to have exceeded 6000, has now fallen apart into splinter groups whose influence among students is visibly waning. And as for "the scattering of new organizations," what it really amounts to is only a few miniscule grouplets — the so-called Seattle Liberation Front is as good an example as any — whose membership runs from about ten to twenty people. From this sorry state of affairs one cannot but conclude that in an organizational sense the New Left scarcely exists.

Hence it's no use glossing over the fact that the New Left today is still little more than a mood and an oppositional rhetoric, and that, furthermore, their significance is vastly overrated by rightists and leftists alike whenever a student confrontation with authority (such as those that occurred at Columbia, Cornell, and Harvard) is overdramatized by the media and instantly turned into a topic of endless and wearisome reports and analyses. To be sure, the oppositional mood prevailing among a sizeable number of students is much to be preferred to the complacence and political indifference characteristic of their state of mind in the late forties and fifties. Still, it is my impression that the student movement has already exhausted itself in demonstrations and that Nixon's apparent defusion of the Vietnam issue through his tricky (now you see it now you don't) policy of withdrawal has had the effect of disorienting that movement. Nor can it be said that the wildly demagogic "law and order" campaign of the Nixon-Agnew-Mitchell team has entirely failed to curb and intimidate the student population. After all, it was chiefly the war in Vietnam that galvanized the student actions of protest and dissent, and now they are bound to pay the price of their rather limited political focus. It should be kept in mind, too, that students are in a sense only "temporary people," and though they can be quite effective in starting a movement they can hardly be relied on to keep it going and make it stick. Moreover, it is impossible for anyone to claim with even the slightest degree of accuracy that at any time during the past decade American universities were actually seething with revolutionary fervor; what they were seething with is anti-Vietnam sentiments, which can by no means be equated with the much broader and more comprehensive outlook of consistent and authentic radicalism.

Nonetheless a few militantly activist groups that might loosely be described as belonging to the New Left do exist after all, and it is therefore all the more unfortunate that so far they have shown no understanding whatsoever of the first rule of revolutionary strategy, which is the education, build-up, and preservation of its leading cadres. Thus the Weatherman faction of the SDS has with unseemly haste managed to bury itself underground, effectively cutting itself off from any participation in the work of agitation and propaganda on the college campuses. (At this time it would be wholly premature to speak seriously of mass-propaganda or mass-contacts on the part of the Left.) Insofar as the Weathermen believe that they are in fact engaged in an armed struggle with the American state power, they are simply indulging themselves in an excessively youthful kind of romantic absolutism. The governing class is not all afraid of the tantrums they call trashing nor of the bombs planted in a few buildings. It can well afford to replace broken windowpanes and even to rebuild any number of buildings while using these same shenanigans to rationalize its policy of repression.

The same goes for the Black Panthers, whose heedless rhetoric of violence and gun-toting tactics have brought them a great deal of publicity while costing them the loss of very valuable and not so easily replaceable cadres. It is pointless to discuss violence in the abstract, but long historical experience has shown that violent assaults on the class-enemy are not only useless but even criminally "counter-productive" if undertaken prematurely, in isolation from any mass movement, that is to say before the challengers of the status quo can count at least on an even chance of victory in an armed struggle with the police. The police are nothing but simple agents of the state, and behind them stand the National Guard and the armed might of the federal government. The employment of force can only be justified within a revolutionary situation, and no such situation can even remotely be said to exist in the United States at present.

Lenin once summed up the conditions of any genuine revolution, and no one has ever denied that in this respect he was exactly right. The three conditions are (a) that the ruling elite should be seriously split on most major issues and unable to proceed as in the past; (b) that the suffering, despair, and anger of the masses should drive them to an outright refusal to continue their former existence; and (c) there must exist a revolutionary party able and willing to exploit its historical opportunity. Now it is obvious that despite Vietnam and all the turmoil it has caused and despite the extravagant and cacophonous claims made in behalf of the so-called counterculture, none of the conditions enumerated by Lenin are present in the United States today. However, only political philistines will conclude that this lack offers definitive proof that the conditions of revolution will *never* come into existence.* Historically we are living on volcanic ground and we may expect all sorts of reversals and surprises. In a purely objective sense, the American system of neocapitalism has long been ripe for fundamental structural change. What is missing, mainly, is the subjective factor. And one's disappointment with the experience of the New Left comes down precisely to this: that it has failed to crystallize from within itself a guiding organization — one need not be afraid of naming it a centralized and disciplined party, for so far no one has ever invented a substitute for such a party — capable of engaging in daily and even pedestrian practical activity while keeping itself sufficiently alert on the ideological plane so as not to miss its historical opportunity when and if it arises.†

Failing in this pivotal task, some few youthful adherents of the New Left have gone in for individual terrorism, thus confirming both their

---

* In speaking of the political philistines one cannot leave out of account certain ex-Marxists, of whom Sidney Hook is a prime example, who at opportune moments still choose to call themselves socialists but who in practice support and defend the American capitalist drive for world hegemony. The favorite trick of such types is to substitute the word "democracy" for the word "capitalism" when writing or talking about the American system. In this way they make it appear that any opponent of capitalism is *ipso facto* an enemy of democracy.

† While looking through Tom Hayden's recent book *Trial*, I was struck by the fact that the necessity of building such an organization does not even occur to him. In any case, it is not mentioned. There can be no doubt of Hayden's personal courage and dedication, but he seems to be almost totally devoid of strategic sense. The only programmatic idea he insistently advocates is the setting up of "free territories," as he calls them, in such areas as "Berkeley, Haight-Ashbury, Isla Vista, Madison, Ann Arbor, rural Vermont, the East Village, and the Upper West Side." And for some reason that escapes me he persists in referring to these areas as "internal colonies" for which he demands "self-determination." This is unfortunately all too characteristic of the fashion in which certain New Leftists play with words and concepts that will not stand even the most cursory analysis. Hayden does not trouble himself explaining in detail how his scheme of "free territories" might be realized, since that would surely require detaching them from the jurisdiction of both the states and the federal government. Any attempt thus to detach them would of course amount to no less than insurrection, and it is prefectly obvious that no such insurrection is in sight. Moreover, if insurrection is the order of the day why be so modest as to content oneself with a few scattered "free territories"? Why not go all out and aim at seizing the power in Washington? Hayden's scheme is so thoughtless and ridiculously utopian that he might as well have issued a call for the restoration of Brook Farm and the Fourierist phalansteries.

desperation and, above all, their total ignorance of revolutionary history. For this history fully illustrates the futility of such methods. In his polemic against the Russian terrorists Trotsky once put it very well indeed in stating that "the chemistry of high explosives cannot take the the place of mass action." And in his autobiographical work *My Life* he recalls that the decade of the 1860s began in Russia with revolutionary propaganda among the people only to end with terrorism. "The 1870's passed into history mainly as the years of the 'People's Will,' a terrorist party. The best elements of that generation went up in the blaze of dynamite warfare. The enemy held all his positions. Then followed a decade of decline, of disenchantment and pessimism, of religious and moral searchings — the 1880's."

The methods of terrorism have a certain aura of heroism about them, to be sure, but in the long run they can only alienate the people at large. The secret terrorist cell is a perfect breeding ground for informers and *agents provocateurs*. Individual terrorism is not a short cut to revolutionary goals but only a blind alley.

Modern Occasions, 1971

INDEX OF NAMES

Index of Names